GARLAND LIBRARY OF SOCIOLOGY
VOL. 27

RAPE, INCEST, AND CHILD SEXUAL ABUSE

GARLAND REFERENCE LIBRARY
OF SOCIAL SCIENCE
VOL. 904

GARLAND LIBRARY OF SOCIOLOGY

PETER W. COOKSON, JR.
Series Editor

RACE AND ETHNIC RELATIONS
An Annotated Bibliography
by Graham C. Kinloch

THE CLINICAL SOCIOLOGY
HANDBOOK
by Jan M. Fritz

JEWISH FAMILY ISSUES
A Resource Guide
by Benjamin Schlesinger

SOCIAL SUPPORT AND HEALTH
An Annotated Bibliography
by John G. Bruhn, Billy U. Philips, Paula
L. Levine, and Carlos F. Mendes de Leon

THE SOCIOLOGY
OF MENTAL ILLNESS
An Annotated Bibliography
by Richard K. Thomas

DIMENSIONS OF COMMUNITIES
A Research Handbook
by Dan A. Chekki

THE SOCIOLOGY OF WORK
A Critical Annotated Bibliography
by Parvin Ghorayshi

THE SOCIOLOGY OF RELIGION
An Organizational Bibliography
by Anthony J. Blasi
and Michael W. Cuneo

THE POLITICAL ECONOMY
OF THE SOCIAL SCIENCES
by Frederick H. Gareau

SUBSTANCE ABUSE AMONG
AMERICAN MINORITIES
An Annotated Bibliography
by Howard M. Rebach

LABOR MARKET
SEGMENTATION
AND ITS IMPLICATIONS
*Inequity, Deprivation,
and Entitlement*
by Dahlia Moore

FEMALE CRIMINALITY
The State of the Art
by Concetta C. Culliver

THE RELIGIOUS ROOTS
OF AMERICAN SOCIOLOGY
by Cecil E. Greek

AMERICAN SOCIETY
IN THE BUDDHIST MIRROR
by Joseph B. Tamney

ORGANIZATIONAL AND
INTERORGANIZATIONAL
DYNAMICS
by Jacob Peters and Doreen L. Smith

THE BLACK FAMILY
IN A CHANGING
BLACK COMMUNITY
by Richard A. Davis

RAPE, INCEST, AND
CHILD SEXUAL ABUSE
Consequences and Recovery
by Pat Gilmartin

RAPE, INCEST, AND CHILD SEXUAL ABUSE

*Consequences
and Recovery*

Pat Gilmartin

GARLAND PUBLISHING, Inc.
New York & London / 1994

Library of Congress Cataloging-in-Publication Data

Gilmartin, Pat, 1950–
     Rape, incest, and child sexual abuse : consequences
and recovery / by Pat Gilmartin.
          p.   cm. — (Garland library of sociology ;
vol. 27)   (Garland reference library of social
science ; vol. 904)
     Includes bibliographical references and index.
     ISBN 0–8153–1326–8
     1. Rape.   2. Incest.   3. Child sexual abuse.
4. Sexual abuse victims.   5. Women—Crimes
against.   I. Title.   II. Series.   III. Series: Garland
reference library of social science ; v. 904.
HV6558.G55   1994
362.7'6—dc20   93–33582
                                                                    CIP

Printed on acid-free, 250-year-life paper
Manufactured in the United States of America

Contents

Series Editor's Preface

The Garland Library of Sociology is proud to include Pat Gilmartin's new book *Rape, Incest and Child Sexual Abuse* in its evolving series of top flight sociological studies. Now more than ever, there is a need for publishing sociological research that addresses the critical issues of our era. Clearly, our society is undergoing very rapid cultural, political, social, and economic change; social science can help illuminate the future by carefully examining the present. It is our hope that the books published in this series will reach not only professional sociologists but all those readers who are deeply concerned about the present condition of society and the future direction of our culture. Society can be analyzed as a series of problematics which result in considerable human suffering; we ought to face these problems with courageous realism. One of the strengths of sociology is that it seeks to uncover potential solutions to social problems without resorting to sentimentality or illusory wishful thinking. Empiricism and tough-mindedness are more likely to lead to enlightenment then the expression of good feelings. Thus, the role of the Garland Library of Sociology is to bring to the public those books that will advance our thinking and propel us to engage more actively in the resolution of those contradictions and dilemmas that keep our society from reaching its potential.

The topics that Professor Gilmartin writes about are critically important; the rate of sexual victimization in American society is truly shocking. Women in particular are victims of many forms of sexual aggression that range from verbal abuse to murder. To understand the effects of victimization it is critical to move beyond statistical analyses alone and acknowledge the depth of the effects of victimization by listening to the voices of those who have suffered through the experience of rape, incest and childhood sexual abuse. As Professor Gilmartin makes clear through her use of case studies, individuals who have been sexually victimized undergo a series of psychological and social experiences that affect every aspect of their lives and the lives of those around them. Individuals who have been sexually victimized have been robbed of their innocence and disempowered in ways that are fundamental to their sense of self. As Professor Gilmartin points out, these experiences are not rare; in fact, the rate of sexual victimization is so high that we must ask ourselves what it is about our society that creates the conditions whereby victimization becomes an on-going social fact.

The major goals of this book are to identify the prevalence of sexual victimization in American culture, to uncover the causes of these offenses, to illuminate the impact of victimization on those who have survived, to examine recovery and treatment issues, and to suggest how sexual victimization can be prevented. These topics are treated with scholarly thoroughness, empathy, and a legitimate sense of righteous indignation by the author. The mixture of tough mindedness and a hope for a better future sets the tone of this book so that one is outraged, but not depressed. Key to this sense of realistic optimism is the author's notion of "victory." She is not content to simply acknowledge that sexual victimization occurs, but she is determined that victims should triumph over the destructive impact of sexual abuse by rediscovering the self. She urges victims to transcend feelings of passivity and helplessness and to embrace a view of themselves that emphasizes strength and growth.

It is my hope that this book will be widely read by those who have been sexually victimized, by their victimizers, and professionals who seek to end sexual victimization and encourage the constructive treatment of those who have been victimized. I also hope that this book will be read by the public-at-large because until our society is free of sexual violence, we will not have achieved the kind of ethical environment that is critical for creating a just and humane society.

Peter W. Cookson, Jr.

Preface

Since this book is about the experiences of girls, adolescent females, and adult women who have been sexually victimized, as well as their responses to and recovery from these traumatic events, a good place to start is to illustrate what it is that we really are talking about. Accordingly, the following accounts depict how the lives of individuals can be transformed by rape, incest, and child sexual abuse.

First are the words of "Mrs. X" which first appeared in Russell's (1974:19–21) book. Mrs. X is a fifty-five-year-old white woman who is divorced and has four grown children; she works as a teacher. She was raped seven years prior to being interviewed and, during the ensuing years, told only one person about the assault:

> . . . I felt that I was outside my body, watching this whole thing, that it wasn't happening to me, it was happening to somebody else. It was a strange feeling, absolutely unreal. I was terrorized, but it's very hard to describe the shock of what was happening. At first, I went into a state of shock where I just shook and shook and shook. And I was freezing cold . . . [After he left,] I called my friend . . . She came up to the house and stayed with me, and I poured the whole thing out to her, and we cried together, and held each other. She never told her husband because she said she knew his attitude toward me would change. He . . . thought a woman couldn't be raped . . .
>
> Then I went straight down to the nearest town, and into the sporting goods store, and I bought a forty sentinel gun and a small Browning automatic. Incidentally, I told the man who raped me that I was going to do this. I told him that I would kill him if he ever came back, and I know I

ix

would. And that was a shock to me, to know that this peaceful person who had never known anything but love was capable of killing a human being. But I knew that I could.

The following are my words regarding the impact that incest and child sexual abuse can have. The focus is on the "intangibles" that abusers often steal from the children that they molest:

> They take away your innocence; you no longer can look at the world through unjaded eyes. They also take your zest or that inner quality which gets manifested by a twinkle in your eye or a bounce in your step. In some cases, they even take away your sense of who you are and what is real.

> Perhaps it wouldn't be so bad if they "just" took parts of you away. But, it's *not* that simple; they also leave things behind. They leave you with a series of contradictions where positive and negative ideas and feelings get fused together. Love and hate become one; so do self and others; ecstacy and despair become synonyms; fear and safety become one and the same; and affection gets all mixed up with sex. They also can leave you with the horrible memories of the actual abuse incident(s), memories to be relived again and again via flashbacks and abreactions, and perhaps even admonitions of future violence if you "tell."

> In sum, the consequences of incest and child sexual abuse are so insidious because the children (as we once knew them) no longer exist (Gilmartin 1991:13).

What we really are talking about is the personal devastation that can occur after sexual victimization. Equally important is the courage, the determination, and the undaunted effort that it takes to rebound from these sorts of potentially life-shattering experiences. In other words, after being sexually victimized, yes, we may experience extreme alterations in our lives, have great difficulty rebuilding ourselves and our worldviews, and spend a considerable amount of time disrupted afterwards. But, this is only part of the story; the other half is that many of us can and do recover and go on to lead happy, healthy, and productive lives. These changes are *not* easy ones to make, and this is *not* a quick, simple process; rather, my message is that rape, incest, and child sexual abuse do *not* have to be life sentences of misery.

Although we have been increasingly willing to investigate the topics of rape, incest, and child sexual abuse during the last twenty years, few sources have attempted systematically to summarize all three of these literatures. Notable exceptions include: Katz and Mazur's (1979), *Understanding the Rape Victim: A Synthesis of Research Findings*, Liz Kelly's (1988) *Surviving Sexual Violence*, and Diana E.H. Russell's (1984) *Sexual Exploitation: Rape, Child Sexual Abuse, and Workplace Harassment.* Due to the rapidly changing nature of these literatures, though, some of this information has become outdated, and several critical issues have been ignored. For example, by today's standards, we also should address such topics as acquaintance rape, the likelihood of so-called normal men to rape and sexually abuse (rather than focusing solely on incarcerated populations of rapists and child molesters), and ritualistic child sexual abuse. These comments are *not* meant to downgrade these earlier works; they were and remain important and authoritative sources on the subject of sexual victimization. Rather, the purpose is to highlight how drastically our ideas and our knowledge about the topics of rape, incest, and child sexual abuse have changed during a relatively short period of time.

Thus, my major goals in this book are to determine how these literatures have changed, to update where we are now in that process of change, and to speculate about the future. In order to achieve these goals, I have included what we currently know about: (1) the incidence and prevalence of rape, incest, and child sexual abuse in our culture; (2) the factors believed to cause these offenses; (3) the impact of these forms of sexual victimization on the girls and women who have survived them; (4) recovery and treatment issues; (5) prevention of sexual victimization; and (6) future prognostications. Please note that I am *not* attempting to include all facets of these problems. Rather, due to the voluminous nature of our current knowledge about rape, incest, and child sexual abuse, as well as my own biases regarding the issues which I regard as more critical ones, I have elected to *exclude* certain subjects. As examples, I do *not* focus much on the perpetrators of these offenses; the social control agents (e.g., police, medical and court personnel, and rape crisis counselors) who process "cases" of sexual victimization; and the attitudinal dimension or how our attitudes shape and exacerbate the problem. I am *not* inferring that these are unimportant concerns; rather, I have opted to select issues which are oriented toward the concerns of the girls, adolescent females, and adult women who have been sexually victimized.

Caveats about This Book

Before presenting a detailed overview of what this book is about, it is important for me to add some caveats about it and to clarify what to expect. First of all, since the vast majority of the victims and the survivors of rape, incest, and child sexual abuse are girls and women, and an overwhelming majority of the perpetrators of these offenses are males (Blume 1990; Finkelhor 1984; Russell 1984), I have elected to make the female victims and survivors the predominant focus of this work. This, though, becomes a problem for a number of reasons. One, I do *not* wish to imply that these offenses are less troublesome or disruptive when committed against boys or men. Rather the point is that, since the experiences and the lives of females and males are so different in our society (Arliss 1991; Belenky et al. 1986; Faludi 1992; Gilligan 1982; Jack 1991; Josselson 1987; Kamen 1991; Kaschak 1992; Reis 1991b; Sanford and Donovan 1985; Sidel 1990; Steinem 1992; Tannen 1990; Tavris 1992), to assume that the experience of sexual victimization would be the same for both sexes is likely to be a serious distortion.[1] Two, when the perpetrators of rape, incest, and child sexual abuse are mentioned in this book, my assumption is that they are males. Although there is an increasing awareness that women can be assailants in cases of incest and child sexual abuse, the overwhelming majority of the perpetrators continue to be men.[2] Three, including both girls and women in this book is somewhat cumbersome. Although there are similarities among the offenses of rape, incest, and child sexual abuse, there also are some very real differences.[3] Notwithstanding the differences, I decided to include girls in this work because I believe that it is important to view all three forms of sexual violence as experiences which, more often than not, are directed at the powerless members of our culture; girls and women both clearly qualify.

A second caveat about this work is that, sometimes, the language is problematic. Throughout this book (and as is detailed in Chapter One), I use the terms rape, sexual assault, sexual coercion, child sexual abuse, and incest to highlight the variety of forms sexual victimization can take. In addition, although the concepts of victim and survivor are employed in this book, I also explore new language which goes beyond the notions of victimization and survival and affords us the oportunity to include the experiences of the girls and the women who have recovered from the trauma of sexual victimization.

An added issue regarding the language used in this book is that I have chosen to write in different "voices" and "persons." That is to say, throughout this book I speak of "those of us" who have been sexually victimized, "they" who have been victimized, and, sometimes, I directly address "you." My reasons for this switching back and forth are twofold. One is to underscore the fact that sexual victimization is a problem for all of us, *not* "just" the ones who have been assaulted; two, I am avoiding distancing myself from this subject and the girls, adolescent females, and adult women who have survived these experiences. This latter issue is critical, particularly in feminist circles, because so many victims and survivors of rape, incest, and child sexual abuse complain about and resent how the experts, their loved ones, and this society want to deny, minimize, and/or euphemize their experiences and their resultant pain.

My third concern is that we must remain sensitive about the ways in which sexual victimization affects us as individuals. In other words, when studying subjects such as rape, incest, and child sexual abuse (particularly post-victimization responses), we must keep in mind that these are highly sensitive topics, so sensitive, in fact, that many of us do *not* report our experiences, even in situations where anonymity is promised. As such, we must take great care that we do *no* further harm to the girls and the women who have been sexually victimized. The flip side of this issue is that, if we are ever to improve the quality of our information about these subjects, increase our understanding of the consequences of sexual victimization, and augment our ability to assist the girls and women who have been so victimized, we need to know more about these issues. If done carefully and sensitively, though, I believe that all of these are attainable goals.

A fourth issue is to be as clear as is possible about my beliefs and biases, as well as to inform you about the theoretical perspective which I employ throughout this work. Therefore, my major assumptions are that: (1) although rape, incest, and child sexual abuse are horrifying and demeaning experiences which can disrupt the lives of their victims and survivors, girls and women can and do recover from them; (2) rape, incest, and child sexual abuse are very serious crimes, and the perpetrators of these acts should be punished severely; (3) we have extensive, well-documented histories of sexism, misogyny, and discrimination against women and children in American society, and these histories are linked in very clear ways to the contemporary factors which cause and perpetuate sexual victimization; and (4) to control and to prevent the sexual victimization problem will require structural changes, *not* just superficial or ameliorative prevention programs which focus on self-defense for girls and women and/or increasing their awareness of their vulnerability. As may be obvious from this list, I have written this book from a feminist perspective. I have done so because I, as well as a *legion* of others, agree that rape, incest, and child sexual abuse are feminist issues, issues that are clearly linked to and caused by social and cultural forces (Bass and Davis 1988; Blume 1990; Briere 1989; Brownmiller 1975; Butler, S. 1985; Clark and Lewis 1977; Connell and Wilson 1974; Courtois 1988, 1992; Dinsmore 1991; Estrich 1987; Finkelhor 1979, 1984; Griffin 1971; Herman 1981, 1992; Katz 1984; Kelly 1988; Koss and Harvey 1991; Madigan and Gamble 1991; Medea and Thompsom 1974; Reis 1991b; Roberts 1989; Rose 1977; Rush 1980; Russell 1984, 1986; Schwendinger and Schwendinger 1983; Walker 1985; Weis and Borges 1973; Williams and Holmes 1981). Therefore, issues such as the deleterious effects of living in a patriarchal society, the negative consequences of misogyny (of which sexual victimization is but one symptom), and the devaluation of the female population are underlying assumptions throughout this book.

A fifth caution is that the sexual victimizers will be mentioned only briefly in this work. As noted earlier, although I regard this subject as an important one, it comprises a large literature in and of itself and falls outside of the purview of this book (i.e., the girls and women who have been sexually victimized). More frankly, if I focus on the perpetrators of rape, incest, and child sexual abuse (their attitudes, characteristics, motivations, and behaviors), perhaps I lend credence to the destruction and devastation that they cause.[4]

Sixth, reading this book will *not* be easy. For those of you who are sensitive and empathic, this book may upset and/or depress you; these are difficult subjects because they force us to acknowledge our own vulnerabilities, as well as those of our children. If you are a victim or a survivor of sexual violence, although I do *not* intend for this work to be a self-help manual, it may aid you in understanding and coping with your own victimization. I would recommend, though, that you be fairly far along in your recovery before reading it and/or that you have someone to talk to about its content.[5] If you are a loved one or a friend of someone who has been sexually victimized, try to be supportive of her; she needs that and you will play a major role in her process of recovery.[6] If you are a police officer, a member of the medical professions, a therapist, a court official, or a rape crisis counselor who interacts with the victims and the survivors of rape, incest, and child sexual abuse, treat them with the respect, consideration, and sensitivity that they deserve because failing to do so can cause a second even more insidious assault for the women and children who are struggling to patch together the various pieces of their lives (Williams and Holmes 1981).

As a final note, although I explore very difficult issues in this book, I have tried to do so in a hopeful and optimistic fashion. I firmly believe that those of us who have suffered the traumatizing experiences of rape, incest, and/or child sexual abuse can and do recover from them. I also believe that we can make the changes necessary to make the world a safer place for all of us in which to live. Accordingly, I have devoted three chapters to the more optimistic issues of recovering from sexual victimization, treatment of post-sexual victimization trauma, and prevention of rape, incest, and child sexual abuse.

An Overview of This Book

Based upon the changes which have occurred during the 1970s and 1980s in the rape, incest, and child sexual abuse literatures, it is important not only to update and synthesize what we now know about these offenses and their aftereffects, but also to add to this knowledge base by rethinking some of our extant ways of looking at these issues. In order to achieve these goals, then, several topics are examined. In Chapter One, for example, recent changes and trends in these literatures are explored, as are the inherent problems which make some of these works both disturbing and misleading.

In Chapter Two, I investigate what we currently know about the incidence and the prevalence of rape, incest, and child sexual abuse. For example, in an earlier time, we simply assumed that data gathered by police and social service agencies reflected the true rates of sexual victimization. Now, though, we know that these figures are abysmal estimates and that they reflect only the very "tip of the iceberg." Based on the results of victimization surveys conducted during the last two decades, recent surveys of college students, and investigations of various community samples, we now can conclude that the "real" rates of rape, incest, and child sexual abuse are much higher than we ever imagined. In addition, I explore a major factor which affects the counting of these offenses (i.e., whether acts which qualify as rape, incest, and child sexual abuse are reported and included in these data bases).

Chapter Three is an examination of historical and current explanations for rape, incest, and child sexual abuse. In earlier times, legal definitions and the victim-precipitated view of rape reigned supreme, while Freud regarded incest and child sexual abuse as "female fantasizing" and/or "wishful thinking." We now, though, have alternate models (e.g., feminist and social learning ones) which have realigned our thinking and have redirected our attention toward the structural and social forces believed to cause and perpetuate these problems.

In Chapter Four, I explore what we currently know about the consequences and the aftermath of sexual victimization. As examples, recent works suggest that we react across a variety of dimensions in our lives, including the psychological, somatic, behavioral, interpersonal, cognitive, self-perceptual, sexual, political, and spiritual spheres, as well as by subsequent victimization(s). In addition, we now know that these harrowing experiences can cause extensive long-term damage and that a sizable percentage of girls and women do *not* recover from them.

On a brighter note, the issues of recovering from sexual victimization and treating these problems are examined in the next two chapters. Although it may seem somewhat arbitrary and artificial to separate the consequences of rape, incest, and child sexual abuse from the issues of recovery and treatment of these problems, I have elected to do so because of the complexity and the enormity of these issues. Therefore, in Chapter Five, I explore the issue of recovering from sexual victimization: what recovery entails, the various dimensions across which we may need to recover, models which explicate this process of growth and healing, and how the process may differ for girls and women. The focus of Chapter Six is treating post-sexual-victimization trauma (i.e., both self-help and professional approaches), or the extant ways which have been found to be effective in facilitating recovery and healing for the victims and survivors of rape, incest, and child sexual abuse.

In Chapter Seven, the important, yet confusing, topic of prevention of sexual victimization is outlined. Since so many of the early works examined this issue primarily at the individual level of analysis (i.e., what individual girls and women could do to safeguard themselves from ever being victimized), the inference was that prevention was solely their "job." Equally troublesome was the fact that many of these early works offered contradictory advice. More recent efforts, though, and rightfully so, tend to view the various forms of sexual victimization as interpersonal and structural problems for *both* sexes and gear their suggestions for prevention accordingly. In other words, in addition to the myriad of caveats which are directed at girls and women as individuals, we now also underscore interpersonal and structural strategies (e.g., restructuring our society, equality for women, eliminating sexist child-rearing methods and socialization practices, and altering current dating patterns) as efficient ways to reduce the prevalence of these crimes.

Finally, in Chapter Eight, I explore what lies ahead. Although we have learned a great deal about rape, incest, and child sexual abuse during the past twenty years, have altered the laws for these crimes, and have changed the medical, social, and legal services extended to the victims and survivors of these offenses, plenty of room for change remains. As examples, it is only recently that we have begun to study the efficacy of rape and child sexual abuse education and prevention programs and how to facilitate the recovery process of the girls and women who have been sexually victimized. In order to improve the current situation, then, much more work needs to be done in these areas, as well as in many others.

By detailing *not only* the negative aspects of sexual victimization (i.e., being a victim and the negative ramifications of the experience) but also the positive outcomes that can occur (i.e., recovery, healing, growth, victory), I have tried to write a book which helps rather than hurts. I hope that you will agree that I have achieved this goal.

Acknowledgments

When I said that I intended to write a book, I scared myself senseless, and the self-doubts began. After a time of hesitation and convincing myself that writing a book is nothing more than writing a "series" of articles, though, I began this work; and what you hold in your hands is the result. This has *not* been an easy book to write, but I am very proud of it. I hope that you learn as much from reading it as I have while writing it, and also develop a deeper empathy for the infants, girls, adolescent females, and adult women who have been sexually victimized.

Like anyone who has ever written a book, I have people to whom I am indebted; and I want to thank them for their support and influence. While some of these folks have sparked my interest in writing this book, others have extended their love, kindness, in-process "pep talks," and words of encouragement along the way.

First, I would like to say a few words about one of the people to whom I dedicate this book. While a student during the late 1970s and the early 1980s in the sociology department at Kent State University, Elizabeth "Liz" Mullins was one of my professors. I have a deep respect for her, and I deeply appreciate the interest that she took in me. I thank her for what she taught me about being a feminist, what it means to be a good teacher, and striving for that which we are unsure we can attain. Liz died in May of 1990. Her death has left a gap in my life and in the lives of everyone that she ever touched. I think of her often, and I wish that she could have read this book and told me what she thought about it.

I also dedicate this book to Jennifer Gilmartin Zena. I love you; I am very proud of you; and you have taught me so much about the joys of living a real life. No Mom could ask for a finer daughter. My hope is that this book will help to create a better understanding of the topics of rape, incest, and child sexual abuse, as well as make your life and the lives of your contemporaries freer from sexually coercive experiences.

Finally, I dedicate this work to my parents, James J. and Mary Alice Gilmartin. I thank you for your encouragement and support over the years. I wouldn't be where I am today without you. My father died earlier this year; I deeply miss his presence in my life.

I also acknowledge and express my thanks to Dr. Richard O'Toole who chaired my dissertation committee at Kent State University. He was and remains a kind man who offers much of himself to his students. From him, I learned that academic "types" can be good people, as well as good scholars.

In addition, I have a truly wonderful group of friends who have aided me, in one way or another, during the writing of this book. In alphabetical order, they are: Danna Bozick, Rosemary D'Apolito, Kerri Griffin, Terry Johnson, Nicole "Nikki" Raeburn, L. J. "Tess" Tessier, and Pat Tomillo. Each of you has been a source of inspiration, encouragement, and/or comfort along the way; I thank you for believing in me, for the valuable gift of your friendship, and, generally, for being who you are. In particular, I thank Danna Bozick. I appreciate your support and kindnesses, your willingness to read so many drafts of these chapters along the way (even when I'm sure you were very tired of doing so), and how you convinced me that this one day would be a published work.

I also would like to acknowledge the groundbreaking contributions of the many women and men whose writings have forced all of us to be more aware of the problems of rape, incest, and child sexual abuse and whose ideas have been instrumental in shaping my own. In particular (and in alphabetical order), I value the works of: Ellen Bass, E. Sue Blume, John Briere, Ann Wolbert Burgess, Sandra Butler, Christine Courtois, Laura Davis, Christine Dinsmore, Yvonne Dolan, David Finkelhor, Susan Griffin, Ronnie Janoff-Bulman, Judith Lewis Herman, Linda Lytle Holmstrom, Sedelle Katz, Liz Kelly, Dean Kilpatrick, Mary

Koss, Linda Ledray, Mary Ann Mazur, Patricia Reis, Florence Rush, and Kathy Steele.

Next, I would like to extend my thanks to Youngstown State University and the members of the 1989–90 Sabbatical Selection Committee for awarding me the sabbatical which made the writing of this book possible. Without this precious time, I might have published this book anyway, but *not* during this century.

Finally, I extend sincere and heartfelt thanks to Dr. Arlene Brewster; you are the one I needed to show me the way. Without your valuable advice, "gentle nudgings," and insights, chances are good that I would *not* have had the clarity it took to write this book. Thank you for being who you are.

It is interesting to note that several of the aforementioned people that I have thanked and acknowledged are fairly recent influences in my life. Perhaps that is fitting because this book really is about new beginnings and growth, and many of you have been instrumental in helping me to strive for those goals. I thank you.

Rape, Incest, and Child Sexual Abuse

CHAPTER ONE

Introduction

> The 'classic' rape involves a stranger who attacks a woman
> late at night in the street and threatens to kill her; the
> assault involves physical violence and the woman is
> expected to resist throughout. This 'definition' prevent[s]
> many women from defining their experiences of forced
> sex as rape (Kelly 1988:148).

> Incest and other forms of sexual abuse of children are
> subjects clouded by myths, contradictions, and confusion.
> There is disagreement . . . as to whether as many boys as
> girls are molested, whether they are equally traumatized,
> whether child molesters are normal, neurotic, psycho-
> pathic or psychotic, whether the child victim in some way
> offers herself for a sexual encounter or whether the
> molester derives his behavior from a disturbed mother or
> a fractured family (Rush 1980:2).

These quotes illustrate the general confusion and the mythology
which surround the subject of sexual victimization. In fact, the
literatures which summarize the topics of rape, incest, and child
sexual abuse, although extensive and complicated, are replete
with contradictions and, in some cases, blatant examples of
misinformation. In part, this is due to the variety of historical
and contemporary definitions and explanations of these
phenomena, as well as how our knowledge about these issues
has changed during the last twenty years. Accordingly, in this
chapter, my major goals are to: pinpoint the recent trends in
these literatures, discuss the methodological flaws which exist in
many of the extant works, and present working definitions of the
terms to be used throughout the remainder of this book.

Recent Trends and Issues in the
Sexual Victimization Literature

As previously noted, even though the vast majority of works in the literatures on rape, incest, and child sexual abuse have been published since 1970, our knowledge about these subjects has changed dramatically during the ensuing years. In order to clarify these changes and to underscore their importance, in the following section I explore four trends which have occurred, including: (1) the imagery used to discuss sexual victimization; (2) our definitions of what constitutes sexual violence; (3) our assumptions about the scope of these problems; and (4) the language that we use to examine these issues.

Prior to 1970, the *predominant imagery* used to explain these offenses was a case-by-case analysis of each crime with the implicit inference that being sexually victimized was the "problem" of girls and women as individuals rather than collectively. In addition, many people (professionals and the lay public alike) perceived these offenses to be victim precipitated (i.e., if sexually assaulted, the woman must have "done something" to cause it). The situation for girls was even more dire; if they "claimed" to have been sexually abused, they were regarded (via Freud's legacy) as fantasizing or perhaps even lying. Even though these viewpoints were and remain replete with flaws and instances of circular reasoning, they did serve to call attention to the fact that rape, incest, and child sexual abuse are serious and highly misunderstood social problems. Perhaps more importantly, though, these sorts of explanations made many of us angry enough to develop new perspectives to explain these phenomena.

As an example (detailed fully in the next chapter), in the early 1970s, American feminists outlined why rape and other forms of violence against women and children were rampant in our culture. Specifically, they argued that these problems were caused and perpetuated by such structural factors as misogyny, male domination, and the devaluation of women and children, factors which are part and parcel of any patriarchal society. As a result of their writings, as well as the activism of many people during the most recent women's movement, definitions of sexual victimization (both legal and attitudinal ones) began to reflect an increasing concern for the welfare of its victims and survivors and a declining emphasis on the issue of them being "at fault." In addition, and to put these views into practice, during the 1970s feminists began to develop rape crisis centers across the country.[1] Their goals were to offer comfort, advocacy, and assistance to victims of rape and child sexual abuse. For the times, these were unprecedented innovations.

A second change has been to *broaden our focus as to what constitutes sexual violence.* Although Kempe formally opened the door on the subject of child abuse in 1961 by coining the term the "battered child syndrome" (cf. Conrad and Schneider 1980; Courtois 1988), it was *not* until the mid- to late 1970s that we opened that same door on the topic of the sexual abuse of children. In addition, we did *not* acknowledge the possibility that "nonstereotypical" rapes (e.g., acquaintance and marital rapes) could be "real" ones. Now, though, we are more likely not only to admit the presense of these problems, but also to categorize them as parts of the same, larger social problem of how our society is structured to devalue and exclude women and children (cf. Kelly 1988; Russell 1984), issues which are detailed further in Chapter Three.

The third change has been our belated realization regarding the *scope of the problem.* Prior to 1970, for example, we relied predominantly on police data and statistics gathered by various social agencies to enumerate rape, incest, and child sexual abuse problems. As will be explored further in Chapter Two, though, we now know that these figures reflect miniscule portions of the total problem. Based upon relatively new data collection tactics and new populations being sampled, recent figures indicate that the true prevalence of rape, incest, and child sexual abuse may be anywhere from *five to ten times higher* than was originally thought (Courtois 1988; Finkelhor 1979, 1984; Johnson 1980; Koss and Harvey 1991; Russell 1984, 1986; Warshaw 1988).

The final and most complicated trend is the *language that we use to discuss sexual victimization.* One example is the terminology that we use to describe the girls and women who have been sexually victimized and how that language has evolved over the years. During the 1970s, we labeled them *victims* or innocent parties who were attacked without provocation. Although the intent of this term was to emphasize the criminal nature of sexual assault, while simultaneously deemphasizing her role in "causing" it, it also carried certain negative connotations (Janoff-Bluman 1985; Koss and Harvey 1991). In other words, this term made "invisible the other side of . . . victimization: the active and positive ways in which [we] resist, cope and survive" (Kelly 1988:163). Other experts add that the concept implies passivity and perhaps even permanence as it can be construed as a life-long status (Blume 1990; Finney 1990; Sanford 1990).

During the 1980s, the term of choice became *survivor*. By drawing our attention to the strength and resiliency of the girls and women who had been sexually assaulted, thankfully, this newer term shifted our focus to the active nature of the social and psychological struggle to recover from the trauma of sexual victimization. Thus, rather than viewing them as passive victims, we began to describe them as active participants in the process of recovery (Bass and Davis 1988; Blume 1990; Finney 1990; Herman 1992; Kelly 1988).

This concept, though, is more complicated than it appears. As Kelly (1988:162–163) applies it to women who have been raped:

> I use it to refer to physical survival, in that the woman is not killed by the man, and women's physical and emotional survival after the assault(s). In this latter sense, too, not every woman survives. Some take their own lives . . . many more experience profoundly negative impacts on their lives . . . Emotional survival, therefore, refers to the extent to which women are able to reconstruct their lives so that the experience . . . does not have an overwhelming and continuing impact on their life.

Poston and Lison (1989:23) highlight the process of survival but do so for adult women who suffered childhood sexual victimization: "We feel that any woman who is not in a cemetery is a survivor. Even the institutionalized women have, in a way, survived, because they developed a mental disorder to escape an intolerable situation ... The fact that they have all chosen *life* over self-inflicted death makes them survivors ..."

I regard these conceptualizations as realistic and accurate for a number of reasons. First of all, many of us who have been sexually victimized remain "stuck" at the victim stage (for a variety of reasons to be discussed in a later chapter), and never achieve the status of survivor. As such, our lives (particularly children's) may be replete with: (1) subsequent victimizations (Blume 1990; Briere 1989; Burgess and Holmstrom 1979b; Poston and Lison 1989); (2) highly distorted cognitions and self-perceptions (Bass and Davis 1988; Browne and Finkelhor 1986; Courtois 1988, 1992; Herman 1992; Janoff-Bulman 1992; Kelly 1988); (3) chronic depression (Ellis et al. 1981; Finkelhor and Browne 1986; Herman 1992; Kilpatrick et al. 1981, 1985; Koss and Harvey 1991); and (4) the serious psychiatric problems of multiple personality[2] (Braun 1989; Braun and Sachs 1985; Cohen et al. 1991; Putnam 1989) and borderline personality disorders (Briere 1989; Kroll 1988).

Second, several authors pinpoint the positive intent of this term. They emphasize the fact that survival is an active process and that many of us can and do make it to the "other side" and begin to live full lives again; yes, we are different afterwards, and we have been forced to develop new views of ourselves and the world around us, but we have survived the ordeal of sexual victimization. And, as noted by Briere (1989), Dinsmore (1991), and Dolan (1991) these are highly important issues: We must *not* forget about *how* the girls and the women who have been victimized actually go about surviving, and we must celebrate each and every one of their efforts to do so, even the ones that at first glance may seem negative.

This term, as well, though, has its flaws. One example is that, while focusing exclusively on the recovery process of those of us who have been sexually victimized, the concept of survivor minimizes the role of the perpetrator, an omission that potentially can be dangerous. In other words, if we focus solely on the girls and women who have been sexually victimized, we unintentionally may infer that they are the sole "problem." In addition, the term survivor (like the earlier one of victim) can imply passivity (i.e., we never *fully* recover or we continue to survive forever). Sanford (1990: xvii) elaborates upon this latter criticism: "'Survivor' connotes nothing of the vibrant colors and textures of their lives today. They have transformed their childhoods into adulthoods that are rich with strength, courage, compassion, wisdom, humor, and impressive self-awareness." In sum, our language falls short in that we do *not* have a specific term for those of us who have moved through the recovery process and are fully functioning human beings.

Bass and Davis (1988), Blume (1990), Briere (1989), Dinsmore (1991), Kelly (1988) and Sanford (1990) are exceptions to this criticism because they have begun to talk about "triumphing" over the destructive impact of incest and child abuse, learning to "thrive" afterwards, or moving "beyond survival." My offering is the term *victory*. Since it infers that we already have gone through the frightening process of rediscovering a self and that we have integrated the nightmare of sexual victimization into that new vision, the concept of victory accurately depicts the experiences of many of us who have worked so diligently to recover (Gilmartin 1991). Furthermore, this term eliminates the emphasis on us as passive and helpless victims and moves us beyond the notion of a continual or life-long process of survival. The true joy of this term, though, is that it does *not* infer that the process of "getting there" was an easy one or that we go through it unscathed. In other words, although victory is an optimistic concept, it also includes the realistic issues of: (1) us as changed beings; (2) the assumptions about ourselves and our world that we were forced to reframe; and (3) the new lives (which by necessity) we had to develop. As such, the focus remains on the facts that we have worked through the trauma and that we have put it into a framework with which we can live in the present.

Another problem with the language is that many works infer that we must pick one of these terms, that they are competing for "best" conceptualization. A better way to do this may be to view all three of them as part of a *process of victimization and recovery*. Rather than debating about which of these terms is most accurate or politically correct, our time would be better spent conceptualizing them as parts of the same whole (Gilmartin 1991). Specifically, the first stage is the passive one of being victimized and the subsequent feelings of helplessness and being out of control that come with the territory of sexual victimization. The second step, or survival, can be regarded as the more active stage of recovery or the lengthy period of time during which we attempt to: regain a sense of equilibrium, integrate the experience of sexual victimization into our lives, and develop new views of ourselves and the world around us. The third and final stage of victory, then, is the outcome of this process; it connotes that the dynamic process of recovery is completed and that we have moved to another level of existence. This is *not* to say that the impact of the experience has disappeared; rather, the emphasis is on us as changed beings who have integrated and learned to live with the experience.

We must be careful, though, in our application of these terms. Our primary concern should be to help rather than to harm the girls, adolescent females, and women who already have been victimized. Hypothetically speaking, if a woman remains disrupted five years after being raped, we should *not* blame her; instead, our focus should remain on individual differences (i.e., some women recover rapidly and fully, while others remain trapped in a state of perpetual disruption). In addition, we must be careful that we do *not* apply these terms rigidly; rather, we must remain cognizant of the fact that some girls and women may proceed through this recovery process in a different sequence of stages and/or may do so with relative ease. Thus, although this reconceptualization seems sound, it remains untested; I offer it solely as a heuristic device which may clarify our thinking about what it means to be sexually victimized and to recover from that experience.

The final problem with the language is the terminology that we use to describe the *aftermath* of sexual victimization. For example, Kelly (1988) prefers the term consequences because it emphasizes what we do *after* we have been sexually victimized (i.e., our attempts to cope), as well as our visible "symptoms" of disuption. She, though, rejects concepts such as "effects" and "reactions" (I would add "symptoms" to this list) because they do *not* take into account the range and the complexity of the impact that sexual victimization can have on our lives, nor do they include the prospect of positive outcomes that some girls and women can achieve during and after recovery. In effect, what we have is the same split that was mentioned earlier: The terms victim and effects are similar because they infer passivity and helplessness, while the concepts of survivor and consequences can be paired because they denote active involvement on the parts of the girls and women who have been sexually victimized.

Taken together, I believe that all of these aforementioned trends and changes indicate that we are working toward a sexual victimization literature which is increasingly accurate and sensitive to the concerns of the women and girls who have been assaulted. We no longer view rape, incest, and child sexual abuse exclusively as attacks involving "strangers who jump out of the bushes." Instead, and rightfully so, we examine the realities of these offenses, as well as the respective roles the assailants and this society play in causing, perpetuating, and hiding them. And, in the process, we have begun to exert greater care in the language that we employ when talking about the girls and the women who have been sexually violated.

Flaws in the Sexual Victimization Literature

Since the sexual victimization literature is in a state of flux and continues to evolve, we must be careful that we do *not* reify the information that we have. From the outset, we must acknowledge that many of these works are replete with flawed reasoning, questionable empiricism, and serious methodological flaws (Asher 1988; Briere and Runtz 1988a; Finkelhor and Browne 1986; Haugaard and Reppucci 1988; Katz and Mazur 1979; Kelly 1988; Koss and Harvey 1991; Ledray et al. 1986; Peters et al. 1986; Russell 1984, 1986; Schetky 1990; Schwartz 1980). As examples, a number of criticisms have been leveled against all three of these literatures. They include: (1) the variety of offenses that are examined; (2) the ages of the girls and women that are studied; (3) the various definitions of rape, incest, and child sexual abuse that are employed; (4) the problem of reportability; (5) the samples that are used; (6) the problematic assumptions that we have regarding the females who have been sexually victimized;

(7) the view that rape, incest, and child sexual abuse are "out-there" phenomena; (8) the dearth of well-done systematic studies; (9) the divergent data collection techniques that are employed; and (10) the number of questions used to determine whether someone has been sexually victimized.

Regarding the first issue, several experts now conclude that the most serious forms of sexual victimization are rape and incest (Katz and Mazur 1979; Peters et al. 1986); yet, what they define as the "less serious" offenses (e.g., nonbodily contacts including verbal insults and exhibitionism) often are studied alongside these more serious infractions. This becomes a problem because combining such disparate offenses can create inaccuracies and distortions, particularly regarding the potentially life-altering impact that rape, incest, and child sexual abuse can have on our lives.

The second issue is the ages of the subjects that are studied. As Katz and Mazur (1979:9–10) explain this problem:

> Even when the type of offense is the same . . . the event is different in many ways for child . . . as opposed to adult victims. The time and place of the event, the prior relationship of the offender to the victim, family background, sexual history, and events occurring during the assault are vastly different for each age group. Even more important are the differences between children and adults regarding the aftereffects of the assault . . . [Thus,] data relating to children from child studies are misleading when applied to adult victims.

Although they recommend that rape, incest, and other forms of sexual victimization be studied separately, I have reservations about doing so. Notwithstanding the fact that the different types of sexual victimization and the aftermath of them may be dissimilar for the various age groupings (e.g., infants, children, adolescents, young adults, middle-aged women, and elderly women), the factors at work which cause these problems are quite similar. In other words, girls and women both possess extensive histories of being devalued and are viewed as the property of men. Therefore, whenever possible, I deal with the various age groupings and the different types of sexual victimization together, but, when the divergencies are clear-cut, I discuss them separately.

The third problem is the diverse explanations and definitions of rape, incest, and child sexual abuse that exist. For example, the victim-precipitated view posits that women cause (or at least contribute to) their sexual victimizations, while the feminist perspective suggests exactly the opposite, that social, structural, and/or cultural factors are the culprits. In addition, it is but a slight exaggeration to conclude that no two studies utilize the same conceptualization and operationalization of these various types of sexual victimization. In effect, when we try to compare studies which employ varying definitions and measurements of these phenomena, we may end up giving misleading information and inaccurate impressions about the causes and consequences of sexual victimization.

The fourth and fifth problems, reportability and the samples that we study, overlap. The former refers to whether cases of rape, incest, and child sexual abuse are reported to official authorities (e.g., police or social agencies), while the latter focuses on the variety of potential populations that can be studied (e.g., police data, information from emergency rooms and psychiatric wards, court records, data from social agencies, investigations of college students, and studies of the general population). Since we now are reasonably certain that rape, incest, and child sexual abuse are vastly underreported crimes (Johnson 1980; Kilpatrick et al. 1985; Koss and Harvey 1991; McDermott 1979; Russell 1984, 1986; Schetky 1990; Warshaw 1988), it is logical to suggest that girls and women who report their sexual victimizations to official agencies may differ in significant ways from those who do not (an issue which is examined in Chapter Two). Regarding the sampling issue, Peters et al. (1986) indicate that these divergent sources not only garner quite different information but that some are better than others, with the best and most reliable estimates coming from probability samples administered in the general population. Thus, what we have had is an abundance of information about the girls and women who *have reported* their assaults to official authorities (particularly assaults involving strangers), while there has been a dearth of knowledge about the "hidden" (or more accurately, ignored) victims and survivors of rape, incest, and child sexual abuse.

The sixth problem focuses on a bias that has existed for some time in the rape literature: If she has been sexually assaulted, there must be something "wrong" with her. Although adult women who have been raped often are regarded as being different, Weis and Borges (1973:74) suggest that they really are *not*: "[A] frequent research hypothesis . . . is that the woman who is the victim of rape is somehow peculiar and psychologically different from others . . . Maintenance of this bias in the findings of such research then serves to justify the status of the raped woman as a legitimate victim and reinforces a rationale for the manner in which society treats her." This notion can be extended to girls, as well, in that Freud originally concluded that many of the "hysterical symptoms" reported by his adult, female patients were rooted in their early experiences of incest and child sexual abuse. Later, though, he recanted and declared that their "reports" simply were childhood "fantasies" about their fathers (Courtois 1988; Dinsmore 1991; Herman 1992; Masson 1984; Miller 1984; Rush 1980; Summit 1988). The obvious outcome of this sort of reasoning is that, as long as this society continues to devalue the female population, and stereotypical child-rearing practices remain the norm, all of us are potential victims of sexual abuse.

Similar to the problem just stated, another criticism is that rape, incest, and child sexual abuse often are viewed as "out-there" phenomena, as offenses which affect only a few of us. If, though, as Kelly (1988) and Russell (1984) do, we expand our definition to include all types of sexual violence, the conclusion becomes that sexual victimization is a very real part of all of our lives. Verification of this claim comes via Gordon and Riger's (1989) analysis of how women's fears about rape alter their daily lives. For example, they found that only 8 percent of the women (versus 22 percent of the men) reported feeling very safe when out alone at night in their own neighborhoods, while 26 percent of them (as opposed to only 9 percent of the men) said that they often restrict going out to the daytime. Thus, Gordon and Riger conclude that you do *not* have to be raped or sexually abused to experience the "fallout" from sexual victimization.

The eighth problem is the lack of well-done, systematic studies (Asher 1988; Haugaard and Reppucci 1988; Katz and Mazur 1979; Peters et al. 1986; Schetky 1990; Schwartz 1980). As examples, few of the early studies employed the methodological strategies of control groups or longitudinal research designs, and many of these early reports included so few cases that any statistical analysis was absurd.[3] As summarized by Katz and Mazur (1979:27), our current knowledge about rape, incest, and sexual abuse victims has been "limited to clinical impressions, anecdotal reports, and a few empirical studies [and] even the empirical studies present contradictory data." Although the situation has improved somewhat, in large part their words still apply today.

The ninth flaw is the variety of ways that the data are collected. Although diversity often is regarded as positive or good, in this case, it adds considerably to the confusion. Specifically, many studies employ self-administered question-naires; others use face-to-face interviews, while a few gather their data via telephone interviews. As noted by Peters et al. (1986) and Russell (1986), though, these divergent research methods also garner quite different estimates as to the prevalence of rape, incest, and child sexual abuse, with the higher numbers being found via the face-to-face interview format. As such, many empirical analyses *underestimate* the extent of these problems and lead people to believe that these offenses are rarer than they actually are.

The final problem in the rape, incest, and child sexual abuse literatures is the number of questions used to elicit the data. Although at first glance this may seem to be a minor point, it is *not*. As examples, Peters et al. (1986:57–59) cite the Keckley market research which asks only one question: "Thinking back on your own childhood, do you think that you were ever asked to participate or do anything sexually as a child that you did not want to do or felt uncomfortable about?" At the other extreme is Russell's (1984, 1986) work which includes fourteen highly specific questions, a format which is regarded as eliciting higher and more accurate estimates of these problems (Courtois 1988; Koss and Harvey 1991). To dramatize the difference in these approaches, the former study found that only 11 percent of the respondents had been assaulted, while Russell's work concluded that 44 percent of the women in her sample, at some time during their lives, had been sexually victimized.

Other critics have suggested flaws that are specific to the incest and child sexual abuse literatures. One is the oftcited claim that one out of four girls and one in nine boys have been sexually abused. The problem is that these estimates are "attributed to unnamed experts, got passed around from article to article, and took on authority simply from being cited so often" (Peters et al. 1986:15). Second, since many "unfounded" cases of incest and child sexual abuse (which indeed are valid ones) do *not* stand up to evidentiary criteria and legal definitions, they are excluded from the official estimates (Wyatt and Powell 1988). A third issue is that it is nearly impossible to discern the actual volume of sexual abuse of children. Since a sizable number of these victims and survivors remain silent and tell no one about their abuse (Engel 1989; Haugaard and Reppucci 1988; Poston and Lison 1989; Wyatt and Powell 1988), others do *not* have access to the memories of their abuse (Bass and Davis 1988; Blume 1990; Cohen et al. 1991; Peters et al. 1986), while others do *not* interpret what happened to them as sexual abuse [even though the acts clearly qualify (Bass and Davis 1988; Dinsmore 1991)], it is unlikely that we will ever know the true extent of the problem (Haugaard and Reppucci 1988; Wyatt and Powell 1988).

The numerous aforementioned criticisms are *not* meant to "prove" that all of the information that we have about rape, incest, and child sexual abuse is unreliable or faulty. Rather, the point is to illustrate that some aspects of it are suspect and that there are vast differences in the quality of the extant information. In addition, since we have begun only recently to study the topic of sexual victimization in a systematic fashion, methodological problems are bound to be present. Rather than discarding this information, I am suggesting that we be forewarned; that way, we can decide for ourselves which studies are the better ones.

There also is an upside to this discussion. As noted by Peters et al. (1986) and Russell (1984, 1986), more and more quality studies are being done now, and the most accurate information about sexual victimization today comes from: (1) investigations of the general community rather than specific subgroups of it; (2) studies which employ face-to-face interviews; (3) reports which utilize multiple screening questions; and (4) works which employ the research strategies of control groups and follow-up assessments. Examples of studies which employ many of these strategies are ones authored by Burgess and Holmstrom (1979a, 1979b); Finkelhor (1979, 1984); Kilpatrick and his colleagues (1979, 1981, 1983, 1985); Koss and her associates (Koss 1985b, 1988; Koss et al. 1987, 1988); Russell (1982a, 1984, 1986); and Wyatt (1985).

In addition, although some of the aforementioned problems remain as serious flaws today (e.g., studying nonrandom groups, divergent definitions of these problems, and anecdotal information rather than empirical verification), others have been corrected. As examples, burgeoning literatures on the recently acknowledged issues of acquaintance rape (Koss 1988; Sanday 1990; Warshaw 1988), the ritualistic sexual abuse of children (Braun 1989, 1990; Cohen et al. 1991; Faller 1990; Kelley 1988, 1989, 1992; Finkelhor and Williams with Burns 1988; Mayer 1991; Snow and Sorensen 1990), and adult survivors of incest and child sexual abuse (Bass and Davis 1988; Blume 1990; Briere 1989; Courtois 1988; Dinsmore 1991; Dolan 1991; Engel 1989; Finney 1990; Poston and Lison 1989; Russell 1986), afford us the opportunity to view sexual victimization within populations which historically have been ignored. Accordingly, we now have a better understanding of both the causes and the consequences of these types of victimization, as well as how to implement plans for preventing them.

Existing Definitions of Rape, Incest, and Child Sexual Abuse and My Working Definitions of These Problems

Currently, consensus does *not* exist regarding how to define the various forms of sexual victimization. Some of the experts choose to discuss all of them as parts of the same whole (Herman 1992; Kelly 1988; Russell 1984), while others prefer to study the different types of sexual victimization as separate entities. Regarding rape victimization, Koss and Harvey (1991) suggest that rape is a particularly difficult and complex term to define and to categorize, that we must be careful that we do *not* oversimplify its meaning, and that we must be clear about our definitions of it. To resolve these dilemmas, they suggest a number of different conceptualizations: (1) it can differ in *form* (e.g., individual rape or one assailant, pair rape or two perpetrators, or multiple rape with three or more offenders); (2) rapes also can differ based upon their *spontaneity* (i.e., some are planned, others are unplanned); and (3) they suggest that we can distinguish between cases of rape based upon whether they become *known to the public*, i.e., reported versus hidden rapes. Please note, though, that hidden rapes are further complicated by the fact that they can be acknowledged (i.e., the woman knows that what happened is rape but for whatever reasons declines to report it), or unacknowledged (the objective characteristics or the assault clearly qualify it as a rape, but she does *not* define or perceive it as such).

Another way to discuss the variety of acts which qualify as rape (and seemingly the most popular one) is to focus on the *interpersonal context*. To be specific, Koss and Harvey (1991) divide rape into the categories of: stranger, acquaintance, date, multiple, and marital. This is a particularly useful categorization because it not only reflects the biases of the involved professionals and social control agents, but also includes the views of the general public and our significant others as to acts which qualify as "real" rapes. In other words, based upon the well-documented biases that many people have, the most "believable" case of rape (i.e., stranger rape) is at one extreme, while the least "credible" one (i.e., marital rape) is at the other end of the continuum. The "in-between" instances (i.e., acquaintance, date, and multiple rapes) present more difficulties because they tend to be viewed as less "clear-cut" by the *not-so-objective* observers who do the defining and labeling (Burt 1980; Gilmartin-Zena 1988; Holmstrom and Burgess 1978; Madigan and Gamble 1991).[4]

Although these categorizations of rape are valuable ones, I would hasten to add that Koss and Harvey (1991) focus predominantly on how the women who have been assaulted

perceive and define their sexually-coercive experiences.
Although I agree with this format, we also must be cognizant of
whether a reported case of rape is *believed and counted* by the
various social control agents in the rape processing system (i.e.,
police officers, medical personnel, court officials, and rape crisis
counselors). In other words, what gets confusing is that it is
usually the legal definition of rape rather than our self-
perceptions of it which carries more weight and determines
whether a sexual assault is regarded as a "real" one. Again, the
aforementioned social control agents (i.e., their biases,
prejudices, preconceived images, and perceptions), are critical
players in this "definition game" (Burt 1980; Holmstrom and
Burgess 1978; Madigan and Gamble 1991).

Efforts to sort out the various definitions of incest and
child sexual abuse are even more confusing because some of the
criteria used to differentiate between these types of sexual
victimization are so different. As examples, the critical issues are:
(1) the ages of the victim and the perpetrator(s); (2) how well the
parties knew each other; and (3) the nature of the sexual acts
involved. Regarding the issue of age, some experts qualify acts
as incest or child sexual abuse *only* if they occurred before the
child or adolescent was sixteen years of age (Finkelhor 1984),
while others use the upper limit of eighteen (Gomes-Schwartz et
al. 1990; Russell 1986). In addition, and in order to exclude acts
which could be viewed as "normal" or "exploratory" ones,
several extant definitions of incest and child sexual abuse require
that the assailant(s) be at least five years older than the victim
(Gomes-Schwartz et al. 1990; Russell 1986). We also divide up
the sexual abuse of children based upon whether the parties
know each other. In cases where they do *not* and/or are
unrelated, we usually discuss these offenses as child sexual
abuse, while we tend to reserve the incest label for instances
wherein the child or adolescent is victimized by someone who is
biologically or legally related to her (Poston and Lison 1989;
Russell 1986). Not all of the experts, though, agree with this
distinction. As examples, Blume (1990), Dolan (1991), Engel
(1989), and Swink and Leveille (1986) believe that the blood or
legal relationship is *not* the critical factor; rather, it is the trust or
the emotional bond that exists between the parties. The final way

to categorize cases of incest or child sexual abuse is to focus on the content of the acts. Please note that some of the language used herein is quite odd and value laden. For example, some experts use terms such as "garden variety" to refer to "typical" instances of child sexual abuse, while others talk about cases of incest or child sexual abuse as being "extraordinary," "atypical," "bizarre," "unusual," or "creative" (cf. Blume 1990; Courtois 1988; Steele 1987). The former terms are used to discuss cases where related or unrelated adults fondle, caress, and/or perform vaginal intercourse upon children or adolescents, while the latter terms refer to cases of child sexual abuse or incest which include ritualistic elements, sadistic acts, organized groups (i.e., cults), and/or "unusual" sexual acts.

Based upon the aforementioned trends and problems which exist in the rape, incest, and child sexual abuse literatures, as well as the variety of acts which qualify as sexual victimization, it is important for me to be clear regarding *my definitions* of these offenses. Throughout this book, I use the general terms rape, sexual assault, and sexual coercion to refer to acts which are committed against women (i.e., eighteen years of age or older). More specifically, I employ the terms *rape* and *sexual assault* to refer to attacks during which the assailant(s), via force or the threat of force, tries to or succeeds in penetrating the woman's body with his penis, other body part, or an object. Other types of sexual acts committed against women which take place under duress (e.g., kissing, touching), or are achieved via force, are labeled *sexual coercion*.

In addition, following the standard set by many of the experts in the field, I use the term *sexual abuse* to refer to all unwanted sexual acts involving bodily contact committed by nonfamilial adults who are at least five years older than the girls or the adolescents (i.e., sixteen years of age or younger) that they assault. I reserve the term *incest* for unwanted sexual acts involving bodily contact which are committed by family members and others who have parental types of roles or are in positions of trust. Finally, when I wish to include all girls, adolescents, and women who have experienced rape, sexual assault, sexual coercion, child sexual abuse, and/or incest, I employ the inclusive term of *sexual victimization*.

Summary and Conclusions

As has been shown in this chapter, we have come a long way in altering our definitions and conceptualizations of the problems of rape, incest, and child sexual abuse. As an example, we have begun to move away from victim-precipitated notions of these problems by redirecting our attention to the perspectives of the girls, adolescent females, and adult women who have been so victimized. Second, we have expanded our definitions to include a variety of types of sexual victimization that historically have been excluded, and we also have widened the net regarding the scope of these problems. Third, we have become increasingly aware of the power of the language that we use to describe the girls and the women who have been sexually victimized. Finally, we have started to assess the quality of the information that we currently have about rape, incest, and child sexual abuse, as well as undertaking better studies of these problems.

Obviously, there is plenty of room for improvement, and there are several issues about which we as yet know very little. In the next chapter, then, I outline what we currently know about the prevalence of these problems, while the foci of Chapter Three are the causes of rape, incest, and child sexual abuse.

CHAPTER TWO

Rates of Sexual Victimization

> Nationally, a *conservative* estimate is that, under current conditions, 20–30 percent of girls now twelve years old will suffer a violent sexual attack during the remainder of their lives . . . In fact, the average American woman is just as likely to suffer a sexual attack as she is to be diagnosed as having cancer, or to experience a divorce (Johnson 1980:145–146).

> According to the figures from the now-famous August 1985 *Los Angeles Times* survey, it is estimated that nearly *38 million adults* were sexually abused as children. Current research . . . [also] indicates that one in every three women and one in every seven men are sexually abused by the time they reach the age of eighteen (emphasis in original) (Engel 1989:1).

There is much disagreement regarding the extent of the problems of rape, incest, and child sexual abuse. Some sources regard these offenses as rarities, while other reports, particularly feminist ones, suggest that they have reached epidemic proportions. In part, this divergency can be accounted for by how the various sources which estimate these problems differ in collecting their data, the different types of groups that they study, and how they define and measure sexual victimization. Accordingly, it should *not* be surprising that their findings about the "real" rates of sexual victimization also differ.[1] In order to clarify this issue, I investigate in this chapter a variety of sources which give estimates of all of these forms of sexual victimization.[2]

It is also important to acknowledge from the outset that there are problems whenever we attempt to estimate the volume of sexual victimization. For instance, some girls, adolescent females, and adult women (regardless of the data collection technique utilized) do *not* disclose the fact that they have been victimized; that is to say, some of them may *not* remember their assaults, while others do *not* define what happened to them as sexual victimization. In addition, some studies focus on the incidence of rape, incest, and child sexual abuse (i.e., figures or rates for a specific time frame such as one year), while other reports indicate the prevalence of these problems (i.e., the percentage of girls or women who ever have been sexually victimized). The former approach has the effect of making these problems "look" smaller, while the latter strategy makes them appear to have reached epidemic proportions. Finally, most of the extant estimates of these problems count the different forms of sexual victimization separately, making it impossible to determine the true scope of the problem.

Notwithstanding these caveats, there are a variety of current estimates of the sexual victimization problem in the U.S. Please note, though, that since most of these estimates summarize the volume of rape, incest, and child sexual abuse separately, I, too, will do so. For the topic of *rape*, data sources to be examined include: (1) official police data or the Federal Bureau of Investigation's Uniform Crime Reports; (2) victimization data gathered via surveys of various communities across the country; (3) findings based on surveys of college students; (4) studies which investigate the prevalence of marital rape; and (5) community estimates of rape. For the *incest* and *child sexual abuse* problems, the data sources to be discussed are: (1) official estimates; (2) community studies which examine both incidence and prevalence; (3) surveys of college students and other special populations which focus solely on prevalence; and (4) clinical samples. For all of these data sources, I summarize what they have found regarding the volume of sexual victimization, as well as the inherent flaws within each one. Finally, the issue of the likelihood to report being sexually assaulted and how it affects rates of rape, incest, and child sexual abuse is examined.

Various Estimates of the Rape Problem

Official Police Data

Since it began to collect data during the 1930s, the Federal Bureau of Investigation (hereafter FBI) has published annual Uniform Crime Reports (hereafter UCR) which summarize the volume of crime in this country. Although done on a voluntary basis, these data focus on reported Part I offenses (e.g., murder and nonnegligent manslaughter, forcible rape, robbery, aggravated assault, burglary, larceny-theft, motor vehicle theft, and arson), and Part II crimes (e.g., the less serious and white-collar crimes, simple assaults *not* included under Part I, embezzlement, and curfew violations) for 97 percent of the population (O'Brien 1985).

To give a more balanced perspective, as well as to compare how the official rate of rape in the U.S. has changed in relation to other types of violent crimes in this country, Table 2.1 reflects the FBI's estimates of violent crime, as well as rates for the specific crimes of murder and nonnegligent manslaughter, forcible rape, robbery, and aggravated assault per 100,000 people for even numbered years from 1940 to 1990. As is shown in column one, there has been a tremendous increase in the *overall rate of violent crime* during this time frame. Specifically, although this rate increased during the 1940s, it declined slightly during the latter part of that decade. Throughout the 1950s, the rate remained fairly constant, but it began to skyrocket during the mid- to late 1960s. During the 1970s and 1980s, the upward spiral continued, and, as a result of this trend, many experts now suggest that the problem of violent crime in our country has reached epidemic proportions.

Regarding the crime of *forcible rape*, the FBI UCR: (1) defines it as carnal knowledge of a female forcibly and against her will (O'Brien 1985); (2) excludes statutory rapes (i.e., either no force is used or the victim is a minor); and (3) calculates this rate per 100,000 *persons* rather than focusing exclusively on its incidence among women. The figures in column three show that our rate of forcible rape was relatively low in 1940; it increased

Table 2.1: FBI Crime Rate Data for Even-Numbered Years from 1940 to the Present, per 100,000 Persons

Year	Overall Rates of Violent Crime	Rates of Murder and Non-Negligent Manslaughter	Rates of Forcible Rape	Rates of Robbery	Aggravated Assault
1940	100.3	6.5	5.2	46.4	42.2
1942	113.0	6.4	6.1	46.6	53.9
1944	114.2	5.6	7.9	43.6	57.1
1946	142.0	6.9	8.7	59.4	67.0
1948	135.9	5.9	7.6	51.9	70.5
1950	132.9	5.3	7.3	48.7	71.6
1952	139.1	5.3	7.1	51.5	75.2
1954	146.5	4.8	6.8	57.6	77.3
1956	136.0	4.7	8.5	46.7	76.7
1958	147.6	4.6	9.3	54.9	78.8
1960	159.0	5.0	9.4	59.9	84.7
1962	160.5	4.5	9.3	59.4	87.3
1964	188.2	4.8	11.0	67.9	104.5
1966	217.2	5.6	12.9	80.3	118.4
1968	294.6	6.8	15.5	131.0	141.3
1970	361.0	7.8	18.6	171.5	163.1
1972	398.0	8.9	22.3	180.0	176.9
1974	396.0	8.6	20.5	188.0	179.0
1976	467.8	8.8	26.6	199.3	233.2
1978	497.8	9.0	31.0	195.8	262.1
1980	596.6	10.2	36.8	251.1	298.5
1982	571.1	9.1	34.0	238.9	289.2
1984	539.2	7.9	35.7	205.4	290.2
1986	617.7	8.6	37.9	225.1	346.1
1988	637.2	8.4	37.6	220.9	370.2
1990	731.8	9.4	41.2	257.0	424.1
Percent changes in rates:					
1940-90	629.6	44.6	692.3	453.9	905.0
1950-90	450.6	77.4	464.4	427.7	492.7
1960-90	360.3	88.0	338.3	329.1	400.7
1970-90	102.7	20.5	121.5	49.9	160.2
1980-90	22.7	-7.8	12.0	2.4	43.6

Sources: Bureau of the Census: U.S. Department of Commerce, Economic and Statistics
  Administration: Statistical Abstract of the United States (102d ed.)
Bureau of the Census: U.S. Department of Commerce, Economic and Statistics
  Administration: Statistical Abstract of the United States (111th ed.)
Federal Bureau of Investigation (1992)
Hindelang and Davis (1977)

slightly during the middle of that decade, but declines were noted toward the end of the 1940s and early 1950s. During the mid-1950s, the rate of forcible rape increased and continued to do so until the mid-1970s; there was, though, a slight decline in 1974. Throughout the remainder of the 1970s and the early 1980s, rates upwardly spiraled again. Inexplicably, in 1982, the rate of forcible rate again dipped a bit, but it continued its upward climb throughout the remainder of the decade. In effect, since 1940, there was a 692 percent increase in the rate of reported forcible rapes, while the comparable increase from 1970 until the present is 122 percent. Regarding the most recent data from 1990: (1) there was a rape victimization rate of 41.2 per 100,000 persons; (2) the crime of forcible rape constituted about 6 percent of the total volume of violent crime; and (3) this is the highest rate of forcible rape ever reported by the FBI UCR (Koss and Harvey 1991).

Although the rates for several *other types of violent crimes* also have increased dramatically during this same time frame, the rate of forcible rape has increased even more so (Baron and Straus 1989; Hindelang and Davis 1977). For example, from 1933 until 1973, our rate of murder and nonnegligent homicide increased by nearly 22 percent; the rate of robbery increased by 94 percent, while the rate of aggravated assault increased nearly 310 percent (Hindelang and Davis 1977). During that same time frame, though, the rate of forcible rape increased by nearly 557 percent (Hindelang and Davis 1977). The same pattern is evident during the last twenty years. Again, based upon the data in Table 2.1, since 1970, we see that the murder rate increased by about 21 percent; the rate of robbery increased by 50 percent; the rate of aggravated assault skyrocketed by nearly 160 percent, while the incidence of forcible rape increased by almost 122 percent.

These data, though, are difficult to interpret for a number of reasons. As examples, we could conclude that: (1) the number of forcible rapes being committed actually is increasing; (2) these increases reflect changes in the laws which make reporting the crime of rape easier; (3) the criminal justice system is now more responsive to women's charges of rape and is more likely to regard allegations of rape as "founded" cases; (4) these increases could be due to the emphasis of rape crisis centers on clients officially reporting their sexual assaults; and (5) some combination of these factors may be true. Thus, the debate continues as to whether these observed increases are "real" or whether they simply reflect changes which have taken place in this society and our rape processing system. Notwithstanding this disagreement, there is little doubt that these official data show that the crime of rape has increased significantly in recent times.

    In addition, and as has been discussed in detail elsewhere (cf. O'Brien 1985; Baron and Straus 1989), several serious problems exist with the FBI UCR estimations of the crime problem, particularly for forcible rape. First and foremost, to be included in this data base, crimes must be reported to the police, yet many rape victims fail to do so for a variety of reasons (e.g., fear of recriminations from the perpetrators, the consequences of negative publicity from official authorities, and distress about going through the trial process). These explanations have been substantiated by O'Brien (1985), who found that women reported their completed and attempted rapes only 43 percent of the time, and Warshaw (1988), who has shown that a shockingly low number of women who were assaulted by acquaintances (i.e., 10 percent) officially reported them to official police agencies. Second, to be counted in the FBI data base, police must regard the reported act as a crime. The problem herein is the "unfounding" process whereby individual police officers and/or police departments are unwilling to view an act as a crime. As has been noted by Baron and Straus (1989), this is a common practice, particularly in rape cases, and has the effect of reducing the official estimate of the problem. Third, it is difficult to compare and contrast rates of forcible rape across the country because this crime is defined differently from one jurisdiction to another and sometimes even among jurisdictions within the same state (O'Brien 1985). Fourth, many victims and survivors of rape have so bought the mythology surrounding the subject of rape that they do *not* define what happened to them as rape; thus, they do *not* report their attacks to official agencies (Russell 1984; Warshaw 1988). The final problem is that police jurisdictions vary in their level of professionalism, which in turn creates different rates of rape. That is to say, the more professional police departments are likely to be concerned with accurate record keeping and validating the volume of crime (mostly for funding purposes) which, in turn, causes them to report higher levels of crime (O'Brien 1985).

Notwithstanding these criticisms, the FBI UCR data base is the sole source of information regarding the rate of rape for most jurisdictions across the country (Baron and Straus 1989; O'Brien 1985), as well as the most readily available measure. As is noted in the following sections, though, we now have other ways to measure this problem, and many of these newer approaches draw quite different conclusions.

Results Derived from Victimization Surveys

In part as a response to crimes being underreported, the National Crime Surveys (hereafter NCS) were initiated by the Law Enforcement Assistance Administration and the U.S. Census Bureau in the early 1970s (Koss and Harvey 1991; O'Brien 1985). Random samples were gathered in twenty-six large cities from 1972 until 1975, while national household surveys began in 1972 and continue to be conducted at the present time. Even though the NCS classifies crimes in a manner that is similar to that of the FBI UCR, please note that the two data sources are difficult to compare for several reasons. As examples, Hindelang and Davis (1977) indicate that: (1) UCR rates of rape are reported per 100,000 persons, while NCS data report information only for females; (2) UCR data include persons of all ages, while the victim survey data include only females who are twelve years of age or older; (3) the victim survey rates are based on results from at least thirteen major cities across the U.S., while information for other large cities and smaller communities is excluded; (4) the victim survey results include rapes reported to the police, as well as ones which were *not*; and (5) rapes reported to survey interviewers are *not* subject to unfounding.

With these shortcomings in mind, via representative samples of residents in twenty-six cities, McDermott (1979) reports rape victimization data for nearly 10,000 households (20,000 individuals) for 1974 and 1975. She suggests that 39,310 rapes and attempted rapes were reported to interviewers and that 82 percent of these attacks were committed by strangers. When compared to FBI UCR data, these results reflect a much higher rate of rape victimization; in fact, the NCS rape victimization rate is nearly double what the FBI reports (Koss and Harvey 1991; McDermott 1979; O'Brien 1985).

More recent victimization data show that nearly 36 million victimizations occurred in each year from 1988 to 1990, while the comparable FBI UCR figures for the same years are about 14 million victimizations (Adler et al. 1991; U.S. Department of Justice 1992). Regarding the crime of forcible rape, NCS data show a rate of 1.2 per *1,000 women* in 1989 and 1.0 in 1990, while the FBI data for 1988 reflect only a rate of 37.6 per *100,000 persons* (Adler et al. 1991; U.S. Department of Justice 1992).[3]

Victimization surveys go a step further by providing information about the demographic characteristics of the women who were raped, as well as information about the nature of their assaults. For instance, McDermott (1979) reports that young women between the ages of sixteen and twenty-four who were nonwhite, single, never married, and poor were overrepresented. In addition, most of the rapes occurred outdoors or in public settings and at night; 40 percent of the women indicated that a weapon was present during the assault; and most of the women reported that they had incurred injuries during their assaults. Finally, she notes that only 56 percent of the women who experienced completed or attempted rapes reported their assaults to the police.

As noted by O'Brien (1985), Koss and Harvey (1991), and Russell (1984), though, there also are problems with this data base. First of all, the data are derived via face-to-face interviews which could cause some respondents to withhold information, a likely situation with a crime such as rape which may cause guilt or embarassment for its victims. Second, since people are asked about criminal victimizations which occurred during the last six months (or the last year), it is possible that some events simply may have been forgotten. Third, the questions asked in these surveys are, at best, oblique measures of forcible rape. Finally, since one member of each household is interviewed, it is possible that he/she may be unaware of victimizations experienced by other members of that domicile. Notwithstanding these flaws,

O'Brien (1985:59) notes that "the NCS survey data have provided us with a rich source of data on victimization[; t]hey have helped provide a sense of the size of the dark figure of unreported crime and have provided some sense of the rate of victimization suffered by various groups."

Surveys of College Students

Surveys of college students generally are of two types. One format is to ask the women about whether they ever have been sexually victimized, while the other approach is to ask male students about their actual, as well as their projected, sexually coercive behaviors. Table 2.2 reports the relevant figures for the women, while Table 2.3 shows the data for the men.

Although Kanin and Kirkpatrick alerted us to the problem of acquaintance rape among college students some thirty-five years ago (Kanin 1957; Kirkpatrick and Kanin 1957), it is only recently that we have resumed an active interest in this subject. As is shown in Table 2.2, current estimates of this problem among *college-age women* include: (1) Allen and Okawa's (1987) random sample of undergraduate and graduate students at the University of Illinois, Urbana-Champaign, which shows that 12 percent of the women had been sexually harassed; (2) Baier et al.'s random sample of undergraduate and graduate students at an unspecified university which shows that 35 percent of the women had been forced to kiss and/or pet, while 12 percent of the women had been forced to have sexual intercourse; (3) data gathered by Berger et al. (1986) at an unspecified Wisconsin university which finds that 25 percent of the women had experienced unwanted sexual contact; (4) Cammaert's (1985) report from a random sample of women enrolled at the University of Calgary which concludes that 30 and 23 percent of the undergraduate and graduate students, respectively, had experienced inappropriate sexual behavior; (5) Fenstermaker's (1989) probability sample of students at an unspecified college which shows that 25 percent of the women reported having experienced some sort of sexual coercion; (6) Koss' (1985a, 1985b) investigation of one Midwestern university which finds that nearly 37 percent of the women had been sexually victimized; (7)

Table 2.2: Recent Studies which Examine the Prevalence of Acquaintance Rape among Women College Students

Author and Year of the Study	Type of Sample Utilized	Sexual Coercion	Prevalence
Allen & Okawa (1987)	Random sample of undergraduate and graduate students at the University of Illinois, Urbana-Champaign	Sexually harassed	12%
Baier et al. (1991)	Ten percent random sample of students at a large, public, residential university	Physical force used to make her engage in kissing or petting that she did not want	35%
	Physical force used to make her have intercourse		12%
Berger et al. (1986)	Ten percent random sample of students at a Wisconsin university	Unwanted sexual contact	25%
Cammaert (1985)	Random sample of students at the University of Calgary	Inappropriate sexual behavior	30% = Undergraduate 23% = Grad.
Fenstermaker (1989)	Probability sample of students at an unspecified college	Sexual coercion	25%
Koss (1985a, 1985b)	Nonrandom sample of undergraduate students at a Midwestern university	Sexually victimized	37%
Lane & Gwartney-Gibbs (1985)	Systematic sample at unspecified college	Coitus under pressure	25%
Lott et al. (1982)	Random sample of students, faculty, staff and administrators at the University of Rhode Island	Sexual assault	25%
Mahoney et al. (1986)	Nonrandom sample of introduction to sociology students at an unspecified university	Forced to have intercourse against their wills	20%
Muehlenhard & Linton (1987)	Nonrandom sample of introduction to psychology students	Unwanted sexual behavior	17%

Table 2.2 (con.)

Author and Year of the Study	Type of Sample Utilized	Sexual Coercion	Prevalence
Soeken & Damrosh (1986)	Nonrandom sample of students at an unspecified university	Rape	15%
MS. *magazine* Project on Campus Sexual Assault (Koss 1988; Koss et al. 1987; Warshaw 1988)	Nearly 6,000 students at 32 representative institutions of higher education across the country	Unwanted sexual contact	53%

Lane and Gwartney-Gibbs' (1985) data, gathered via a systematic sample of students at an unspecified state college, which indicate that 25 percent of the women had experienced coitus under pressure; (8) Lott et al.'s (1982) study of randomly selected students, faculty, staff, and administrators at the University of Rhode Island which concludes that 25 percent of all women will experience at least one sexual assault; (9) Mahoney et al.'s (1986) nonrandom survey of introduction to sociology students at an unspecified institution of higher education which shows that 20 percent of the women had been forced to have intercourse against their wills; (10) Muehlenhard and Linton's (1987) study of undergraduate students enrolled in introduction to psychology courses which determines that 17 percent of the women said that, on recent dates, the men had attempted to engage in sexual behavior that the women did *not* want; and (11) Soeken and Damrosh's (1986) report which concludes that 15 percent of the women at their university had been raped.

The most comprehensive study of the acquaintance rape problem to date is the *MS. Magazine* Project on Campus Sexual Assault. Conducted by Koss and her associates (Koss 1988; Koss et al. 1987), this study included nearly 6,000 students at 32 representative institutions of higher education across the country. And the findings are alarming: *53 percent* of the women reported experiencing unwanted sexual contact. Specifically, 15 percent reported a completed rape; 12 percent had been involved in attempted rapes; 11 percent had experienced sexual coercion; and 15 percent reported having been touched sexually against their wills (Koss 1988; Koss et al. 1987; Warshaw 1988). Equally important, these data show that: (1) 84 percent of the women who had been the victims of *completed* rapes knew their assailants; (2) 57 percent of these assaults took place while the women were on dates; (3) only 27 percent of the women whose sexual victimizations met the *legal* criteria for the crime of rape labeled them as such; and (4) many of these women remained silent about their assaults [i.e., 42 percent never told anyone, while only 10 percent officially reported their attacks to the police or rape crisis centers (Warshaw 1988)].

Regarding studies which have examined the attitudes and behaviors of *male college students*, the results are equally insidious. As is shown in Table 2.3: (1) Briere and Malamuth (1983) report that 41 percent of the men in their sample self-reported *no* likelihood to rape or to use force during sex; 30 percent said they would use *some* force but would *not* rape, while a shockingly high 28 percent said that they would use force and commit rape; (2) similarly, Check and Malamuth (1983) conclude that 30 percent of the male students in their study admitted that they would rape, if guaranteed that no one would find out; (3) in his study of seventy-one college men who were self-disclosed (but undetected) rapists, Kanin (1984, 1985) reports that 77 percent of them knew that they had committed rape; (4) Koss (1988) shows that 25 percent of the men that she surveyed, at some point in their lives, had been sexually aggressive; (5) according to Mosher and Anderson (1986), nearly 20 percent of their male respondents had forced a woman to have sex, while two-thirds of them said that they had gotten a woman drunk in order to have sex with her; (6) Rapaport and Burkhart (1984) note that, on at least one occasion, 15 percent of the 201 men enrolled in their undergraduate psychology classes had forced a girl or a woman to have sex; and (7) Wilson et al. (1983) found that 26 percent of their male students reported securing sex via "forceful and offensive" tactics.

These data, as well, though, are problematic. For example, some of the studies employ random samples of college students, while others utilize accidental samples. In addition, these studies use different measures for sexual coercion and violence (i.e., some of them report sexual harrassment data; others focus on

Table 2.3: Major Studies which Examine the Attitudinal or
Behavioral Likelihood of College-Age Men to be Sexually Coercive

Author and Year of the Study	Type of Sample	Sexual Coercion	Prevalence
Briere & Malamuth (1983)	Nonrandom sample of 352 males in introductory psychology classes at the University of Manitoba	Attitudinal likelihood to use force and/or to rape	30% = would use force but would *not* rape; 28% = would use force and commit rape
Check & Malamuth (1983)	Nonrandom sample of 289 students enrolled in introductory psychology classes at the University of Manitoba	Attitudinal likelihood to commit rape	Overall = 30% some likelihood to commit rape; of men with traditional views about sex roles = 44%; of men with non-traditional views about sex roles = 12%
Kanin (1984, 1985)	Nonrandom sample of 71 undetected rapists	Knew that they had committed rape	77%
Koss (1988)	Nearly 6,000 students (2,972 men) at representative institutions of higher education in the U.S.	Had been sexually aggressive	25%
Mosher & Anderson (1986)	Nonrandom sample of 175 college men	Had forced a woman to have sex	19% = had forced a woman to have sex; 66% = had gotten a woman drunk in order to have sex with her
Rapaport & Burkhart (1984)	Nonrandom sample of 201 college males enrolled in introductory psychology courses	On at least one occasion, had forced a girl or a woman to have sex	15%

Table 2.3 (con.)

Author and Year of the Study	Type of Sample	Sexual Coercion	Prevalence
Wilson et al. (1983)	Nonrandom sample of 103 male undergraduate students at a medium-sized regional university in the South	Secured sex via forceful and/or offensive tactics	26%

unwanted touching, while still others examine rape as it is defined legally). Notwithstanding these flaws, the results are strikingly similar; on the average, approximately 30 percent of the college-age women reported that they had experienced coercive and/or unwanted sexual activity. (What makes this figure even more amazing is that Kirkpatrick and Kanin reported the same one thirty-five years earlier.) These data also suggest that the self-reported likelihood of college-age men to rape, as well as their admissions that they actually have done so, are *not* the idiosyncratic or abberant attitudes and/or behaviors of a few; rather, these are commonplace notions and actions for many men.

These studies differ dramatically, though, in how they explain the men's attitudes and proclivities. For instance, Briere and Malamuth (1983:322) offer a structural explanation: "[P]reventing rape may be tantamount to revamping a significant proportion of our societal values, as opposed to placing primary emphasis on treating 'sexual psychopaths' or other 'deviant' individuals." Rapaport and Burkhart (1984: 220), though, employ psychological and social-psychological variables to explain these same patterns: "[S]exually coercive males act on a system of values wherein females are perceived as adversaries, and that this system is potentiated by the characterological dimensions of irresponsibility and poor socialization."

In sum, the prevalence of the acquaintance rape problem among college students is quite real. In addition, although the aforementioned studies only reflect data for college students, albeit disheartening, similar results have been found among high school students (cf. Alder 1985; Levy 1991; White and Humphrey 1991). Yet, as is to be discussed in Chapter Seven, it is only recently that we have begun to openly acknowledge this issue and try to do something about it within these two populations.

The Prevalence of Marital Rape

Our willingness to acknowledge (attitudinally as well as legally) that another type of acquaintance rape, marital rape, is possible is even more recent (Finkelhor and Yllo 1985; Russell 1991). As Russell (1982b:2–3) suggests, "[W]ife rape has presumably been with us as long as the institution of marriage—at least in Western culture," and the basis for this type of rape is "the idea that females are the property of males," a major tenet of any patriarchal society. Even though the first wave of feminism brought this subject to the public's attention during the *1850s*, by 1980, only three states (New Jersey, Oregon, and Nebraska) had eliminated the marital rape exemption in their laws; four other states (California, Hawaii, Minnesota, and Iowa) had partially eliminated this restriction (Russell 1991), while in thirteen states, "legislators . . . had quietly extended the privilege of husbands to rape their wives to men who are cohabitating with women with whom they are not legally married" (Russell 1982b:21). As of 1990, the situation has improved somewhat. Currently, in seventeen states, "wife rape is a crime . . . regardless of whether the couple lives together or apart;" in twenty-six states, "men can be prosecuted for raping their wives in some circumstances, but they are totally exempt from prosecution in others that are prosecutable for nonmarital rapes," while in the remaining seven states raping one's wife is *not* defined as a crime (Russell 1991:133).

The empirical investigations of this problem have shown that marital rape is a more frequent problem than anyone imagined. In her analysis of its prevalence within a group of randomly selected women residing in the San Francisco Bay Area, Russell (1982b) concludes that 14 percent of them had been raped by a husband or an ex-husband, while Finkelhor and Yllo

(1985) have reported the comparable figure of 10 percent. Interestingly, though, and *not* surprisingly, only 7 percent of the women in Russell's study whose experiences qualify as marital rape perceived that they had been raped. Since the same tendency has been observed among college-age women who have been victims of acquaintance or date rapes, Russell concludes that this has more to do with the *mythology* which surrounds the subject of rape, particularly when the parties know each other (i.e., women "cause" it by their attitudes, dress, and behaviors), than it does with the particular group of women that she studied.

Community Surveys

During the late 1970s (via the same random sample of 930 women cited earlier), Russell and Howell (1983) investigated the prevalence of the rape problem in the San Francisco Bay area (Russell 1982a, 1984; Russell and Howell 1983). They concluded that nearly one-half (44 percent) of the women had experienced at least one attempted or completed rape. Although some experts question this figure and regard it as being too high, it is important to reiterate that Russell employed *fourteen* probe questions. And as was noted in the last chapter, the more questions you ask and the better the quality of those questions, the higher is the likelihood of obtaining a high rate of rape (Peters et al. 1986).

In addition, Kilpatrick and his associates (1983) conducted telephone interviews of a random sample of nearly 2,000 women residing in Charleston County, South Carolina. They found that 15 percent of the women had experienced one or more attempted or completed rapes.

Siegel and her associates (Burnam et al. 1988; Siegel et al. 1990) conducted a random sample of 3,132 adults (eighteen years of age and older) residing in two Los Angeles mental health catchment areas. Please note that the residents of one catchment area are predominantly Spanish-speaking (83 percent), while the majority of the residents of the other district are white (63 percent), with a smaller, yet sizable, Spanish-speaking population (21 percent). Subjects were asked: "In your lifetime, has anyone ever tried to pressure or force you to have sexual contact" (Siegel et al. 1990:234)? And 13 percent of them said yes (i.e., 17 percent of the women and 9 percent of the men). Note, as well, that 80 percent of these assaults occurred before the respondents were twenty-five years of age [i.e., "13 perent between ages six and ten, 19 percent between ages eleven and fifteen, 34 percent between ages sixteen and twenty, and 15 percent between ages twenty-one and twenty-five" (Burnam et al. 1988:845)].

Ageton (1983) conducted a survey of a national, random sample of adolescents (ages eleven thru seventeen), and she concluded that 7 to 9 percent of the females had experienced one or more sexual assaults. There are, though, theoretical and methodological drawbacks in this study. For instance, Ageton makes *no* effort to differentiate between cases of rape and child sexual abuse; she simply assumes that all of them are rapes.[4] Second, she engages in a great deal of victim blaming in her interpretation of these data: "The findings . . . indicate . . . that engaging in delinquent behavior and being part of a delinquent network influence the risk of being sexually assaulted . . . It appears that teenage females who are generally delinquent are advertising their unconventionality in ways that jeopardize their control of sexual situations" (Ageton 1983:132–133).

Comparing and Contrasting These Data Sources

When examining and comparing these data sources, several conclusions may be drawn. First of all, FBI data reflect the lowest rate of rape victimization; victim surveys rank second, while surveys of college students and members of the community offer the highest estimates of the problem. We must keep in mind, though, that the FBI UCR would be likely to count fewer cases of rape due to their parochial definition of rape, as well as the "unfounding" process which exists in many police departments across the country. Obversely, investigations conducted on college campuses and in the general community often ask about less specific issues such as "unwanted sexual activity" or "sexually coercive behaviors," while victimizat. surveys are in between with a fairly oblique measure of t.

problem. Therefore, it should *not* surprise us that these divergent sources also report vastly different estimates of the problem.

Second, all of these investigations are, at best, estimates of the rape problem. This is because many women never report their sexual assaults to official authorities; they fail to disclose them to researchers who investigate the "hidden" rape problem; and/or they do *not* label what happened to them as rape. As such, we can only make calculated guesses about the "real" volume of this problem.

Third, as readily can be seen, we have a great deal of information about FBI UCR data, victimization survey results, and the acquaintance rape problem, while we have much less data regarding the incidence and prevalence of rape and attempted rape within randomly selected, community-based samples. In order to gain a better understanding of the true volume of sexual assault, then, future research needs to correct this situation.

Fourth, these data sources tend to include different types of rape victimizations. For example, FBI data focus almost exclusively on stranger rapes because cases of acquaintance rape are much less likely to be reported as well as more likely to be "unfounded." Although NCS data include both stranger and acquaintance rape, recent data show that less than half (45 percent) of the assaults disclosed to interviewers were committed by strangers (Koss and Harvey 1991), while surveys of college students and women who have been raped within marriage usually are estimates of the acquaintance rape problem.

Regardless of which data source we investigate, and regardless of the inherent flaws within each of them, forcible rape can be viewed as a problem that some now suggest has reached epidemic proportions. As Johnson (1980:146) articulates this perspective: "The numbers reiterate a reality that American women have lived with for years: Sexual violence against women is part of the everyday fabric of American life."

Are Some Women More at Risk than Others?

Several experts have tried to determine whether some women are more vulnerable to being raped than are others. Let me, though, be very clear about this issue; I am *not* suggesting that women cause their assaults to happen. Rather, the focus is on whether patterns have been found, and the data do show certain trends. For example, NCS data show that victims of rape are more likely to be young, poor, nonwhite, and single.

Regarding the likelihood of a woman experiencing acquaintance rape, vulnerability factors include: (1) being a first-quarter, first-year student; (2) being in a "risky" situation with a new date (e.g., being alone with him in a relatively isolated environment); (3) failing to remain sober; (4) failing to learn much about a potential dating partner; (5) traditional or gender-stereotyped dating patterns (e.g., he initiates and pays for the date); and (6) miscommunications about sex (Allgeier 1987, 1988; Koss 1988; Parrot 1990; Sanday 1990; Warshaw 1988). In addition, the sex-role attitudes of both parties (i.e., the more traditional the attitudes the higher the likelihood of acquaintance rape), having experienced or witnessed violence in one's family of origin, and jealousy on the man's part have been associated with a higher likelihood of acquaintance rape (Allgeier 1987; Sugarman and Hotaling 1991; Warshaw 1988).

A few markers also have been found among women who have experienced marital rape. For instance, Russell (1982b) reports that women who have been raped within marriage are more likely to have had histories of childhood sexual victimization as well as prior adult victimization(s). In addition, she found that the "traditionality" of the woman was significant, but only as a predictor of why women remain in these relationships. Specifically, the prevalence of marital rape was *equal* among nontraditional and traditional women, but traditionality determined whether they stayed in their marriages: "The more traditional women (more traditional by virtue of having fewer resources) are more likely to stay" (Russell 1982b:171).

Estimates of the Incidence and Prevalence of Child Sexual Abuse

Although many people would have us believe that the incest and child sexual abuse problems are fairly recent phenomena, Peters et al. (1986) note that estimates of these problems in the U.S. date back to 1929. Before outlining some of the early data, as well as some of the more current estimates of these problems, though, it is important to acknowledge from the outset that these estimates are even more questionable and variable than are the ones which enumerate the rape victimization problem. In effect, these data, too, are replete with definitional problems and methodological flaws, and they reflect an even larger range of estimates of this problem [i.e., the lowest estimate is that 6 percent of girls and 3 percent of boys have been sexually abused, while the highest estimates are that 62 and 31 percent of girls and boys, respectively, have been sexually abused (Peters et al. 1986)].

Notwithstanding these problems, we now have a multitude of studies which investigate the incidence and prevalence of incest and child sexual abuse, and Table 2.4 includes several of the important studies which estimate the extensiveness of these problems. In addition, the following sections summarize the data from *six different sources*: early estimates of the problems; reported cases (i.e., cases known to the police or social service agencies); community surveys; studies involving college students; clinical populations; and other estimates.

Early Estimates of the Problem

In the U.S., several of the major studies which examined the prevalence of the child sexual abuse problem among females were conducted in the 1940s, 1950s, and 1960s (Russell 1984). As examples, (1) Landis et al.'s 1940 study of middle-class hospital patients and controls shows that 36 percent of the female respondents had been sexually abused, with 13 percent having experienced incest (i.e., among what the authors call the "abnormals" or the psychiatric hospital patients the ever-abused percent is 39, while the percentage among the "normals" or control group participants is 33 percent); (2) in 1953, Kinsey et al. determined that 24 percent of their female respondents had been sexually victimized before the age of fourteen, with 3 percent of them having been the victims of incest; (3) in 1956, Landis found that 35 percent of the women that he surveyed had been sexually abused; and (4) Gagnon's 1965 data show that 28 percent of the

Table 2.4: Studies which Examine the Prevalence of Incest and Child Sexual Abuse in a Variety of Samples

Author & Date of Study	Sample Studied	Prevalence
The early studies:		
Landis, C. et al. (1940)	Nonrandom sample of psychiatric patients and a control group	36%=sexually abused 13%=victims of incest
Kinsey et al. (1953)	Nonrandrom sample of nearly 2,000 women	3%=incestuous abuse before age fourteen 24%=sexually victimized or approached for sex by age fourteen
Landis, J. (1956)	Sample of 1,800 college students	35%=of the women had one or more experiences with a sexual deviate
Gagnon (1965)	Subgroup of Kinsey et al.'s sample (N = 333)	28% = had been sexually abused as a child by an adult
Random surveys of the community:		
Los Angeles Times survey (see Finkelhor et al. 1989)	Random sample of 2,627 U.S. residents	22%=had experienced some form of child sexual abuse (27% of the women and 16% of the men)
Russell (1986)	Random sample of households in the San Francisco Bay area	16%=at least one experience of incestous abuse 31%=at least one experience with extrafamilial abuse 38%=combined figure
Finkelhor (1984)	Random sample of parents in Boston, MA	15%=of the women had been sexually abused before age sixteen 5%=had been sexually abused by a relative
Wyatt (1985)	Random sample of women in the Los Angeles area	21%=sexually abused by a relative 32%=extrafamilial abuse 45%=combined figure
Peters (1988)	Random sample of women residing in Los Angeles County	60%=at least one episode of sexual abuse by age 18
Kercher & McShane (1984)	Random sample of registered drivers in Texas	11%=of the women had been sexually abused as children

Table 2.4 (con.)

Author & Date of Study	Sample Studied	Prevalence
Bagley & his associates (cf. Bagley & King 1990)	Random sample of adults residing in Calgary, Canada	22%=of the women reported at least one serious event of sexual abuse as children
Saunders et al. (1992)	Community sample of adult women residing in Charleston County, South Carolina	34%=of the women had been victims of at least one form of sexual assault before age eighteen

Recent surveys of college students:

Finkelhor (1979)	Nonrandom sample of women students enrolled in six New England colleges and universities	10%=had been sexually abused as children
Bagley (cf. Bagley & King 1990)	Nonrandom sample of female college students	19%=had been sexually abused as children
Briere & Runtz (1988b)	Nonrandom sample of undergraduate females at unspecified school	15%=had been sexually abused as children
Fromuth (1986)	Nonrandom sample of women students in psychology classes at Auburn University	22%=had been sexually abused as children

Clinical Samples:

Briere (1989)	Women requesting counseling at an out-patient crisis intervention center	50%=had been sexually abused as children
	Women seen at a psychiatric emergency room	Nearly 2/3=had been sexually abused as children
Jehu (1988)	Nonrandom sample of women seeking treatment at the University of Manitoba's Sexual Dysfunction Clinic	All=had been sexually abused as children

Other estimates:

Bagley (cf. Bagley & King 1990)	Nonrandom sample of former prostitutes	73%=had been sexually abused before age sixteen

Table 2.4 (con.)

Author & Date of Study	Sample Studied	Prevalence
Briere (1989)	Nonrandom sample of teenage mothers	60%=had been sexually abused as children
	Nonrandom sample of former prostitutes	50%=had been sexually abused as children
Simons & Whitbeck (1991)	Nonrandom sample of adolescent runaways	43%=had been sexually abused as children
	Nonrandom sample of homeless women	24%=had been sexually abused as children

women in his sample had been sexually abused before puberty. Please note that, although we have known about the problems of incest and child sexual abuse for some time now, it is only recently that we have begun to acknowledge that these figures may be "real," and have tried to do something to stem these problems.

Reported cases. As noted by Peters et al. (1986), Jehu (1988), and Crewdson (1988), there have been three national attempts to determine the incidence or prevalence of the child sexual abuse problem. First was the American Humane Association which, until 1985, operated as a national clearinghouse for statistics on child abuse and neglect. In 1976, the incidence of these problems was nearly 7,600 cases, while the comparable figure in 1983 was almost 72,000 cases, a nearly tenfold increase. The second effort was the National Incidence Study (a random sample of residents in twenty-six U.S. cities), and the findings show an incidence rate of .7 per 1,000 children. Third was the 1985 *Los Angeles Times* survey of 2,627 randomly selected U.S. residents. The results showed that 22 percent of the respondents had experienced some form of child sexual abuse: 27 percent of the women and 16 percent of the men [see Finkelhor et al. (1989) for details of this study].

Community Surveys

In her ground-breaking work on incest and child sexual abuse, Russell (1986)[5] determined that 16 percent of the women in her random sample had experienced incest before the age of eighteen years, while 31 percent reported at least one episode of extrafamilial child sexual abuse. When these figures are combined (and since there is an overlap between the two categories), a total of *38 percent* of these women reported having experienced either incestuous or extrafamilial sexual abuse as a child. As Russell (1986:61) comments, "Shockingly high as these prevalence figures for child sexual abuse are, they would have been still higher had we used definitions of incestuous and extrafamilial child sexual abuse as broad as those used in some other studies."

Several other studies have examined the prevalence of the child sexual abuse problem. For instance, Finkelhor (1984) investigated this problem within a group of 521 randomly selected parents in the Boston area. He found that 15 percent of the women had been sexually abused before the age of sixteen and that 5 percent had been abused by a relative. Second, in 1985, Wyatt published the results from her randomly derived sample of 248 women who reside in the Los Angeles area. Via interviews, she determined that 21 percent of the women had been sexually abused by relatives, and that 32 percent of them had experienced extrafamilial sexual abuse (Wyatt 1985). When combining these two groups, the prevalence figure was 45 percent. Third, Peters (1988) investigated the prevalence of this problem within a sample of 122 randomly selected women residing in Los Angeles County, and she concludes that 60 percent of the women had experienced at least one episode of sexual abuse prior to the age of eighteen. Fourth, Kercher and McShane (1984) studied a random sample of registered drivers in Texas. Although their response rate was only 53 percent and the authors do *not* provide information about the people who declined to participate, they found that 11 percent of their respondents had been sexually abused as children. Fifth, Bagley and his associates have conducted a series of prevalence studies in Canada (cf. Bagley and King 1990:123–125). One example is a random sample of adults residing in Calgary, and the authors determine that 22 percent of the women reported at least one "serious event" of sexual abuse as children. Finally, Saunders and his associates (1992) conducted a random survey of adult women residing in Charleston County, South Carolina. They found that, before the age of eighteen, 34 percent of the women had experienced some sort of sexual assault [i.e., 68 percent of these attacks involved physical sexual contact, and nearly 28 percent were rapes (Saunders et al. 1992)].

Recent Surveys of College Students

In 1979, Finkelhor reported the results of his survey of 530 women students enrolled in social science classes at six New England colleges and universities. Although a nonrandom sample, he determined that 10 percent of the women had been sexually victimized by a relative during their childhoods. When he used an inclusive definition of childhood sexual victimization (i.e., no age difference between victim and perpetrator), though, this figure climbed to 28 percent. In a replication of Finkelhor's study in Calgary, Canada, Bagley and his associates determined that 19 percent of the female college students had been sexually abused as children (cf. Bagley and King 1990:122).

Briere and Runtz (1988b) and Fromuth (1986) drew similar conclusions. For example, Briere and Runtz (1988b) studied a nonrandom sample of 278 female undergraduate students at an unspecified university. Utilizing Finkelhor's Family Experiences Questionnaire, they conclude that 15 percent of the women had been sexually abused as children. Via her survey of women enrolled in undergraduate psychology courses at Auburn University, Fromuth shows that 22 percent of them reported at least one sexually abusive experience as children. By including such diverse issues as "noncontact" experiences (e.g., exhibitionism) all the way through the most extreme form of bodily contact (sexual penetration), though, this report does employ a fairly inclusive definition of sexual abuse.

Clinical Populations

Many of the studies which investigate the subjects of incest and child sexual abuse do so via clinical sample, and these studies represent children who were recently abused or studies of adult women who have histories of child sexual abuse. As such, these reports are biased in that they investigate the girls and women who are disrupted enough to seek assistance for these problems or ones who sought help for other problems, but during the course of therapy, their histories of sexual victimization came to light. For example, Briere (1989) reports that almost 50 percent of the women requesting counseling services at an out-patient crisis intervention center and nearly two-thirds of the women seen at one psychiatric emergency room had been sexually abused as children. In addition, Jehu (1988) investigated a nonrandom sample of 51 women who sought treatment at the University of Manitoba's Sexual Dysfunction Clinic, and he found that all of them had been sexually victimized as children.

Although we can sort out all sorts of issues by studying clinical samples (e.g., presenting complaints, long-term consequences of childhood sexual victimization, and the therapeutic interventions which seem to be most effective), we cannot address the distribution of these problems within the general population. I offer these data as evidence, though, that often women who enter into treatment for "other" presenting problems may be survivors of rape, incest, and/or child sexual abuse, an issue which is detailed further in the next section.

Other Estimates of the Problem

Other estimates of the incest and child sexual abuse problems have been found within specific subgroups of the population. As examples, Bagley and King (1990) investigated former prostitutes and showed that 73 percent of them had been sexually abused before age sixteen (and prior to entering prostitution). In addition, Briere (1989) concluded that more than one-half of teenage and adult prostitutes that he studied had histories of childhood sexual victimization, while the comparable figure within a group of adolescent mothers was 60 percent. Finally, Simons and Whitbeck (1991) have shown that a history of prior childhood sexual victimization is linked not only to prostitution and a history of running away as adolescents but also to homelessness among adult women.

In sum, the range of estimates of the prevalence of child sexual abuse is anywhere from 10 percent to 60 percent. Although this sort of disparity may confuse rather than clarify the issue, it is important to reiterate that some of these studies are better than others. With that in mind, and based upon the methodologies employed by Russell and Wyatt, we can conclude that theirs are two of the stronger studies that have been mentioned. In addition, their findings are strikingly similar. Specifically, Russell (1986) found that 16 percent of the women in her sample had been victims of incest; 31 percent reported at least one episode of extrafamilial child sexual abuse, while the combined figure was 38 percent. Similarly, Wyatt (1985) found that 21 percent of the women in her study had been victims of incest, 32 percent had experienced extrafamilial sexual abuse, and the combined prevalence figure was 45 percent.

The Risk Factors Associated with Childhood Sexual Victimization

Several experts have noted that there also may be characteristics which put children at higher risk for sexual victimization. Finkelhor and Baron (1986), for example, have noted that children who are: female, between the ages of eight and twelve, isolated from their peers, residing in homes where there is a great deal of conflict, residing with a stepfather, and/or experiencing poor relationships with her parents are significantly more likely to be sexually abused; they also conclude that there are *no* differences by race and class. Moreover, a number of works cite the "absent" mother (i.e., one who is ill, differently abled, emotionally absent, or working outside of the home) as a "risk" factor, particularly for incest (cf. Butler, S. 1985; Herman 1981; Russell 1986). As will be discussed in detail in the next chapter, though, we must be careful with this assumption; regardless of the mother's role, ultimately, it is the father/stepfather who must be held accountable for his own behavior.

Likelihood to Report Cases of Rape and Child Sexual Abuse

It is important to reiterate that none of the aforementioned data collection techniques is perfect. Regardless of the ones that we use to estimate the scope of these problems, they all have the same problem of girls and women failing to report their sexual victimizations. As noted by Kilpatrick et al. (1985), only 29 percent of the women that they studied reported their rapes to the police, while Russell (1982a) and Warshaw (1988) found that a mere 10 percent of the women in their studies officially reported their attacks. Although the following factors may be more reflective of why women and girls do *not* report to official, police agencies, several of them also apply to why they do *not* report their attacks to researchers via questionnaires or interviews.

When determining whether *women are likely to report being raped*, several studies have shown that the characteristics of the assault are critical predictors (Lizotte 1985; Randall and Rose 1981; Skelton and Burkhart 1980; Williams 1984). Specifically, if a woman has experienced a "classic" or "stereotypical" rape (i.e., the attack was sudden and violent; the assailant was a stranger; and she was injured), she is significantly more likely to officially report the assault. When we consider the stereotypes that some social control agents in the rape processing system have, this makes a great deal of sense. Holmstrom and Burgess (1978), for example, note that the earlier-mentioned "classic" type of sexual assault often is the one which is regarded as more "credible," "ideal," or "real" by police officers, medical personnel, and court officials. Accordingly, in these sorts of rape cases, the officials are much more likely to treat rape victims with respect and sympathy, thereby increasing the likelihood that women will report these types of sexual assaults and/or that these cases will be regarded as "founded."

Other reports suggest that the victims' perceptions of the criminal justice system are important in determining whether they report being raped (Lizotte 1985; White and Mosher 1986). In their now-classic study, Dukes and Mattley (1977) have found that women's perceptions about several police characteristics are significant determinants of whether they reported being raped. These factors include whether the police were perceived to be: sympathetic and concerned, likely to believe her, efficient, and considerate. If the women's views about the police were positive, and if they thought that the police would be able to do something, they were significantly more likely to report being sexually assaulted.

Additional factors which have been suggested are the level of fear experienced by the victim immediately after the rape (Dukes and Mattley 1977) and her beliefs regarding her "moral duty" to report the attack (White and Mosher 1986). Thus, if the woman experiences a high level of post-rape fear and/or if she believes that reporting her rape will protect other women from similar experiences, she is much more likely to report the assault to the police.

Regarding the likelihood of children to report cases of incest and child sexual abuse, the problem is more complicated. First and foremost, ofttimes, children are *not* permitted to be the decision makers about whether to report being sexually abused. Rather, their parents often chose to "informally" or "unofficially" handle these matters, thereby hoping to reduce the levels of shame and humiliation experienced by them and their children (Peters et al. 1986). Additional factors which explain why cases of incest and child sexual abuse are *not* reported to official authorities are that: (1) many of us do *not* recall our childhood sexual victimizations until many years later; (2) child sexual abuse tends to be hidden, particularly if the perpetrator is a member of the immediate family; and (3) often children "tell" (whether directly or indirectly via their behavior) that they have been sexually abused, but they are *not* believed by their significant others and/or their teachers (Bass and Davis 1988; Blume 1990; Dinsmore 1991). Based upon all of these factors, it is fairly easy to determine why cases of incest and child sexual abuse are even less likely to be reported than are cases of rape. In effect, we are back to the idea that many observers and professionals alike are even *less* likely to believe "allegations" of incest or child sexual abuse than they are to believe "claims" of rape.

Summary and Conclusions

The data are quite clear. The sexual victimization of girls, adolescent females, and women is a problem which has reached epidemic proportions in this country. FBI data show that the official rate of forcible rape has increased dramatically since the 1970s. In addition, NCS data show that many of us do *not* report our sexual assaults to official authorities and that the calculated rate of rape is at least double that of the FBI UCR. Recent surveys of college students also have shown us that anywhere from 30 to 50 percent of the women have experienced unwanted sexual contact, while a sizable percentage (the range is 15 to 30 percent) of the males report attitudes which support the use of force or coercion in securing sex and/or an actual proclivity for being sexually assaultive in their relationships with women. Finally, we have random samples of various communities across the country which conclude that a considerable number of women have experienced either attempted or completed rapes. The child sexual victimization data are equally disturbing. As is evidenced by the better estimates of the problem (e.g., Finkelhor et al. 1989; Russell 1984, 1986; Wyatt 1985), anywhere from 27 to 45 percent of women report having been sexualy victimized during their childhood years. In addition, a sizable percentage of the women who seek mental health services have similar histories, as do women who are or were prostitutes and/or are homeless.

To simply count the incidence and prevalence of rape, incest, and child sexual abuse and/or to estimate the extent of them, though, is *not* enough. Accordingly, in the next few chapters, I explore the causes of these problems, as well as their consequences for the girls, adolescent females, and women who have been victimized. In addition, and since these numbers should frighten all of us, in a later chapter the critical issue of how to reduce or prevent the problem of rape, incest, and child sexual abuse is explored.

Historical and Contemporary Explanations of the Causes of Rape, Incest, and Child Sexual Abuse

> A central feature of feminist work around male violence
> has been to challenge male definitions . . . In extending the
> definition of sexual violence, feminists have challenged
> men's power to define and [have] drawn attention to the
> role of male-dominated legal systems in constructing and
> reinforcing limited definitions (Kelly 1988:27).

> Sigmund Freud, whose theories have had such enormous
> influence on modern thinking, knew that the sexual
> abuse of children existed, but he could not reconcile the
> implication of that abuse with either his self-image or his
> identification with other men of his class, and thus he
> altered his telling of reality. Eventually he succeeded in
> gaslighting an age into ignoring a devastating childhood
> reality and a very serious social problem (Rush 1980:82).

It is important to acknowledge from the outset that widely
accepted explanations of rape, incest, and child sexual abuse do
not exist; rather, there are a number of divergent definitions and
conceptualizations of these various forms of sexual violence. In
part, these variations can be accounted for by the numerous
emphases and biases of the disciplines that explain these
problems, as well as the various levels of analysis at which they
operate. As examples, many works investigate sexual victimization exclusively at the interpersonal level, viewing it as an
"interaction" between two or more participants, while a number
of other reports focus on the structural components of these
problems. In addition, since the topics of rape, incest, and child
sexual abuse have been "claimed" by a number of different

disciplines (e.g., criminology, women's studies, psychology, public health, and sociology) and since there has *not* been a great deal of sharing of the findings among these various groups, divergent perspectives of and explanations for these traumatizing experiences have emerged.

A second reason why a single definition of these offenses does not exist is that there are some very real differences between rape and acts which qualify as incest or child sexual abuse. As examples: (1) many of the motives which rapists have reported are different from those expressed by child molesters (Groth 1979; Finkelhor 1984; Horton et al. 1990; West et al. 1978); (2) although many of the responses that survivors have to all three forms of forced sex are similar, there also are differences in that children usually are more disturbed by these experiences than are adolescents and adults who have been raped (Courtois 1988; Finkelhor 1984; Kelly 1988; Shengold 1989); and (3) the history of our awareness and acknowledgment of these acts (again, although similar) also reflect differences (Finkelhor 1984; Herman 1992; Russell 1984).

Third, the emphases of the rape literature are different in many ways from those which exist in the incest and child sexual abuse literature. One glaring example is that the former body of knowledge is more likely to examine the causes of, the prevalence of, and women's reactions to rape, while much less attention has been paid to the issue of recovering from the experience. On the other hand, the major foci in the incest and child sexual abuse literatures are the prevalence of these problems and recovering from and treating the long-term aftermath. Although it is difficult to know for sure why this is the case, one possibility is that we are much less willing to examine the reasons why incest and child sexual abuse occur. Although we may be willing to acknowledge that rape is a serious problem and that it occurs with astounding frequency and that perhaps the social order is involved in causing and perpetuating the problem, we are much more hesitant to openly discuss why the sexual abuse of children occurs. Perhaps it simply is more frightening to admit that this latter problem exists and that adults who should be able to be trusted *cannot* always be.

In the next section, I will begin by examining the historical and the legal perspectives which explain rape (i.e., the FBI definition, as well as an overview of some of the recent reforms in our statutory definitions of this offense). At least five other conceptualizations, though, are important deviations from the historical and legal ones; they include: the victim-precipitated view, the feminist perspective, rape as part of the larger continuum of sexual violence against women and children, psychodynamic theories, and sociocultural explanations. Later in this chapter, I explore the historical evidence thought to "prove" the *nonexistence* of the child sexual abuse problem. In addition, legal definitions are presented, as are a number of contemporary explanations of these problems, including: feminist, psycho-dynamic, and structural perspectives.

Various Conceptualizations of Rape

Historical and Legal Views

We have four divergent historical or legal definitions of the crime of rape. They are: the historical, legal perspective; modern, yet traditional laws; the reform movement which changed rape statutes across the country; and the recently "discovered" types of rape (e.g., acquaintance and marital rapes).

Since our legal system traces its roots back to English common law, the *historical legal perspective* readily explains why claims of rape have been so difficult to make. As an example, during the early stages of English society (as was the case in most modern societies), women, quite simply, were viewed as the property of their men. Koss and Harvey (1991:125) illustrate this point by noting that rape was *not* defined as a crime until the tenth century, and, even then, the law applied mostly to slaves: "Free men who raped were obligated to pay fines to both owner and king, [while] slaves who raped slaves were sentenced to castration." During the ninteenth century, Hale's dictum that claims of rape, though "easy" to make, were very difficult to "prove," reigned supreme. In effect, he gave credibility to the view of rape that assumed that women were lying, seeking revenge, and/or being vindictive, while men, concomitantly, were *not* held responsible for their actions (cf. Koss and Harvey 1991). And, until very recently, this perspective summarized how we viewed many if not most allegations of rape.

During the twentieth century, although we began to define rape as a crime, simultaneously, we also continued to view victims of rape as "somehow" responsible. Specifically, the *modern, yet traditional, legal definition* had three criteria to qualify an act as rape: carnal knowledge, force or the threat of force, and lack of consent on the part of the victim (Carrow 1980; Koss and Harvey 1991; Largen 1988). The problem was that these issues usually were interpreted rigidly: Rape involved specific, heterosexual contact (i.e., vaginal penetration by a penis) between or among participants who did *not* know each other and were of the legal age of majority. Thus, and as summarized by Koss and Harvey (1991:125), the implicit assumption that women "caused" their rapes to occur continued to reign supreme until the antirape movement of the 1970s:

> As recently as 1975 . . . prevailing law (a) allowed the victim's sexual activity with men other than the defendant to be presented as evidence for the defense; (b) required that the occurrence of rape, resistance on the part of the victim, and/or the identity of the accused be established not by belief in the victim's testimony but by independent, corroborating evidence (e.g., the testimony of an eyewitness observer!); and (c) provided for judges to instruct juries of the difficulties faced by defendants seeking to disprove a charge of rape.

As was noted in the last chapter, though, before the 1970s and due largely to this parochial definition of rape, official estimates of the problem were fairly low (Baron and Straus 1989; Hindelang and Davis 1977); and few of the acts which women who were assaulted might define as rape could meet these stringent criteria.

Due primarily to the efforts of feminists in the recent women's movement of the 1970s, *rape reform laws* were passed in most states across the country. The predominant result has been that these statutes now reflect an increasing concern for the victims and survivors of rape (Carrow 1980; Cobb and Schauer 1977; Koss and Harvey 1991; Russell 1974, 1984). For example, following the lead of Michigan's 1974 Degrees of Sexual Conduct Act, many states *eliminated*: (1) their corroboration requirements, (2) in-court examinations of the victim's sexual history (if that history does *not* involve the alleged assailant), and/or (3) cautionary instructions to juries about how "easy" it is to make a claim of rape (Cobb and Schauer 1977; Rose 1977; Largen 1988; Koss and Harvey 1991). In addition, several states expanded their definitions of rape to include a variety of sexual acts which had been excluded (e.g., oral and anal intercourse), as well as "new" types of rapes such as same-sex assault and marital rape (Carrow 1980; Koss and Harvey 1991; Largen 1988; Russell 1991).

Regarding the motives for instituting these changes, Estrich (1987) and Temkin (1986) suggest that there were two. First of all, based upon the prior wording of rape statutes, the difficulties women had in "proving" that their rapes had occurred and the victims' theretofore legitimate fears that nothing would be done by the criminal justice system, many assaults went unreported. Second, evidence showed that many cases of rape would *not* reach the court system because of the "sensitive" circumstances of these crimes and the unwillingness of jurors to find men guilty of rape. Thus, the two hoped-for results were that more rapes would be reported and that the conviction rates for the crime of rape would increase.

Although all this sounds well and good, Largen (1988) indicates that several critical problems remain. One is that many of the states never responded to the call for change. As examples, spousal exemptions in cases of rape remain today in nearly thirty states, and a fairly traditional legal definition of rape remains in twenty-five states and the District of Columbia. Second, based on her survey of criminal justice personnel in three states (Michigan, Florida, and Georgia), Largen found that police officers continue to wield a great deal of discretionary power in "nonstereo-typical" cases of rape (i.e., ones involving victims and assailants who have prior or current sexual relationships, assaults by spouses, rapes within same-sex couples, and acquaintance rapes), and that they remain unwilling to investigate and make arrests in these "sorts" of cases. Finally, she found that jurors remain hestitant to convict defendants in cases of acquaintance rape, but that they are more likely to do so in "stereotypical" or "classic" rapes (i.e., ones in which the victims are "blameless" and the parties are complete strangers).

There also, though, is an upside to this discussion. For instance, the Sexual Coercion and Assault Staff (1986) examined the impact of reform laws in California and Michigan. In California, between 1975 and 1982, they found that arrests for the crime of rape which resulted in filings by prosecutors increased, as did arrests and sentencing for rapists. Findings gathered in Michigan, though, produced mixed results. Although more sexual assault cases were being filed, a significant difference between rape cases and nonsexual assaults remained, with the latter ones being more likely to be regarded as "real" assaults and to be filed as official cases. As the authors conclude: "[S]tatute change alone does not fully bring about the desired objectives of making the handling of the two types of assault comparable. For full change to come about, change must take place not only in criminal justice personnel, but in the wider society that makes up juries and elects prosecutors" (Sexual Coercion and Assault Staff 1986:28).

In sum, although many changes have been enacted in rape statutes across the country, a number of problems still remain. They include: (1) the fact that many police officers and court officials continue to interact with women who have been sexually assaulted in problematic fashions (Koss and Harvey 1991; Madigan and Gamble 1991); (2) these same social control agents have pronounced biases regarding what constitutes a "real" rape (Holmstrom and Burgess 1978; Madigan and Gamble 1991; McCahill et al. 1979); (3) since men predominate as the aggressors and women usually are the victims, sex-neutral language clouds the realities of rape and deemphasizes the fact that power and powerlessness are *not* gender-neutral terms when applied to the crime of rape (Estrich 1987); and (4) the hoped-for increases in reporting and conviction have *not* materialized (Estrich 1987; LaFree et al. 1985).

Most recently, we have begun to acknowledge the existence of *types of rapes which previously have been ignored*. For example, and as previously noted, although Kanin and Kirkpatrick originally brought the issue of *acquaintance rape* to our attention thirty-five years ago (Kanin 1957; Kirkpatrick and Kanin 1957), it took us a very long time to replicate their findings. Interestingly enough, we find that their results are strikingly similar to the more recent ones of Koss and her associates in that approximately 25 percent of women college students have experienced an attempted or a completed rape (Koss 1988; Koss et. al. 1987; Koss et al. 1988; Warshaw 1988). What differs dramatically, though, are the authors' respective explanations for this phenomenon. Kanin (1957), for example, emphasizes personal issues (i.e., the "girl's" role in "causing" her assault), while Koss (1988) and Warshaw (1988) pinpoint interpersonal and structural issues (e.g., gender-stereotyped socialization practices and our sexist dating patterns) as factors which cause the acquaintance rape problem.

In addition, we have begun to acknowledge that married women can be raped by their spouses.[1] Although some states continue to ignore *marital rape* as a crime and our willingness to believe these sorts of "claims" remains low, many states have moved toward legally admitting that marital rape is possible (Estrich 1987; Russell 1991). As noted by Koss and Harvey (1991: 125), "In 1990, twenty-six states still treat as noncriminal at least some forms of wife rape and eight states have not criminalized wife rape at all." Yet (and as is noted in the last chapter), Finkelhor and Yllo (1985) and Russell (1982) have shown that these are problems for a sizable proportion of women in this country.

Contemporary Perspectives which Explain Rape

Drawing from Wolfgang's (1958) work on homicide,[2] Amir (1967, 1971) devised the *victim-precipitated view* of rape:

> Once the victim and the offender are drawn together, a process is set in motion whereby victim behavior and the situation which surrounds the encounter will determine

the course of events leading to the crime. If the victim is
not solely responsible for what becomes the unfortunate
event, at least she is often a complementary partner . . .

Theoretically, victim precipitation of forcible rape means
that in a particular situation the behavior of the victim is
interpreted by the offender either as a direct invitation for
sexual relations or as a sign that she will be available for
sexual contact if he will persist in demanding it . . .

Thus, wrongly or rightly a woman's behavior, if passive,
may be seen as worthy to suit action, and if active it may
be taken as an actual promise of success for one's sexual
intentions. The offender then will react as seems
appropriate (Amir 1967:493–494).

Amir (1967:502) also deemphasizes the culpability of the
assailant and asks us to focus more closely on the victim's role in
"causing" her assault:

[T]he notion of negligent and reckless behavior on the part
of the victim is as important to understanding the offense
as is the appearance of these types of behavior in the
offender. It does not make any offender innocent but
allows us to consider some of these men, at least, less
guilty and leads us to consider that the victim is perhaps
also responsible for what happened to her.

Finally, Amir (1967:495) includes such value-laden and suspect
notions as the woman's prior "reputation" and her "chasteness"
as issues which determine whether a "real" rape occurred.

I have quoted Amir's words extensively for a very specific
reason: I wanted to make sure that I did *not* take his ideas out of
context. Thus, the message that he did wish to impart was that
many women, via their characteristics, behaviors, and bad
judgments, cause their rapes to occur. This conceptualization,
though, is replete with flaws, examples of circular reasoning, and
illogical hypotheses. In effect, "Amir converted the theretofore
unformalized beliefs about rape into 'scholarly' proof'"
(Gilmartin-Zena 1988:280). Moreover, Amir's view reinforces the
existing mythology of the day: If she was raped, she must have
done something to deserve it, while he simultaneously
minimizes the respective roles of men and our society in causing

and perpetuating the rape problem. Second, although Amir (1971) found that a *minority* of the cases in his sample met his criteria for victim precipitation (i.e., 19 percent), he leads his readers to believe that most rapes are of this ilk. Third, he assumes that it is the perceptions of the assailant which are critical in defining (what he would label) a sexual encounter, while he downplays the perceptions of the woman and many of the objective characteristics of the rape. Fourth, Amir suggests (and *not* so implicitly) that women must be the gatekeepers of sex via his inference that men really cannot "help themselves" or be "held accountable" for their sexual behaviors.[3] Fifth, many of Amir's assumptions are blatantly sexist and misogynistic. Finally, Amir creates the perfect "Catch-22": If women are "passive" in their encounters with men and are raped, they are wrong because they should have been more forceful; on the other hand, if they are "active" and are raped, they can be viewed as having "asked for it." Based on these criticisms, the consequences of this view of rape for its victims and survivors are likely to be devastating: "Others' expression of these . . views will exacerbate the victim's immediate reactions to rape, while delaying her long-term recovery. . . Due to these possible and negative consequences for the victim, those interacting with her, at all costs, must avoid such a stance . . . [T]he damage that could be done to her might be very well irreparable" (Gilmartin-Zena 1987b:2).

In part as a response to Amir's work, a number of *feminist definitions* of rape emerged during the 1970s (Brownmiller 1975; Clark and Lewis 1977; Connell and Wilson 1974; Griffin 1979; Medea and Thompson 1974; Millett 1970; Russell 1974). Although written in different "voices," all of these works have the starting point that the world in which we live is patriarchal, masculinist, and misogynistic. They also suggest that the lower status of women is endemic in many modern societies and that "women's" problems (of which rape is but one) are caused and perpetuated by social rather than biological or psychological factors. In other words, feminist explanations have moved us away from a case-by-case analysis of who does or says what to whom and focus instead on rape as a social problem caused by structural factors. As Johnson (1980:137) summarizes this viewpoint: "A feminist interpretation [of rape] does not attribute violence to the aberrant behavior of a lunatic fringe of normal male society; rather, it locates the etiology of sexual violence in the everyday fabric of relations between men and women in patriarchal society."

Now regarded as classics, four early feminist works have been instrumental in altering our thinking about rape. They are: (1) Brownmiller's ground-breaking opus, *Against Our Will: Men, Women and Rape*; (2) Millett's *Sexual Politics*; (3) Griffin's article, "Rape: The All-American Crime"; and (4) *The Politics of Rape: The Victim's Perspective* by Russell. According to Brownmiller (1975:391), for example, rape readily can be explained via social factors:

> [R]ape is not a crime of lust. . . but is a deliberate, hostile, violent act of degradation and possession on the part of a would-be conquerer, designed to intimidate and inspire fear. [W]e must look toward those elements in our culture that promote and propagandize these attitudes, which offer men . . . the ideology and psychologic encouragement to commit their acts of aggression *without awareness, for the most part, that they committed a punishable* crime, let alone, a moral wrong. (Emphasis in the original.)

By linking patriarchal elements to sexual offenses committed against women, Millett (1970:33) concurs with this view about the "social acceptability" of rape:

> What goes largely unexamined, often even unacknow—ledged . . . , is the birthright priority whereby males rule females. Through this system a most ingenious form of 'interior colonization' has been achieved. It is one which tends moreover to be sturdier than any form of segregation . . . [or] class stratification, more uniform, certainly more enduring. However muted its present appearance may be, sexual dominion obtains nevertheless as perhaps the most pervasive ideology of our culture and provides its most fundamental concept of power.

With these sorts of ideological and cultural supports, crimes against women (particularly rape) should be endemic in patriarchal societies because the rules and the rulers rarely protect those who are being ruled.

In self-reflective language, Griffin (1971:3) notes the pervasiveness of rape in our society, as well as the cultural supports for the victim-precipitated explanation of it: "From a very early age I, like most women, have thought of rape as part of my natural environment—something to be feared and prayed against like fire or lightning. I never asked why men raped; I simply thought it one of the many mysteries of human nature." Thus, Griffin suggests that the reality of rape is ever-present, and, if it occurs, the current mythology dictates that women have to be blamed.

Russell (1974:44), too, highlights one of the inherent double binds which exist for women: "No man is ever guilty; if he did something bad, it must have been invited." In other words, while the societal expectation is that women are supposed to make themselves attractive to men and are rewarded for doing so, they simultaneously are blamed if these same men view them as sex objects and/or attempt to sexually assault them. At first glance, Russell's words seem to lend support for Amir's victim-precipitated view of rape, but there is a major difference: She *knows* them to be false and victim-blaming, while Amir simply states his viewpoint as "fact."

More recent feminist works continue to specify the cultural influences which operate to cause and perpetuate rape. For instance, we have Russell's (1984) analysis of the various psychological, social-psychological, and structural factors involved in the rape problem. They include: the biological capacity and desire of men to rape, a history of childhood sexual victimization (which they then repeat), the socialization of males into stereotypical sex roles which encourages their acts of aggression, and the linkage of rape and pornography, as well as other forms of the mass media which support rape as a way to control women. In effect, she argues that the factors at work which cause the rape problem are complex indeed and cut across several different levels of analysis.

We also have Sanday's (1981, 1986) work which questions the accuracy of sociobiological or evolutionary theories of violence and rape (i.e., male aggression is genetically based).

Instead of selecting biology and genes as the culprits, she highlights the distinctive, cultural features of what she calls "rape-prone" societies. Specifically, these societies have highly divergent roles and statuses for men and women, and they exclude women from participating in the public decision-making process. Conversely, in "rape-free" societies, the "maternal features of nurturance and childbearing are valued" and the "relationship between the sexes tends to be symmetrical and equal" (Sanday 1986:85).[4] Thus, she argues for a *social* rather than a biological or a genetic explanation of rape by suggesting that men in many societies have been taught to objectify women and to treat them as sex objects which creates the "perfect" environment for sexual violence.

Klein (1981:64), too, acknowledges that violence against women is but one outcome of a "social structure and ideology of gender domination." She adds that this negative history is lengthy and has been evidenced not only in explicit ways (e.g., the raping and battering of women), but also in more subtle, covert ways such as attempts to control women's reproduction and the devaluation of the nurturing roles of women. In order to reduce or eliminate the problem of violence against women, then, she suggests that we must radically reorder the existing social structure.

Penultimately, we have Burt and Katz's (1987:60–61) perspective which states that rape is *not* idiosyncratic behavior; rather, it is "an extreme exaggeration of the prescribed and accepted sexual and social roles played by women and men . . . [which are] centered around power and control [and] grow out of a structural disparity in status and power held by men as a class versus women as a class." In addition, they depict rape as having its "roots in [the] patriarchal societal structure" and that it is tolerated so readily because it is both a "manifestation of and a tool for the perpetuation of the dominance of men . . . over women."

Most recently, we have Koss and Harvey's (1991:124–127) summary of the major elements needed to qualify an analysis of rape as a feminist one. They include: (1) taking as a given that ours is a patriarchal society which permits not only the subjugation of women but also violence against them; (2) a need to acknowledge that our gender-coded socialization practices teach girls/women and boys/men to be victims and assailants, respectively; (3) the notion that "rape and the fear of rape function to reinforce male power and help to ensure the social control of women"; and (4) being cognizant of the role of the various "social institutions (e.g., hospitals, police precincts, district attorneys' offices, and courts) [which] have dismissed the seriousness of a rape victim's experience and have denied her the right to interpret that experience herself and to chart her own course of recovery."

In sum, each of these authors has argued that our patriarchal society plays a critical role in causing rape. But how does all of this work? According to many feminists, we must pay particular attention to the negative images of women replete throughout American society (particularly those promulgated by the advertising and the pornography industries), as well as the importance of our problematic socialization practices which set all of us up for sexually coercive experiences. Regarding current images of women, for some time now, the advertising industry has been regarded as a major culprit in creating negative, objectified images of women. As an example, Kilborne (1979, 1987) depicts how this linkage between negative images of women and violence works: As a result of the *cumulative* impact of these images, people can become immune to their content; even more specifically, men learn to objectify women. Moreover, this "learned objectification" diminishes the likelihood that we will view women as "real" victims, if and when they are sexually assaulted.

The insidious role of pornography in rape causation is quite similar. Pornographic materials (particularly ones that equate sex with violence) have been found to lower women's self-esteem (Jack 1991; Mayerson and Taylor 1987), while simultaneously increasing men's likelihood to accept inter-personal violence as a way of life and/or to excuse their tendencies to be sexually assaultive in their relationships with women (Baron and Straus 1987, 1989; Check and Malamuth 1983, 1985; Donnerstein and Linz 1989; Donnerstein et al. 1987; Finkelhor 1984; Malamuth 1981, 1989; Malamuth and Dean 1991; Rapaport and Posey 1991). In other words, pornography creates "perfect" rape situations because it conditions women to think less of themselves and to be passive, while simultaneously encouraging inaccurate images of women and aggressive behaviors among men.

As for the role of the socialization process in causing and perpetuating the rape problem, if we educate our sons and daughters into gender-stereotyped roles, we are asking them to think and to act in ways which may be harmful to them. As examples, if men buy into gender stereotypes (Alder 1985; Burt 1980; Check and Malamuth 1985; Lundberg-Love and Geffner 1989),[5] are involved in highly eroticized peer groups (Kanin 1984, 1985), and/or have a macho personality (Lottes 1988; Mahoney et al. 1986; Mosher and Anderson 1986), they are more likely to be sexually coercive or assaultive in their relationships with women. These same gender-specific roles cause women to discount themselves and their ideas, as well as to be passive, particularly in their encounters with men (Gilligan 1982; Jack 1991; Steinem 1992). An added, negative effect of socializing our children into gender stereotypes is that the scripts to which these roles dictate end up creating potential rape situations. In other words, traditional dating practices (e.g., boys/men paying, driving, and making all of the decisions) are not only vestiges of an upbringing which teaches active roles for boys/men and passive ones for girls/women, but they also set all of us up for sexually coercive experiences (Allgeier 1987, 1988; Koss and Harvey 1991; Muehlenhard 1989; Muehlenhard and Linton 1987; Parrott 1990; Warshaw 1988). In effect, "rape tolerance" is rooted in the general sexist attitudes replete throughout our society, i.e., we teach males to be the "initiators" of sex, while women are relegated to being "weak, passive, and compliant toward men and therefore more vulnerable to rape" (Hall et al. 1986:102).

Although these feminist explanations of rape are considered to be quite credible, they do have their detractors. One critic is Ellis (1989), who criticizes these perspectives because they downplay the sexual component of men's motivation to rape as well as overestimate the role of sexist attitudes and/or acceptance of the rape myths in causing men to rape. Regarding this first issue, Ellis notes that, although feminists prefer to view rape as a crime of violence (rather than one of sex), many rapists credit their behaviors to sexual motives, particularly in cases of acquaintance rape. In response, I would suggest that, although many feminists do conceptualize rape as a crime of violence rather than one of sex or passion, it also is a fact that there is a lack of consensus among them on this issue. Some feminist analyses, for example, emphasize the sexual component of men's motivation to rape (Marolla and Scully 1986), while other feminist works focus on rape as a crime of violence which uses sexual acts as weapons (Brownmiller 1975; Groth 1979; Koss and Harvey 1991). Accordingly, this is *not* a particularly valid criticism because there is *not* "one" feminist perspective of rape; rather, there are several.[6] In addition, it is instructive to note that in the case of rape, Ellis is willing to permit the assailants to interpret and explain their actions, while for most crimes, the typical scenario is that we want the experts to explain why the criminals do what they do.

Regarding Ellis's latter point, it is true that some scales which measure our views about rape are inherently flawed and that some of them may create spurious support for the notion that attitudes "cause" rape, but Ellis does *not* go far enough with this criticism. That is to say, he ignores the very real linkage which exists between our attitudes and our behaviors. Nor does he "get" the attitudinal dimension of patriarchal culture: If we truly "buy" as fact that American society is patriarchal, along with this awareness comes the entire package of devaluing women, creating negative images about them, and viewing them as sexual objects. I would place my support with the extensive summary of Donnerstein and his associates (1987) which clearly shows a causal linkage between men's views about women and their subsequent likelihood or willingness to commit rape.

When interacting with women who have been raped, what are the consequences of a feminist perspective? Typically, they are positive for the girls and women who have been assaulted: "The resultant effects for her will include fewer reactions and a speedier recovery from the assault. This is *not* to say that she will not feel bad or be disrupted, but her reactions will be easier for her to bear, as she will be accepted by her significant others, as well as treated well by involved social control agents" (Gilmartin-Zena 1987b:3).

Another way to conceptualize rape is to view it as *part of the continuum of sexual violence*. As Kelly (1988:24) suggests: "Rape no longer has a privileged place in analysis as the full range of men's use of force and coercion." Rather, we also must pay close attention to what she calls the nonroutine assaults which really are "extensions of more commonplace intrusions" because doing so aptly describes the experiences of many, if not most, women. Along this continuum, Kelly (1988) includes: (1) the threat of violence; (2) sexual harassment; (3) pressure to have sex; (4) sexual assault; (5) obscene phone calls; (6) coercive sex; (7) domestic violence; (8) sexual abuse (including that of children); (9) flashing; (10) rape; and (11) incest. Please note that Kelly has *not* ordered these acts by their severity or seriousness; instead, her ranking reflects the *frequency* with which they were experienced by the women that she interviewed (i.e., 100 percent of them had received threats of violence, while the smallest group, or 22 percent, had been victims of incest as children).

I believe that this conceptualization has a great deal of merit: We should *not* perceive rape as an extraordinary event because our lives are filled with many forms of sexual violence. By viewing rape as part of this continuum of violence against girls and women, we not only demystify the processes which cause and perpetuate sexual violence, but also make the solutions to the problem clearer. In addition, this perspective forces us to examine the *systems* which contribute to these forms of violence, thereby reducing the element of blame accorded girls and women who are so victimized. There is, though, a very real danger inherent within this perspective. As I noted earlier, Katz and Mazur (1979) suggest that we may minimize the effects, as well as the seriousness of rape and incest, if we clump them together with other less "serious" forms of sexual coercion; yet this is exactly what Kelly is prescribing. Perhaps a solution to this dilemma is to continue to conceptualize sexual violence as a continuum of possible behaviors but to examine women and children's responses to and long-term consequences from these experiences separately.

Russell (1984) and Koss and Harvey (1991) offer excellent overviews of the *psychological typologies* which explain the assailant's motives to rape. First is *Gebhard et al.'s 1965 study* of men who have been convicted and imprisoned for the crime of rape. This theory is automatically problematic because prison samples now are regarded as a miniscule subgroup of the population which engages in these behaviors. Notwithstanding this flaw, they offer six categories of sexually assaultive behaviors: (1) assaultive rape, which is the most common type, as well as the most violent variety; (2) amoral delinquents or rapists who want sex and are unconcerned about the wishes of the girls or women involved; (3) the drunken rapists or the disinhibition model which suggests that alcohol "releases" these sorts of actions; (4) the explosive rapists or men whose aggression suddenly appears out of nowhere (i.e., they do *not* have histories of violence); (5) the double-standard rape (i.e., men who divide women into two groups—good women who should *not* be raped and bad women who are "legitimate targets"); and (6) other rapes (their catch-all category).

The most popular of the psychodynamic models to explain why men rape is *Groth's (1979) now-classic perspective.* His viewpoint, though, suffers from the same problem as Gebhard et al.'s because he bases it on interviews with incarcerated rapists. Notwithstanding this problem, Groth's categorization of rape includes three types: (1) the "anger rape" which usually includes a great deal of force and is "just" another way to express violent tendencies; (2) the "power rape" which refers to men who have inadequate images of themselves, feel a need to prove their masculinity, and attempt to compensate for their failings by sexually assaulting women; and (3) the "sadistic rape" in which sexual arousal is achieved by inflicting pain (this type of attack can result in the death of the woman). Groth (1979) adds that most rapes which occur in the U.S. are of the power variety (55 percent); anger rapes comprise 40 percent of all rapes, while, thankfully, sadistic rapes are the least frequent type (5 percent of all rapes).

Kanin (1984, 1985) offers insights about a different type of rapist, the *"undetected rapist"* (i.e., the college-age man whose behavior clearly qualifies as rape but is *not* known publicly as a rapist). For this group, Kanin found that "sexual conquests" were associated with feelings of self-worth and that they were "externalizers" in accounting for their sexually assaultive behaviors (i.e., they believe that the women and/or alcohol caused the attacks rather than they or their behaviors). I would argue that Kanin (1984:105), too, is externalizing because he believes that the victim-precipitated model of rape is credible because "it stresses an interactionist dimension . . . [and it] represents reality . . . [which] is patently reflected in the widely shared stereotypes of female behavior that permit the ascription of fault to those seen as contributing, however unwittingly, to their own victimization."

In sum, psychodynamic theories explain rape via the personality characteristics of the offenders. Although this may be a viable perspective for certain types of sexual assaults (particularly for what Groth has called the sadistic rape), this viewpoint does little to explain the frequency with which most rapes occur. In other words, if rape were the problem of a few, "sick" men, we would expect the incidence of it to be quite low, and this perspective might be valuable in accounting for the rape problem. As was shown in the last chapter, though, particularly regarding the extensiveness of the acquaintance rape problem, this simply is *not* the case, which reduces the viability of psychological explanations.

Social learning and subcultural explanations of rape depict rape as a learned response. That is, rape is one more form of aggression that can be learned through imitation and maintained via intermittent reinforcement from such sources as our culture, subcultures to which we belong, and the mass media. But what are the specifics involved in this process? As was noted earlier in this chapter, our culture plays a decided role in causing violence against women because our culture has an extensive history of sex discrimintion, misogyny, and the devaluation of women (Brownmiller 1975; Faludi 1991; Jack 1991). These factors not only are problems in and of themselves, but they also influence how men interact with women in sexual as well as nonsexual ways. As an example, Scully and Marolla (1985:262) suggest that:

> The [incarcerated rapists that we studied] force us to acknowledge that rape is more than an idiosyncratic act committed by a few 'sick' men. Rather, rape can be viewed as the endpoint in a continuum of sexually aggressive behaviors that reward men and victimize women . . . Our

data demonstrate that some men rape because they have learned that in this culture sexual violence is rewarding.

Second, Kanin (1984, 1985) notes the powerful and reinforcing influence of the "macho" subculture for college men who are "undetected" rapists. Specifically, "scoring" has a high priority within this group; one's peers encourage, celebrate, and reward sexually coercive behaviors. In a similar vein, several experts have validated the role of the mass media in creating and sustaining negative, objectified, and sexualized images of women (Baron and Straus 1987, 1989; Donnerstein and Linz 1987; Donnerstein et al. 1989; Jack 1991; Reis 1991b; Russell 1984). In sum, these sorts of images affect us in a cumulative manner and cause some men to be coercive in their relationships with women, as well as make most of us more callous and immune to the suffering of others.

Ellis (1989:12–13) outlines the specific learning variables involved in this process of learning to be a rapist:

> [It is] part of aggressive behavior toward women learned through four interrelated processes: (a) by imitating rape scenes and other acts of violence toward women, as one may see in real life or as depicted in the mass media, (b) by associating sexuality and violence as when viewing sex and violence repeatedly depicted in the same context (as in many pornographic and slasher/horror films), (c) by perpetuating various 'rape myths,' such as 'No means Yes,' and 'Women secretly desire to be raped,' and (d) by desensitizing viewers to the pain, fear, and humiliation of sexual aggression.

He refers to these components, respectively, as the modeling, sex-violence linkage, rape myth, and desensitization effects. In sum, Ellis suggests that any culture which permits and encourages such messages, as well as devalues one-half of its population, will have a high rate of violence (physical as well as sexual) against women.

Russell (1984:137–145), also cites a number of cultural forces and values that encourage sexually coercive behaviors for some men. These factors include: (1) female sexuality being viewed as a "commodity" (i.e., if men objectify women it makes it easier to inflict pain upon them); (2) rape as a "natural" consequence of our rape-supportive culture (i.e, our beliefs in the various rape myths are one more part of the cultural support for gender-stereotyped roles and behaviors); (3) subcultural norms which encourage violence (i.e., interpersonal violence, including rape, is a learned response); and (4) rape as one more "symptom" of our violent culture (i.e., structural, economic, and political factors such as "unemployment, poverty, and marginality" cause high levels of violence in the U.S.).

The aforementioned relationships are more than mere speculation because there is a great deal of current evidence which shows that many of these cultural elements indeed are linked causally to our rape problem. As examples, there is little doubt that adversarial sexual beliefs and support for the existing rape myths are attitudes that are learned in this culture (Burt 1980; Check and Malamuth 1983; Lottes 1988; Mosher and Anderson 1986). In addition, the acceptance of interpersonal violence that is rampant in our culture has been found to be a critical factor (Adler 1985; Briere and Malamuth 1983; Burt 1980, 1991; Malamuth 1989; Rapaport and Burkhart 1984). That is to say, if we encourage and fail to work toward eradicating violence at all levels in our society, then we should *not* feign surprise when we see that we have high rates of all sorts of violence, not "just" rape.

In sum, subcultural models are powerful in that they: (1) demystify the processes whereby people learn all sorts of deviant behaviors, including rape; (2) pinpoint the salient role of reinforcement in causing and/or maintaining negative behaviors; and (3) offer hope, because if behaviors such as rape are learned, there also is the prospect that they can be "unlearned." In addition, this perspective rightfully places the spotlight on the assailants and how they learn to be rapists rather than emphasizing the victims of rape and what they did, how they were dressed, and/or their characteristics which historically have been regarded as "causing" their assaults.

Although I, too, agree that social learning and subcultural theories of rape are powerful explanations of rape causation, they also have their flaws. For example, some learning theories minimize the role society plays in causing and perpetuating the rape problem by focusing almost exclusively on interpersonal causal factors. Furthermore, although social factors are included in Kanin's model, the mechanisms whereby men actually learn to be violent, criminal, and/or deviant operate predominantly at the interpersonal level and in small groups. In addition, since the primary concern of this type of theory is why some men rape, little attention has been paid to the girls and women who are raped and the aftermath of these experiences for them.

Regarding the consequences of this perspective for the women who have been sexually victimized, it may ease their minds somewhat to realize that the onus of responsibility and blame is placed on the rapists. That is to say, if we focus on how and why men learn to rape while simultaneously minimizing the roles of women, we no longer blame the victims of this crime or look for "evidence" of how they may have precipitated their assaults. Perhaps the more important consequence of this perspective is that it offers hope for reducing the likelihood that some men will continue to be rapists. This, though, is a complex issue. First of all, if they are willing to change, we can create programs and offer counseling which would help them unlearn their sexually coercive behaviors. This, though, only works if the boy or man is a known rapist and is motivated to change his behavior. Herein lies the problem, because many men who are sexually coercive are *not* known or regarded as rapists (Kanin 1984, 1985; Warshaw 1988), nor do they have a desire to alter their behaviors.

Comparing These Perspectives

It is important to acknowledge that all of these explanations of rape operate at quite different levels of analysis. For example, the legal, victim-precipitated, psychological, and learning/subcultural views explain rape individually or interpersonally, while the feminist perspective and the explanation of rape as part of a continuum of sexual violence pinpoint the social or structural factors involved in rape causation. In order to truly understand the phenomenon of rape, as well as to reduce or eradicate it, though, I believe that we need all of these levels of analysis. For example, and as is to be detailed in Chapter Seven, there are tactics that individuals can implement to either safeguard themselves from being raped or to reduce the likelihood that they will rape. Also included in this analysis, though, is the larger issue of restructuring our society so that we can eliminate the very roots of the problem. Although it is absurd to exclude either level of analysis, many of the suggestions given by rape prevention experts detail the former issues, while virtually ignoring the latter ones.

A second consideration is that there is a great deal of overlap among the feminist, social learning, and the sexual violence as a continuum explanations of rape. As noted by Ellis (1989:13), feminist and learning theories are similar in that they: (1) emphasize the role of social and cultural factors in causing the rape problem; (2) acknowledge the various aspects of modern, Western culture which lead to the sexual exploitation of women by men; and (3) "repudiate any suggestions that nonlearning, extra-cultural variables are responsible for variations in male propensities to commit rape." These views diverge, though, in that feminist theory clearly pinpoints the socioeconomic and/or political variables which lead to rape, while the social learning model focuses more on "cultural traditions [being] more directly linked with interpersonal aggression and sexuality as responsible for sexual assault" (Ellis 1989:13).

Finally, most of these perspectives have merit and have improved our understanding of the rape problem. For instance, the legal model clearly outlines the nature of the laws surrounding sexual coercion and lays out the parameters for "acceptable" behavior; the feminist and sexual violence as a continuum models clearly detail the social and cultural factors involved in creating and perpetuating the rape problem, while the social learning view and the psychodynamic typologies present a clearer picture of how some men come to be rapists and some women learn to be victims. Regarding Amir's victim-precipitated explanation of rape, though, it not only fogs and distorts our vision, but it also does damage, particularly to women who have been sexually assaulted.

The following section outlines the historical and current perspectives which explain the phenomenon of incest and child sexual abuse. Although some of these models are similar to ones mentioned earlier, they are different enough in their application to merit separate consideration. Specifically, the major difference is that many adult women who make accusations of rape are *not* believed, and their cases are regarded as unfounded. For incest and child sexual abuse, though, the situation is even more insidious because we have tried desperately to deny the very existence of these problems.

Historical and Contemporary Perspectives which Explain the Sexual Abuse of Children

Although we have "known" about the the sexual victimization of children for a very long time, we have been quite unwilling individually and collectively to admit that these problems exist and that they have reached epidemic proportions. In order to clarify our understanding of this movement from ignorance toward enlightenment, in this section I explore several early explanations of incest and child sexual abuse, as well as contemporary ones. As was the case with the historical and current explanations of rape, some of these perspectives explain the sexual abuse of children by focusing on the individual level of analysis, while others look toward social and cultural variables to explain these phenomena.

A Historical Overview

Although the road to our awareness of the incest and child sexual abuse problems has been a meandering, confusing one, some experts would have us believe that this awareness is recent. This, though, simply is *not* true. Indeed, the history of how, why, and when we began to admit that these problems existed is even more ignominious than it was for the crime of rape. For example, de Young (1982), notes that ancient societies, particularly the Roman empire, were replete with examples of child abuse (e.g., infanticide, particularly female children, the selling of children into slavery, and extreme corporal punishment for acts of "disobedience"). Since the Bible and the

Talmud were used to sanction harsh treatment of children, Judeo-Christian societies were *not* much better (de Young 1982; Rush 1980). More recently, in 1860, Tardieu, the dean of forensic medicine in France, published a treatise which detailed the epidemic proportions of the child sexual abuse problem. His documentation, though, virtually was ignored, and his ideas were scorned and discredited. In effect, people were able to continue to label children as liars who were attempting to defame "innocent" adults (Asher 1988; Goodwin 1985; Masson 1984; Summit 1988, 1989).

If we look at the pattern of acknowledgment in *our country*, several experts have argued that the standard child-rearing philosophies and practices in colonial America, by today's standards, were abusive. Part of the problem is that at that time the "value" of children tended to be calculated almost exclusively in economic terms rather than in social or emotional ones, and this, reportedly, prevented parents from becoming emotionally attached to their children (Empey 1978; Zinn and Eitzen 1990). According to de Young (1982), even then, though, there was the nascent awareness of child abuse, including the sexual victimization of children. She cites a case that occurred in 1641 where three men were believed to have sexually abused two school-age sisters over an extended period of time; this was a difficult case, though, because the existing legal codes did *not* include such acts as crimes. Notwithstanding this "technicality," the men were sentenced and punished (without ever being charged): "[E]ach was whipped repeatedly and had to pay a monetary restitution to the father of the two girls. On the day they were sentenced, the court created a law which made the 'carnal copulation with a woman-child under ten years' punishable by death, even if the victim 'had consented to the act'" (de Young 1982:106).

More recently, our first "official" case of child abuse and neglect poignantly illustrates our earlier views about children as well as our unwillingness to acknowledge the existence of these problems. As is reported by Conrad and Schneider (1980:162), in the early 1870s, a nine-year-old girl named Mary Ellen was being maltreated by her foster parents; church workers tried to secure help for her from a number of different social agencies, but all of them refused to get involved "because they viewed the right of parents to chastize their children as absolute, and there was no law under which they could intervene to protect the child." Eventually, they took Mary Ellen's case to the American Society for the Prevention of Cruelty to Animals: "[They were] able to intervene because Mary Ellen was a member of the animal kingdom, and thus could be included under the laws which protected animals from human cruelty" (Conrad and Schneider 1980:162). As a result of this case and the resultant publicity it received, many states enacted laws which began to protect children, not only from parental maltreatment, but also from the then-standard labor practices which permitted children to work long hours in unsafe conditions.

More recently, for that brief moment in time, we had Freud's "seduction theory" which suggested that father-daughter incest was occurring at an alarming rate. Based upon the accounts of several of his female patients, Freud concluded that incest and child sexual abuse were not only real problems but that these experiences had traumatic consequences for them as girls, as well as years later as adults. Due to the unwillingness of his peers to believe his accounting of the problem and the professional pressure that they put on him, though, Freud recanted this explanation and replaced it with his drive and Oedipal theories. The resultant effects were to place the onus of responsibility back onto the female children by viewing them as having sexual "fantasies" about and "seductive desires" for their fathers and to absolve adults as the perpetrators of these heinous acts (Asher 1988; Bagley and King 1990; Carmen and Rieker 1989; Courtois 1988; Crewdson 1988; Dinsmore 1991; Finkelhor 1984; Goodwin 1985; Herman 1992; Lerman 1988; Masson 1984; Miller 1984; Rush 1980; Summit 1988, 1989).

Miller, a former Freudian psychoanalyst who now vehemently rejects that perspective, argues that via this reversal, Freud did serious damage to all of us. Based upon his inability to tolerate being shunned by his peers, "A few months later, . . . he described his patients' reports on sexual abuse as sheer fantasies attributable to their instinctual wishes. Humanity's briefly disturbed sleep could now be resumed" (Miller 1990:54–55). She adds that this switch "institutionalized the denial that endowed the lies of pedagogy with alleged scientific legitimacy" and that this was a grievous error because it gave credence to the widely-held (yet inaccurate) belief that children "by nature [are] wicked and bad and must be trained by adults to be good" (Miller 1990:57). Masson (1984:xxi-xxii) concurs but argues that Freud's motivations were more complex and included: "a fear of standing up for the least advantaged in society; . . . a fear of the wrath of the more powerful men of the middle class elite whom Freud's patients were accusing of sexual abuse, and a desire to remain in the good graces of these men so that he could continue to practice his profession." Masson concludes that Freud's recantation of his earlier perspective showed a lack of moral courage.

Others posit that the real blame lies in the social and political climate of late nineteenth century Europe. Herman (1992:15), for example, suggests that "it is necessary to understand something of the intellectual and political climate that gave rise to the investigation in the first place." Specifically, she cites the political conflict between a monarchy with religious ties (i.e., Catholicism) and a movement toward a republican, secular type of government, a movement which did *not* include equal rights for women and children. Thus, Herman (1992:18) argues that it is inappropriate to regard Freud's reversal "as an act of personal cowardice . . . [because] to engage in this kind of ad hominem attack seems like a curious relic of Freud's own era, in which advances in knowledge were understood as Promethean acts of solitary male genius." Instead, she suggests that we consider the fact that: "No matter how cogent his arguments or how valid his observations, Freud's discovery could not gain acceptance in the absence of a political and social context that would support the investigation of hysteria, wherever it might lead" (Herman 1992:18).

Even more recently, when we have been willing to admit that incest and child sexual abuse do exist, we also have tended to believe that they really do *not* "harm" children and/or that the victims are somehow "complicitous." As an example of this view, we have Gagnon's (1965:180–181) investigation of the problem. He bifurcated sexual abuse into "clearly accidental" (i.e., "[t]he fundamental criterion was a single event with a single offender without any buildup of social interaction apparent in the record"), and "collaborative," which refers to children being "involved in the events through a provoked or mutual desire." He also attempted to "prove" that incest and child sexual abuse really are not all that damaging for children:

> The lack of negative outcomes regardless of the type of participation suggests that participation [of the child] may not be a central consideration in determining the quality of the outcome of the experience, and that other aspects of the child's personality . . . produce a protection against negative effects whether the contacts were short-lived or extensive, except for the small number of coerced females where the exposure to aggression over time seems to be extremely disorganizing in its impact (Gagnon 1965:192).

Although it was the 1950s before Kempe and Steel "officially" discovered the problem of physical child abuse (cf. Conrad and Schneider 1980; Goodwin 1985; Pfolh 1977; Summit 1988), it was the mid-1970s before we began to open that same door on the subjects of incest and child sexual abuse (Finkelhor 1979, 1984; Rush 1980). This acknowledgment, though, did *not* come from professional circles; rather, it came from personal, first-person accounts of women's lives (Bagley and King 1990; Rush 1980; Summit 1989). Most notably books such as Armstrong's *Kiss Daddy Goodnight,* Butler's *Conspiracy of Silence,* and Allen's *Daddy's Girl* made us aware that something was drastically wrong. At the same time, we had the women's and the children's protection movements which forced us to admit that the sexual victimization of children was a reality that had far-reaching consequences for all of us (Dinsmore 1991; Finkelhor 1984; Pfohl 1977).

Even more recently, we have had several works which began to "discover" the most horrible form that the maltreatment of children can take—ritualistic or cultic child sexual abuse (Bass and Davis 1988; Faller 1990; Kelley 1988, 1989, 1992; Mayer 1991; Snow and Sorenson 1990; Steele 1987; Summit 1989). Specifically, ritualistic sexual abuse refers to abuse which "occurs in a context linked to some symbols or group activity that have a religious, magical, or supernatural connotation, and where the invocation of these symbols or activities, repeated

over time, is used to frighten and intimidate the children"
(Finkelhor and Williams, with Burns 1988:59). Ritualistic child
sexual abuse also can include such nefarious acts as isolating the
child; torture; brainwashing the child to convince her that she is
bad, evil, and/or negatively magical; and animal and human
sacrifices (Kelley 1988, 1989, 1992; Finkelhor and Williams, with
Burns 1988; Summit 1989).

As you might suspect, we are even less willing to
acknowledge that this type of child abuse is possible and that it
is happening with a frequency that astounds, and many lay
people and experts alike are trying to discredit the children who
make these "allegations." As expressed by Summit (1989:418):
"Our present consternation over ritualized abuse is not
necessarily different from earlier denial of widespread
incestuous abuse or the age-old rejection of even the most basic
concept of child abuse." Yet again, many of us are choosing
complacency and denial over what Miller (1990:172) calls
becoming "enlightened witnesses" (i.e., being aware that these
sorts of atrocities exist and being willing to act as advocates for
the children who experience them). Summit (1989:418) outlines
the critical need for us to acknowledge the problem rather than
continuing to deny it: "We can challenge deliberate ignorance
only if we pursue and test the unknown at least as logically as
we protect the known and only if we are willing to challenge
what we have been comfortable in knowing in deference to
premonitions of what we least want to accept."

Thus, we have a lengthy history of: (1) ignoring the fact
that incest and child sexual abuse exist; (2) minimizing the
serious impact and the traumatizing nature of these experiences;
(3) buying into the mythology which surrounds this subject[7;] (4)
ignoring the structural roots and causes of these forms of sexual
victimization; and (5) acknowledging the "less serious" forms of
child sexual victimization while denying that organized or cultic
forms can be real. Even today there are detractors who would
have us believe that: incest and child sexual abuse do *not* exist,
child sexual abuse and incest are rare occurrences, and the
impact of these experiences is minimal (cf. Goodwin 1985; Miller
1984; Rush 1980; Summit 1988). Notwithstanding the naysayers,
a multitude of works published since 1970 has focused on incest

and child sexual abuse and has made it increasingly difficult for us to deny the existence and the consequences of these problems (Bass and Davis 1988; Blume 1990; Briere 1989; Courtois 1988; Dinsmore 1991; Engel 1989; Finkelhor 1979, 1984, 1986; Finkelhor and Williams, with Burns 1988; Finney 1990; Herman 1992; Miller 1990; Poston and Lison 1989; Rush 1980; Russell 1984, 1986; Sanford 1990; Tower 1988; Women's Research Centre 1989).

In sum, it has taken us centuries to acknowledge that incest and child sexual abuse exist, and it has taken us decades to recuperate from Freud's legacy of blaming the victim. Now, though, we have come full circle to the realization that incest and child sexual abuse do exist and that they are unwanted realities forced upon children by their adult caretakers (Armstrong 1978; Finkelhor 1984; Rush 1980; Summit 1989). Blume (1990:26) eloquently articulates this perspective and has angry words for the people who do *not* acknowledge the reality and the seriousness of these problems:

> I have something to tell you about those children who society claimed were lying, fantasized the abuse, who wanted the abuse. They are the women who I see as adults trying to repair their shredded souls, struggling to survive . . . believing they're crazy so it won't be true. They come to therapy, week after week after week, crying, struggling, denying, and finally with a combination of relief and sadness, admitting to the truth of their pasts . . .
>
> And finally the wounded child is free of the lies . . . and the silences, and her voice is heard. She is the confirmation of the truth that these children are forbidden to tell.

So, why all the denial? It is *not* enough to admit that we have been uninterested in exploring or acknowledging the problems of incest and child sexual abuse; we also need to examine *why* this has been the case. Finkelhor (1986) and Stein et al. (1988) offer fairly scientific rationales for these "tendencies." As examples, they suggest that the changing nature of our knowledge about these problems and the divergent methods by which we have gathered information about them are the primary reasons. In addition, Finkelhor (1988:61) suggests that we already have passed through two phases of explanations: (1) the initial or "catalogue phase" in which "clinicians recorded the wide range of symptoms and problems that they observed in children and adults who had been sexually abused," and (2) the "documentation phase" wherein researchers began to "measure the impact using recognized indices of psychopathology, comparison groups, and statistical procedures to try to partial out the specific contribution of the abuse." According to Finkelhor, though, only recently have we begun to enter the third phase of "modeling" whereby researchers and clinicians alike propose models to account for the incidence and the impact of child sexual abuse.

    Although these explanations are credible, they are *not* the whole story. As has been argued for some time now by a multitude of feminist authors, if we acknowledge that incest and child sexual abuse are real problems and fairly common occurrences, then we also are forced to admit that something is drastically wrong with this society, that these are *not* "just" the infrequent acts of a few sick men (Blume 1990; Briere 1989; Courtois 1988, 1992; Dinsmore 1991; Finkelhor 1979, 1984; Herman 1992; Rush 1980; Russell 1984, 1986). We also are forced to come to see the very real linkages among the rape, incest, and child sexual abuse problems and that many of the same factors are at work to cause and perpetuate all three of them, as well as a number of other issues which get depicted as "women's" problems (Brownmiller 1979; Herman 1992; Kelly 1988; Russell 1984). In sum, many of the experts now regard the problems of incest and child sexual abuse to have reached epidemic proportions and view them as being deeply rooted in the very fabric of this society. These more recent explanations are summarized in the following section.

Current Explanations of Incest and Child Sexual Abuse

    Although there are a number of recent explanations for the problems of incest and child sexual abuse, many of them focus predominantly on one of two issues. Either they offer psychological explanations as to why individual abusers do what they do (i.e., models of individual pathology), or they focus on why sexually abused children and adult survivors react in the ways that they do. Much less attention, though, has been paid to the structural underpinnings of these problems.

Several of the extant *psychological models* which explain incest and child sexual abuse focus on the pathology of the individual perpetrator. One example is *Groth's (1979) conceptualization* which assumes that the offender is a pedophile who uses children to gratify his need for power and love. He also differentiates between "fixated" and "regressed" pedophiles; the former type refers to molesters who evidence signs of infantile personality and are unable to relate well with adults, while the latter category refers to perpetrators who usually interact with peers but under stress regress and use children to meet their "needs." Although logical, Groth's theory is inherently flawed because he bases his conclusions on a prison population of convicted child molesters; this is problematic because many (perhaps most) child sexual abusers go undetected, much less convicted for their actions (Dinsmore 1991; Russell 1986).

Another individualistic explanation of incest and other forms of child sexual abuse is that if you were sexually abused as a child, your chances of *repeating this pattern* as an adult are quite high (Gebhard et al. 1965; Miller 1990; Russell 1984). There may be some basis in fact for this line of reasoning because studies of incarcerated males who have histories of being sexually victimized as children show that, as adults, they are likely to commit crimes of sexual violence against women and children (Gebhard et al. 1965; Groth 1979). There also, though, are very serious flaws with this view. In addition to the problem of utilizing prison populations, we have a number of recent works which show that girls predominate over boys as the victims of incest and child sexual abuse (Bass and Davis 1988; Finkelhor 1984; Russell 1984). If this perspective is accurate, women should predominate as the perpetrators of these acts; this, though, is *not* the case. Second, although "common sense" dictates that if abused as a child, you will be an abusive adult, studies which examine this issue have found that, on average, only about one-third are "repeaters" (Steinem 1992; Ziegler et al. 1988). Accordingly, one of the important issues that we need to address is why many people (particularly women who were sexually abused as children) do *not* repeat these patterns. This group really is the more noteworthy one because they have *not* done what is "expected"; more importantly, they are the ones from whom we can learn about breaking this "cycle" of violence.

In contrast to models which focus on individual pathology, several other experts have noted that child sexual abuse, more specifically incest, can be readily explained via *social psychological factors*. The most popular social-psychological explanation seems to be the *dysfunctional family or family systems model* (Bograd 1986; Courtois 1988; Dinsmore 1991; Dolan 1991; Finkelhor 1984; Kaschak 1992). Specifically, this perspective suggests that many family problems, including incest, result from a "'family system' gone wrong . . . [and] that each family member own[s] a piece of the problem" (Dinsmore 1991:15). In other words, pathology in the family is *not* regarded as the idiosyncratic behavior of a single member of that unit; rather, the family system is implicated as causing and perpetuating whatever problem that exists.

When we began to notice that incest appeared in "good," as well as "bad" families, though, Dinsmore (1991) notes that this type of theory became less "popular." She also adds that this is when the negative images about the mother's role in the incestuous family began to appear: "What was particularly noticeable about the emergence of this theory was that we began to see such terms as the complicitous mother; the distant, detached wife; the absent, disabled mother; the frustrated father" (Dinsmore 1991:15). The not-so-subtle implication of this line of reasoning is that (yet again) "mothers were somehow to blame when fathers committed incest, and that fathers were victims who were attempting to meet their needs inappropriately" (Dinsmore 1991:15).

Regarding the role that the mother may play, this issue is far from understood, much less agreed on. As an example, some experts suggest that many mothers know (sometimes consciously, other times unconsciously) that their daughters are being victimized, but for a variety of reasons (e.g., more often than not, their own powerlessness), they do *not* or *cannot* do anything to stop it (Bograd 1986; Finkelhor 1979; Forward and Buck 1978; Herman 1981). Other experts, though (particularly ones who embrace feminist explanations of the problem), regard this emphasis as one which confuses the real issues; they suggest that it is yet another example of blaming mothers while simultaneously minimizing the importance of the real culprits [i.e., the men who commit these behaviors, as well as this society which permits, encourages, and perpetuates the problem (Blume 1990; Dinsmore 1991; Russell 1984)].

There also are a number of *structural perspectives* that explain the incest and child sexual abuse problems. As was the case with rape, *feminism* has played a major role in defining incest and child sexual abuse as real problems. Via consciousness-raising groups of the 1970s, women began to talk to each other about their lives; and, not surprisingly, they came to realize that their "personal" problems and life experiences (e.g., wife battering, rape, incest, and child sexual abuse) also were the experiences of many other women (Dinsmore 1991; Kaschak 1992). Accordingly, major goals among feminists have been to make us more aware of the connections between our individual lives and outside political forces, and to reconceptualize the sexual victimization of children as a social problem rather than a problem of individuals.

In addition, we have Russell's (1984) work. Although she acknowledges several psychodynamic theories of child sexual victimization (e.g., poor impulse control, sexual frustration of the perpetrator), she suggests that structural factors are more effective explanations. As examples, she notes the importance of male sex-role socialization, exposure to child pornography, and the historical devaluation of children in this country as causal agents: "Just as females are viewed as the property of males, children are almost universally seen as the property of their parents [and s]ome fathers assume that this includes the right of sexual access, particularly to their daughters" (Russell 1984: 248).

By focusing on "male norms," Dinsmore (1991:17) concurs about the role that society plays in causing the problems of incest and child sexual abuse: "[This] does not mean that all men, or even most men, sexually abuse children. But it does acknowledge and hold accountable norms for men that encourage and in fact urge men to be aggressive, dominant, victorious, sexual, and powerful and to see sexual involvement as an entitlement." She also suggests that, until we are willing to acknowledge and name these issues as structural ones, all girls and adolescent females will continue to have difficulty developing into mature, healthy adult women. Courtois (1988:119) agrees regarding the role society plays in causing and perpetuating the sexual victimization of children: "Incest is seen as the tragic and most extreme manifestation of this power imbalance [between the sexes] and a within-the-family conditioning of women to their roles in society."

As was noted in the last chapter, Kelly (1988) has developed the *continuum of sexual violence*. Her model, too, is a feminist interpretation which highlights the importance of structural factors. She goes a step further, though, by suggesting that we should stop thinking about rape, incest, and child sexual abuse as separate topics; rather, she contends that the same forces cause all three forms of sexual violence. Again, if we follow this line of reasoning, we are able to demystify the processes which cause and perpetuate all of these problems, as well as make the solutions to them clearer. I also would add that we may be able to rouse people's anger more readily if we focus on the sexual victimization of women *and* children. That is to say, although some people continue to cling to the archaic notions that a child is "seductive" and that she plays a role in "causing" her victimization, most people today seem to be more sympathetic to the plight of the sexually abused child than they are to the adult woman who is raped. Perhaps if we combine these issues, some of this "understanding" may spill over and create a more humane situation for the woman who has been raped.

There also are models *which combine psychological and structural elements*. One example is *Finkelhor's (1984:54) Four-Preconditions Model of Sexual Abuse*. It includes the following emphases:

1. A potential offender needed to have some motivation to abuse a child sexually.
2. The potential offender had to overcome internal inhibitions against acting on that motivation.
3. The potential offender had to overcome external impediments to committing sexual abuse.

4. The potential offender or some other factor had to undermine or overcome a child's possible resistance to the sexual abuse.

Although this model appears to be a psychological one, Finkelhor (1984:56) does include social and cultural elements. For example, Precondition I emphasizes not only the issue of the "arrested emotional development" of the perpetrator but also the structural factor of the "masculine requirement to be dominant and powerful in sexual relationships." The second precondition focuses on such individual characteristics of the molester as psychosis, alcohol usage, and impulse disorder, as well as the structural factors of this society's "tolerance of sexual interest in children," "weak criminal sanctions against offenders," and child pornography. Regarding the third precondition, Finkelhor (1984: 57) includes the psychological factors of a "mother who is absent or ill" and/or the "social isolation of the family," but also adds the structural variable of "barriers to women's equality." Finally, the components of Precondition 4 are psychological concerns such as the "child who is emotionally insecure or deprived," as well as the structural issues of "unavailability of sex education for children" and the "social powerlessness of children."

Based on nearly twenty years of investigating the causes and the consequences of family violence, *Gelles and Straus* (1988) have developed a model which draws from *social exchange and social inequity theories*. They posit that: (1) the tenets of exchange theory show that people will use violence toward family members when the rewards (e.g., the immediate reward of releasing one's anger, as well as the rewards of increased power, control, and self-esteem) outweigh the costs (e.g., detection and punishment); and (2) sexual and intergenerational inequalities within the family (e.g., physical differences in size and inequities in status and power) make it a breeding ground for violence. Therefore, although acted out individually, Gelles and Straus are aware of how deeply imbedded family violence is in this culture.

We also have a number of theories which explain incest and child sexual abuse that are quite similar to ones that were mentioned earlier in this chapter. That is to say, *learning theories* focus on the cultural elements which cause us (particularly men) to learn that these behaviors are "acceptable." As one example of this type of explanation, several authors have noted that our *current socialization practices* encourage boys and men to be aggressive, while girls and women are taught to be compliant—"complementary" characteristics which easily can lead to victimizations (Bass and Davis 1988; Courtois 1988; Russell 1984, 1986). No one argues that this is the intended goal of such practices, but when we teach our boys that they are superior and that their aggression is acceptable, while we simultaneously inform our daughters that they are inferior and that they should be passive, the resultant categories of victimizer and victim can be the respective, unintended consequences.

A related variation of this perspective is *child pornography* which, in addition to being a type of child sexual abuse itself, is viewed as a cause of other forms of child sexual victimization. In other words, if we involve children and use them to make pornographic images, we are committing an act of sexual abuse, while the existence of pornographic materials which focus on children causes some males to think that the sexual abuse of children is acceptable (Donnerstein et al. 1987). Russell (1984: 242) summarizes the nature of this connection:

> By the simple laws of classical and instrumental conditioning, stimuli portraying adult sexual behavior in repeated association with portrayals of children enjoying or accepting this behavior can make sex with children an exciting idea. Such portrayals [then] likely feed the self-serving belief—common among child sexual abusers—that the children aren't hurt by such experiences, and that the experiences are enjoyable to both adult and child.

Another way that learning theory can explain participation in a particular type of child sexual abuse is to examine the *shared context of the ritualistic abuse of children*. Since these rituals usually take place in groups, Finkelhor and his associates (1988) have noted that the involvement of people in acts that should be regarded as disgusting and repugnant to them is normalized and reinforced. To state this a bit differently, the individual's guilt is assuaged not only by the presence of these others but also by their messages that the activities are acceptable. This notion reinforces what we have known for some time: That many people act differently in groups than they do as individuals and that this group context can normalize violence as well as other forms of deviance for the participants (e.g., delinquent gangs, the Ku Klux Klan).

Comparing these Perspectives

Although all of the aforementioned theories increase our understanding of how incest and child sexual abuse can occur, some of them are better than others. For instance, the psychologically-oriented perspectives (e.g., Groth and Gebhard et al.) help us to comprehend how some adolescent boys and men can perpetrate such offenses, but they afford little opportunity to understand from whence such urges and tendencies arise. These sorts of explanations also present problems because they often employ prison populations (i.e., convicted child molesters), while ignoring what is now regarded as a huge group of unidentified abusers.

The social-psychological explanations (e.g., models which underscore the dysfunctional family or the family as a system) clarify why the sexual abuse of children seems to "run" in certain families as well as the role of familial power imbalances. This sort of explanation, too, though, keeps the focus on individual families as the problem and ignores the societal power imbalances which many families mimic. Regarding this issue, Bograd (1986:100) has lots to say, and most of it is negative. First of all, she notes that although these theories assume that families are embedded in a larger social context, they do little to integrate this message into their treatment approaches: "[I]n practice, family therapists tend to focus on the nuclear family as a relatively closed system . . . This focus . . . leads to the family being viewed as an interpersonal event, detached from the sociohistorical context, which privitizes the family and ascribes responsibility to individual family members for their transactional patterns" (Bograd 1986:100). She has even more problems with family system models which assume that the mother "knew" but "chose" to do nothing, and that the daughter "complies" with her father's wishes: "It is the father who has failed as parent and husband . . . The mother takes no action, not because she supports the incest, but because she is immobilized and lacks power in and out of the family. The daughter complies with father because she has little choice by virtue of being a female child" (Bograd 1986:100).

To correct these problems, Bograd (1986:96) suggests that family systems theories and treatment modalities will need to do more than just include a "sensitivity" to women's issues. Rather, a complete restructuring is needed, a restructuring which includes the feminist concerns of: (1) the impact of living in a patriarchal society; (2) the deleterious impact of the "expected" roles for women in the family (e.g., disregard self and nurture everyone else); (3) viewing women as a class grouping and being aware of all that this implies; and (4) regarding women's qualities (e.g., nurturance and a capacity for communication) as strengths rather than deficits. In sum, "The feminist systemic reformulation . . . is not simply a question of semantics. Such a formulation challenges family therapists to evaluate the biases they bring to their examination of family process and structure" (Bograd 1986:96).

Although the notion that people can reduce their individual responsibility by taking part as a member of a group in the ritualistic or cultic abuse of children is an important one, it does little to clarify our thinking about the origins of this type of abuse. In other words, this perspective may be helpful in explaining how people who engage in this type of abuse of children can stand themselves (i.e., they find others who are equally reprehensible), but it does little to explain why and/or how people are motivated to get involved and remain involved in these sorts of insidious activities.

Finally, models which examine structural variables (e.g., sex-role socialization, power imbalances in the society, and the continuum of sexual violence) and ones which combine social-psychological and structural variables (e.g., the models of Finkelhor and Gelles and Straus) do the best job of describing how incest and the sexual victimization of children can happen. Not only do they examine the role of various learning variables, but they also pinpoint the flaws in the larger social structure which cause and perpetuate these problems.

Summary and Conclusions

When you examine historical and contemporary explanations for a given phenomenon, you get a pretty good idea about how that particular issue is accounted for, as well as how it can be resolved. In the cases of rape, incest, and child sexual abuse, what we see historically is avoidance and failing to name these problems as problems. This should *not* surprise us, though, particularly if we buy into feminist explanations of these types of crimes. In other words, feminists have shown us how patriarchy can lead to ownership notions about women and children, which in turn legitimates all sorts of negative attitudes about and behaviors toward them. Sexual victimization, then, becomes a given in societies which do *not* support notions of equality, justice, and fairness for all of its members.

Although many of the current legal views and theoretical explanations have improved the situation, problems remain. As examples, we still see a tremendous emphasis (particularly in the rape literature) on how women "tease" men; "cause" their own assaults via their characteristics, behavior, and/or dress; and make "false" accusations of rape. In addition, although different, the historical development of how we came to regard the sexual victimization of children as a "real" problem is quite similar to what we see in the rape literature: We tried desparately to ignore the problem, and until very recently, we failed to do much to protect children.

Now, though, the doors are open on these subjects, and I sincerely hope that there is *no going back*. We have come to realize that many of our cultural patterns, our gender-coded socialization practices, the extant negative attitudes about women and children, and the existing, objectified depictions by the various media are related to the problem of sexual victimization. And, finally, we have begun to do something about these issues—*not* enough to eliminate them yet, but we are beginning to address them in very direct ways.

CHAPTER FOUR

The Immediate and Long-Term Consequences of Sexual Victimization

> There is a loneliness that can be rocked. Arms crossed,
> knees drawn up; holding on, this motion, unlike a ship's,
> smooths and contains the rocker. It's an inside kind—
> wrapped tight like skin. Then there is loneliness that
> roams. No rocking can hold it down. It is alive, on its own.
> A dry and spreading thing that makes the sound of one's
> own feet going seem to come from a far-off place
> (Morrison 1987:274).

> In situations of terror, people spontaneously seek their
> first source of comfort and protection. Wounded soldiers
> and raped women cry for their mothers, or for God.
> When this cry is not answered, the sense of basic trust
> is shattered . . . Thereafter, a sense of alienation, of
> disconnection, pervades every relationship, from the
> most intimate familial bonds to the most abstract
> affiliations of community and religion. When trust is lost,
> traumatized people feel that they belong more to the dead
> than to the living (Herman 1992:52).

These quotes illustrate the severity of the possible consequences when girls and women are sexually victimized. In order to aid them through these experiences, it is essential that we have a better understanding of the nature, specific content, and duration of these consequences. The goal of this chapter, then, is to summarize what we know now about the aftermath of sexual victimization. Let me be clear from the outset, though; I regard this issue as a *stepping stone* to the more important one of recovering from sexual victimization, a topic which is addressed in the next two chapters. In other words, it is *not* enough to speak about the possible damage that can result when girls, adolescent females, or adult women are victimized sexually; we also must focus on the steps that they can take to heal from these experiences.

Caveats about This Information

Before beginning this summary of the post-sexual-victimization consequences, it is important to reiterate a few of the problems with this information, as well as to offer some additional caveats. First of all, regarding the quality of many of the works in this literature (and as was detailed in Chapter One), many of them possess a variety of flaws and lack scientific rigor. In part, this can be explained via the relative infancy of these bodies of knowledge, the complexity of the tangled web of issues that they sort out, and the diverse research methodologies that are used to study these topics.

An additional caution is that we must be careful about the biases and assumptions that we have regarding the consequences of sexual victimization. For example, several studies conclude that, after such traumas, most girls and women experience fairly "typical" or "normal" responses. As an example, Scurfield (1985) notes that the time-limited reactions of denial, numbing, and intrusive or repetitive thoughts and memories are typical post-trauma responses. Using feminist notions, Kelly (1988:187) makes a similar point by suggesting that many works examine post-assault responses such as frigidity and promiscuity while virtually "ignoring the male-defined assumptions implicit in these words and their place within a system of negative cultural meanings surrounding women's sexuality." Instead, she regards these responses "as a chosen period of celibacy ('frigidity') and a choice not to make emotional commitments in relationships with men ('promiscuity')," while she views women's post-sexual-victimization distrust of men as a positive reaction or "a healthy and self-protective response to the reality of sexual violence" (Kelly 1988:187). Other experts, though, depict these same responses as "symptoms" of pathology. Therefore, it is important that we be careful *not* only about the language that we use to describe the consequences of rape, incest, and child sexual abuse, but that we also need to exert caution regarding the implicit messages inherent in some of the "popular" terminology in these literatures.

A third concern is that we do a huge disservice when we focus solely on "average" responses to rape, incest, and child sexual abuse. When reviewing studies which summarize the consequences of sexual victimization, for example, we must remember that these conclusions are based upon averages, which in turn are derived via a *range* of scores (i.e., everybody is *not* at the midpoint or the mean level of anything). As Blume (1990:15) expresses this point, "Some . . . rally their strengths and survive their abuse relatively unscathed. Some stubbornly refuse to surrender, and go on to experience lives of satisfaction. Some are so damaged and endure such repeated horrors that they must rebuild themselves almost from scratch." By remaining aware of the heterogeneity of possible responses, we will be able to understand better the experiences of these girls and women as individuals as they react to and recover from their traumas.

Fourth, we need to underscore the fact that all forms of sexual victimization affect all of us and that they are social as well as personal problems. In the words of Burt and Katz (1987:58), "Rape may be a social/political phenomenon, but its reality is acted out in an intensely personal and personalized manner." Dinsmore (1991:31) concurs but applies this notion to the survivors of incest:

> There is a tendency to focus on the most brutal cases of incestuous rape when presenting a picture of the destructiveness of incest, but this is a disservice to the many more women who were sexually abused in ways that led them to doubt the legitimacy of their pain. Most cases of incest are not torturous. Yet I know of no incest survivor, regardless of the degree of violence, who has been left unscarred.

Therefore, it is essential that we remain aware of the fact that sexual victimization diminishes all of us, not "just" its victims and its survivors.

A fifth caveat is that, whether consciously or unconsciously, many of the early works which examined the aftermath of sexual victimization downplayed its impact (cf. Blume 1990; Finkelhor 1984; Koss and Harvey 1991). Miller (1984) offers the poignant example of Bell's biography of his late aunt, Virginia Woolf. Although he does acknowledge Ms. Woolf's well-documented history of child sexual abuse, he minimizes its consequences on her life. In truth, though, and as was evidenced via her life-long battle with depression, angst, and ultimately her suicide, the consequences for her were devastating (DeSalvo 1989). The life, as well as the demise, of Virginia Woolf, though, is *not* an isolated example: More than likely, this same scenario has been played out over and over again in the lives of not-so-famous girls and women, and many more lives have been lost. These, though, are "facts" that we will never be able to substantiate.[1]

Sixth, we have begun prematurely to divide our discussion of sexual victimization into "types" of assaults. Take for instance the fact that we now have a burgeoning literature on the topic of acquaintance rape, and some of these works infer that our responses to this type of assault may be different from (i.e., less serious than) the responses of women who have been raped by strangers. An example of this view is Ageton's (1983:62) analysis of the acquaintance rape problem among adolescents and her preconceived notions about the "minimal" impact of this form of rape:

> One unexpected finding . . . was that so many victims of attempted assaults by dates or boyfriends reported fear of being alone and fear of other men, often two to three years . . . [later] . . . [I]t was surprising how often . . . [these reactions] were reported by victims of attempted rapes that involved little physical force. This type of sexual assault is fairly common among the adolescent population and appears to be an almost standard feature of dating. If a sizable proportion of female adolescents react to these attempted seductions [?] with some generalized fears, the effect of these seemingly mild sexual experiences may be more serious than previously imagined.

The reality of the situation, though, is that adolescents and women who experience acquaintance rapes have at least the same amount of difficulty, if *not* more, recovering from them. As proof of this perspective, Warshaw (1988) cites the possible long-term consequences among college-age women who were raped by acquaintances, while Russell (1982b) concludes that women who have been sexually victimized by their husbands or ex-husbands experience more post-rape difficulties than do women who are involved in any other type of rape.

Some works also bifurcate the topic of child sexual abuse into the categories of incest and nonfamilial forms (Blume 1990; Courtois 1988; Russell 1986), and one possible implication of doing so is that the consequences of the former type of sexual victimization may be perceived as being more devastating than are those of the latter type. The bottom line, though, is that we do a disservice to everyone involved if we infer that some girls' and women's experiences have been less serious than were others.

These criticisms are *not* meant to negate the fact that there are some very real differences among the various types of sexual victimization. As examples, we do know that acquaintance rape victims and survivors are much *less* likely to report their sexual assaults and that the level of violence involved in these types of rapes tends to be lower (Koss 1988; Koss et al. 1988; Warshaw 1988). We also know that girls and women who have histories of *severe* child sexual abuse (particularly instances which were sadistic or ritualistic in nature and/or abuse which occurred over an extended period of time) are significantly *more* likely to develop borderline personality or multiple personality disorder (Blume 1990; Braun 1985; Braun and Sachs 1985; Briere 1989; Courtois 1988; Finney 1990; Janoff-Bulman 1992; Kroll 1988; Mayer 1991; Putnam 1989). Finally, being a victim of incest does seem to cause more severe consequences than does being the victim of nonfamilial child sexual abuse (Blume 1990; Courtois 1988; Russell 1986). Our goal, though, should *not* be to show that some girls and women have "worse" responses to sexual victimization than do others; rather, we would do better to remember that all forms of sexual victimization produce trauma for their victims and survivors, as well as make this world a much less safe place for all of us in which to live.

Seventh, many works which explain reactions to rape, incest, and child sexual abuse focus almost exclusively on "symptoms" or "signs" of disruption (e.g., physiological and/or psychological changes which are measured via a number of objective tests).[2] As noted by Kelly (1988:159), though, this approach is flawed because it does *not* consider the "range and the complexity of the impact of abuse on women or the fact that women and girls who have been abused are actively engaged in a struggle to cope with the conseqences." Dinsmore (1991:23) concurs by viewing women's post-incest consequences as survival skills: "They are symptoms of incest and need to be addressed[;] . . . they are not pathological. These behaviors are learned skills that were necessary for survival."

Although I, too, will summarize what we know about the "signs" or "symptoms" that are associated with rape, incest, and child sexual abuse, I take this discussion a step further by hypothesizing about the possible *underlying meanings* of these consequences. Please note that this is more than an issue of semantics; what I am suggesting is a different way of conceptualizing post-sexual-victimization "symptomatology." In other words, the aforementioned "symptoms approach" emphasizes the medical model of illness and assumes pathology rather than normal reactions to very real life events. By focusing instead on such issues as the consequences (rather than the "symptoms") of sexual victimization, as well as the underlying meanings that these responses may represent, our attention is redirected to the merits that some of these responses have, as well as the purposes that they serve. In addition, in the next two chapters, I examine what we know about the more optimistic issues of how girls and women can and do cope with sexual victimization, the healthy outcomes which are possible for them afterwards, and various treatment strategies which seem to work. Since I do *not* want to leave you with the erroneous impression that victims and survivors of rape, incest, and child sexual abuse remain disrupted forever, these positive emphases are a critical and an intentional component throughout this book.

Penultimately, I believe that it is important that we view ourselves as multifaceted human beings. This then dictates that we highlight the immediate and long-term consequences of sexual victimization across all of the different yet interrelated spheres of our lives. Accordingly, in the section which follows, I examine possible post-assault consequences across several spheres or dimensions of our lives, including: (1) psychological aftereffects; (2) somatic complaints; (3) behavioral changes; (4) interpersonal problems; (5) cognitive difficulties; (6) altered self-perceptions; and (7) sexual difficulties. Although most sources seem to agree that girls and women can and do experience consequences across these seven spheres, far fewer works acknowledge the prospect of political and spiritual ramifications, as well as subsequent victimization(s).[3]

Finally, it is important to keep in mind that, contrary to the stereotypes, many survivors of sexual victimization are *not* so "different." Rather, many of their post-trauma responses are similar to ones reported by people who have experienced a variety of other crisis situations or negative life events (Cohen 1988; Herman 1992; Horowitz 1986; Janoff-Bulman 1992; Lifton 1967, 1986; Mannarino et al. 1989, 1991; Thoits 1983). In other words, it is important to keep in mind that the traumatizing experience itself may *not* be the critical variable. Rather, the primary issues seem to be whether we are put into situations which make us feel helpless (particularly as children) and whether we have confronted death or the potential for death (either our own or someone else's); if these variations are present, the long-term ramifications can be quite severe (Herman 1992; Janoff-Bulman 1992). Thus, fairly recent works which attempt to explicate the nature of trauma, as well as its consequences, are combining such divergent experiences as being kidnapped as a child, surviving the Holocaust, being a political prisoner, and being sexually victimized (Herman 1992; Janoff-Bulman 1992; Terr 1990).

What is unique about the girls and women who are sexually victimized, though, is the victim-blaming and the mixed messages that get directed at them. Tower (1988:16) illustrates this point by specifying the confusing interactions that can take place after it becomes known that a child has been sexually abused: "The victim is usually viewed with curiosity, guilt, fear, and ambivalence by friends, neighbors, and even family. In addition to assuming that the child is *different*, people are unsure how to treat the child . . . Unable to sort out this dilemma, adults may actually withdraw from the child—if not physically, at least emotionally." These sorts of responses are insidious because they can reduce the empathy and the assistance accorded the girls and women who have been sexually victimized, intensify their confusion, and impede their recovery.

Notwithstanding these caveats, we now know a great deal about the consequences of sexual victimization. In the discussion which follows, though, I have elected to bifurcate this subject. Specifically, I have chosen to divide this issue into: (1) the immediate and long-term consequences of rape for adolescent females and women and (2) the aftermath of incest and child sexual abuse for children and adolescents, as well as for adult women years later. Although there are similarities in how we respond to these different forms of sexual victimization, I have elected to analyze them separately for a specific reason: Several studies now conclude that our responses to these different types of sexual victimization vary based upon such factors as our age at the initial attack, the nature of the assault, and our relationship to the offender. Thus, it would be misleading to assume that the consequences of rape, incest, and child sexual abuse are identical.

The Consequences of Rape

Currently, there is a multitude of empirical studies which investigate the post-rape recovery process of adolescent females and women, and several of them[4] are listed in Table 4.1. Please note, though, that there is a great deal of diversity among these works regarding the time frames analyzed (i.e., immediate responses versus long-term consequences); the groups that they study (adolescents versus adults); whether methodological strategies such as follow-up investigations and/or control groups are employed; and whether responses to rape are

Table 4.1: Major Studies which Investigate Women's and Girls' Post-Rape Reaction Processes

Studies: By Authors, Dates and Sources of Samples	Sample Size	Offenses Included	Ages of Victims	Control Group	Time Frame	Variables Included	Statistical Analyses	Theoretical Perspectives
Atkeson et al. (1982) Rape crisis center	115	Unclear	Adolescents and adults	Yes	One-year follow-up	Changes in level of depression, characteristics of assault, demographic data, & pre-rape crises	ANOVA & multiple regression	Do not specify
Becker et al. (1982) Rape crisis center	40	Attempted and completed rapes	Adolescents and adults	No	Initially studied one year post-rape	Acute symptoms, long-term reactions, & sexual dysfunction	Percentages	Do not specify
Burgess and Holmstrom (1974, 1978, 1979b) Hospital emergency room	146	Forcible and attempted rapes	All ages	No	Five-year follow-up	Victim's characteristics, assault factors, & views of significant others and social control agents	Percentages and Chi Square	Crisis and labeling theories
Burt & Katz (1987) Rape crisis center and ads	113	Unclear	Adults only	No	Retrospective analysis	Depression, anxiety, recovery, & self-esteem	Factor analysis	Developmental psychology and feminist view of rape
Calhoun et al. (1982) Rape crisis center	115	Unclear	Adolescents and adults	Yes	One-year follow-up	Fear reactions	ANOVA	Social learning

Table 4.1 (con.)

Studies: By Authors, Dates and Sources of Samples	Sample Size	Offenses Included	Ages of Victims	Control Group	Time Frame	Variables Included	Statistical Analyses	Theoretical Perspectives
Cohen & Roth (1987) Responses to an ad	72	Completed rapes	Adults only	No	Retrospective analysis	Demographic characteristics, assault factors, & social adjustment	Percentages, correlations, & t-tests	Do not specify
Ellis et al. (1981) Rape crisis center	27	Completed rapes	Adults only	Yes	Retrospective analysis	Depression, mood states, social adjustment, & fears	ANOVA	Do not specify
Frank & Anderson (1987) Rape crisis center	154	Unclear	Adults only	Yes	Six-week follow-up	Anxiety, depression, substance abuse, & phobias	t-tests	Do not specify
Gidycz & Koss (1990, 1991) National nonrandom sample of college students	44	All types of sexual coercion	Adults only	Yes	Retrospective analysis	Characteristics of the attack & post-victimization responses	ANOVA & Chi square	Do not specify
Gilmartin-Zena (1983, 1985) Rape crisis center	42	Attempted & completed rapes	Adults only	No	Two-month follow-up	Behavioral, interpersonal, psychological, & somatic reactions	t-tests	Life events & crisis view

Table 4.1 (con.)

Studies: By Authors, Dates and Sources of Samples	Sample Size	Offenses Included	Ages of Victims	Control Group	Time Frame	Variables Included	Statistical Analyses	Theoretical Perspectives
Girelli et al. (1986) Unclear	41	Unclear	Adults only	No	Retrospective analysis	Characteristics of assault & long-term fears & anxieties	Multiple regression	Social learning
Kilpatrick & associates (1979, 1981) Rape crisis center	40 & 83	Unclear	Adults only	Yes	Four-year follow-up	Standardizes tests measuring fears, mood states, & anxiety	ANOVA	Social learning
Koss et al. (1988) National nonrandom sample of college students	489	Attempted & completed rapes	Adults only	No	Retrospective analysis	Differences in reactions to acquaintance & stranger rapes	ANOVA & Chi squares	Do not specify
Kramer & Green (1991) Hospital emergency room	100	Completed rapes	Adults only	No	Two-month follow-up	Psychological symptoms, whether PTSD present, assault factors, & social support	Percentages & correlations	Do not specify
McCahill et al. (1979) Rape crisis center	1400	Unclear	All ages	No	Retrospective analysis	Victim & assailant characteristics	Percentages	Conflict & Feminist theories

Table 4.1 (con.)

Studies: By Authors, Dates and Sources of Samples	Sample Size	Offenses Included	Ages of Victims	Control Group	Time Frame	Variables Included	Statistical Analyses	Theoretical Perspectives
Nadelson et al. (1982) Rape crisis center	41	Unclear	Adolescents and adults	No	Retrospective analysis	Post-rape responses and life changes made	Percentages	Do not specify
Norris & Feldman-Summers (1981) Responses to an ad	179	Unclear	Adults only	No	Retrospective analysis	Symptoms, severity of assault, & social support	Multiple regression	Do not specify
Notman & Nadelson (1976) Clients from private practice	Unclear	Completed rapes	Adults only	No	Few months	Victim adjustment	None	Crisis theory
Resick et al. (1981) Rape crisis center	93	Completed rapes	Adolescents and adults	Yes	One-year follow-up	Demographic characteristics, assault factors, & social adjustment across seven areas of life	ANOVA	Do not specify
Ruch & associates (1980, 1983) Rape crisis center	138	Completed rapes	Adults only	No	Two-week follow-up	Traits of the woman, assault factors, prior life events, & rape impact	ANOVA perspective	Life events

Table 4.1 (con.)

Studies: By Authors, Dates and Sources of Samples	Sample Size	Offenses Included	Ages of Victims	Control Group	Time Frame	Variables Included	Statistical Analyses	Theoretical Perspectives
Sales et al. (1984) Rape crisis center	127	Attempted & completed rapes	Unclear	No	Retrospective analysis	Pre-rape symptoms & characteristics of the assault	t-tests & correlations	Crisis theory
Sutherland & Scherl (1970, 1972) Public mental health center clients	13	Completed rapes	Adults only	No	Few months follow-up	Reaction patterns of the women	None	Crisis theory
Williams & Holmes (1981) Rape crisis center	61	Attempted & completed rapes	14 & older	No	Retrospective analysis	Post-rape adjustment, characteristics of the woman, assault factors, & community attitudes	Multiple regression	Conflict & feminist theories
Wirtz & Harrell (1987b) Rape crisis center	56	Unclear	Adolescents and adults	No	Six-month follow-up	Assault factors, fears, anxiety, & stress	LISREL	Social learning
Wyatt et al. (1990) Probability sample	55	Attempted & completed rapes	Adults only	No	Retrospective analysis	Assault factors, attribution of responsibility, & outcomes	Correlations & path analysis	Do not specify

examined prospectively or retrospectively. Thus, some of these studies include the better research strategies of standardized symptom checklists, random samples, multivariate analyses, control groups, and/or longitudinal examinations of reactions to rape,[5] while others rely solely on clinical samples, univariate or bivariate analyses, and/or anecdotal data. We must *not*, though, downplay the importance of this latter type of investigation because it, too, has merit in that it keeps us grounded to and aware of the actual words and feelings of individual victims and survivors of rape.

Immediate Reactions to Rape

Some experts have found that many women show a number of signs of disruption almost immediately after being raped, while others are numb and show few "visible" signs of distress (Burgess and Holmstrom 1979b; Katz and Mazur 1979; Koss and Harvey 1991).[6] Although people may question the "credibility" of the women who evidence this latter response pattern, Scurfield (1985: 231) "normalizes" it by noting the variety of reported consequences: "Some [women] collapse on the spot; others collapse once refuge is attained; some 'freeze' and are literally immobilized; still others 'click' into a machine-like state and efficiently carry through in their actions; others enter with emotions raging." Thus, many women react immediately after being raped (which is defined as anywhere from moments to a few months later), while others experience a delayed response pattern or chronic, long-term consequences.

Notwithstanding these variations, numerous reports have found a similar range of possible post-rape consequences across at least seven dimensions of our lives. First of all, our immediate *psychological aftereffects*, typically, are quite severe and can include any combination of the following: anxiety, crying, and sadness (i.e., the early signs of depression); increased moodiness; fears; feelings of guilt, shock, embarrassment, and/or humiliation; and, in some cases, wanting to seek revenge (Atkeson, et al. 1982; Burgess and Holmstrom 1979b; Calhoun and Atkeson 1991; Ellis 1983; Frank and Anderson 1987; Gilmartin-Zena 1983b; Katz and Mazur 1979; Kilpatrick et al.

1985; Koss and Harvey 1991; Ledray 1986; Resick 1983; Sales et al. 1984; Wirtz and Harrell 1987a). Many women also report a multitude of *somatic complaints* shortly after being raped, including: pelvic pain, gastrointestinal difficulties, disrupted sleep and/or eating patterns, headaches, and muscular tension (Becker et al. 1982; Burgess and Holmstrom 1979b; Calhoun and Atkeson 1991; Ellis 1983; Gilmartin-Zena 1983b; Katz and Mazur 1979; Ledray 1986). Third, many victims and survivors of rape evidence *behavioral changes* immediately thereafter, including spending more time alone or with others, and absenteeism from work or school (Burgess and Holmstrom 1979b; Gilmartin-Zena 1983b). Fourth, many women experience *interpersonal problems* shortly afterwards, particularly in getting along with and/or trusting members of their social network (Burgess and Holmstrom 1979b; Ellis 1983; Gilmartin-Zena 1983b). Fifth, many women report the beginning stages of a number of different post-rape *cognitive difficulties* [e.g., trying to deny that the rape has occurred or the obverse of intrusive thoughts about the attack (Burgess and Holmstrom 1979b; Ellis 1983; Ledray 1986)]. The sixth area of immediate consequences are *changed self-perceptions*, particularly problems with self-esteem (Burgess and Holmstrom 1979b; Kilpatrick et al. 1985) and self-blame (Ellis 1983; Janoff-Bulman 1985). The final category of possible immediate post-rape responses are *sexual difficulties*, and oftcited complaints are that women may have less interest in sex, as well as experience less satisfaction with their sexual encounters (Calhoun and Atkeson 1991; Ledray 1986).

Although most of the works in the rape literature have examined the consequences for women, an exception is Ageton's (1983) analysis of the impact of rape among adolescent females. Specifically, she found that these girls experienced several initial responses including: feelings of anger, embarassment, and/or guilt; depression; and fears. In sum, the presence of all of these responses illustrates that many, if not most, adolescent females and adult women experience numerous consequences shortly after being raped. Yet, many studies stop here and leave us with the impression that long-term consequences do *not* exist. The rest of the story, though, is that a multitude of reports now shows that the long-term aftermath of rape can be quite severe, and this issue is summarized below.

The Long-Term Aftermath of Rape Victimization

Since the late 1970s, we have begun to rethink our views about the potential for long-term, post-rape consequences, and several reports now conclude that this process is neither a quick nor an easy one (Burgess and Holmstrom 1979b; Herman 1992; Kilpatrick et al. 1981, 1985; Koss and Harvey 1991; Ledray 1986). As Burt and Katz (1987:62) explain it:

> After the immediate task of regaining equilibrium and simply being able to function in daily life, the much longer task of rebuilding begins. There is tension and exchange between a woman's life as it was and as it looked to her before the rape, and all the new things that she is forced to learn and to confront in her post-rape life, [i.e.,] asserting control over the situation and accepting that there are in fact some things beyond her control.

Prior to this "rebuilding" phase, though, many women evidence numerous long-term consequences which readily illustrate the arduous and difficult nature of the post-rape recovery process. In fact, an astounding number of studies concur that rape can have highly devastating long-term effects. (Please note, though, that "long term" is defined as anywhere from two months to six years later). These reports show that many of us who are the victims and survivors of rape continue to evidence a variety of consequences across the seven dimensions mentioned earlier (i.e., psychological, somatic, cognitive, interpersonal, behavioral, self-perceptual, and sexual), as well as across the added dimensions of political consequences and subsequent victimization(s). When compared to immediate responses, though, what is different about the long-term ramifications is that their content typically reflects chronic "conditions" rather than acute "symptomatology."

The most frequently observed, long-term consequences of rape are *psychological*, including intense fears (particularly of stimuli reminiscent of the attack), anxiety, phobias, tension, nightmares, anger, hostility, suicidal ideation and/or suicide attempts, dissociative symptoms (e.g., feeling disconnected and/or "outside" of our bodies), and chronic depression (Atkeson et al. 1982; Becker et al. 1979, 1982; Burgess and Holmstrom 1979b; Braswell 1989; Calhoun and Atkeson 1991; Calhoun et al. 1982; Ellis 1983; Cohen and Roth 1987; Ellis et al. 1981; Girelli et al. 1986; Janoff-Bulman 1992; Katz 1984; Katz and Mazur 1979; Kelly 1988; Kilpatrick et al. 1979, 1981, 1985; Koss and Harvey 1991; Ledray 1988; Ledray et al. 1986; Nadelson et al. 1982; Norris and Feldman-Summers 1981; Resick 1983; Resick and Schnicke 1990; Stekette and Foa 1987; Wirtz and Harrell 1987a, 1987b).[7] Based on the content of these "symptoms," many of us seem to: (1) remain stuck at the victim stage; (2) have difficulty resolving and/or integrating the fact that we have been raped, and/or (3) feel responsible and are blaming ourselves for having been raped. Therefore, the underlying themes of most of these responses seem to be the senses of loss and confusion that come when we are placed in situations that are not only disruptive and traumatic but also ones for which we have *no* prior experience or knowledge.

Although most *somatic complaints* tend to diminish after a few months, some of them can and do persist. For example, two frequently cited responses (which may or may *not* have physiological bases) are fatigue (which usually is caused by continued sleep difficulties and nightmares) and gynecological problems [particularly pelvic pain during intercourse (Burgess and Holmstrom 1979b; Calhoun and Atkeson 1991; Norris and Feldman-Summers 1981; Williams and Holmes 1981)]. Again, these long-term physical responses underscore the fact that some women may have difficulty recovering from their rape experiences. They also may indicate women who have trouble doing their pain "out loud." That is to say, the pain does get examined but only when they are in "altered states" (e.g., asleep, sexual arousal), or when they are exhibiting stress-related physical "symptoms."

Behavioral changes, too, are part of the long-term, post-rape response picture. Some of the reactions which have been observed are positive ones (e.g., changing residences and increasing activities related to personal safety and security), while many women also experience the negative responses of substance abuse and an inability to enjoy life (Burgess and Holmstrom 1979b; Ellis 1983; Ledray 1986; Nadelson et al. 1982; Root 1989). Although the former changes are positive ones and should be viewed as attempts to gain back some sense of control in our lives, the latter ones, particularly substance abuse, reflect the fact that some of us get and remain "numb" after being raped and that we are able to feel little joy in our lives. Therefore, it behooves us to rethink our current biases about substance abuse because it may be yet another "symptom" of post-rape disruption rather than the woman's "sole" problem (Root 1989). (This issue is explored further in the next chapter.)

Many women also evidence long-term *interpersonal problems*. Oftcited issues are: difficulties achieving and/or sustaining intimacy; problems getting along with and/or trusting people; and work adjustment issues (Ellis et al. 1981; Gilmartin-Zena 1985; Girelli et al. 1986; Katz 1984; Kelly 1988; Koss and Harvey 1991; Ledray et al. 1986; Resick 1983; Resick et al. 1981; Stekette and Foa 1987). The probable underlying issues of these consequences are that many women, after having been sexually assaulted, tend to isolate themselves, feel misunderstood, and lose the ability to trust others. We must keep in mind, though, that a great deal of this imputed confusion is based in reality. As was noted earlier in this work, many lay people and professionals alike have been found to have in-accurate attitudes about rape (i.e., they believe the rape myths); blame the victim for her misfortune, and disbelieve her "allegation" of rape (Burt 1980, 1991; Lottes 1988; Madigan and Gamble 1991). These sorts of negative responses can intensify the woman's post-rape consequences (Gilmartin-Zena 1985; Holmstrom and Burgess 1978; Lottes 1988).

The long-term, post-rape *cognitive difficulties* are particularly problematic; not only do they warp our images of ourselves and the world around us, but they also work to diminish our chances for recovery. Frequent responses include: a distorted view of the world, confusion, being haunted by traumatic memories or intrusive thoughts, hypervigilance to danger, and altered beliefs about our power and/or sense of mastery (Ellis 1983; Herman 1992; Janoff-Bulman 1979, 1985,

1992; Koss and Harvey 1991). These "symptoms" probably reflect that we not only view ourselves and the world around us differently but that we also may regard ourselves as lesser beings. According to Janoff-Bulman (1985), the underlying meaning of these distorted patterns of thinking is that our original assumptions about the world have been shattered; in effect, we no longer have a "cognitive map" which acts as a blueprint for everyday living.

Understandably, many of us also evidence long-term *changes in our self-perceptions.* The most frequently cited ones are: self-blame; lost senses of security, safety, and self-respect; poor self-esteem; and an increased awareness of our vulnerability, as well as the fragility of our lives (Burgess and Holmstrom 1979a, 1979b; Burt and Katz 1987; Girelli et al. 1986; Herman 1992; Janoff-Bulman 1979, 1985, 1992; Kelly 1988; Koss and Harvey 1991; Ledray 1986; Wyatt et al. 1990). Although some of these responses are to be expected, as well as realistic (e.g., lost senses of security and safety, an increased awareness of our own vulnerability), others such as self-blame, loss of self-respect, and low self-esteem infer that women who have been raped *not* only blame themselves for their attacks but also view themselves as "lesser" or "diminished" human beings afterward. One possible interpretation of these issues is that some women may be buying into the extant stereotypes regarding women and rape and may be viewing themselves as "damaged goods."

Sexual difficulties, too, persist as part of the long-term aftermath of rape. Frequently cited problems are fear of sex, sexual abstinence, "frigidity," "promiscuity,"[8] "confusion" about sexual identity, and flashbacks during sexual activity (Becker et al. 1979, 1982; Burgess and Holmstrom 1979b; Calhoun and Atkeson 1991; Ellis 1983; Katz 1984; Katz and Mazur 1979; Kelly 1988; Koss and Harvey 1991; Ledray 1986; Nadelson et al. 1982; Norris and Feldman-Summers 1981; Stekette and Foa 1987). Even though rape currently is defined by many experts as a crime of violence, many women report long-term difficulties with the sexual content of the crime, and have difficulty separating their current sexual encounters from their past rape experience(s). If we consider that many (perhaps most) women equate sex with love, closeness, and intimacy, though, it should be easier for us to understand why so many of them later feel so differently about their sexuality, sexual identity, and sexual relationships. The underlying meaning of these "symptoms," then, is that their sexual experiences become problematic because someone has stolen their ability to regard sex, love, closeness, and intimacy as parts of the same whole; rather, based upon very real experiences, sex and sexuality take on dire meanings.

An interesting long-term post-rape effect (and one that I as well as many others would argue is *not* a "symptom" at all) is the *political consequences*. As an example, Kelly (1988) suggests that some of us gain a new awareness regarding the political underpinnings of rape (e.g., an increased understanding of the need for a wider role for women in our society), and that some of us even go so far as to become political activists to try to stem the rape problem. Rather than "signs" of pathology, these responses can be beneficial because they help women who have been sexually assaulted to better understand the societal factors which cause and perpetuate rape (Herman 1992). This, in turn, can reduce their likelihood to engage in the negative and destructive patterns of self-blame, self-denigration, and guilt. In other words, the underlying themes of these consequences are positive: Some women attempt to facilitate their recovery by immersing themselves in "speaking out" about the issue of rape and trying to do something concrete about it.

The final, frequently cited long-term consequence of rape is *subsequent victimization(s)*. Although the experts are unclear as to the exact hows and whys of this one, it has been shown time and time again that many women who have histories of sexual victimization (including childhood experiences) have a significantly higher likelihood of future victimization [i.e., physical violence in their intimate relationships and even subsequent sexual assaults (Briere 1989; Burgess and Holmstrom 1979b; Jehu 1988; Kelly 1988; Koss and Harvey 1991; Russell 1986; van der Kolk 1989)]. Possible interpretations of these findings are that women have taken on the role of victim and that the self-fulfilling prophecy is in effect. In other words, when we view ourselves as victims, along with this comes the cognitive and behavioral "baggage" of passivity, helplessness, and feeling as if we have no control over our lives, and these sorts of attitudes and behaviors can lead to subsequent victimizations. Let me add, though, that we are *not* alone in doing this to ourselves. Other people (e.g., significant others and involved social control agents) encourage and facilitate these counterproductive images and actions if and when they blame us for our assaults and/or question the credibility of our "claims" of rape because, at times like these, we are more susceptible to the definitions of others. Ergo, we can end up believing that and living as if we are less than we were.

Again, although the vast majority of works which analyze long-term, post-rape responses focus on adult women, Ageton (1983) provides us with information regarding the adolescent victims and survivors of rape. She suggests that they have particular difficulty with anger, embarassment, guilt, and depression. She also notes that afterwards these girls tended to date less frequently and slacked off on their work and school responsibilities.

Each of these long-term consequences clearly reflects the depth of the pain which can result from rape, the severity of the impact of the experience, and the multitude of ways that rape can affect us afterwards. Although many, if not most, of us can and do recover completely from being so victimized, we also can conclude that for some adolescent females and adult women, rape can be a life-altering or even a life-shattering experience. As proof of this claim, we have Burgess and Holmstrom's (1979b) follow-up study which shows that nearly one-third of the women in their sample remained disrupted five years after they were raped, as well as Kilpatrick et al.'s (1981) report which finds that approximately 75 percent of the women that they studied continued to evidence serious, post-rape "symptoms" one year later.

I also would hypothesize that some of these consequences wreak more havoc in our lives than do others. To be specific, the problems which arise in the *cognitive and self-perceptual dimensions* of our lives seem to be the most critical long-term post-rape consequences, as well as the ones from which all of our other responses arise. In other words, if we experience extreme changes cognitively (e.g., distorted views about the world around us and a general sense of confusion), as well as self-perceptually (e.g., self-blame and poor self-esteem), we also are more likely to experience reactions in the psychological, somatic, behavioral, interpersonal and sexual spheres of our lives, as well as via subsequent victimization(s). This is so because the ways that we define and regard self and the world around us are critical in explaining how we will adapt in these other dimensions of our lives.

In addition, some of our responses to sexual victimization are *not* negative consequences at all; rather, they are signs of growth and indicators that healing has begun. As an example, we should regard some behavioral changes (e.g., changing residences) as attempts to increase our safety, a laudatory goal for anyone whose illusion of safety has been shattered. Regarding the long-term political consequences of rape (i.e., when we come to an awareness of its structural underpinnings and feel a need to do something about them), these are even more graphic signs of growth and evidence that recovery has begun, and we do a tremendous disservice if we pathologize them.

Factors which Increase or Decrease Our Post-Rape Reactions

Several studies have addressed the issue of the variability of our post-rape consequences by investigating mediating variables that may reduce our responses. Kilpatrick and his associates (1985:122), for example, have noted that these sorts of studies begin with the assumption that women "bring to the rape a certain ability to cope with stress in general and with the stress of a rape situation in particular," and that these pre-existing tendencies are "based on her previous life history, certain constitutional factors, and level of psychological functioning at the time of the rape." Moreover, they suggest that one's post-rape adjustment depends not only on the "immediate impact and the victim's continuing ability to cope with rape-induced stress," but also on the quality and content of her interactions with significant others and involved social control agents who "can serve as additional sources of stress, enhancers of coping ability, or some combination of the two" (Kilpatrick et al. (1985:122). In other words, these sorts of studies highlight the fact that women who have been raped are *not* "just" rape victims; they had lives prior to their assaults, and they will continue to have lives afterwards.

The discussion of these issues is extremely important for a couple of reasons. First of all, if we are cognizant of the fact that certain types of rapes may be more difficult ones from which to recover, we can do more for the survivors of these sorts of assaults. In addition, this topic offers positive and optimistic messages because it focuses our attention on factors which lead to salutogenesis or health. Again, rather than spending our time exploring why many of us do *not* recover from being raped, this emphasis switches our attention to the factors which can facilitate recovery, healing, growth, and victory.

The model that I have developed to illustrate many of the factors believed to affect our post-rape responses include such issues as: (1) pre-rape demographics; (2) pre-rape indicators of adjustment and functioning (e.g., prior self-perceptions and stressors); (3) characteristics of the assault (e.g., level of violence, presence of a weapon, whether the woman sustained injuries, and relationship to the assailant); (4) women's reactions immediately afterwards; (5) post-rape self-perceptions and views about the world (e.g., self-esteem and sense of coherence); and (6) the post-assault attitudes and responses of our significant others and involved social control agents (Gilmartin-Zena 1983b:54). We, though, must be careful in our application of this model. It is *not* a "profile" which will always "work," or determine which women will experience the more severe, long-term consequences of rape; rather, it is offered as a heuristic device which may improve our understanding of the possible post-rape responses of adolescent females and adult women. In addition, to date, there are no reports which investigate this model as a totality. Rather, several reports have posited similar models, but they do *not* investigate them in a multivariate format, or they only examine certain segments of this model (e.g., Burgess and Holmstrom 1979; Koss and Harvey 1991; Sales et al. 1984). Thus, its predictive value is as yet unknown.

Notwithstanding these caveats, several investigations have concluded that the *demographic characteristics* of *marital status* (Kilpatrick et al. 1985; McCahill et al. 1979), *race* (Kilpatrick et al. 1985; Ruch and Chandler 1983; Williams and Holmes), *age* (Cohen and Roth 1987; Kilpatrick et al. 1985; McCahill et al. 1979), and *class* (Stekette and Foa 1987) affect our post-rape reactions. To be specific, more severe responses have been observed among women who are: married, members of minority groups and/or the lower class, and/or older. Please note, though, that other experts have concluded that demographic characteristics are relatively unimportant in predicting recovery from rape (Calhoun and Atkeson 1991; Koss and Harvey 1991).

Second, *pre-rape adjustment variables* have been found to be important issues which mediate the long-term consequences of rape. As examples, a number of reports have found that prior victimization(s), a history of psychiatric difficulties or emotional problems, being differently abled, and/or the presence of chronic life stressors are associated with more severe post-rape responses (Burgess and Holmstrom 1979b; Calhoun and Atkeson 1991; Janoff-Bulman 1992; Ledray 1986; Koss and Harvey 1991; Resick 1983; Popiel and Suskind 1985).

Regarding the *characteristics of the assault*, again, the findings are contradictory. Although many studies have concluded that assault factors are *not* good predictors of immediate or long-term post-rape responses (Calhoun and Atkeson 1991; Gilmartin-Zena 1983b; Kilpatrick et al. 1985; Koss and Harvey 1991; Kramer and Green 1991; Resick 1983; Ruch and Chandler 1983; Stekette and Foa 1987), other reports have found that some of them are. These latter studies, for example, show that women who experience particularly "brutal" rapes (i.e., the presence of a weapon, severe injuries, the use of force) tend to evidence greater difficulty recovering from them (Cohen and Roth 1987; Ledray 1986; Norris and Feldman-Summers 1981; Wyatt et al. 1990). To further complicate the picture, McCahill et al. (1979) have found a curvilinear relationship between assault type and long-term responses: If women experience what they label as "less serious" sexual acts (e.g., fondling, caressing), or if they experience more "deviant" sexual acts (e.g., anal intercourse), they are much more likely to report high levels of post-rape disruption.

Koss and Harvey (1991) and Girelli et al. (1986) have tried to explain these discrepant findings by suggesting that the level of brutality or violence involved in a rape is *not* the critical issue; rather, it is the *level of felt threat* or the woman's subjective experience of her assault which predicts her post-traumatic consequences. In effect, we are back to the issue of permitting women who have been sexually victimized to define for themselves what their concerns are. This solution seems such an obvious and simple one, but some of the experts in the field of rape victimology historically have preferred to superimpose their own views and values onto the experiences of the women that they study.

Another characteristic of the assault which has produced confusing results is the relationship to the assailant(s). Some experts have found that involvement in "stranger rapes" is more unsettling and produces more disuption because these sorts of experiences explode our ideas about personal safety and our ability to trust people (McCahill et al. 1979). Others, though, have suggested that recovery from acquaintance rapes is a more difficult process because someone that we have known and trusted has violated that trust. As examples, Burt (1991), Gidcyz and Koss (1991), and Katz (1991) report severe, long-lasting responses among women who have experienced acquaintance rapes, while Russell (1982b) concludes that women who have experienced marital rapes suffer more long-term consequences than do women who are involved in other types of rapes.

Fourth, some studies report that the higher the woman's *initial post-rape* responses the more difficulty she will have in recovering from the assault (Kilpatrick et al. 1985; Stekette and Foa 1987). That is to say, if she exhibits high levels of disruption immediately afterwards, she also is more likely to report high levels of reactions at follow-up assessments one to four years later (Kilpatrick et al. 1985).

Fifth, our *post-rape self-perceptions* are believed to be important predictors of recovery from rape. In particular, after being raped, if someone evidences *poor self-esteem, character-ological self-blame* (i.e., the belief that the person is a problem as a whole rather than "just" having problematic behaviors), and/or a *weak sense of coherence* (i.e., a worldview which includes a lack of meaning and a lack of commitment to others, as well as an emphasis on the unmanageable aspects of life), she also is more likely to report more signs of disruption, as well as a delayed recovery pattern (Burgess and Holmstrom 1979b; Frank and Anderson 1987; Gilmartin-Zena 1983b, 1988; Janoff-Bulman 1979, 1985; Ledray 1986; Resick 1983).

Last but not least, the *attitudes and the responses of significant others and involved social control agents* have been found to be importantly related to post-rape reactions. Sociologists who support a symbolic interactionist perspective of human development and social interaction have long understood the importance of the attitudes and the responses of our significant others in the development and the maintenance of our sense of who we are (Calhoun and Atkeson 1991; Charon 1977; Cooley 1902; Mead 1932, 1934; Meltzer, Petras, and Reynolds 1977; Stryker 1980). Relating this issue to rape, several reports now highlight the salient role that significant others play in the rape recovery process (Burgess and Holmstrom 1979b; Gilmartin-Zena 1983b, 1988; Janoff-Bulman 1992; Katz 1984; Ledray 1986; Popiel and Suskind 1985; Resick 1983; Williams and Holmes 1981; Wyatt et al. 1990). In sum, if the important people in our lives respond favorably toward us, support us, and do *not* blame us for being sexually assaulted, we tend to exhibit fewer post-rape reactions.

A similar effect has been reported for social control agents (e.g., police officers, medical personnel, court officials, and rape crisis counselors) who interact with women after they have been raped (Holmstrom and Burgess 1978; Madigan and Gamble 1991). The problem, though, is that many members of these groups (particularly police, medical, and court personnel) possess stereotypes or negative, preconceived notions about the "ideal" rape victim or the "believable" rape case, i.e., the woman is expected to: be *visibly* upset when she talks about the rape, have medical evidence which substantiates her "claim" of rape, report the attack in a "timely" fashion, have *visible* signs of physical injury, and have *not* known the perpetrator(s). In turn, these images and notions predict how these authority figures interact with the victims and survivors of rape; if the women meet the criteria for being "ideal," "real," or "credible" rape victims, they are generally treated well, while women who do *not* meet these socially-constructed standards are typically treated less equitably by the various social control agents. As probably is obvious, the former response from authority figures tends to reduce post-rape aftermath, while the latter one intensifies it. The role of one expert, the rape crisis counselor, is unique because, usually, she understands the experience of being raped; plus, she does *not* have the "cultural baggage" which dictates that she question the credibility of the woman's "claim" of rape. Accordingly, her involvement is critical not only because she acts as a source of support and advocacy for women who have been sexually assaulted but also because she provides accurate information about the realities of sexual victimization.

In summary, what we have is a model which specifies the profile of the adolescent girl or the adult woman who is more likely to recover fully from the trauma of rape. Again, though, we must be very careful about some of the implicit assumptions of this model because we could end up blaming the victim for not recovering quickly or fully enough. Notwithstanding this problem, the profile which appears to facilitate recovery from rape includes: a fairly "healthy" existence and a strong self-concept prior to being sexually assaulted; experiencing a "less traumatic" or a "less brutal" type of rape; certain post-rape self perceptions such as positive self-esteem, a strong sense of coherence, and/or a fairly low level of self-blame; and the support and loving kindness, as well as favorable and approving responses, from significant others and social control agents. In addition, this model should help practitioners and clients alike to determine the frequently observed "trouble areas" encountered after rape. That is, practitioners who are aware of these issues should be better equipped to aid these adolescent girls and women to recover, while for women who have been sexually assaulted, simply knowing about these issues should make it clear to them that they are responding in "normal" fashion to the trauma of rape.

A Summary and Critique of These Findings

Based on the foregoing discussion, we can conclude that our knowledge about possible post-rape consequences has improved dramatically during the last two decades. As an example, a multitude of recent works has validated the seriousness of rape by showing that we can experience post-rape consequences across several dimensions of our lives immediately afterwards, as well as months and even years later. In addition, we now know that a number of variables (prior psychiatric history and post-rape self-esteem, to name two) can intensify the aftermath of rape.

These findings, though, also have some very serious limitations. One problem that I already have alluded to is that many if *not* most of these works investigate our post-rape consequences via what I call the "symptoms approach." In other words, when we utilize standardized measures of psycho-pathology or symptom checklists to determine the specific content and duration of the aftermath of rape, we focus mostly on the psychological, physiological, behavioral, interpersonal, and sexual dimensions of our lives. While this approach has merit (i.e., it highlights the range of possible post-rape reactions in these areas), it also can minimize other salient dimensions of our lives such as our cognitions and self-perceptions. In addition, this approach really only "scratches the surface" because it tends to ignore the underlying meanings that these "signs" and "symptoms" often represent. To simply enumerate and list post-rape responses is inadequate because women who have been raped are more than a sum of these issues. Thus, it behooves us to take this discussion a step further by permitting the women who have been raped to define for themselves (if they can) what their "symptoms" mean to them.

A few examples should clarify this point. As previously noted, after experiencing traumas such as rape, a serious aftereffect can be the shattering of our assumptions about the world in which we live (Antonovsky 1979, 1987; Janoff-Bulman 1979, 1985, 1992; Steele 1987). This underlying theme, though, is masked if we only focus on the "visible" signs of sleep disruption, confusion, depression, and/or tension. In addition, after being sexually assaulted, many of us experience altered self-perceptions and an increased awareness regarding our vulnerability and lack of control over our lives (Fuller 1990; Kelly 1988; Ledray 1986; Resick and Schnicke 1990).[9] Yet, if we continue to focus solely on the "symptoms" of poor self-esteem, low levels of mastery, interpersonal difficulties, and depression, these deeper meanings are overlooked. Thus, what we historically have labeled as the "symptoms" or "aftereffects" of rape can be viewed equally well as *metaphors* which represent (often unconsciously) the core, underlying issues with which those of us who have been raped must grapple while trying to put ourselves and our worlds back together again.

My second criticism is that too much emphasis has been placed on post-rape reactions and *not* enough attention has been paid to the coping strategies that many adolescent girls and women attempt afterward. Thus, the message has tended to be a negative one: They passively experience their sexual assaults. When we investigate issues such as the specific tactics that they use to cope with having been raped, though, this reflects not only a more positive approach but also one which views them as active participants in the process of their own recovery (Burt and Katz 1987). As an example, if we utilize a "coping perspective" rather than a "symptoms approach," the post-rape responses of denial and intrusive thoughts can be regarded as attempts to control one's pain and to achieve mastery over the trauma (Janoff-Bulman 1992) rather than as "signs" of pathology.

My final criticism is that many works in the rape victimization literature have studied reactions to rape without intersecting with the stress or life events literature. This becomes a problem because the stress literature has shown that, if we experience a number of negative and/or uncontrollable life events in a relatively short period of time (i.e., six months or one year), there is a good chance that we will become physically and/or psychologically ill (cf. Brown and Harris 1978; Dohrenwend and Dohrenwend 1984; Kaplan 1983; Kessler et al. 1985; Thoits 1983). Yet, few works in the rape literature have acknowledged, much less explored, this issue. A notable exception to this criticism is the work of Ruch and her associates which focuses on the relationship between prior life events and post-rape reactions (Ruch and Chandler 1983; Ruch et al. 1980; Ruch and Hennessy 1983; Ruch and Leon 1983). They report a curvilinear relationship between these two variables, i.e., women who report either few *or* many pre-rape stressors evidence more severe post-rape reactions, while women who report a moderate number of pre-rape stressors experience fewer reactions after being sexually assaulted.[10] Mental health professionals should heed this information because it can aid them in understanding why women respond to rape in certain ways, as well as prompt them to make inquiries about other current or chronic life stressors in the women's lives.

In sum, if we only examine post-rape consequences and ignore the issues of coping with and recovery from rape, we do a serious disservice, and we do little to improve our understanding of the most important post-rape consequence of all—recovery. We have more than enough research which validates the seriousness of the consequences of rape; what we need now is to increase our understanding of how we can facilitate women in recovering from these consequences and reclaiming their lives, issues which are explored in the next two chapters.

The Aftermath of Incest and Child Sexual Abuse

Table 4.2 lists a number of the recent works which investigate the consequences of incest and child sexual abuse. As can be seen, many if not most of these works are even more recent than are the ones which examine our post-rape consequences. As such, many of the flaws previously noted about the rape literature (see discussions in Chapters One and Three, as well as earlier in this chapter) apply equally well to the incest and child sexual abuse literatures.

As examples, since several diverse definitions of incest and child sexual abuse have been offered, the victims and survivors of these experiences have been studied across a number of divergent time frames, and since many of these studies are based almost exclusively upon clinical impressions, some of these works lack scientific rigor (Asher 1988; Russell 1986). In addition, many reports examine the consequences of child sexual abuse within child and adolescent populations (Gomes-Schwartz et al. 1990; Kelley 1989; Mannarino et al. 1989, 1991), while a sizable number of these studies investigate its aftermath years, even decades later among adult women who were sexually abused as children (Bass and Davis 1988; Briere and Runtz 1988a, 1988b; Finkelhor 1984; Jehu 1989; Peters 1988). While making comparisons across these groups may prove interesting, it is methodologically unwise to do so because the experiences of children who currently are being or were sexually abused fairly recently have been found to be quite different from those of adult women who were maltreated decades earlier (Asher 1988; Briere 1989; Courtois 1988). Finally, many of the definitions of the aftermath of child sexual abuse are distinctively different from the ones used in the rape literature. For example, several reports define "immediate" reactions to child sexual abuse as ones which occur during the first two years (Courtois 1988; Finkelhor and Browne 1986; Gomes-Schwartz et al. 1990), while most of the works which examine post-rape consequences limit their discussion of immediate reactions to a few weeks or perhaps a few months later.

In sum, as was the case with the rape literature, our current knowledge about the aftermath of incest and child sexual abuse is less than perfect. In addition, due to the relative recency of our willingness even to acknowledge and investigate these issues, we are just beginning to look at certain aspects of childhood sexual victimization. As examples, we now have recent, yet growing literatures on topics such as: (1) ritualistic or cultic forms of child sexual abuse (Braun and Sachs 1985; Faller 1990; Finkelhor and Williams with Burns 1988; Kelley 1988, 1989, 1992; Mayer 1991; Snow and Sorenson 1990; Steele 1987), and (2) the possibility of developing multiple or borderline personality disorder after experiencing the more severe forms of abuse (Bass and Davis 1988; Briere 1989; Kluft 1990; Mayer 1991; Putnam 1989). Although these are difficult topics, when you open the door on the subjects of incest and child sexual abuse, you must be willing to hear about all facets of it, regardless of how dire they may be.

Table 4.2: Recent Studies which Investigate Girls' and Women's Post-Sexual Abuse or Post-Incest Reactions

Studies: By Authors, Dates and Sources of Samples	Sample Size	Offenses Included	Ages of Victims	Control Group	Time Frame	Variables Included	Statistical Analyses	Theoretical Perspectives
Bass & Davis (1988) Case studies	15	Incest & child sexual abuse	Women	No	Retrospective analysis	Reactions & recovery issues	None	Feminist theory
Briere & Runtz (1988a) Public mental health center clients	152	Incest & child sexual abuse	Women	Yes	Retrospective analysis	History of suicide attempts, substance abuse, fears, & depression	t-tests & factor analysis	Do not specify
Briere & Runtz (1988b) Women college students	278	Incest & child sexual abuse	Women	Yes	Retrospective analysis	Characteristics of the abuse, anxiety, depression, & dissociation	ANOVA & correlations	Do not specify
Conte & Berliner (1988) Sexual assault center	369	Incest & child sexual abuse	Children & adolescents	Yes	Seen within six months of the abuse	Post-abuse symptoms	Percentages, factor analysis, & multiple regression	Do not specify

Studies: By Authors, Dates and Sources of Samples	Sample Size	Offenses Included	Ages of Victims	Control Group	Time Frame	Variables Included	Statistical Analyses	Theoretical Perspectives
Conte & Schuerman (1987 & 1988) Sexual assault center	369	Incest & child sexual abuse	Children & adolescents	Yes	Seen within six months of the abuse	Self-esteem & behaviors of the victims	Percentages & multiple regression	Do not specify
Coons et al. (1990) Women's counseling center	46	Any type of abuse or trauma	Women	Yes	Retrospective analysis	Post-abuse psychiatric disorders, PTSD symptoms, & dissociation	Percentages	Do not specify
Finkelhor (1984) College students	796	Incest & child sexual abuse	Young adults of both sexes	Yes	Retrospective analysis	Sexual self-esteem, subsequent victimizations, & homosexuality	Percentages	Feminist theory & life events view
Finkelhor et al. (1989) National random sample	2630	Incest & child sexual abuse	Adults (men & women)	No	Retrospective Analysis	Assault factors, marital disruption, sexual satisfaction, & participation in organized religion	Chi-square and discriminant analysis	Do not specify
Finkelhor & Williams, with Burns (1988) Day care facilities	266	Child sexual abuse and ritualistic sexual abuse	Children (boys & girls)	No	Retrospective analysis	Risk factors of children, factors of day care facilities, abuse factors, and post-abuse symptoms	Percentages, t-tests, ANOVA, & multiple regression	Do not specify

Table 4.2 (con.)

Studies: By Authors, Dates and Sources of Samples	Sample Size	Offenses Included	Ages of Victims	Control Group	Time Frame	Variables Included	Statistical Analyses	Theoretical Perspectives
Fromuth (1986) College students	106	Incest & child sexual abuse	Women	Yes	Retrospective analysis	Parental support, self-esteem, & depression	Correlations & semi-partial correlations	Does not specify
Gold (1986) Responses to an ad	103	Incest & child sexual abuse	Women	Yes	Retrospective analysis	Demographic characteristics, self-blame, locus of control, & social support	ANOVA	Does not specify
Gomes-Schwartz et al. (1990) Children referred to a crisis agency	156	Incest & child sexual abuse	Children & adolescents	No	Seen within six months of the abuse	Characteristics of the abuse, responses from social control agents, self-esteem, and short-term and long-term reactions	Percentages	Do not specify
Greenwald & Leitenberg (1990) Nurses (5.4 percent had been abused as children)	1500	Incest & child sexual abuse	Women	No	Retrospective analysis	Characteristics of the abuse & whether symptoms of PTSD present now or ever present	Percentages	Do not specify

Studies: By Authors, Dates and Sources of Samples	Sample Size	Offenses Included	Ages of Victims	Control Group	Time Frame	Variables Included	Statistical Analyses	Theoretical Perspectives
Jehu (1989) Women in treatment for psychiatric problems	51	Had to have known the abuser	Women	No	Retrospective analysis	Family of origin, characteristics of the abuse, self-esteem, cognitions, treatment, and depression	Percentages	Does not specify
Kelley (1989) Recruited nationally	134	Day care abuse & ritualistic sexual abuse	Children (ages four to eleven)	Yes	Recently abused	Parental view of children's behavior, current symptoms, impact of event, & type of abuse	Percentages & t-tests	Does not specify
Kelly (1988) Source of sample unclear	60	Incest	Women	No	Retrospective analysis	Coping strategies, resistance, and current symptoms	Percentages	Feminist theory
Mannarino et al. (1991) Girls in treatment	94	Incest & child sexual abuse	Girls (ages six to twelve)	Yes	Seen within six months of the abuse	Parents' and girls' perceptions about self-concept, anxiety, and depression	ANOVA	Do not specify

Table 4.2 (con.)

Studies: By Authors, Dates and Sources of Samples	Sample Size	Offenses Included	Ages of Victims	Control Group	Time Frame	Variables Included	Statistical Analyses	Theoretical Perspectives
Peters (1988) Random community sample	122	Incest & child sexual abuse	Women	Yes	Retrospective analysis	Psychiatric hospitalization, substance abuse, abuse factors, self-esteem, & depression	Percentages & multiple regression	Does not specify
Russell (1986) Random community sample	930	Incest & child sexual abuse	Women	No	Retrospective analysis	Characteristics of the abuse & long-term effects	Percentages	Feminist theory
Simons & Whitbeck (1991) Adolescent runaways & homeless women	40 & 95	Incest & child sexual abuse	Adolescent girls & women	No	Retrospective analysis	Substance abuse, involvement in prostitution, and prior sexual victimization	Percentages, correlations, & multiple regression	Do not specify
Snow & Sorenson (1990) Clients from an outpatient treatment clinic	39	Incest & ritualistic sexual abuse	Children (ages four to seventeen)	No	Occurred between 1985 & 1986	Characteristics of the abuse and post-abuse reactions	Percentages	Do not specify

Studies: By Authors, Dates and Sources of Samples	Sample Size	Offenses Included	Ages of Victims	Control Group	Time Frame	Variables Included	Statistical Analyses	Theoretical Perspectives
Tsai et al. (1990) Clinical & nonclinical groups	90	Incest & child sexual abuse	Women	Yes	Retrospective analysis	Characteristics of the abuse and impact of the abuse	Percentages	Do not specify
Wyatt & Mickey (1988) Probability sample	248	Incest & child sexual abuse	Women	No	Retrospective analysis	Characteristics of the abuse & impact of the abuse	Percentages	Do not specify

Notwithstanding these criticisms, we now have a better understanding of how these experiences affect us as children, as well as later in adolescence and adulthood. In addition (and as was the case in the earlier discussion of our post-rape responses), child sexual abuse can cause immediate consequences and/or delayed or compounded reactions years later. One reason for this latter phenomenon is that it is quite common for children who have been sexually abused to "bury" their memories of the abuse. In effect, their experiences were so painful that they could *not* or would *not* let themselves remember them until it was safer to do so [e.g., when the perpetrator dies (Bass and Davis 1988; Blume 1990; Courtois 1988; Dolan 1991; Engel 1989; Finney 1990; Kendall-Tackett 1991; Mayer 1991; Snow and Sorenson 1990)].[11] Thus, in the discussion which follows, it is important to separate these findings into immediate responses among infants and children, the consequences for adolescent females, and the aftermath for adult women years later.

Immediate Reactions among Infants and Children

Based on several recent reports, we now know that children who have been sexually abused exhibit immediate aftereffects across many of the dimensions that were mentioned in the prior discussion of post-rape consequences. These include: (1) the *psychological aftereffects* of anxiety, fear, confusion, guilt, anger, dissociation, and depression (Asher 1988; Browne and Finkelhor 1986; Conte and Schuerman 1987, 1988; Courtois 1988; Finkelhor 1988; Forward and Buck 1978; Gil 1988; Gomes-Schwartz et al. 1990; Haugaard and Repucci 1988; Kelley 1988, 1989; Lipovsky et al. 1989; Mannarino et al. 1991); (2) *somatic complaints,* particularly signs of physical injury to body parts which were traumatized (e.g., sexually transmitted diseases, injuries to the genitals); sudden weight gain or loss; urinary tract infections; headaches; sleep disorders, and self-destructive behaviors (Asher 1988; Conte and Schuerman 1987, 1988; Courtois 1988; Finkelhor 1988; Gil 1988; Gomes-Schwartz et al. 1990; Kelley 1988, 1989); (3) the *behavioral changes* of increased dependency, sleeping more, clinging behaviors, loss of toilet training, temper tantrums, aggressive behaviors, withdrawal, and/or crying for "no reason" (Asher 1988; Finkelhor and Williams, with Burns 1988; Friedrich 1990; Gil 1988; Haugaard and Repucci 1988; Kelly 1988); (4) *interpersonal problems* such as difficulty getting along with family members and adjustment issues at school (Browne and Finkelhor 1986; Courtois 1988; Friedrich 1990; Gomes-Schwartz et al. 1990); (5) *cognitive difficulties* including difficulty determining what is real, feeling confused, and a distorted body image (Conte and Schuerman 1987; Finkelhor 1988; Friedrich 1990; Gomes-Schwartz et al. 1990); (6) *changed self-perceptions,* particularly low self-esteem (Conte and Schuerman 1987; Lipovsky et al. 1989; Mannarino et al. 1991); and (7) *sexual problems,* typically precocious sexual attitudes and behaviors and/or confusion about sex (Asher 1988; Browne and Finkelhor 1986; Courtois 1988; Finkelhor 1988; Gil 1988; Gomes-Schwartz et al. 1990; Haugaard and Reppucci 1988).

Several experts, though, have begun to suggest that we need to differentiate between infants' and children's responses because age and developmental level mediate how they respond to incest and child sexual abuse (Asher 1988; Courtois 1988; Friedrich 1990; Gomes-Schwartz et al. 1990). Courtois (1988), for example, has found that *infants* only can react in pre-verbal ways via failure to thrive, withdrawal, fretfulness, feeding disturbances, and clinging behaviors. Among *toddlers and preschoolers,* frequently observed responses include: thumb-sucking, scratching and picking behaviors, immaturity, self-injurious behaviors, enuresis, speech problems, conduct disturbances, anxiety, withdrawal, hyperactivity, difficulty separating from parents, disrupted sleep patterns, inappropriate sex play and/or showing an understanding of sexual activity that is well beyond their years (Courtois 1988; Gomes-Schwartz et al. 1990). Finally, children in their *middle childhood* years can exhibit one or more of the following symptoms: depression, nightmares, anxiety, hostility, sleep disturbances, difficulty concentrating, fears, phobias, eating disorders, impaired functioning socially and/or at school, low self-esteem, somatic complaints, running away, unruly acts or delinquent behaviors, substance abuse, and pseudomature behaviors, as well as the more serious signs of suicidal ideation, antisocial behavior, multiple or borderline personality disorder, and psychotic states

(Asher 1988; Conte and Berliner 1988; Courtois 1988; Gomes-Schwartz et al. 1990; Haugaard and Repucci 1988).

We must be careful in our application of these age-specific findings, though, for several reasons. First, infants and children can exhibit these same responses but for vastly different reasons; that is, although these "symptoms" seem to be everpresent when infants and children have been sexually abused, they also can infer a variety of other physiological, social, and/or psychological problems unrelated to child sexual abuse. Second, some of the aforementioned authors (e.g., Asher and Courtois) do *not* clarify whether they are describing children who were sexually abused *earlier* and are reacting in their toddler or middle childhood years or whether these children were abused only recently. Third, some of these reports focus exclusively on children who were the victims of incest (e.g., Courtois), while others include all types of child sexual abuse (e.g., Conte and Berliner 1988; Gomes-Schwartz et al. 1990). Until we do more prospective studies which determine the nature of the consequences of incest and child sexual abuse over time, as well as how these consequences change as children age and mature, this criticism will continue to apply to most works in this literature.

Immediate or Delayed Responses among Adolescents

Although adolescents, too, show signs of disruption across several dimensions of their lives, the content of many of their responses is quite different from those evidenced by infants and girls. To be specific, the immediate and delayed consequences of incest and child sexual abuse for adolescents can include: (1) the *psychological aftereffects* of depression, anxiety, hostility, phobias, panic attacks, anger, nightmares, amnesia for small or large parts of their childhoods, trance states or dissociative episodes, flashbacks, and multiple personality disorder (Conte and Berliner 1988; Courtois 1988; Gomes-Schwartz et al. 1990); (2) *somatic complaints,* particularly eating disorders, migraine headaches, fainting spells, and digestive problems (Asher 1988; Courtois 1988; Runtz and Briere 1989); (3) *behavioral problems* such as antisocial behavior, drug and/or alcohol abuse, aggression, delinquency, doing poorly in school, and running away (Asher 1988; Courtois 1988; Gomes-Schwartz et al. 1990; Herman 1981; Runtz and Briere 1986); (4) the *interpersonal problems* of disrupted peer relationships, difficulty getting along with family members, and problems developing intimate love relationships (Courtois 1988; Gomes-Schwartz et al. 1990; Runtz and Briere 1986); (5) the *cognitive difficulty* of being unsure as to what is real (Courtois 1988); (6) *changed self-perceptions*, particularly low self-esteem and depersonalization or seeing self from afar (Conte and Berliner 1988; Courtois 1988; Gomes-Schwartz et al. 1990); (7) *sexual problems* such as "promiscuity," adolescent pregnancy, involvement in prostitution, and homosexual contacts (Asher 1988; Gomes-Schwartz et al. 1990; Herman 1981; Runtz and Briere 1986); and (8) *subsequent victimization(s)* via violence in dating relationships, as well as additional sexual assaults (Asher 1988; Sugarman and Hotaling 1991).

Differences in Response Patterns between Children and Adolescents and Their Post-Victimization Reactions Over Time

As has been noted in the above analyses, infants, children, and adolescents respond differently to sexual victimization, and they do so in fairly age-specific ways. As Asher (1988:9) has summarized the findings:

> Young children generally present with behavioral symptoms that are manifestations of anxiety. As children enter latency and early adolescence, aggressive and impulsive behavior begins to appear. Older children seem to be more disturbed by sexual victimization than are younger children, perhaps because of their increased awareness of the meanings of sexual behavior. As children reach adolescence, acting out becomes more common as a way of expressing overwhelming feelings and also as a plea for help.

To reiterate an earlier point, though, we must be careful in how we apply these findings. Are these the responses of adolescents who have been abused sexually only recently, or is this the delayed aftermath among adolescents who were abused earlier in their lives? Because so many of the extant studies examine such diverse samples, as well as explore these issues for relatively short periods of time, we are unable to answer this question with any certainty. In effect, we end up comparing and contrasting groups which should *not* be compared (e.g., children who were sexually abused during the last six months all the way through clinical and nonclinical samples of children and adolescents who were abused when they were much younger).

Notable exceptions to this criticism are the longitudinal analyses of Gomes-Schwartz et al. (1990) and Mannarino et al. (1991). Gomes-Schwartz et al.'s study, for example, focuses on 156 children who were recent victims of sexual abuse; and their findings show that eighteen months later, most of the children:

> showed a significant decrease in overall psychopathology and an increase of positive self-esteem. In all, 75 percent of the youngsters in the four– to thirteen–year old range did not exhibit significant psychopathology when compared with the general population. More individualized assessment of change indicated that the majority of the children showed significant improvements in overall behavioral disturbance and in self-esteem during the follow-up period. Some children [though] did not improve and another group actually exhibited significantly worse problems at follow-up (Gomes-Schwartz et al. 1990:135).

Thus, there is considerable variability in the possible outcomes of childhood sexual victimization.

Mannarino et al. (1991) also have studied children who were recent victims of child sexual abuse and have compared them to a control group of "normal" children and a clinical control group of children in therapy for non-abuse issues. Interestingly, at both the six-month and twelve-month follow-ups, children who had been sexually abused were found to differ significantly from the control group of normal children on several measures (e.g., self-concept and social competence), but they did *not* differ appreciably from the clinical control group. In addition, these authors found a within-group difference or "sleeper effect": Children who had experienced the more serious form of sexual abuse (e.g., intercourse) reported more difficulties than did children who had experienced "lesser" forms (e.g., fondling).

We must keep in mind, though, that both of these groups of children were involved in combined research *and* treatment programs. The inevitable question is: Do children who are sexually abused but *not* involved in treatment programs fare as well six, twelve, and eighteen months later? Again, although the experts at this time cannot answer this question with certainty, their best guess seems to be *no*.

The Long-Term Effects of Child Sexual Abuse for Adult Women

At the present time, there also is uncertainty as to why some of us respond to sexual abuse during our childhood and adolescent years while others do *not* do so until many years later. What is certain, though, is that, if left untreated, the impact of childhood sexual victimization does *not* just go away; it eventually is felt, and in many cases, the long-term aftermath can be serious and even life-threatening (Bagley and King 1990; Bass and Davis 1988; DeSalvo 1989; Engel 1989). Blume (1990:15) succinctly summarizes this issue:

> Time does not cure the effects of incest. Although the memories go underground, the consequences of the abuse flourish. Sometimes they are buried under other problems . . . But they lie waiting, waiting for the clarity that sobriety brings; waiting for release from thought-confusion and phobias, the lifting of depression, the opening that comes through therapy or intimacy. They also may erupt on their own. Untreated, they can lead to suicide, or even murder. And, in the saddest paradox of all, the aftereffects that comprise [the] Post-Incest Syndrome usually spell continuing victimization—for the survivor herself, for her lovers, even for her children.

Notwithstanding the debate of *when* these reactions surface, a multitude of studies has examined adult women's long-term responses to having been sexually victimized in childhood, and there is a great deal of agreement among these studies. To be specific, consequences have been found across all ten dimensions of our lives, including the psychological, somatic, behavioral, interpersonal, cognitive, self-perceptual, sexual, political, and spiritual ones, as well as via subsequent victimization(s). These consequences, as well as the underlying meanings that they may represent, are summarized below.

The more common, long-term *psychological aftereffects* of incest and child sexual abuse include: anxiety; depression; denial; intrusive thoughts; loneliness; dissociative symptoms (e.g., depersonalization and feeling unreal); feelings of anger, hostility, sadness, isolation, and guilt; suicidal ideation and/or attempted suicides; phobias; and fears of both men and women (Allender 1990; Asher 1988; Bagley and King 1990; Barringer 1992; Bass and Davis 1988; Braun 1989; Briere 1989; Briere and Runtz 1988a, 1988b; Browne and Finkelhor 1986; Courtois 1988; Dinsmore 1991; Dolan 1991; Donaldson and Gardner 1985; Engel 1989; Farmer 1989; Finkelhor 1987, 1988; Finkelhor and Browne 1988; Finney 1990; Gil 1988; Gold 1986; Haugaard and Reppucci 1988; Herman 1981, 1992; Janoff-Bulman 1992; Jehu 1988, 1989; Kunzman 1990; Peters 1988; Poston and Lison 1989; Powell 1988; Ratner 1990; Russell 1986; Sanford 1990; Siegel et al. 1990; Steele 1987; Stein et al. 1988; Swink and Leveille 1986; Tower 1988; Wisechild 1988; Wyatt and Powell 1988). These "symptoms" probably reflect the underlying issues of women who remain stuck at the victim stage, have *not* resolved or accepted the fact that they were sexually abused as children, and more likely than not are blaming themselves for having been abused. In addition, these consequences illustrate the poor quality of adult life which can ensue after childhood sexual abuse, as well as the depth and all-encompassing nature of the trauma. In effect, and as was noted earlier, if left untreated during our childhood or adolescent years, the aftermath of incest and child sexual abuse not only persists but can intensify during our adult lives (Bass and Davis 1988; Blume 1990; Engel 1989; Herman 1992).

Commonly observed *somatic complaints* are weight problems (obesity or being underweight); sleep disturbances (e.g., insomnia, nightmares, or early morning wakenings); dizziness; and a number of other stress-related symptoms such as gastrointestinal problems, migraine headaches, difficulty breathing, hypertension, and aches, pains, rashes, and/or infections which defy diagnosis and sometimes even treatment

(Allender 1990; Bagley and King 1990; Bass and Davis 1988; Briere and Runtz 1989; Browne and Finkelhor 1986; Carmen and Reiker 1989; Courtois 1988; Engel 1989; Finkelhor 1987; Gil 1988; Poston and Lison 1989; Ratner 1990; Siegel et al. 1990; Swink and Leveille 1986; Tower 1988). Regarding the underlying meaning of these consequences, many of them point to the fact that some women continue to relive their experiences of incest and child sexual abuse, but they do so (usually unconsciously) in highly physical ways. Moreover, if we support a holistic view of health, these physiological responses readily can be linked to psychological ones in that long-term bouts of anxiety and/or depression often take their toll in physical ways.

The chronic *behavioral problems* which have been linked to incest and child sexual abuse are eating disorders (e.g., anorexia nervosa, bulimia, and overeating); substance abuse; self-destructive behaviors; homelessness; and increased aggressiveness (Asher 1988; Bagely and King 1990; Bass and Davis 1988; Browne and Finkelhor 1986; Dolan 1991; Finkelhor 1987, 1988; Finkelhor and Browne 1988; Gagnon 1989; Herman 1981, 1992; Peters 1988; Poston and Lison 1989; Powell 1988; Ratner 1990; Simons and Whitbeck 1991; Stein et al. 1988; Swink and Leveille 1986; Tower 1988; Women's Resource Centre 1989; Wyatt and Powell 1988). Again, these "symptoms" probably reflect the deeper, underlying issues of women continuing to "take out" their abusive histories on themselves rather than refocusing their attention, anger, and rage at the appropriate sources (e.g., the perpetrator, as well as this society which continues to implicitly encourage such actions and to hide them once they occur). This probably means that self-hatred, guilt, and a shattered view of self are the real underlying issues, or, as Briere (1989) calls them, the "core effects" of these earlier experiences.

The long-term *interpersonal problems* which have been reported among adult survivors of incest and child sexual abuse include: difficulties getting along with others; problems in relationships, particularly with achieving and/or sustaining intimacy; dissatisfaction with current relationships with lovers, husbands, family members, and friends; difficulty parenting; and sexualized and/or conflicted relationships (Allender 1990;

Asher 1988; Bagley and King 1990; Blume 1990; Browne and Finkelhor 1986; Courtois 1988; Dinsmore 1991; Farmer 1989; Finkelhor 1987; Finkelhor et al. 1989; Finney 1990; Gagnon 1989; Gil 1988; Herman 1981; Jehu 1988; Kunzman 1990; Ratner 1990; Russell 1986; Sanford 1990; Swink and Leveille 1986; Tower 1988; Wyatt and Powell 1988). Regarding the underlying meanings of these consequences, they probably reflect the tremendous difficulties that many adult women experience when they attempt to get close to and/or trust someone.

As Courtois (1988:111) suggests, the rationales for these interpersonal difficulties are fairly "easy" to explain, particularly for the survivors of incest:

> Difficulty trusting others due to the past betrayal by one or more family members is at the core of problems in interpersonal relating. The attitude that many survivors hold is: 'If I couldn't trust my family, who can I trust? No one is trustworthy.' Unfortunately, this conclusion becomes self-fulfilling if the survivor does not come into contact with others [who] are honorable or if she is revictimized. Survivors also may not have had the opportunity to develop relationship skills in their families and may relate according to the role they played in family interactions.

Courtois also adds that a disproportionate number of women who were sexually abused as children remain unmarried; she credits this to the tremendous difficulty that they have in developing and/or maintaining close relationships. Finkelhor et al. (1989) concur and report that women with histories of childhood sexual abuse have a significantly higher likelihood to have "disrupted" marriages (e.g., separations or divorces).

Some of the most disabling of the long-term consequences of incest and child sexual abuse that can occur are the *cognitive difficulties*. Frequently reported issues are: distorted cognitions such as chronic perceptions of danger and confusion; illogical thinking (e.g., the belief that reality is externally determined rather than being within our control and/or related to what we do); inaccurate images about the world around us; shattered assumptions about the world; and difficulty determining what is real (Allender 1990; Bass and Davis 1988; Blume 1990; Briere

1989; Briere and Runtz 1988b; Courtois 1988; Dinsmore 1991; Dolan 1991; Engel 1989; Farmer 1989; Fine 1990; Finkelhor 1987; Finney 1990; Herman 1992; Janoff-Bulman 1992; Jehu 1989; Kunzman 1990; Poston and Lison 1989; Sanford 1990; Swink and Leveille 1986; Women's Resource Centre 1989; Wyatt and Powell 1988). The primary reason why these "symptoms" are so insidious is that they leave us with a highly distorted view of the world around us, thereby making it difficult (if not impossible) for us to function well in a world that we do *not* comprehend. As noted by Briere (1989:108), though, these responses do make a great deal of "sense:"

> Because the victim must attend to the difficult task of surviving . . . she . . . has little time or energy available to interact with the environment and master its surmountable challenges . . . Instead she becomes developmentally conservative—taking as few risks as possible and limiting her activities to those that are immediately relevant to safety and/or escape. In this context maturation is difficult, and . . . the individual is, to some extent, frozen in childhood.

Tragically, the bottom line is that some women who were sexually abused as children, particularly if they experienced the more "severe" forms of abuse, become adults trapped in children's bodies and minds; they have aged, but they have *not* "grown up."

Changed self-perceptions also have been found to be a serious long-term consequence of incest and child sexual abuse. Oftcited ones are: self-disgust or self-denigration; feeling ashamed, guilty, bad, out of control, unlovable, helpless, and/or worthless; low levels of self-esteem and/or mastery; self-hatred; self-blame; and inaccurate body images (Allender 1990; Asher 1988; Bagley and King 1990; Bass and Davis 1988; Blume 1990; Briere 1989; Browne and Finkelhor 1986; Carmen and Rieker 1989; Celano 1992; Courtois 1988; Dinsmore 1991; Dolan 1991; Donaldson and Gardner 1985; Engel 1989; Farmer 1989; Finkelhor 1987, 1988; Finkelhor and Browne 1986, 1988; Finney 1990; Gagnon 1989; Gil 1988; Gold 1986; Herman 1992; Janoff-Bulman 1992; Jehu 1989; Kunzman 1990; Peters 1988; Putnam 1990; Ratner 1990; Russell 1986; Sanford 1990; Swink and Leveille

1986; Tower 1988; Women's Resource Centre 1989; Wyatt and Powell 1988). The underlying meaning of these consequences is that many of us who were sexually abused as children have lost a sense of who and what we are (more precisely, it was stolen from us), and this makes it nearly impossible to have positive and accurate images about ourselves.

An additional self-perceptual response that has been noted among some adult survivors of childhood sexual victimization is the feeling that they are magical. Briere (1989: 44) calls this "negative specialness" or an "almost magical sense of power [or] the ability to do harm," while Courtois (1988:102) labels this response as "negative power" (i.e., "feeling powerful but in a malignant way"). These consequences reflect the depth of the messages that many of us were forced to incorporate as children—that you are bad, you caused this to happen, I will know if you ever tell anyone—and that some of us continue to subscribe to as adults. The role of our society in perpetuating these sorts of images again, though, must be acknowledged: Many of the victims and the survivors of incest and child sexual abuse are left to walk around in a zombie-like condition thinking that they are worthless, bad, and evil, while we as a nation try to deny that incest or child sexual abuse exists and that their consequences can be severe.

Sexual "problems" such as frigidity, promiscuity, dissatisfaction with or an inability to enjoy sex, negative attitudes about sex, homosexuality, an impaired motivation to be sexually active, becoming a prostitute, a variety of orgasmic disorders, pain during intercourse, and confusion regarding sexual identity and sexual norms and standards have been suggested as possible long-term consequences for women who were sexually abused as children (Asher 1988; Bagley and King 1990; Browne and Finkelhor 1986; Blume 1990; Briere 1989; Courtois 1988; Dinsmore 1991; Dolan 1991; Engel 1989; Farmer 1989; Finkelhor 1987, 1988; Finkelhor et al. 1989; Finney 1990; Fromuth 1986; Gil 1988; Gold 1986; Haugaard and Reppucci 1988; Herman 1981; Jehu 1988; Kunzman 1990; Poston and Lison 1989; Powell 1987; Ratner 1990; Siegel et al. 1990; Simons and Whitbeck 1991; Swink and Leveille 1986; Tower 1988; Tsai et al. 1979; Wyatt and Powell 1988). In effect, these problems show that women have difficulty as adults recovering the sexual aspects of themselves that were stolen from them during their childhood years.

Blume (1990:246) summarizes what I, too, believe is the root of most post-abuse sexual problems, particularly for survivors of incest:

> She does not know the difference between liking someone and *liking* someone. Early on, her parent or caretaker inappropriately introduced a sexual component into their relationship which robbed the child-victim of the natural pace and order of the introduction of sexuality into her relationships . . . Her view is that the two are synonyms, that relationships all become sexual.

This view is also substantiated by Finkelhor and Browne (1986:181) who indicate that many post-sexual-abuse difficulties are due to "traumatic sexualization" or the "process . . . [by] which a child's sexuality (including both sexual feelings and sexual attitudes) is shaped in a developmentally inappropriate and interpersonally dysfunctional fashion as a result of sexual abuse." Therefore, if our childhood relationships are sexualized, as adults, many of us have great difficulty determining when, how, and/or why to engage in intimate relationships, and issues such as affection, intimacy, and closeness get confused with sex [i.e., if anyone is affectionate with or tries to get close to us, we assume that we should respond sexually (Bass and Davis 1988; Briere 1989; Courtois 1988; Finney 1990; Jehu 1988)].

As already has been noted, though, many of these sexual "symptoms" and "diagnoses" reflect the value-laden and tacit biases of others (particularly medical and mental health professionals) rather than the women's perceptions about themselves and their lives. Yet again, we must be careful with such labels as "frigidity" and "promiscuity" because they not only ignore feminist principles and theories but they also fail to reflect what women who have been sexually victimized as children have to say about their own behaviors (Kelly 1988).

Even more care must be taken with the "expert opinion" that women become lesbians because of their histories of incest or child sexual abuse (Courtois 1988; Herman 1981). Jehu (1988: 162), for example, notes that: "Although previously sexually abused women may or may not be more likely to be predominantly homosexual in adulthood . . ., there are certainly some abused women who become practicing [?] lesbians and their abuse and its associated circumstances may have contributed to this sexual orientation in a number of ways." Bass and Davis (1988:268) counter this notion by suggesting that it distorts and minimizes what many reports now regard as a decision, a preference, or a biological predisposition:

> It is true that being abused by men has influenced some women to relate sexually and emotionally to women rather than men. However, no one becomes a lesbian solely because she was abused by a man. After all, many heterosexual women were abused by men, and they continue to choose men as their mates and sexual partners. If abuse were the determining factor in sexual preference, the lesbian population would be far greater than it is now.

Added evidence that incest and child sexual abuse do *not* "cause" lesbianism is offered by Dinsmore (1991:108) who notes the similarity in the research findings of Loulan and Russell. Specifically, Loulan (via a nonrandom sample of lesbians) and Russell (by way of her analysis of a randomly selected group of women) found that 38 percent of the women in their respective studies had been sexually abused as children. If child sexual abuse "caused" lesbianism, then, Loulan should have found that the vast majority of the lesbians that she studied had experienced either incest or sexual abuse as children; this, though, was *not* the case.

As was noted earlier in this chapter, some of the more interesting "aftereffects" of rape are the *political consequences* (i.e., the awareness that rape is caused by social and structural factors); and the same outcome has been observed among adult survivors of incest and child sexual abuse. I refer again to Kelly's (1988:228) idea of moving from what she calls "individual survival to collective resistance." This refers to a three-step process whereby: (1) women come to see that their personal experiences are caused by "oppressive social relations"; (2) they begin to believe that "social change is both necessary and possible"; and (3) they come together to form a "collective organization that is directed towards achieving the necessary change." As a result of making these "quantum leaps," some women come to: be more independent or stronger, blame themselves less, the awareness that men's violence is a political issue, empathize with the plight of other women who have similar histories, and know that they are not alone, that theirs is a social problem rather than an individual one (Kelly 1988). From this perspective, then, it makes much more sense to view these sorts of consequences as positive results or signs of recovery rather than viewing them as "symptoms." In other words, coming to understand that incest and child sexual abuse have political underpinnings can have liberating effects: It can free us from individual lives of guilt and sadness and redirect us toward the issue of others who have had similar experiences and perhaps trying to do something for or with them.

Although *spiritual devastation* is much less likely to be discussed, it, too, can be a serious long-term consequence of incest and child sexual abuse. We must be careful in our analysis of this "symptom," though, because some sources employ fairly parochial definitions of the spiritual dimension and spirituality. As examples, Finkelhor et al. (1989) and Russell (1986) infer that spirituality is the same thing as religiosity and that, if we reject organized religion, we have "lost" our sense of the spiritual. Others, though, do *not* concur. One example is Coles (1990:100), who focuses on the perspectives of children; more specifically, he explains the complex intersection of their spiritual and religious notions: "Children try to understand not only what is happening to them, but why; and in doing that, they call upon the religious life they have experienced, the spiritual values they have received, as well as other sources of potential explanation." He cites his work during the 1950s with children who were stricken with polio: Some children were angry; others cried, and still others tried to comprehend where their God was. Coles (1990:101) concludes that we cannot view these solely as psychological "symptoms"; rather, we must remain aware of the fact that "psychological themes connect almost imperceptibly, but quite vividly at moments, with spiritual inwardness."

An added problem is that many children (due to their levels of cognitive and emotional development) employ literal interpretations of sin and punishment. In other words, if something "bad" (e.g., incest and child sexual abuse) happens to them, they tend to regard themselves as "bad" (i.e., they are being punished for their "sins"). Please note, though, that this is *not* something that children do to themselves; rather, this message is learned and reinforced by many Western, Christian religions (Sanford 1990). In addition, many adults evidence similar cognitive distortions. As an example, Lerner's (1980) "just world hypothesis" illustrates how and why adults tend to feel safer if they can find "something" that other people did to "cause" their misfortunes. Thus, if observers view others' misfortunes as random happenings, they feel vulnerable; and in order to resolve their discomfort and to try to make sense of the world, they look for something that these people did to cause their problems; this, in turn, reduces their own sense of vulnerability.

The point is that we must *not* limit our discussion solely to women who are members of organized religions and/or subscribe to traditional religious belief systems. Instead, we must develop and use inclusive definitions of the terms spiritual and spirituality, ones which permit those of us who no longer subscribe to traditional religious beliefs to be involved in this discussion. I particularly like Tessier's (1992:15) definition: "In accord with the sense of body/mind/spirit relationality emerging from feminist relational theology, I use 'spiritual' to refer to our most fundamental identity and connections to ourselves, to others, and to the world, whether or not that identity involves a relationship with some transcendent power." This sort of emphasis focuses on diversity, as well as belief systems that some may *not* regard as religious ones (e.g., commitment to other people or causes, a worldview, a spiritual connection to nature); and it allows us to include the women who have rejected "formal" religions.

So, what becomes of children who are sexually abused; as adults, how do they perceive the world and themselves spiritually? Some authors indicate that many of them have lost their sense of faith, not just a religious belief in a divine being, but also their faith in themselves, other people, and the world in general (Bass and Davis 1988; Janoff-Bulman 1992). As noted by Tessier (1992:15), these sorts of consequences occur because "[c]hildhood sexual abuse affects us at the core—at the very deepest center of our reality." In addition, some experts now speak of such issues as soul murder (Miller 1984; Shengold 1988), the shattered soul (Blume 1990; Steele 1987, 1988), and soul pain (Allender 1990) in relation to incest and child sexual abuse (issues which will be explored further later in this chapter). They use this graphic language to refer to the complete shattering of self and reality that can occur, particularly when children are involved in the more "serious" forms of incest and child sexual abuse (e.g., ritualistic abuse).

Thus, regardless of whether you focus on religious or secular conceptualizations of this term, the possible spiritual outcomes of incest and child sexual abuse include: less interest and participation in organized religions; a lack of faith in self, others, and the world; and soul murder, the shattered soul, or soul pain. And, as will be discussed in detail in the next chapter, these are some of the most serious of the post-sexual-victimization consequences that can result.

Subsequent victimization(s) (e.g., being battered in adult relationships and/or additional sexual assaults), as well as becoming the victimizers by physically abusing their own children, are all too common experiences for women who have histories of childhood sexual victimization (Asher 1988; Briere and Runtz 1988b; Browne and Finkelhor 1986; Dolan 1991; Fromuth 1986; Herman 1981; Jehu 1988; Kunzman 1990; Lundberg-Love and Geffner 1989; Russell 1986; Swink and Leveille 1986; Tower 1988; van der Kolk 1989; Wyatt and Powell 1988). Please note, though, that the underlying bases of many of these responses are not only behavioral but also cognitive: *Via our early experiences with incest and sexual abuse, we are conditioned to believe that we lack value and that anyone can do whatever they want to us. Moreover, we learn to be helpless, to be victims, and to think that we deserve to be treated poorly.* Let me be quick to add, though, that this is *not* yet another instance of victim blaming; instead, I would suggest that we develop these sorts of cognitions and behaviors when we are encouraged to do so via others who reward us for thinking and acting these ways. And, unless we (or someone else) do something to break this cycle of victimization, it will continue.

In sum, the long-term consequences of incest and child sexual abuse can be quite severe. Via their summary of a number of works which investigate these issues within clinical and nonclinical child and adult populations, Browne and Finkelhor (1986:164) summarize what we currently know:

> In the immediate aftermath of sexual abuse, from one-fifth to two-fifths of abused children seen by clinicians manifest some noticeable disturbance. When studied as adults, victims as a group demonstrate more impairment than their nonvictimized counterparts (about twice as much), but less than one-fifth evidence serious psychopathology. These findings give reassurance to victims that extreme long-term effects are not inevitable. Nonetheless, they also suggest that the risk of initial and long-term mental health impairments for victims of child sexual abuse should be taken very seriously.

Thus, although many girls and women do recover from being sexually abused for a variety of reasons to be discussed later, some of them can and do remain seriously impaired for a very long time.

The Most Serious Consequences of Child Sexual Abuse

The prior analyses show that the consequences of incest and child sexual abuse can be long-lasting and severe. We also must acknowledge, though, that even more insidious long-term effects are possible, particularly when the abuse is "serious" or "severe." Although this language is troublesome and I suggested previously that our goal should *not* be to rank order sexually abusive experiences, the reality of the situation is that there are different levels of post-sexual-abuse devastation, as well as degrees of sexual abuse (i.e., one-time episodes involving strangers through the long-term ritualistic abuse of children which may include animal and even human sacrifices). In other words, although we must regard all forms of child sexual victimization as serious and severe, there are instances that are extraordinary both in their content and duration. It is this latter type of incest or child sexual abuse which has been associated with the devastating effects of: (1) *borderline personality disorder*

(Briere 1989; Courtois 1988; Dolan 1991; Kreisman and Straus 1989; Kroll 1988; Stone 1990); (2) the most serious of the dissociative disorders, *multiple personalities or multiplicity* (Bagley and King 1990; Bass and Davis 1988; Bliss 1986; Blume 1990; Braun 1990; Braun and Sachs 1985; Briere and Runtz 1988a; Dolan 1991; Fine 1990; Janoff-Bulman 1992; Kelley 1988, 1989; Mayer 1991; Putnam 1985, 1989, 1990; Putnam et al. 1986; Snow and Sorenson 1990); and (3) what some experts now refer to as *soul murder* (Miller 1984; Shengold 1989) *or the shattered soul* (Steele 1987, 1988).

According to Briere (1989:39), the most recent edition of the American Psychiatric Association's Diagnostic and Statistical Manual (DSM III-R), *borderline personality disorder* (hereafter BPD) includes the "symptoms" of:

> (1) 'impulsiveness in at least two areas that are potentially self-damaging,' (e.g., sex, substance use, reckless spending, shoplifting, overeating, etc.), (2) 'a pattern of unstable and intense interpersonal relationships' (e.g., idealization, manipulation, and marked shifts in attitude), (3) 'inappropriate, intense anger,' (4) 'marked and persistent identity disturbance' manifested by uncertainty about several issues related to self (e.g., self-image, gender identity, friendship patterns, and values), (5) 'affective instability: marked shifts from baseline mood to depression, irritability, or anxiety,' (6) 'recurrent suicidal threats, gestures, or behavior or self-mutilating behavior,' (7) 'chronic feelings of emptiness or boredom,' and (8) 'frantic efforts to avoid real or imagined abandonment.'

It is important for us to examine and to understand this disorder because it is *the* diagnosis most frequently applied to women seen in psychiatric settings who also exhibit severe signs of post-sexual-abuse trauma (Briere 1989; Stone 1990).

Briere, though, points out that there are problems with this diagnosis, particularly as it is applied to women suffering from post-sexual-victimization trauma. As examples, all of the aforementioned "symptoms" are nearly identical to "symptoms" reported by girls, adolescent females, and adult women who have been sexually abused as children; most members of the psychiatric community do *not* acknowledge the linkage between childhood sexual victimization and the development of BPD; and many psychiatrists (as well as other mental health professionals) define BPD via such outdated Freudian concepts as "early object loss" and "'difficulties in the separation-individuation period of childhood" [i.e., yet again, Mom did something wrong (Briere 1989:37)]. Briere (1989:39) suggests an alternative model; rather than "positing contingent 'libidinal supplies and gratification' by the inevitably disordered mother, a survivor-oriented perspective [of child sexual abuse] suggests that the cognitive, affective and interpersonal effects of severe child abuse are sufficient to account for many cases of what is referred to as 'borderline' behavior."

Regarding dissociative disorders, a number of recent sources suggest that many (if not most) girls, adolescent females, and adult women who were sexually abused in childhood are quite adept at the dissociative, defense mechanisms of "compartmentalizing" their lives, "getting outside" of their bodies, and "fading away" (Bass and Davis 1988; Blume 1990; Briere and Runtz 1988b; Dolan 1991; Dinsmore 1991; Faller 1990; Finkelhor and associates 1986; Finney 1990; Gomes-Schwartz et al. 1990; Wyatt and Powell 1988; Wisechild 1988). We also must acknowledge, though, that there are degrees of dissociation and that the most extreme version is *multiple personality disorder* (hereafter MPD).

Although historically MPD has been regarded as a relatively rare disorder, current investigations offer conclusive evidence that it is *not* as rare a condition as we once thought (Herman 1992; Kelley 1989; Kluft 1990; Mayer 1991; Putnam 1989; Putnam et al. 1986; Summit 1988). In addition, multiplicity now is regarded as one possible consequence of incest or child sexual abuse, particularly when the abuse was sadistic or overtly violent, lasted a long time, involved multiple perpetrators, and/or had ritualistic components (Bass and Davis 1988; Bliss 1986; Blume 1990; Braun 1990; Braun and Sachs 1985; Briere 1989; Cohen et al. 1991; Courtois 1988; Dolan 1991; Finkelhor et al. 1988; Finney 1990; Gil 1988; Kelley 1989; Kluft 1985a, 1985b, 1985c; Mayer 1991; Putnam 1985, 1989; Summit 1989).[12] In fact, some experts now suggest that 95 to 98 percent of *known multiples* also have histories of severe physical and/or sexual child abuse (Braun 1989, 1990; Putnam et al. 1986).

Although MPD is regarded by many as a truly disruptive and serious disorder, as well as one that entails a lengthy period of expert intervention, there is an upside to this discussion. That is to say, MPD now is regarded by some experts as a logical, positive adaptation. For example, Braun and Sachs (1985:44) suggest that: "The adaptive function of the symptomatology of multiple personality disorder becomes more obvious when one considers that . . . [these] patients are exposed to events that produce anxiety overwhelming enough to cause a psychotic decompensation in most normal people." Rather than allowing the traumas of incest and child sexual abuse to destroy them, children who develop MPD do so out of necessity: They survive in the only way open to them; they split off from themselves so that the pain becomes more "bearable." Though arguably a logical solution for children involved in highly illogical situations, multiplicity is considered to be "maladaptive . . . in an adult world that stresses continuity in memory, behavior, and sense of self" (Putnam 1989:54). Accordingly, many (but clearly *not* all) of the experts believe that integration of the various parts of the shattered self should be the goal of therapeutic intervention.

Soul murder and the shattered soul are *not* clinical categorizations or diagnoses; rather, they are metaphors which highlight the shattering of the "spirit" which can occur during and after particularly severe cases of incest or child sexual abuse. Regarding "soul murder," Shengold (1989:24–25) suggests that:

> What happens to the child . . . is so terrible, so over-whelming, and usually so recurrent that the child must not feel it and cannot register it, and resorts to a massive isolation of feeling, which is maintained by brainwashing (a mixture of confusion, denial, and identifying with the aggressor). A hypnotic living deadness, a state of existing 'as if' one were there, is often the result . . .

Soul murder also refers to: an inability to determine what is real; a changed, if not a shattered, sense of self; confusion about identity issues (e.g., sexual identity, as well as a more general sense of who you are); an inability to love or be loved; and distorted images of oneself and the world. In effect, "murdering someone's soul means depriving the victim of the ability to feel joy and love as a separate person" (Shengold 1989:2).

Steele (1989: 19) prefers the term "shattered soul" to illustrate the long-term aftermath which can ensue, particularly after brutal cases of incest or child sexual abuse: "[I]magine what happens when one's entire childhood is a composite of . . . torments. These kinds of trauma often fragment the psychological collage we call the 'self' . . . I believe it also shatters, or at least deeply wounds, the soul [or] that essential being of a person that is more than [just the] psychological self."

Although at first glance these two concepts appear to be quite similar, there is at least one distinction between them. Shengold infers that one's soul is gone, that it is dead; Steele's approach, on the other hand, is a bit more optimistic because she suggests that one's soul is *not* gone or dead but rather shattered. In other words, the implication is that "soul murder" is a permanent condition from which we cannot recover, while Steele's conceptualization of the "shattered soul" suggests that, with a great deal of commitment, time, and effort, people can recover from their abusive histories (i.e., perhaps they will never be "normal" or completely healed, but they can come to have lives that are richer and fuller).

In sum, although all cases of child sexual abuse must be regarded as serious and severe, there are some instances which are more extreme in both their content and duration. Therefore, we must remain aware of the fact that there are "stories" out there that are so horrible, so sickening, that many of us may *not* even want to hear them. As I suggested before, though, when you open the door on subjects such as incest and child sexual abuse, you must be willing to open that door all the way and to hear all aspects of the problem.

Factors which Explain Our Post-Sexual Abuse Consequences

As was noted in the summary of post-rape reactions, there are factors which can reduce or intensify our long-term responses, and the same is the case with incest and child sexual abuse. As examples, several experts have found that the aftermath of childhood sexual victimization is *more pronounced* when the abuse involves: (1) *close relatives*, particularly fathers and stepfathers (Asher 1988; Briere and Runtz 1988b; Browne and Finkelhor 1986; Courtois 1988; Friedrich 1990; Greenwald and Leitenberg 1990; Jehu 1988; Schetky 1990; Tower 1988; Wyatt and Powell 1988); (2) *genital contact and/or penetration* (Briere and Runtz 1989; Courtois 1988; Finkelhor and Browne 1986; Gomes-Schwartz et al. 1990; Greenwald and Leitenberg 1990; Mannarino et al. 1991; Schetky 1990; Wyatt and Powell 1988); (3) *the use of force* (Asher 1988; Briere and Runtz 1988b; Courtois 1988; Haugaard and Reppucci 1988; Jehu 1988; Schetky 1990; Siegel et al. 1990; Wyatt and Powell 1988); (4) *multiple perpetrators and/or ritualistic components* (Braun 1990; Braun and Sachs 1985; Briere and Runtz 1988b, 1989; Cohen et al. 1991; Finkelhor and Browne 1986; Finkelhor and Williams, with Burns 1988; Jehu 1988; Mayer 1991); (5) *male perpetrators* (Courtois 1988; Finkelhor and Browne 1986; Russell 1986); (6) *victimization which lasts over an extended period of time* (Briere and Runtz 1988b, 1989; Cohen et al. 1991; Courtois 1988; Finkelhor and Browne 1986; Gomes-Schwartz et al. 1990; Haugaard and Reppucci 1988; Jehu 1988; Russell 1986; Schetky 1990); and/or (7) *disbelief by others or the abuse is viewed as insignificant once the child discloses it* (Bagley and King 1989; Cohen et al. 1991; Finkelhor and Browne 1986; Haugaard and Reppucci 1988; Janoff-Bulman 1992; Tower 1988; Wyatt and Mickey 1988).

Although these variables clarify our thinking about why incest and child sexual abuse can produce such devastating responses, the more important contribution is for practitioners who come into contact with the girls, female adolescents, and adult women who have histories of childhood sexual victimization. If it is understood that these factors may be related to the onset of the more severe forms of post-sexual-abuse consequences (i.e., they pinpoint the issues that are particularly troublesome and which make recovery more difficlut), practitioners should be better equipped to aid these girls and women in their search for healing and growth.

A Summary and Critique of These Findings

As can be concluded from this discussion: (1) our responses to incest and child sexual abuse can occur over an extended period of time, beginning in childhood and lasting well into adulthood; (2) some of these consequences can be life-threatening (e.g., suicidal ideation and suicide attempts, subsequent victimizations, substance abuse, and eating disorders); (3) responses occur in each and every sphere of our lives; (4) several variables are known to increase the severity of the aftermath of incest and child sexual abuse; and (5) some of these consequences are more serious than others (e.g., the development of borderline and multiple personality disorders, as well as soul murder and the shattered soul).

As was the case with the rape literature, though, problems also exist with what we know about post-sexual-abuse or post-incest consequences. For example, we just now are beginning to examine such issues as why: (1) some children recall their abusive experiences and react to them almost immediately while others bury their memories until they are adults; (2) children of different age groupings react differently to child sexual abuse; and (3) some of us have more serious long-term consequences than do others. Due to the relative recency of our interest in and our willingness to explore these issues, the variety of definitions which describe the various forms sexual victimization can take, and the diversity of the groups which have been studied, though, it is no wonder that we as yet are unable to sort out many of these issues.

An additional problem which was mentioned in the foregoing discussion of the rape literature also applies to how we conceptualize the aftermath of incest and child sexual abuse. Specifically, I am referring to the fact that the majority of the studies which investigate the issue of childhood sexual victimization do so via the "symptoms approach." With its emphases on standardized, objective measures of psychological, behavioral, and somatic changes, this becomes a problem because we never really come to understand the deeper meanings that these "symptoms" may represent. In other words, this approach keeps us at a level of analysis which focuses mostly on our "symptoms" (e.g., sleep disturbances, increased tension, anxiety) or "diagnoses" (i.e., depressive disorder), while we do *not* dig deeper to determine what these indicators and diagnoses mean to the girls and women who have been sexually victimized.

At present, there seems to be a growing awareness of this problem in the *child* sexual victimization literature. Briere (1989:39–40), for example, uses the term "core effects" to refer to the "impacts of sexual victimization thought to underlie the clinical problems or 'symptoms' of abuse survivors" (e.g., other-directedness or thwarting the child's self-awareness or ability to individuate; a chronic perception of danger; self-hatred). Similarly, Poston and Lison (1989:189) discuss the plight of women who for years have lived with or ignored the impact of incest on their lives: "Most [of them] were treating *symptoms*, circling round and round in a pattern of discomfort and complaint, occasionally getting help, but more often than not having one symptom clear up only to have two others take its place." Dinsmore (1991:23) presents a similar argument. Rather than regarding post-sexual-abuse consequences as signs of pathology, she depicts them as "survival behaviors," and she cautions therapists about acknowledging the utility of these sorts of efforts: "Instead of identifying incest in the life of the client, they dance around that issue and look only at the 'problem behaviors' . . . But it is essential to acknowledge and understand these 'symptoms' as survival behaviors, for without them there is little possibility for the child-victim to have become the woman-survivor . . . "(Dinsmore 1991: 24). If they heed this advice, practitioners can enlist and encourage these coping mechanisms or use these "negatives" to create positive outcomes.

In sum, if we focus solely on the psychological problems, physical ailments, distorted cognitions, etc., we do a disservice to the infants, girls, adolescent females, and adult women who have survived sexual abuse and/or incest; and we end up obfuscating the real issues which underlie these "symptoms." If we truly aspire to the lofty goals of "treating" and "fixing" the resultant psychic, physical, and spiritual damage of incest and child sexual abuse, as well as repairing the shattered souls and lives with which some of these girls and women end up, we must be willing to go below the surface; we must begin to examine and directly address the underlying issues that these consequences represent.

Let me, though, be very clear about something; I am *not* suggesting that we ignore such serious "symptoms" as substance abuse and suicide attempts. If children, adolescent females, or adult women are actively suicidal, or if they are killing themselves more slowly via alcohol, drugs, and eating disorders, these "symptoms" are important ones in and of themselves and they merit our immediate attention. After that, though, there is the added step of moving to a deeper level of analysis and attempting to understand what these responses have meant for them. This latter step is critical because if we fail to investigate and determine the underlying meanings of these "symptoms" and "conditions," we will never come to a full awareness of why survivors of sexual victimization develop them in the first place; in effect, we will be applying "Band-Aids" to serious "wounds."

Similarities and Differences in Response Patterns

Many of the aforementioned immediate and long-term consequences of incest and childhood sexual abuse are similar to the ones reported by adolescent females and adult women who have been raped. As examples, all three groups of survivors are very likely to experience: the psychological responses of fear, anxiety, and depression; numerous stress-related, somatic complaints (e.g., headaches and gastrointestinal problems); altered behavior patterns such as spending more time alone; a variety of interpersonal problems, particularly with intimacy; cognitive distortions (e.g., believing that they are bad and/or deserved what happened to them); self-perceptual difficulties, usually problems with self-esteem and self-blame; and a number of age-specific sexual problems. Although the content of their "symptoms" differ across the various age groupings, the underlying significance of them does *not*: Rape, incest, and child sexual abuse affect infants, girls, adolescent females, and adult women in virtually all spheres of their lives.

One thing that is different, though, is that the problems which can arise from incest and sexually abusive experiences are considered to be even more insidious than are the consequences of rape. This is due, in part, to the developmental differences between children and adults. That is to say, children have *not* as yet had the opportunity to achieve a full and mature view of self; their notions about themselves are much more fragile and permeable (Celano 1992; Janoff-Bulman 1992; Ledray 1986; Shengold 1989). As Blume (1990:12) explains this issue: "An adult is fully formed. Her sense of herself as a separate yet interrelated individual, as well as her sexuality, are more advanced than that of the child; a child victim of incest [or sexual abuse], however, experiences a course of development that is shared, everyday, with premature sexuality, lack of safety (even terror), and deformities of many life skills." Briere (1989) and Ledray (1986) go so far as to suggest that children can get "frozen" or "stuck" in time, i.e., their psychosocial development comes to a screeching halt. Although they age and grow taller, in some cases (particularly if nothing was done to help them when they were younger), the adult survivors of incest and child sexual abuse remain children trapped in adult bodies.

Second, there is a debate regarding whether the characteristics of the assault make any difference in adolescent females' or women's responses to rape (see earlier discussion of this issue in this chapter), while these same factors have been shown to play a very critical role in predicting post-sexual-abuse consequences. In other words, the experts are not certain about whether different types of rape produce different consequences, while a very clear pattern emerges in the incest and child sexual abuse literatures: The child who experiences the more brutal types of incest or sexual abuse has more serious consequences, particularly in adulthood. Part of this difference can be explained via the aforementioned lower level of cognitive development of children, as well as their unfamiliarity with sex and sexuality. In other words, adult women are more likely to have a sense of who they are, as well as a fairly strong sexual identity, but children have *not* as yet had the opportunity to achieve those levels.

Finally, as additional (yet reverse) "proof" of the difference between response patterns among the various age groupings, I have never come across an example in the rape literature of rape causing an adult woman to "split off" into multiple personalities, develop borderline personality disorder, "become" a lesbian, and/or experience soul murder or a shattered soul. Yet, the incest and child sexual abuse literatures, albeit unfortunate, are replete with such examples. Again, due to developmental differences and the intensified confusion that children can experience after being sexually assaulted, they are more at risk to develop the more serious consequences of sexual victimization.

Summary and Conclusions

The primary goal of this chapter has been to outline the possible consequences of sexual victimization. While doing so, I have described how responses for the various age groups (e.g., infants, pre-school children, school-age children, adolescents, and adult women) differ, as well as the differences across the different categories of sexual victimization (i.e., rape, incest, and child sexual abuse). Notwithstanding this diversity, the conclusions are disturbing: Sexual victimization can wreak havoc in our lives and can cause us to suffer consequences across a number of diverse dimensions. This, though, should *not* be surprising information. Based on what we now know about holistic health, the totality of the person, and the ramifications of negative life events, we should expect traumas such as rape, incest, and child sexual abuse to affect us psychologically and somatically. Moreover, if we are disrupted across these two dimensions, more often than not we also will act differently afterwards (i.e., the behavioral realm), our relationships with others are likely to be strained (i.e., the interpersonal dimension), and our willingness to be involved in intimate relationships (i.e., the sexual sphere) may be diminished.

In addition, although all of the pains that we experience across the various dimensions of our lives are critical, some of them may be more devastating and cause deeper wounds. Specifically, I am referring to the potential for cognitive, self-perceptual, and spiritual consequences. Although none of the "areas" of our lives really can be viewed as distinct or separate entities, these three are particularly interwoven. In other words, our self-perceptions are critically linked to our cognitions about the world and the people around us, as well as what we define as meaningful in our lives; our cognitions about the world affect our views about ourselves and that which we regard as meaningful, while the spiritual component leads us to have specific notions about the world (e.g., it is good versus evil, safe versus unsafe), as well as images about ourselves as good or evil, valuable or worthless. Herman (1992:51) is one of the few voices who regards the interplay among these three dimensions of our lives as critical:

> Traumatic events call into question basic human relationships. They breach the attachments of family, friendship, love, and community. They shatter the construction of the self that is formed and sustained in relation to others. They undermine the belief systems that give meaning to human experience. They violate the victim's faith in a natural or divine order and cast the victim into a state of existential crisis . . .
>
> Traumatic events destroy the victim's fundamental assumptions about the safety of the world, the positive value of the self, and the meaningful order of creation.

If our notions about the world, the people around us, ourselves, and what has meaning to us are shattered, we can end up *without* a center or a core. That which we had previously "known" no longer applies; former rules no longer make sense, and we have difficulty determining who we are, what is real, and what is of value to us (Janoff-Bulman 1992). In sum, we feel as if we no longer fit into our lives and the world around us. When viewed from this perspective, the origins of the more serious consequences of incest and child sexual abuse (e.g., borderline personality disorder, multiplicity, and soul murder or the shattered soul) are much more comprehensible. In fact, it is small wonder that more of us do *not* suffer from them.

Regarding the final dimension across which we can suffer consequences, it makes a great deal of "sense" that many of us have been victimized more than once. If we are placed in incomprehensible situations (e.g., rape, incest, and child sexual abuse) and if steps are *not* taken to ward off the likelihood of long-term damage, it is likely that our views of ourselves and the world around us (i.e., the self-perceptual, cognitive, and spiritual spheres of our lives) will be altered. The "logical" next step in this downward spiral is that we come to believe that we are worthless and that we have little or no control over our lives. When these sorts of distortions are regarded as "facts," girls, adolescent females, and adult women may be unable or unwilling to protect themselves from further victimization, begin to believe that they deserve this sort of negative treatment, and/or may *not* see the "next" victimization coming until it is too late.

In sum, the more brutal the sexual victimization, the more likely it is that these devastating consequences will ensue. Let me, though, end this chapter with an optimistic slant: Due to the stated purpose of this chapter (i.e., to summarize the extant knowledge about the consequences of sexual victimization), by necessity, its tone has been particularly negative and pessimistic. This, though, is *not* the end of the "story" because I have been setting the stage for the more critical considerations of how to heal the wounds of sexual victimization. Accordingly, the subjects of the next two chapters are the issues of recovering from rape, incest, and child sexual abuse and the available treatment strategies which can facilitate the regaining and reclaiming of our lives and ourselves.

Healing, Growth, and Victory: Recovering from Rape, Incest, and Child Sexual Abuse

> And now, having survived, she can begin again. She can go beyond surviving and work for the quality of life that she deserves. She can unlock and break the secret, take her power back, shed the guilt and self-blame of the experience and learn, finally, to be angry at what was done to her—instead of at herself. She can refuse to accept a life that feels confused and out of control. It is not enough to get up each morning and suffer through the day. When she faces her past and reclaims herself, she will not just have survived; she will have triumphed (Blume 1990:20).

For the longest time, whenever I saw or heard words such as survival, healing, thriving, or recovery in relation to sexual victimization, I felt somewhat confused and angry because the meanings of these terms often were quite vague. In addition, until fairly recently, few works outlined the specifics of how you go about achieving these lofty goals. Although many works have defined these terms and listed factors which either impede or facilitate recovery, healing, and growth, far fewer have outlined the tasks that needed to be accomplished or the issues that had to be resolved.[1] In large part, this dearth of information is one reason that motivated me to write this book.

Returning to Blume's words, what they do is offer hope— hope that recovery is *not* only possible but within reach. She does this by illustrating the importance of: acknowledging the ways that girls and women have survived, even the seemingly negative ones; being dissatisfied with "just making it through the day"; redirecting our anger at the appropriate source (i.e., the

157

perpetrator); choosing to reclaim our lives; and triumphing over adversity. Since many of us have moved *beyond* the statuses of victim and survivor toward recovery, thriving, triumphing, or victory, these are the perfect starting points for this chapter because such images depict the reality and the quality of many of our current lives.

In order to clarify the multitude of issues involved in recovering from sexual victimization, in this chapter I explore several topics. They include: (1) caveats about the extant recovery advice; (2) the various meanings and conceptualizations of terms such as recovery, growth, healing, victory, and resolution; (3) healing and growth across the ten dimensions of our lives that were mentioned in the last chapter (psychological, somatic, behavioral, interpersonal, cognitive, self-perceptual, sexual, political, spiritual, and subsequent victimization), or the issues that must be dealt with and the changes that must be made in order to achieve recovery; (4) models which describe the process and the content of recovering from sexual victimization; and (5) how the experiences and the recovery of girls who have been sexually abused (or survivors of incest) may differ from those of adult women who have been raped.

Caveats about Recovery, Healing, Growth, and Victory

Before doing so, though, it is important to offer a few caveats about this information. First of all, what we often see as the major emphases in this literature are the immediate and long-term post-sexual-victimization "symptoms" that many of us experience and the "fact" that we remain victims or survivors forever (i.e., that we are permanently "damaged" after these traumas). Far fewer works, though, focus on the more optimistic goals of coping, recovery, healing, integration, thriving, resolution, victory and/or growth. While it is true that some of us never do recover fully from these experiences and still are striving for that goal, it is equally important to underscore the facts that many of us *not* only have recovered from these experiences but have gone on to lead happy, healthy, and productive lives.

Second, we have tended to conceptualize the negative life events of rape, incest, and child sexual abuse as having life-shattering potential, while an emphasis on the positive outcomes which can result during recovery is a relatively new one. Let me, though, be both careful and clear about this notion: I am *not* suggesting that being sexually victimized is "good" for girls and women, that it "teaches them a lesson," or that it "builds character." Rather, I believe that if and when these sorts of traumatic life events occur, while regrouping from them and by taking specific steps to improve our lives, we can create positive outcomes for ourselves. An example of this hopeful perspective is Kelly (1988:159), who suggests that, "By placing women as decision makers and actors at the centre, the common, although often implicit, assumption that all consequences of sexual violence are, or remain, negative can be questioned and attention can be drawn to the possibility that the process of coping with negative effects may, in the long term, have positive outcomes."

Third, many of the works which examine recovery-related issues investigate only one type of assault. As examples, Braswell (1990), Burgess and Holmstrom (1979b), Koss and Harvey (1991), and Ledray (1986) focus predominantly on the subject of rape; Blume (1990), Courtois (1988), Dinsmore (1991), Ratner (1990), Russell (1986), and Wisechild (1988) examine the topic of incest; Bagley and King (1990), Bass and Davis (1988), Briere (1989), Dolan (1991), Engel (1989) Finkelhor (1984, 1986), Finney (1990), Gil (1988), Jehu (1988), and Tower (1988) explore the issue of child sexual abuse, while the works of Herman (1992), Janoff-Bulman (1992), Kelly (1988), and Russell (1984) are the exceptions in that they examine all three forms of victimization as parts of the same continuum of sexual violence. In effect, most of these works examine how to recover from one type of victimization, and the advice may *not* be applicable to other forms of sexual assault.

Fourth, it is important to keep in mind that there is a great deal of variability in how and why girls, adolescent females, and women initiate the process of recovery, as well as when and why they choose to begin this journey. In other words, there is *not* one way to go about healing; there are a variety of approaches, techniques, and rationales for doing so. As examples, some girls and women seek professional help; others join self-help or support groups, while still others recover from these experiences alone. In addition, some of us begin this process almost immediately while others of us delay it (whether consciously or unconsciously) for many years. Tower (1988:88–89) explains these discrepancies by noting that our motives to change and to initiate recovery can be quite divergent:

> For some it is a conscious decision—one made when they just can't stand living with themselves anymore. Relationships that are negative *or* positive may be factors in the realization that change is needed . . . It [can] happen when the victims develop a new perspective on what is going on. They become aware . . . [that] there . . . [are] better ways to live and relate and they choose to take the responsibility for moving toward them . . .

Fifth, many of the works which examine post-victimization recovery infer that it is automatically a lengthy and arduous process. If the sexual victimization is dealt with when it occurs and if we get the right kind of responses and help from significant others and involve social control agents immediately afterwards, though, this need *not* be the case (Janoff-Bulman 1992). Bass and Davis (1988:34) explain this issue as it relates to the adult survivors of childhood sexual abuse: "If a child's disclosure is met with compassion and effective intervention, the healing begins immediately. But if no one noticed or responded to your pain, or if you were blamed, not believed, or suffered further trauma, the damage was compounded. And the ways you coped with the abuse may have created further problems." The same situation exists with rape: If our significant others and the various social control agents respond to us in positive and supportive ways, we tend to have fewer long-term consequences (Burgess and Holmstrom 1979b; Holmstrom and Burgess 1978; Madigan and Gamble 1991).

Finally, since recovering from rape, incest, and child sexual abuse involves many of the same stages and tasks, I have elected to discuss rebounding from them together. This does *not* negate the fact that recovery must be fitted to the individual needs of each girl, adolescent female, and adult woman who has been sexually victimized; rather, my goal is to simplify what in reality is a highly complex, interrelated set of tasks. Please note, as well, that there are some very real differences in recovering from these different types of sexual victimization and that this issue is discussed later in this chapter.

Recovery, Growth, Healing, and Victory: What Are They?

Notwithstanding these caveats, several conceptualizations of these terms have been developed. For example, Burgess and Holmstrom (1979b:413) define recovering from *rape victimization* as the "psychological work required by rape victims[; it] includes freeing oneself from the fears generated by the rape, acknowledging and bearing the pain caused by the rape, redefining the feelings of vulnerability and helplessness, and gaining control of one's life again." Koss and Harvey (1991:176–177), too, use the term recovery in relation to healing from a rape experience, but they conceptualize it as "the victim-to-survivor process . . . [or] the process by which a victim not only survives a sexual assault but survives standing up." Ledray (1986:98–99) prefers the term resolution and defines it as the process whereby the rape victim puts her life back in order, resolves her negative attitudes and feelings, prevents long-term post-rape social and psychological problems, and has the "opportunity to emerge from chaos and turmoil better able to handle other crises . . ."

Blume (1990:301) uses the terms recovery and healing to describe how a woman can overcome a history of *incest*; she defines it as a "time to grow strong in the broken places, to make friends with her physical self, to reunite her mind and body, to feel safe in her own skin, [and] to develop social skills." Wisechild (1988) also uses the term healing the wounds of incest, but she conceptualizes it as an all-encompassing endeavor that is woven into all of the aspects of our lives (e.g., work, relationships, and the search for new forms of spirituality).

Courtois (1988:170) offers a more clinical definition of this healing process and regards it as "an abreaction of the trauma, which generally involves breaking the secret, catharsis, and reevaluation of the incest, its circumstances, and its effects." She also suggests that it is a process which includes: "remembering, . . . facilitating the change from victim to survivor and beyond . . . and finding meaning in the experience as well as mourning [it]" (Courtois 1988:171). Further, she adds that more often than not, psychotherapy is needed to achieve these goals, and that professional intervention should be "a developmental process involving reparenting in the sense that the survivor reexperiences and reworks the tasks of maturation that were either missed or experienced prematurely" (Courtois 1988:171). During this process, the therapist does *not* act as the survivor's parent, rather, he/she "provides an opportunity to address the past with a supportive ally and to grieve and make up for the losses of childhood" (Courtois 1988:171).

Regarding *child sexual abuse*, Bass and Davis (1988) liken recovering from it to a process of resolution and healing whereby the survivor puts the experience into a manageable perspective. More importantly, they introduce the optimistic goal of thriving, which "means more than just an alleviation of symptoms, more than Band-Aids, more than functioning adequately . . . [It] means enjoying a feeling of wholeness, satisfaction in your life and work, genuine love and trust in your relationships, pleasure in your body" (Bass and Davis 1988:20). Please note that Bass and Davis are *not* suggesting a magical process whereby we automatically return to "normal"; rather, they speak frankly about what it takes to resolve an event that could have shattered your life permanently.

Briere (1989) prefers the terms integration and self-affirmation to describe recovering from child sexual abuse and suggests that these goals can be achieved only via a therapeutic process which assumes growth, i.e., intervention which emphasizes and reinforces the strengths of the woman rather than her weaknesses. In addition, Finney (1990:17) speaks of healing as the process whereby you "confront your fears," "face your pain," and "take control of your life," while Gil (1988) discusses recovery as fixing the woman's self-image, empowerment for her, improving her ability to hope, resolution of the trauma, and affiliation or breaking the pattern of isolation. Finally, Tower (1988:174–176) uses the words of her clients to define the process of survival; it includes a wide range of activities from just "getting up every morning," embracing a "small part of myself," "learning to accept what happened," "recognizing that we have choices," all the way through "learning to trust and feeling good about yourself in spite of it."

Herman offers a different perspective because she focuses on recovering from *all types of sexual victimization* (as well as from a variety of other traumas such as being a prisoner of war or a political prisoner). Specifically, she suggests that:

> The survivor who has accomplished her recovery faces life with few illusions but often with gratitude. Her view of life may be tragic, but for that very reason she has learned to cherish laughter. She has a clear sense of what is important and what is not. Having encountered evil, she knows how to cling to what is good. Having encountered the fear of death, she knows how to celebrate life (Herman 1992:213).

In sum, terms such as recovery, resolution, healing, growth, and victory refer to the process whereby we take whatever steps are necessary to make the changes in our lives that will facilitate happiness and positive images of ourselves, good relationships with others, and hope for the future.

Thus far, I have focused on what we as individuals can do to recover and to heal the wounds of sexual victimization. Several experts, though, particularly feminist ones, have begun to combine this personal journey with something outside of the self, or a *collective approach* to healing. Kelly (1989), for example, has found that many women alter their perceptions about the world after they have been sexually victimized and that they do so in highly politicized terms; she calls this the "transition from individual survival to collective resistance." Specifically, this means that the women were no longer able to believe models that viewed individualized violence, stress, and/or alcohol as the "causes" of the sexual victimization problem; rather, they came to see that structural issues (e.g., the domination of men over women and children, misogyny, the devaluation of women and children, and both groups being viewed as the property of men) are the *real* causes of these problems.

Bass and Davis (1988) present a similar argument by emphasizing that women should become aware of and do something about the structural forces which cause all sorts of crimes of violence. In an interview, Davis notes that: "[H]ealing can't stop with the individual . . . it is about taking that healing and doing something with it . . . [which] includes looking at the political structure of our society that has enabled abuse to run rampant" (Bolz 1991:39). She also notes that there is a very real danger in thinking that child sexual abuse is the problem of individuals and that it requires individual solutions; rather, she believes that we need to develop a "political perspective that sees activism as essential in stopping abuse, and an activism that does not negate individuals who need time out and space to attend to their own healing and pain. Linking the two together is what will create a change in society" (Bolz 1991:39)

Dinsmore (1991) and Herman (1992) label this nexus between the personal and the political as the "survivor's mission," which refers to salvaging something positive out of the rubble of tragedy. Examples include working in child abuse prevention programs and becoming involved with battered women's shelters. They also add that these sorts of activities not only are of service to agencies which so desperately need the help but that they also produce a major benefit for the women who do them: "Commitment to making the world a better, safer place for women and children has helped many survivors become thrivers" (Dinsmore 1991:46).

Miller (1990:172) refers to this process of doing something for others as becoming "enlightened witnesses" or potential helpers: "If I succeed with my books in reaching a few people who were fortunate enough to have had a helpful witness in their childhood, . . . after reading my books, they will become enlightened, *conscious* witnesses and advocates of children . . . [T]hey will become aware of the suffering of children more quickly and more deeply than others who must deny it." More importantly, they will do something about it.

Sanford (1990) examines this issue a bit differently. Drawing on the expertise of practitioners who work with

Vietnam veterans, she notes the importance of the Vietnam War Memorial in Washington, D.C. That is, "[it] represents a 'spiritual breakthrough' because it gave veterans a . . . meeting ground where they could remember and grieve together . . . and [it] marked the end of this country's denial of its experience and a sanction of mourning over the war" (Sanford 1990:174). Sanford (1990:74) also contrasts this with how we historically have conceptualized the child abuse problem: "We largely deny the experience . . . Our society does not sanction the mourning of childhood trauma." To remedy this situation, though, Sanford (1990:174–175) concludes that "[w]e need a wall for survivors of childhood trauma. There we could remember and not be alone. We could grieve in good company." Although I agree with Sanford's ideas, she does *not* take them far enough. Notwithstanding the fact that collectively acknowledging the realities of childhood abuse is an important first step in the process of healing, we need to refocus our attention by taking direct action to eradicate or at least to reduce the problem. As examples, we can: (1) let the perpetrators know that we regard any maltreatment of children as a serious infraction and that they will be punished severely for these behaviors; (2) work to protect our children from these traumas, let them know that they can talk to us if they are so victimized, and, if they make such reports, believe, support, and help them; and (3) focus on how to help the survivors of childhood traumas to recover and reclaim their lives.

These authors who link recovery to larger, collective issues regard it as entailing a multitude of activities, numerous cognitive emphases, changed behavioral patterns, and various levels of involvement (i.e., personal as well as collective approaches). Lest all of this seem overwhelming, though, let me be very clear: The first priority is to heal yourself at a pace with which you are comfortable; the rest can come in good time, if and when you ever desire to go outside of yourself and do something for others who have had similar experiences. Blume (1990:305) clearly expresses this sentiment: "While she struggles, those of us who are strong enough must do the work of declaring that our emperors are naked, of breaking secrets, smashing lies, and working toward change wherever we can. As for the incest survivor, we must support her right to do what she can, when she is able, by her choice, not by our command."

In sum, regardless of whether you speak of recovering from rape, incest, or child sexual abuse, and regardless of which conceptualization of this process you prefer (e.g., healing, growth, victory, triumphing, etc.), there are commonalities and areas of agreement among them. For example, most of these experts focus on the need to: (1) feel whole again by reclaiming a sense of who we are and/or by developing a self-concept which acknowledges and incorporates the experience of sexual victimization; (2) grow strong and get to know ourselves better; (3) reclaim our bodies; (4) put the blame where it belongs (i.e., on the perpetrator and this society); (5) develop healthy relationships (i.e., learn to trust our judgments about people, as well as improve our ability to discriminate between good and bad folks); (6) free ourselves from our fears; (7) redefine the world around us; (8) establish or reestablish a sense of control over our lives; and (9) involve ourselves in collective action geared toward making the world a better, safer place for all of us in which to live. In effect, we are back to the ten spheres or dimensions of our lives that were introduced in the last chapter, or the specific areas across which we experience the consequences of sexual victimization (i.e., psychological, somatic, behavioral, interpersonal, cognitive, self-perceptual, sexual, political, and spiritual, as well as subsequent victimization).

Recovery, Healing, Growth, and Victory Across the Various Spheres of Our Lives

In the last chapter, I examined the possible immediate and long-term consequences of sexual victimization and noted that these consequences can affect us in various spheres of our lives. The focus now switches to these dimensions as the areas across which we need to make changes in order to improve our lives and/or to recover. As is summarized in Table 5.1, in this section, I illustrate the specific issues that must be resolved across all of these different spheres. It is important to reiterate, though, that in "real life" these dimensions or spheres are *not* distinct entities; rather, they are interconnected, overlapping parts of ourselves and our lives.

As for the *psychological sphere*, the most frequently observed post-sexual-victimization "symptoms" are fears, phobias, guilt, shame, and depression (Briere 1989; Burgess and Holmstrom 1979b; Calhoun and Atkeson 1991; Courtois 1988, 1992; Girelli et al. 1986; Herman 1992; Janoff-Bulman 1992; Kilpatrick et al. 1985; Koss and Harvey 1991). As was noted in the previous chapter, possible underlying meanings of these "symptoms" are that: (1) we have *not* as yet dealt with or faced the fact that we have been sexually abused or raped; and/or (2) we are unable (for whatever reasons) to make the shifts which will enable us to imagine ourselves as changed, vulnerable human beings. In effect, we are "stuck" at the victim stage and tend to feel helpless, confused, and immobilized.

Another way to explain these consequences is that changed visions of ourselves and the world around us take their toll; they do *not* come easily, nor do they come without costs; they cause pain. Therefore, these psychological "symptoms" can be viewed as the "costs" involved and the pain that we experience when we have been sexually victimized and begin the struggle toward recovery (Dinsmore 1991; Herman 1992; Janoff-Bulman 1992). Blume (1990:76), who describes the survivors of incest as the "walking wounded," expresses a similar sentiment: "The survivor's responses to the incest are natural and even meritorious . . . *She* is not crazy—incest is crazy. She does not have an 'affective disorder'—she is mourning a murdered childhood. But what has saved her may [now] cripple her." Rather than viewing these consequences as "signs" of pathology, then, we would do better to regard them as the resultant effects of a very real trauma and as responses that should diminish as we begin to experience, sort through, and come to grips with our pain and get closer to achieving the goals of changing our views about ourselves and the world around us. I am *not* suggesting that these changes are ones that we make easily or that we always can make them alone; rather, this may be an arduous and lengthy process which may require the loving

Table 5.1: Recovery Issues: Dimensions or Spheres Affected, Symptoms, Underlying Issues, and Recovery Tactics

Dimension or Sphere	Major "Symptoms"	Underlying Meanings of "Symptoms"	Specific Recovery Issues or Tactics
Psychological	Fears, phobias, anxiety, & depression	(1) Have not as yet dealt with the fact of having been raped or sexually abused (2) Unable to make the shift which enables us to imagine ourselves as changed, vulnerable human beings (3) "Stuck" at the victim stage (4) Costs involved in the struggle toward recovery	(1) These responses should diminish as we come to grips with the pain and change our view about ourselves and the world around us
Somatic	Headaches, fatigue, and gynecological problems	(1) Body's ways of dealing with issues that we do *not* deal with directly and consciously (2) Have *not* as yet incorporated having been sexually victimized into our current views of self (3) Feel as if our bodies let us down	(1) Work toward incorporating our experiences of sexual victimization into our current self-perceptions (2) Begin to view these as historical events rather than current ones (3) "Break the silence" (4) Learn to be comfortable with our bodies
Behavioral	Altering our lives in ways that make us feel safe and/or substance abuse	(1) Altering our lives is *not* a symptom but rather a sign of recovery (2) Substance abuse could be yet another "symptom" of prior sexual victimization, the goal of which is to help us feel numb	(1) Treat the substance abuse problem before trying to deal with the issue of sexual victimization (2) Care must be taken to make sure that substance abuse recovery programs make the connection between addiction to whatever substance and the likelihood of prior sexual victimization

Dimension or Sphere	Major "Symptoms"	Underlying Meanings of "Symptoms"	Specific Recovery Issues or Tactics
Interpersonal	Conflicted relationships, difficulty in developing & maintaining intimacy	(1) Should not be regarded as "symptoms" but rather as logical responses to real-life stressors (2) Residual effect is that we have great difficulty trusting anyone	(1) Deal with self before worrying about relations with others (2) Need to strike a balance between healthy interconnectedness and isolation (3) Deal with family members, particularly in cases of incest which may require "orphanization" (4) If elect to withdraw from family of origin, create a "family of choice"
Cognitive	Feeling powerless, helpless, insecure, & confused	(1) Shattered assumptions about the world	(1) Develop a new world view which includes awareness of our vulnerability to victimization and a realistic view of the randomness of negative life events (2) Learn to have what Antonovosky calls a "sense of coherence"
Self-Perceptual	Low self-esteem & self-blame; if compounded can lead to self-destructive behaviors, depression, and eating disorders	(1) Girls, adolescent females, and adult women may be buying into others' stereoypes of them as "damaged goods" (2) Logical responses given what has happened	(1) Gain what Belenky et al. call "a voice" or constructed knowledge (2) Improve image of self and boost self-esteem (3) Educate girls and women to develop internal locus of control, competency, self-efficacy, optimism, and resiliency

Table 5.1 (con.)

Dimension or Sphere	Major "Symptoms"	Underlying Meanings of "Symptoms"	Specific Recovery Issues or Tactics
Sexual	Variety of sexual dysfunctions, fear of sex, and flashbacks	(1) Logical responses given what has happened	(1) Must come to understand ourselves and what we need
		(2) Women equate intimacy, love, and sex	(2) Learn to be in charge of our own sexual experiences
			(3) Select intimates based on their willingness to be supportive
			(4) Develop relationships that are based on mutual trust and open communication
Political	Becoming politically aware and active (e.g., transition from individual survival to collective resistance, survivor's mission)	(1) Not symptoms but signs of recovery	(1) Achieving this awareness and wanting to become politically active is recovery
			(2) Need to break the silence and tell
			(3) Disservice is done if our pain is privatized

Dimension or Sphere	Major "Symptoms"	Underlying Meanings of "Symptoms"	Specific Recovery Issues or Tactics
Spiritual	End up being unable to believe in anything beyond ourselves can end up feeling hollow or dead inside	(1) Via our experiences of sexual victimization, we learn to shut down our feelings and/or to feel numb	(1) Find something to do, someone to be with, or something to believe in (2) Some of us may find the above in traditional religions; others will need nontraditional practices (e.g., reclaiming the goddess, nature, and/or intimacy) (3) Spirituality through creativity (4) Rebirth and cleansing rituals (5) Forgiving self
Subsequent Victimization	Revictimized in later relationships (e.g., subsequent rapes, domestic violence) or become a victimizer, particularly a child abuser	(1) Come to believe that we should be treated poorly (2) Some of this comes from observers disbelieving our "claims" of sexual victimization (3) Learn to be abusive	(1) Involves psychological issues, behavioral components, interpersonal, issues, cognitive restructuring, changed self-perceptions, and spiritual healing (2) Must come to learn that we have value and that we do *not* deserve negative treatment (3) Must unlearn patterns of abuse

support of significant others and perhaps professional intervention.

Regarding our *somatic complaints,* many of us who have been sexually victimized as children and/or as adults continue to exhibit long-term physiological problems. As was noted in the last chapter, "typical" ones include headaches, fatigue, and gynecological problems. These sorts of responses, though, are *not* mysteries, nor should they be viewed exclusively as physiological ones; rather, they are the body's ways of dealing with issues that we may *not* be able to deal with directly and consciously. As a blatant example, I am reminded of a friend who was sexually abused by her father during much of her childhood. As an adult, she used to say that she "couldn't face things," and she often had the physical "symptom" of facial paralysis to prove it.

Somatic "symptoms" also show that we have *not* as yet incorporated the fact of sexual victimization into our view of ourselves, that we have been unable (again, for whatever reasons) to face our "demons" head on. In order to alleviate these physiological responses, then, we must work toward incorporating our experiences of rape, incest, and/or child sexual victimization into our current self-perceptions, as well as begin to view these experiences as *historical* events, rather than ones which must program every moment of our lives today. Again, this can be a painful, arduous process which necessitates that we "break the silence." If and when we do, though, and as we begin to deal with these issues on a conscious level, many of our physical responses should dissipate.[2]

Another physiological issue for some survivors is that, when they were being sexually victimized, their bodies may have "let them down" by experiencing pleasure and/or orgasm. Although these reactions must be regarded as normal, physiological reflexes, they are difficult ones from which to recover, both cognitively and self-perceptually, because they create the mistaken impression of having "asked for it" and/or of having "enjoyed it." In turn, these sorts of perceptions can intensify post-sexual-victimization guilt and confusion among survivors. Thus, an added component in physically recovering and healing is learning to be more comfortable with our bodies, as well as beginning to view them as our allies rather than our enemies. The specifics of this process of physical reclamation can include such diverse activities as: physical exercise, biofeedback, massage therapy, eating well, and generally taking care of ourselves (Bass and Davis 1988; Engel 1989). The goal, then, is to learn to accept our bodies and to reclaim them as our own.[3]

Behavioral changes, too, are frequently observed "signs" of post-sexual-victimization trauma. Oftcited ones are: (1) altering our lives in ways that may make us feel safer (e.g., changing residences, spending more time alone or with others, and absenteeism from work or school) and (2) substance abuse. Please note that we should *not* regard the former changes as "symptoms" at all, but rather as ways to cope with the trauma of sexual victimization and to increase a sense of control in our lives.

On the other hand, the problem of substance abuse is a serious one that requires immediate attention. There is a dilemma, though, because many of the currently popular treatment approaches for substance abusers are "twelve-step" programs which are based loosely on the Alcoholics Anonymous (hereafter AA) model. Thus, in order to qualify as a "recovering" alcoholic or drug addict, people must be willing to: (1) admit that they are "out of control"; (2) support a medical or a disease model of substance abuse (i.e., it's a problem for the individual rather than a social problem); and (3) give themselves up to some "higher power" (Kaschak 1992; Tallen 1990). Although this type of program works well for many people, we also must admit that it has flaws, particularly for women who have histories of sexual victimization (Root 1989). First of all, if these women try to deal with the "symptom" of substance abuse as if it is their *sole* problem (i.e., they do *not* examine the possible connection between their earlier sexual victimization and their current substance abuse), more than likely, this form of treatment will be *ineffective* for them.[4] Second, the role of the patriarchal social structure in creating and perpetuating such problems as alcoholism and drug addiction is ignored in many of these programs; instead, the focal concern is individual "failings." These sorts of emphases can mask the real reasons many of us "choose" numbness rather than squarely facing the issue of sexual victimization, cloak the social and cultural forces which cause and perpetuate problems such as substance abuse and sexual victimization, and depoliticize these problems (Bolz 1991; Conn 1991; Herman 1992; Kaschak 1992; Root 1989; Tallen 1990). Suffice it for now to say that recent feminist approaches to treatment for all sorts of "women's" problems are increasingly aware of these pitfalls (Bass and Davis 1988; Courtois 1988; Koss and Harvey 1991; Reis 1991b), an issue which will be examined in detail in the next chapter.

In order to recover in the behavioral dimension of our lives, then, we must be willing to explore the long-term ramifications that sexual victimization has had on our lives, as well as to understand all of the ways that these ramifications have been manifested. In addition, if as a result of being raped or experiencing incest or child sexual abuse we develop "problematic" behaviors, these behaviors must be examined within social, cultural, and political contexts; we no longer should be willing to accept explanations which locate the causes of these problems exclusively in individual psyches or the psychopathology of the person. Rather, these are social problems, and the solutions to them must incorporate social factors.

Many girls and women evidence *interpersonal difficulties,* after being sexually victimized, particularly in the areas of developing and maintaining intimate relationships and trusting others. As noted by Kelly (1988:216), though, these responses should be regarded as *positive* ones rather than as "symptoms:"

> Women's coping strategies are directed towards both controlling the impact of sexual violence and protecting themselves from further abuse. Distrust of men and conflicts about heterosexuality are not 'dysfunctional' reactions but part of women's active and adaptive attempts to cope with the reality of sexual violence . . . Whilst sexual violence is so prevalent and the vast majority of men so unwilling to change their attitudes and behavior, it is in women's interests to insist that trust will not be given automatically—it has to be earned. It is the reality of men's violence which creates the necessity of women's distrust.

Thus, Kelly is suggesting (and I heartily concur) that we *should* have interpersonal "symptoms," as these are highly effective ways whereby we take back control of our lives and reconstruct our boundaries—critical issues for anyone who has had their visions of the world and their views of themselves shattered. The other side of the debate is that we cannot go through the remainder of our lives isolated and distrusting everyone around us; rather, in time, we need to strike a balance between these two extremes. This balance, though, should *not* be an early component or an early goal of recovery; rather, it must wait until we have arrived at a clearer sense of who we are.

Our relationships with immediate family members also are regarded as potential trouble spots. This is particularly true for those of us who as children were violated by "loved ones," were *not* protected from them by other family members, and did *not* have supportive significant others once the sexual victimization was acknowledged. In order to resolve these relationships, some experts have suggested the goals of forgiveness and forging healthier relationships with them (Farmer 1989; Finney 1990; Ratner 1990). As Swink and Leveille (1986:135–136) summarize this point of view: "Occasionally, with a new attitude and if there have been some major changes in the family (such as abuser and spouse divorced, or an alcoholic became sober), then a new relationship can be formed." Swink and Leveille are quick to add, though, that these should be goals *only* in situations where: (1) family members are willing to acknowledge their abusive behaviors or roles in permitting the abuse to occur; and (2) we are realistic about what we want from these people.

It is important to add that a much different solution also has been offered: that we need *not* forgive these people at all. In other words, some experts now advise us to have *nothing* to do with them (Dinsmore 1991; Forward with Buck 1989; Herman 1992; Swink and Leveille 1986). Since more often than *not* they are unwilling to admit their involvement, continue to deny the "allegation" of incest, and/or are unwilling to make the necessary changes to improve their relationships with us, we must take drastic action. In these situations, Swink and Leveille (1986:136) offer the option of "orphanization":

> This necessitates giving up the hope that she will someday
> get the . . . [family] that she has always needed . . . Then
> she must break old patterns with [them] . . . Often the
> pressure to return to old patterns is so great, that for her
> own self-protection she must break all ties with the
> family—no longer attending family functions/rituals, no
> longer having contact with the family . . . [S]he must take
> care of herself, not them . . . Then she will feel free of the
> degradations, manipulations and abusiveness. Although
> this may seem to be a difficult solution, for many of us it is
> the only one which can lead to true recovery and healing
> of these old wounds.

I for one am glad to see this latter option "in print"; I have
grown tired of approaches that emphasize forgiveness of the
abuser (and other involved parties), "understanding" his/her
motives, and/or "turning the other cheek." Rather, I prefer the
viewpoint that *there are some things that people do to us that are
inherently unforgivable and that we should not be made to feel guilty
for making that admission and/or for our decision to break these bonds*
(Herman 1992; Miller 1990; Swink and Leveille 1986). As
expressed by Forward with Buck (1989:189): "The more I thought
about it, the more I realized that this absolution was really
another form of denial: 'If I forgive you, we can pretend that
what happened wasn't so terrible.' I came to realize that this
aspect of forgiveness was actually preventing a lot of people [i.e.,
survivors] from getting on with their lives." An added reason
why I like this option is that it affords us the opportunity to
disengage from these "crazy" ties and to select what some now
call a "family of choice" or a "family of creation" (Dinsmore
1991; Swink and Leveille 1986), i.e., surrounding ourselves with
people that we consciously select to interact with in familial
ways. Finally, and perhaps most importantly, this approach
retains the girl or the woman who has been sexually victimized
as the *protagonist* in her own story. Rather than emphasizing
whether and/or how to go about forgiving others, the focus
remains on her—her needs, her desires, and what is best for her
(Forward with Buck 1989).

Similar to what has been said about interpersonal
difficulties, *cognitive difficulties*, in large part, come from what

Janoff-Bulman (1985, 1992) calls our "shattered assumptions" about the world: "As a result of their victimization, . . . the assumptions that formerly enabled them to function effectively no longer serve as guides for behavior" (Janoff-Bulman 1985:22). The specific assumptions that get shattered include our beliefs that we are invulnerable, the world is meaningful and comprehensible, and we are valuable. Shattering the first and third assumptions can result in feelings of powerlessness, helplessness, and insecurity, while the disruption of the second one can cause us to feel confused, particularly if we tended to view ourselves as good people (Janoff-Bulman 1985, 1992).

This, though, is only part of the story. Once we acknowledge that our prior vision of the world has been destroyed, the logical next step is to come up with a new one:

> To a great extent, coping with victimization involves . . .
> reestablishing a conceptual system that will allow the
> victim to once again function effectively . . . While victims
> are not likely to ever again view the world as wholly
> benevolent, or themselves as entirely invulnerable, they
> will still need to work on establishing a view of the world
> as not wholly malevolent and of themselves as not
> uniquely vulnerable to misfortune (Janoff-Bulman
> 1985:22).

This dictates that we must consciously and actively work toward developing a new worldview, one which includes an awareness of our vulnerability to victimization and a realistic assessment of the randomness of such events (Fine 1990; Herman 1992; Janoff-Bulman 1992). This, though, can be a difficult, arduous process, particularly if we experience what Janoff-Bulman (1992) labels "human-induced victimizations." In these situations, someone intentionally sets out to harm us, and this necessitates that we confront and acknowledge the existence of evil, examine the trustworthiness of others, and adapt to the "possibility of living in a morally bankrupt universe" (Janoff-Bulman 1992:78).

An important approach to resolving our shattered assumptions about the world has been offered by Antonovsky (1979, 1984, 1987). He calls it "sense of coherence" (hereafter,

SOC). According to Antonovsky (1987:17), SOC is a worldview or:

> a global orientation that expresses the extent to which one has a pervasive, enduring though dynamic feeling of confidence that (1) the stimuli deriving from one's internal and external environments in the course of living are structured, predictable, and explicable; (2) the resources are available to one to meet the demands posed by these stimuli; and (3) these demands are challenges, worthy of investment and engagement.

In other words, if people believe that the world makes sense, that they are able to manage their lives, and something or someone is important to them, they fare better when confronted with harsh life events.

Although he does not address the merits of applying this social-psychological construct to the survivors of sexual victimization, he and others have shown its value for people who are recovering from other sorts of catastrophic life events [e.g., surviving a Nazi deathcamp, grieving the death of a loved one (Antonovsky 1987; Fiorentino 1986; Margalit 1985; Rumbaut et al. 1981)]. Based upon the content of this perspective, though, I believe that it readily can be applied to girls, adolescent females, and adult women who are recovering from sexual victimization. Moreover, it is *not* easy to arrive at new visions of the world, but if we are to move *beyond* survival (or just "holding on for dear life") and truly heal the wounds of sexual victimization, doing so is an essential component of this process (Janoff-Bulman 1992). The bottom line is that we must develop new "cognitive maps," or attitudes and beliefs which not only acknowledge our misfortune but also move us beyond feeling "sorry" for ourselves or remaining "stuck." Doing so should redirect our attention toward optimistic and healing images, and Antonovsky's SOC, clearly, is one such option.

Our problematic post-victimization *self-perceptions* share many similarities to the aforementioned cognitive and psychological difficulties. That is to say, we also can suffer from a shattered sense of self and have difficulty knowing who we are. It is important to add that some works which examine responses to traumatic events are finding that people do *not* return to "normal" afterwards, that they no longer view themselves in the same way. As examples, Herman (1992) suggests that individuals develop new identities, identities which incorporate the realities of their trauma, while Janoff-Bulman (1992) focuses on how people develop different assumptions about themselves and the world, assumptions that incorporate their negative life experiences. In sum: "Her task now is to become the person she wants to be. In the process, she draws upon those aspects of herself that she most values from the time before the trauma, from the experience of the trauma itself, and from the period of recovery. Integrating all of these elements, she creates a new self, both ideally and in actuality" (Herman 1992:202).

Other experts have offered the metaphors of voice and silence to describe the difficulties with which many women struggle (Jack 1991). For example, Reis (1991b:143) speaks of how entrenched the problem of silence is for many if not most of us, its origins, and how to resolve not having a voice: "What grows out of female fear is a certain kind of female silence. Silence born of fear is what has stopped women dead in our tracks for centuries. Breaking the silence, finding our voice, and speaking our truths are some of the major works for women today." In addition, Belenky et al. (1986) have found that the "silent" women in their study usually had histories of severe deprivation and/or had been the victims of violence as children. In other words, these women had been beaten (sometimes figuratively, other times literally) into "silence" and submission by their home lives, as well as a society that devalued them; and as adults, they continued to live isolated, unfulfilled lives. The solution to this problem comes with gaining a voice or the stage of constructed knowledge, i.e., "attempting to *integrate* knowledge that . . . [is] personally important with knowledge . . . [that is] learned from others . . . of weaving together the strands of rational and emotive thought and of integrating objective and subjective knowing" (Belenky et al. 1986:134).

As for the specific experience of sexual victimization, Barringer (1992:8) eloquently speaks of the value of "breaking the silence" and "coming to voice," particularly if we were victimized as children:

> Speaking is a profoundly significant act for the survivor of
> childhood sexual abuse. To speak of her abuse, the
> survivor must not only defy her perpetrator's threats and
> the societal taboo, but she must also give up the very
> protections that have enabled her to survive—the
> forgetting, the denial, the numbness. She must push
> against the enormous weight of her isolation and shame.
> Just as she trained herself, in childhood, to endure in
> silence, she must now retrain the tongue, the throat, the
> chest, to release the words that choke her into paralysis.

She also adds the healing ramifications of coming to voice and
that the process is "an act of courage" which enables the
survivor to "reclaim herself for herself" (Barringer 1992:8).

Added problems for many of us who have been raped
and/or have histories of childhood sexual abuse are that we
have poor self-esteem and tend to blame ourselves for having
been sexually victimized (Bass and Davis 1988; Burgess and
Holmstrom 1979b; Dinsmore 1991; Steinem 1992). Both of these
consequences, if "compounded," can lead to the added
difficulties of depression, self-destructive behaviors, and/or
eating disorders. In order for women to have good self-images,
some experts now suggest that as adults, they must: (1) go back
and reclaim their girlhood selves [i.e., reclaim who they were
before they were pressured into putting on their "feminine
masks" (Hancock 1989)]; (2) strive to develop egalitarian
relationships with others because doing so affords opportunities
to grow (Hancock 1989; Sanford and Donovan 1984); (3) examine
and let go of negative illusions about themselves [e.g., others'
evaluations as totally accurate and that they have no other
choices (Sanford and Donovan 1984)]; and (4) begin to view self
as a friend rather than an enemy (Sanford and Donovan 1984).

It is important to underscore the fact that although self-
image and self-esteem are problems for many if not most girls,
adolescent females, and adult women in this culture, these are
even more pressing concerns for the survivors of sexual
victimization, particularly the ones who were victimized as
children. As noted by Bass and Davis (1988:178):

> For survivors, these issues are heightened [because y]ou
> were damaged early. Something was broken at a core
> level. The reality that you were precious, that you

> deserved love, that you were capable, that you were okay
> just the way you were, was denied you as a child . . .
> Instead, you were abused. You were left feeling dirty,
> somehow at fault. And the way you were forced to cope
> may have left you feeling even worse about yourself . . .

Bass and Davis (1988:178–190) argue, though, this need *not* be a "life sentence" and that there are very specific steps that she can take to improve her view of self. Examples include changing the negative internalized messages that were placed into her mind during the abuse, positive self-affirmations, setting limits and boundaries, living for herself, doing things that she is proud of, and accentuating the positive.

Other literatures also have a great deal to say about the relationship between self-perceptions and recovering from difficult life events. For example, if we examine the literature which explores the connection between perceived stress and life events, we see that the social-psychological concepts of locus of control, fatalism, mastery, competence, self-efficacy, optimism, and resiliency can buffer us from the devastating impact of our negative life events. Although different, these concepts also are similar in that they tap the dimension of our perceptions of control, as well as beliefs about our abilities to achieve what we set out to do; and they operate to alleviate stress in our lives (Dean 1985). As examples, people who exhibit the pattern of internal *locus of control* tend to cope more effectively with their life events (Lefcourt 1985), while people who believe that their lives are being controlled by external factors are much more likely to become depressed (Becker and Heimberg 1985) or to exhibit the cognitive and behavioral pattern of learned helplessness (Abramsom et al. 1978; Seligman 1975). Similarly, people who evidence a low level of *fatalism* cope well with their life changes (Thoits 1987; Wheaton 1985), while high levels of *mastery* (Folkman et al. 1986; Kessler and Essex 1982; Moos and Billings 1982), *competence* (Dean 1986; Mechanic and Hansell 1987; Moos and Billings 1982), *self-efficacy* (Downey and Moen 1987; Moos and Billings 1982), *optimism* (Scheier and Carver 1985, 1987; Scheier et al. 1986; Seligman 1991), and *resiliency* (Herman 1992; Werner and Smith 1982) are associated with good health and an overall sense of well-being. In sum, each of these constructs has been found to reduce the impact of negative life events, act as a buffer against perceived stress, and predict the utilization of efficient coping strategies.

Regarding sexual victimization, I believe that these concepts are important ones. As was noted earlier in this section, females have *not* been taught and/or encouraged to have good images of themselves or to have a strong "voice;" we also can add to this list that girls, adolescent females, and adult women have *not* been encouraged to develop internal loci of control, mastery, competence, and self-efficacy. Since improving self-perceptions must be a critical component of any program aimed at recovering from sexual victimization, one way to achieve this goal would be to stimulate the development of these sorts of traits. (This issue will be examined further in the next chapter.)

Sexual problems, too, are possible post-sexual-victimization consequences. As was summarized in the last chapter, oftcited ones include a variety of sexual dysfunctions (e.g., impaired desire, inability to achieve orgasm, pain during intercourse), fear of sex, and flashbacks during sex. Recovering sexually, though, is no easy task because to do so we have to learn to trust someone else, and this is often one of the most difficult issues with which we as victims and survivors of sexual victimization grapple. To reclaim our sexual selves, then, we must come to understand ourselves better, learn to be in charge of our own sexual experiences, learn to be clear about what we want sexually as well as what we can and cannot do, and select intimates based upon their willingness to hear our concerns and respect our wishes (Bass and Davis 1988; Herman 1992; Maltz and Holman 1987). Recovering sexually also entails that we separate the past from the present and come to the realization that our current sexual experiences do *not* have to cause pain. These sorts of goals, though, can only be achieved in relationships that are based on mutual trust and respect. This entails open communication with a partner, taking it slowly, and possibly even a period of celibacy during which we examine and clarify what it is we want. Only then can our sexual lives be rewarding and fulfilling.[5]

Regarding the *political ramifications* of sexual victimization, these really are signs of recovery rather than "symptoms" of pathology. As is noted earlier in this chapter, to become politically aware or active (i.e., the transition from individual survival to collective resistance, the survivor's mission, becoming enlightened witnesses) infers that we have come to understand the brutal realities of sexual victimization and its political and structural underpinnings (Bolz 1991; Dinsmore 1991; Herman 1992; Kelly 1988). Yet few of the experts, particularly practitioners who treat the victims and survivors of sexual victimization, acknowledge this very important connection or are aware that discussions of recovery and healing must include issues outside of the individual.

An exception to this criticism is Conn (1991:71), a therapist who speaks of the serious failing of most psychological theories—that they regard the self as a "bounded, masterful agent which is separate from and prior to the 'outside world,' almost as if in a vacuum." The impact of this sort of counterproductive thinking has been to examine personal pain without reference to larger contexts or the social, political, and/or cultural forces which are at work. As Conn (1991:72) expresses this issue, "[W]e as a culture tend to pathologize and individualize personal pain, viewing any 'pain for the world' as a personal and probably pathological experience that has been projected outward." In turn, clients who try to tie their pain to larger, more global concerns are regarded as "ill," or, at least, "projecting." In other words, we need to correct our thinking about this issue: If women increase their awareness of the political components of sexual victimization, come to see the connections between themselves and others who have had similar experiences, link their personal pain to social or structural factors, initiate political activity to do something to stem the problems of rape, incest, and/or child sexual abuse, these are *not* "signs" of pathology. Rather, these attitudes and behaviors are proof that they are well on their way to recovery, growth, and healing, and a tremendous disservice is done by the experts when they try to "privatize" their pain (Herman 1992; Reis 1991b).

As for the *spiritual dimension* of our lives, although most of the works which address this issue appear in the incest and child sexual abuse literatures,[6] many of the ideas apply equally well to adolescent females and adult women who have been raped. The primary conclusion is that many of us who were sexually victimized in childhood end up as adults being *unable* to believe in anything beyond ourselves (if we can manage that), and, in the worst-case scenario, we end up feeling hollow inside or perhaps even dead. This means that in order to survive or to continue living, many of us learned to shut down our feelings and to feel numb or dead inside (Bass and Davis 1988; Dolan 1991; Farmer 1989; Herman 1992). Although these can be effective survival strategies for children, continuing to live in these ways as we age and mature can compound our problems and impede our ability to achieve the goals of healing, growth, recovery, and victory.

In order to recover spiritually, then, we have to fill in the "hollow spaces" and feel alive again. This entails finding something to do, someone to be with, and/or something that we can believe in again. For some of us, religion is the answer. As examples, Finney (1990) found relief in the act and the power of prayer; Bass and Davis (1988:157) suggest that "[i]f you have an established religious path, faith will probably play a strong part in your healing," while Herman (1992:196) notes that "old beliefs that gave meaning to her life have been challenged; now she must find anew a sustaining faith."

But what about those of us who for a long time have rejected formal religion and all of its trappings? In response to this question, Bass and Davis (1988:156) offer options that do *not* involve traditional, religious dogmas or practices:

> A healing spirituality is the opposite of . . . alienation. It's a passion for life, a feeling of connection, of being a part of the life around you. Many people experience this in nature, watching the ocean roll in, looking out over a vast prairie, walking in the desert. When you are truly intimate with another human being, when you are uplifted through singing, when you look at a child and feel wonder, you are in touch with something bigger than yourself . . . And, that's spirituality: staying in touch with the part of you that is choosing to heal, that wants to be healthy, integrated, fully alive.

Another nontraditional option that is offered by Reis (1991b:14–15) is a woman-centered belief system that involves reclaiming the Goddess:

> What I have found . . . is that an awareness of the Goddess helps to awaken women to ways in which our deepest female body experiences, our psyche's realities, and our spiritual quests are all related . . .
>
> What I hope to uncover is a new women-centered awareness of how the archetypal world of Goddess images and myths informs and gives meaning to the seemingly mundane events in our everyday lives.

Other authors contend that creativity plays a critical role in achieving a new sense of spirituality (Wisechild 1988, 1991). For example, Miller (1990) notes that her own healing journey began when she initiated "spontaneous painting." During that process, she not only began to remember her history of childhood physical abuse, but she also began to heal from it. Reis (1991a), a therapist who works with survivors of incest and child sexual abuse, notes the importance of drawing and painting in the recovery from childhood sexual abuse for one of her clients, a woman named Susan. Although some might look at some of Susan's images and see violence, anger, and bitterness, you have only to look a bit deeper to see the healing images which show that she has learned to express her anger and has taken back control of her life.

Still others have begun to employ the very important healing metaphor of rebirth. Blume (1990:304), for example, suggests that: "Facing a problem is a rebirth . . . [; p]urifying a sin that was not hers, she becomes her own parent . . . [and t]hrough healing and finding her power, she is, like the phoenix, reborn." Tessier (1992:18) articulates why this "rebirth" is even necessary: "[W]e must understand that a death has occurred. More than childhood lost or innocence destroyed, our spirits, our selves, our structures of existence have been shattered, and a new life requires rebirth. This requires a communal effort, a relational project . . . We need friends, therapists, communities who will share the [re]birthing." In other words, it may *not* be enough for many of us "just" to change our images of ourselves, to alter our images of the world around us, and to devise "non-traditional" forms of spirituality; in order to return to some semblance of who we were prior to our sexual victimizations and/or to "let go" of these traumas, some of us may need rebirthing ceremonies and cleansing rituals (i.e., actual or allegorical resurrections of the self) to accomplish these goals (Bass and Davis 1988; Dinsmore 1991; Dolan 1991; Reis 1991b; Tessier 1992). I hasten to add that these sorts of ceremonies and rituals should *not* be the starting points of the recovery process; rather, they should occur toward the end, well after you have done much of the work of talking about your pain, understanding its depths and current impact on your life, and have come to accept that sexual victimization is a part of your life.

Once again, some experts emphasize the notion of self-forgiveness and forgiving others as part of one's spiritual recovery. For example, Sanford (1990:173) indicates that: "[S]urvivors must first forgive themselves for being helpless and innocent and cease denial and minimization before they can begin to forgive others . . . [and that f]orgiving others unclutters one's own life." Although a number of authors concur that self-forgiveness is an important component of recovery (Bass and Davis 1988; Dinsmore 1991; Engel 1989; Herman 1992), as was noted earlier in this chapter, we must be *very careful* with the notion of forgiving *others*. It is up to each one of us to make our own determination about whether to expand this notion to anyone other than ourselves; if it works for you, fine; but forgiving others is not for all of us, nor does it need to be.

As was detailed in the last chapter, *subsequent victimization(s)* is clearly linked to several issues including viewing ourselves as victims, devaluing ourselves, and buying into the existing mythology which surrounds the subject of sexual victimization. When we speak of recovery as including warding off subsequent victimization(s), then this is *not* a simple nor an easy task but rather one which involves psychological concerns, behavioral components, interpersonal issues, cognitive restructuring, changes in our self-perceptions, spiritual healing, and perhaps political awareness. In effect, if we heal in these other spheres of our lives (i.e., come to view self as valuable, take charge of our lives rather than feeling helpless, develop healthy relationships, come to have different views of the world and ourselves, recapture or discover a spiritual dimension, and come to a new perspective as to the politics of victimization) chances are good, but *not* certain, that we may be able to avoid future victimizations. Conversely, if we have *not* recovered from being sexually victimized and have *not* healed the resultant wounds, it is likely that we will continue to live in ways that lead to future victimization(s). I am *not* suggesting that this is a conscious decision made by girls, adolescent females, and adult women; rather, I regard subsequent victimization(s) as one more risk that each of us takes *until* we move beyond survival and begin to work toward the more optimistic goals of recovery, healing, triumph, thriving, and victory. It is equally important to underscore the fact that girls and women *cannot* be the only ones making the changes; if this society continues to devalue and disregard us, no matter how many improvements we make as individuals, the prospect of being victimized again and again remains a distinct possibility for all of us.

Thus, concepts such as recovery, healing, growth, or victory refer to a complicated process which demands that we focus on all of the different spheres of our lives. We must not only be aware of how rape, incest, and/or child sexual abuse have affected us in the psychological, somatic, behavioral, interpersonal, cognitive, self-perceptual, sexual, political, and spiritual arenas of our lives, but we also must be willing to make changes in each of these dimensions. Although this is a process which requires great effort, it is facilitated when the people around us support our efforts. In sum, many children who have been sexually abused, as well as many adult survivors of rape and/or childhood sexual abuse, cannot recover from these experiences by themselves (particularly if they were involved in the more brutal and traumatizing abuse situations); they need at least one other person to help them and to support them while they are going through this process (Courtois 1992; Herman 1992; Janoff-Bulman 1992). Yet (and as was noted earlier), two of the most frequently mentioned long-term aftereffects of sexual victimization are problematic views of self and shattered assumptions about the world, both of which can impede our ability to get that help from another person. The obvious question becomes: how can the girls, adolescent females, and adult women who have these "symptoms" accept the kindness and support of anyone else when they have lost their abilities to trust and to love themselves and others? Herein lies the ultimate dilemma: The very things that we need the most (e.g., a soft, nondemanding kind of love and gentle, healing touches) are the very things that we no longer can bear. I believe, though, that our options really are few and far between: Either we make the decision to do whatever it takes to heal ourselves, or we end up living half-lives of misery, loneliness, and despair, or we die.

In sum, recovery is a difficult process, but it also is an achievable one. We, though, cannot be lulled into thinking that we work toward the goals of recovery quickly or without snags; we will have setbacks and the process will, at times, seem unbearable. Often, we move forward one step only to fall back two. But if we continue to aim for the optimistic goals of recovery, healing, thriving, growth, and victory, we will eventually make it, and all of the work will seem worthwhile. These concepts are eloquently expressed by Janoff-Bulman (1992:174–175):

> The inner worlds of victims who have 'recovered' now reflect an acknowledgment of misfortune, an awareness of vulnerability. These survivors know that their prior assumptions were naive, that tragedy can strike and that no one is invulnerable . . . [Thus,] these survivors recognize the possibility of tragedy, but do not allow it to pervade their self and worldviews . . .

> Trauma survivors no longer move through life unmindful of existence; they can more readily relish the good, for they all too well know the bad. They have made their peace with the inevitable shortcomings of our existence and have a new appreciation of life and a realization of what is really important . . . And the trauma survivor emerges somewhat sadder, but considerably wiser.

Models which Explain Recovery, Resolution, Healing, and Victory

During the 1970s and 1980s, experts began to explain our reactions to sexual victimization by focusing on the stages that we go through afterwards, and we now have several models which explain these stages, as well as the issues involved in this process. Although there is *not* consensus regarding the nature of recovery, the steps involved, and the theoretical underpinnings of this process, in the following section I summarize and critique a number of perspectives which examine these issues. Regarding rape, these include three crisis intervention models (i.e., the works of Sutherland and Scherl, Burgess and Holmstrom, and Forman), the social learning approach which is predominantly the contribution of Kilpatrick and his associates, the post-traumatic stress disorder model, and the more recent and eclectic works of Koss and Harvey, Ledray, and Braswell. The models which outline recovering from incest and child sexual abuse are detailed later in this chapter.

The Rape Recovery Process

Early works which detailed the reaction process of adolescent and adult rape victims took their lead from *crisis intervention theory*. Drawing from the works of Lindemann (1944) and Caplan (1964), contemporary proponents of this perspective assumed that reactions to life events were neither signs of illness nor pathological states (Burgess and Holmstrom 1979b, 1985; Calhoun and Atkeson 1991; Golan 1978; Hoff 1978; Resick and Schnicke 1990). Rather, they regarded them as normal, short-term reactions to very real crisis situations in people's current lives.

During the 1970s and early 1980s, several theorists began to relate these ideas to the specific trauma of rape. Three models in particular warrant our attention. First of all, based upon the assumption that recovering from rape is different than recovering from other sorts of crisis events, Sutherland and Scherl (1970, 1972) developed a three-stage model to highlight these differences. They suggest that the initial stage, or acute reactions, includes the responses of shock, disbelief, agitation, incoherence, and anxiety that can last anywhere from a few days to a few weeks. Although labeled outward adjustment, the second step in their model refers to a period of pseudo-adjustment. That is to say, based upon outward appearances, the woman looks and acts "better," yet what usually is happening is that she is denying that the rape occurred and/or suppressing its effects. The final stage is integration and resolution, which begins when the woman develops an inner sense of depression and a need to talk about the rape; this usually starts after an event reminiscent of the attack occurs or when the defenses that she has been utilizing no longer hold her pain at bay.[7]

The second crisis intervention model is Burgess and Holmstrom's (1974, 1979b) now-classic rape trauma syndrome. Their model suggests that our reactions to rape involve a two-stage process.[8] During the impact phase, the woman experiences a variety of "symptoms" (e.g., somatic complaints, behavioral changes, altered interpersonal patterns, fears, and anxiety). The second stage or outcome of this model, reorganization, originally was depicted as putting the realities of rape into a workable perspective and returning to one's *pre-rape* level of functioning. In a later work, though, Burgess and Holmstrom (1979b:35) conceptualized it as "the long-term process in which the victim must reorganize this disrupted lifestyle" (i.e., they moved away from an emphasis on returning to "normal").

The final crisis intervention model is Forman's (1980, 1983) five-stage model of recovery. The initial phase occurs during the rape and shortly thereafter, and the major response is shock. The second stage is denial; although she has an outward appearance of adjustment, the woman really is living her life superficially and mechanically. Third is the decompensation or symptom formation stage which involves the recurring feelings experienced during the rape (e.g., rape-related fears, anxiety, depression, guilt, shame, nightmares, feeling vulnerable, helplessness, alienation, and/or isolation). Fourth is anger which includes not only the visible signs of rage but also the less obvious and underlying issues of despair, hopelessness, and shame. Fifth is the outcome of this model or resolution which "is achieved as the victims accept the sexual assault as a part of their past [and t]he incident itself and circumstances surrounding post-assault behavior should be viewed by victims as a significant life experience, integrated among other experiences" (Forman 1980:310).

A fairly recent approach to explain post-rape reaction process is the *social learning model.* Predominantly the contribution of Kilpatrick and his colleagues (Atkeson et al 1982; Calhoun and Atkeson 1991; Calhoun et al. 1982; Ellis et al. 1981; Kilpatrick et al. 1979, 1981, 1985; Resick et al. 1981), this perspective assumes that rape is a real-life example of classical conditioning: "Any stimuli present during the rape . . . [can] become associated with the fear response through . . . classical conditioning. These cues then become conditioned stimuli which can evoke that same anxiety and fear responses in other situations" (Kilpatrick et al. 1981:110). In other words, anything which reminds the woman of her assault can cause these responses to occur again and again, thereby crystalizing them into a generalized fear response.

Kilpatrick and his associates have conducted several empirical analyses to test the merits of their model and have concluded that it is an accurate representation of what happens after a sexual assault. Their findings suggest that: (1) women who have been raped evidence a multitude of responses initially as well as two weeks later (Kilpatrick et al. 1979, 1981, 1985; Resick 1983); (2) although many of these acute "symptoms" subside two and three months later, problems remain, particularly with anxiety, fears, and work adjustment (Kilpatrick et al. 1979; Resick et al. 1981); (3) six to eight months later, anxiety, fears, and adjustment problems at work remain at high levels (Kilpatrick et al. 1979; Resick 1983; Resick et al. 1981); and (4) one year to four years post-rape, many women continue to evidence difficulties, particularly with anxiety, fears, and depression (Atkeson et al. 1982; Calhoun et al. 1982; Ellis et al. 1981; Kilpatrick et al. 1981, 1985; Resick 1983). As an added feature, these authors have developed a treatment program, the goal of which is to desensitize women's rape-related fears. (This treatment model is discussed in the next chapter.)

Another popular view which examines post-rape consequences is the *post-traumatic stress disorder* (hereafter PTSD) model (Calhoun and Atkeson 1991; Herman 1992; Janoff-Bulman 1992; Koss and Harvey 1991; Kramer and Green 1991; Resick and Schnicke 1990; Saunders et al. 1990; Stekette and Foa 1987; Trimble 1985; Wilson et al. 1985). The traditional definition of PTSD entails reactions to traumatic events that are outside the range of our normal experiences (e.g., natural disasters, being the victim of a crime, war experiences, and being the victim of terrorism). In order to qualify for this diagnosis, though, additional criteria must be present, including: (1) "symptoms" that persist for several months afterward or ones that follow a delayed-onset pattern (i.e., reactions begin six months or more after the negative life event); (2) if exposed to events reminiscent of the earlier trauma, the original event is reexperienced via intrusive thoughts or memories, flashbacks, recurrent dreams, or stress responses; (3) stimuli associated with the original trauma are avoided; and (4) increased arousal is manifested via disrupted sleep patterns, irritability, anger, difficulty concentrating, hypervigilance, startle responses, and a variety of somatic responses (Calhoun and Atkeson 1991; Herman 1992; Koss and Harvey 1991; Kramer and Green 1991). Janoff-Bulman (1992:50), though, suggests that the real importance of this new diagnostic category is that it provides "a single category for traumatic events," and that the earlier tradition in psychology that posited the need for preexisting pathology in order to cause traumatic reactions to current life events is omitted. In sum, "What is clear is that there are extreme life events that will produce psychological difficulties not in a vulnerable few, but in large numbers of people exposed to them" (Janoff-Bulman 1992:50).

Specific to the experience of rape, this model has been found to be an effective explanation for many of the initial as well as the long-term responses of adolescent females and adult women who have been raped. As examples, several experts now conclude that adolescent girls and women can: have a delayed-onset, post-rape response pattern; evidence long-term difficulty recovering from a sexual assault; experience flashbacks which repeat the original trauma; and develop all sorts of long-term, rape-related fears and phobias (Burgess and Holmstrom 1979b; Calhoun and Atkeson 1991; Koss and Harvey 1991; Kramer and Green 1991; Saunders et al. 1990). In fact, more and more works have begun to move away from a crisis explanation of rape and have replaced that earlier view with the PTSD perspective.

In a recent work, Herman (1992:119) cautions that the PTSD model may be too simplistic, particularly when applied to severe cases of trauma: "The current formulation of post-traumatic stress disorder fails to capture either the protean symptomatic manifestations of prolonged, repeated trauma or the profound deformation of personality that occur in captivity." To resolve this dilemma, she proposes the "complex post-traumatic stress disorder syndrome," which better explains the experiences of hostages, prisoners of war, and deathcamp survivors, as well as survivors of domestic violence, organized sexual exploitation, and particularly brutal rapes. Thus, her reconceptualization names and recognizes the potential aftereffects associated with prolonged exploitation and/or terror: "It is an attempt to find a language that is at once faithful to the traditions of accurate psychological observation and to the moral demands of traumatized people. It is an attempt to learn from survivors, who understand, more profoundly than any investigator, the effects of captivity" (Herman 1992:122). This is *not* simply a reformulation of the old PTSD concept; rather, it is an acknowledgment that there are degrees of trauma, as well as degrees of responses to them.

Koss and Harvey's (1991) *eclectic model* explains post-rape consequences as a process which involves working toward and achieving several goals. Specifically, they have developed a four-stage model which is a compilation of the aforementioned works of Burgess and Holmstrom, Forman, and Sutherland and Scherl. It includes: (1) the anticipatory phase "during which the victim's earliest recognition develops into a situation that is potentially dangerous"; (2) the impact phase or the actual rape and its immediate aftermath, i.e., the "disintegration and disorganization" which result from having experienced an "intense fear of death or serious bodily harm"; (3) reconstitution, which begins when the woman attempts to put her life back in order (this stage is similar to Sutherland and Scherl's stage of pseudoadjustment); and (4) resolution, which includes feeling and resolving such emotions as anger, despair, hopelessness, and shame (Koss and Harvey 1991:48–55).

Koss and Harvey also include several goals that they believe must be achieved if one is to recover from rape. They are: (1) gaining "control over the remembering process and *not* the reverse (i.e., the individual can elect whether or not to recall events that previously intruded)"; (2) integrating memories and feelings (i.e., "things are remembered with affect that is appropriate in intensity to the thing remembered"); (3) learning to be tolerant of one's affect (i.e., it no longer overwhelms her); (4) symptom mastery, or reducing one's current symptoms of anxiety, depression, and sexual dysfunction to levels which are manageable; (5) being able once again to attach or reconnect with others; and (6) developing acceptable meanings about the sexual victimization and self as a survivor [i.e., "losses have been named and mourned and given a meaning that allows the victim to move forward through life" (Koss and Harvey 1991:176–177).

Ledray's (1986:100–115) *self-help approach* to recover from rape victimization has four components: (1) evaluating one's resources, internal as well as those in the environment; (2) coping with fear, anger, and depression via the tactics of combatting negative thoughts and feelings, overcoming fears, and expressing anger in positive ways; (3) rebuilding self-esteem; and (4) learning to enjoy sex again. Depending upon the severity of "symptoms," as well as the woman's ability to accomplish all of this alone, Ledray indicates that this process can be achieved a number of different ways, including working with skilled professionals, doing it alone, and/or accomplishing it with the loving support of significant others. More important than with whom you do this work, though, is acknowledging that these are the areas across which we need to recover.

Braswell (1989), as well, offers a *self-help plan* to heal the wounds of rape victimization. For her, the process entails the specific tasks of: (1) feeling the pain, particularly the fears, the anger, and the depression; (2) making new decisions about future safety and sexuality; (3) developing new insights regarding self and friends, as well as insights about how to live; and (4) "letting go," or making the decision to have a good life.

According to Braswell (1989:52), this last step is essential because it allows us to live in healthy ways:

> Holding on to the pain, the anger, and the depression puts limits on your potential growth . . . [and it] can keep you stuck in a place where you have little or no vision. It can color your insight, sour your soul with bitterness, and keep the barriers to freedom rigid . . . From that point of view, you see the world as a hateful place. Letting go of the pain restores you and enables you to reclaim your personal power.

Each of these models has merit and has increased our understanding of reactions to rape. For example, the crisis intervention perspective shows us that responses to traumatic events such as rape victimization are normal and to be expected rather than signs of pathology. This model also is valuable because it can be used to explain crisis responses to a variety of negative life events. The PTSD model, as well, is noteworthy because it emphasizes the normalcy of our reactions to extraordinary or traumatic life events such as rape (Koss and Harvey 1991; Scurfield 1985; Stekette and Foa 1987), focuses on the seriousness of the negative life event, and deemphasizes the weakness of the respondent (Blume 1990). In addition (and as was the case with the crisis perspective), the PTSD model can be used not only to explain post-rape stress responses but also reactions to a number of other negative life events which involve perceived threat and/or loss (Herman 1992). The social learning perspective clarifies the process whereby we develop fears and phobias after being sexually victimized, while the primary contribution of Koss and Harvey, Ledray, and Braswell is to clarify the major issues to be resolved during the process of recovery from rape victimization.

There also, though, are problems with each of these perspectives. The crisis viewpoint, for example, can be attacked theoretically based on: (1) its emphasis that the current crisis of rape may reactivate earlier, unresolved conflicts and lead to "exaggerated" or "inappropriate" responses; (2) the notion that we are supposed to go through a sequence of stages when resolving a rape experience; and (3) the fact that recovery is believed to take only six to eight weeks (Cohen and Nelson 1983;

Kilpatrick and Veronen 1983; King and Webb 1981; Koss and Harvey 1991; Nadelson et al. 1982; Resick and Schnicke 1990; Williams and Holmes 1981). In particular, critics have attacked this latter point, noting that most of us do *not* recover rapidly from a sexual assault. As contraindications, Burgess and Holmstrom (1979b) have found that women took varying amounts of time to recover fully from their rape experiences (i.e., 70 percent said that it took months or years to do so, and the remaining 30 percent continued to be disrupted five years later), while Kilpatrick et al. (1981) have concluded that only 20 to 25 percent of the women that they studied were symptom-free one year after being raped. In effect, this model assumes recovery is achieved once the individual's most noticeable acute symptoms have declined. Yet, as Herman (1992:165) notes, this can be a very inaccurate conclusion: "Though the survivor may make a rapid and dramatic return to the appearance of normal functioning, this symptomatic stabilization should not be mistaken for full recovery, for the integration of the trauma has not been accomplished." An added criticism of the crisis perspective is that it omits important elements of recovery. That is to say, most of the models mark movement from total disruption to some end point (integration, resolution, reorganization, reconstitution, and letting go), while they virtually ignore the active coping strategies of the women who have been raped.

In large part, the social learning perspective has *not* come under much fire because there really is little doubt regarding its accuracy. I would argue, though, that this perspective does *not* go far enough in improving our understanding of the trauma of rape. Although it has shown that many of us do respond by learning the post-rape "symptoms" of depression, anxiety, and fears, the social learning model pays little attention to the *underlying* meanings of these symptoms. In addition, this perspective fails to acknowledge the role of structural factors in causing and perpetuating the rape problem, as well as our responses to it, preferring instead to examine these issues at the psychological level of analysis.

Although the currently popular PTSD model is considered to be a good one, it, too, has its detractors. For one, Finkelhor

(1987) suggests that it does *not* account adequately for all of the "symptoms" experienced after a sexual assault. Specifically, the model locates most of the trauma in the affective realm; yet, it is often the cognitive realm that is the primary problem area for women who have been raped. In addition, although this explanation does outline how and why we develop post-traumatic responses, much less attention has been paid to how to go about reducing these "symptoms." Finally, there is disagreement regarding whether the trauma associated with rape is similar to the "symptomatology" associated with PTSD. Finkelhor (1988), for example, argues that the diagnosis of PTSD does *not* match the experiences of many women who have been raped, while Burgess and Holmstrom (1985), as well as Kramer and Green (1991), have reported that it does. In order to resolve some of these dilemmas, Herman's work is a step in the right direction; not only does she focus on the variability of our responses to a variety of different, traumatic life events, but she also outlines many of the specifics involved in recovering from them.

Regarding Koss and Harvey's (1991) perspective, although the stages and the goals that they include are critical ones, they do *not* illustrate clearly the specifics involved in achieving them. For example, they suggest that professional intervention is *not* always warranted; yet, they detail intervention via individual or group therapy. The models of Ledray (1986) and Braswell (1989), too, suffer from this same problem in that they outline the many goals of recovery but are much less explicit about the specifics involved in achieving them.

Recovery from Incest and Child Sexual Abuse

Several models also indicate why we react the ways that we do to sexual victimization which occurs in childhood, as well as the content of the process of recovering from these experiences. Models to be discussed include: (1) Finkelhor and Browne's traumagenic dynamics model, (2) Summit's child sexual abuse accommodation syndrome, (3) the post-traumatic stress disorder model, (4) Courtois' three-stage recovery process, (5) Bass and Davis' fourteen stages of recovery, (6) Swink and

Leveille's perspective, (7) Dinsmore's stages of incest recovery, and (8) Engel's seven step, self-help program.[9]

Since it clarifies not only how we respond to childhood sexual victimization but also why, the *traumagenic dynamics model* is a particularly important perspective (Finkelhor 1987, 1988; Finkelhor and Browne 1986). The crux of this theory is that incest or child sexual abuse produces devastation because it is "an experience that alters a child's cognitive or emotional orientation to the world and causes trauma by distorting . . . [her] self-concept, world view, or affective capacities" (Finkelhor 1987:354). Specifically, the four factors or traumagenic dynamics which are responsible for most of the damage are: traumatic sexualization, betrayal, stigmatization, and powerlessness.

Traumatic sexualization refers to sexualizing children prematurely (i.e., they come to have knowledge about sex and sexuality well before they are developmentally and cognitively equipped to understand them), and this causes them to acquire warped notions about sexual behavior and sexual morality which are based upon the offenders' views and behaviors. Betrayal includes not only betrayal at the hands of the perpetrator(s) but also via the inaction of nonoffending family members who do *not* protect or save her from harm. Stigmatization refers to the negative messages that are given to the sexually abused girl, i.e., that she is evil, worthless, shameful, and guilty. These messages are rendered not only by the perpetrator(s) but also via the attitudes of involved others if they disbelieve and/or attempt to discredit her "allegations." Finally, the child's powerlessness comes via two sources: (1) during the abuse, her will and sense of efficacy were damaged, and (2) the threat of injury or annihilation which exists in many cases of child sexual abuse.

Finkelhor (1987:359–360) also outlines the psychological and behavioral ramifications of these traumagenic dynamics. For example, traumatic sexualization can result in: a preoccupation with sex, compulsive masturbation and/or sex play, sexual behaviors and knowledge that are inappropriate for the child's age, sexual aggression, and the delayed onset of sexual difficulties (e.g., aversion to sex, flashbacks, arousal and orgasmic dysfunction). Betrayal is associated with: depression, dependency, clinging behaviors, hostility, anger, distrust of men, and a history of failed marriages. Third, stigmatization can cause low self-esteem, isolation, involvement with stigmatized groups (e.g., prostitutes, drug users), and self-destructive behaviors, including suicide attempts. Finally, the dynamic of power-essness can lead to fears and anxiety, impairment of coping skills, and the compensatory reaction of needing to control or dominate others. In sum, unless specific steps to change them are taken, the effects of incest and child sexual abuse can be extensive and may last a lifetime.

Summit's (1983) *child sexual abuse accommodation syndrome* involves five components. Please note that the first two focus on the vulnerability of the child or the preconditions needed for the abuse to occur, while the other three refer to what can happen after the abuse has occurred. First is the issue of secrecy. Since the child often is dependent upon the perpetrator, the abuse may be cloaked in secrecy, and this "proves" to her that what happened was bad and dangerous. The second component is help-lessness; Summit suggests that observers must acknowledge and validate this feeling (i.e., they must reinforce that the girl did *not* cause the abuse and that she was the innocent victim). Third is entrapment and accommodation. Since child sexual abuse (particularly incest) is *not* usually a one-time event, in order to survive, the girl comes to accept the situation, but doing so can exact a heavy toll. That is to say, she can learn to lie, develop MPD, engage in self-destructive behaviors, and/or become a substance abuser. Fourth is delayed, conflicted, and uncon-vincing disclosure. This stage focuses on the fact that many of the child victims of sexual abuse do *not* disclose the abuse when it happens but wait until adolescence to do so. The problem is that by then she is "acting out" and is "out of control." Her "story," then, appears to be an invention to get her out of trouble, and it is *unlikely* that others will believe her. Finally is the response of retraction. Due to all of the "trouble" that telling causes (e.g., being removed from her home, public embar-rassment of her father), the girl often retracts her "allegations" of sexual abuse which has the effect of reinforcing the existing myth that children are *not* to be trusted, that they "lie" about being sexually abused. Since the impact of this syndrome is insidious, change is absolutely necessary:

> ... [L]eft unchallenged the sexual abuse accommodation syndrome tends to reinforce both the victimization of children and societal complacency and indifference to the dimensions of that victimization ... [T]he power to challenge and to interrupt the accommodation process carries an unprecedented potential for primary prevention of emotional pain and disability, including an interruption in the intergenerational chain of child abuse (Summit 1983:188–189).

As was noted earlier in this chapter, *PTSD* refers to the multitude of responses that can arise after we experience extraordinary events such as rape (e.g., reactions can occur shortly after the traumatizing experience, or they can remain dormant for months and even years). This model also has been applied to the victims and survivors of childhood sexual victimization, and it is regarded as an accurate depiction of how children and adolescents react when they are sexually abused (Briere 1989; Coons et al. 1989, 1990; Courtois 1988; Courtois and Sprie 1988; Gomes-Schwartz et al. 1990; Herman 1992). In addition, this model readily explains the delayed-onset pattern among adult women who were sexually abused earlier in their lives but did *not* react (at least *ostensibly*) when it was happening (Blume 1990; Briere 1989; Courtois 1988; Dolan 1991; Farmer 1989; Greenwald and Leitenberg 1990; Ratner 1990; Sanford 1990; Wyatt and Powell 1988). Further, the PTSD model suggests that: (1) if they are exposed to events which remind them of their earlier traumas of sexual victimization, women will experience all sorts of "symptoms" (e.g., disrupted sleep patterns, irritability, anger, difficulty concentrating, hypervigilance, startle responses, and a variety of somatic responses); (2) the original events tend to be experienced over and over again via intrusive thoughts or memories, flashbacks, nightmares, and/or stress responses; (3) stimuli associated with the original traumas (e.g., odors, darkness, words) tend to be avoided (Briere 1989; Courtois 1988; Dolan 1991); and (4) some children and adult survivors will have more intense reactions, particularly if their experiences were of the more traumatizing variety [e.g., involved extreme exploitation, lasted an extended period of time (Herman 1992)].

Courtois (1992) has developed a *three-stage model* which outlines the recovery process for adult women who are grappling with childhood experiences with incest. Stage one, or the "pre-trauma work," refers to the period of assessment, education, and stabilization that must occur before the woman's past can be examined and resolved. Issues to be explored during this stage are: (1) making sure that she is safe in the present, (2) "self-soothing" or helping her to learn how to care for and be good to herself, (3) existing compulsions and/or addictions, and (4) building support. In other words, you do *not* start to remove her old defenses (even if they are counterproductive ones) until she is stabilized (including sober and drug free), has a support system, and is beginning to learn more efficient methods of coping.

The second part of this process is the actual "trauma work" or dealing with the woman's childhood. Included elements are: remembering the traumas and gaining the associated affect (i.e., bringing together the emotional and intellectual spheres); grieving and mourning what she has lost; placing a new meaning or developing a new understanding of the past (i.e., contradict the shame and help her to come to believe that it was the perpetrator's fault rather than hers); involving her in an abuse-focused support group; and building and enlisting the aid of her support system (Courtois 1992).

The final stage in this process is the "post-trauma phase." This refers to: (1) relational rebalancing (i.e., acknowledging and dealing with the fact that a history of abuse can alter the balance in current relationships, particularly with her partner and her children); (2) skill-building, or continuing what was started in stage one with the goal of having her learn better ways to cope with the past, the present, and the future; (3) developing intimacy skills and the ability to be a sexual being; (4) the survivor's mission, or involvement in collective ventures aimed at reducing the problem of child sexual victimization; and (5) helping her to make important post-trauma decisions [e.g., whether to disclose her past, confront the perpetrator, and/or report the crime, as well as deciding about forgiving the perpetrator, *only if* this latter one is an issue with the woman (Courtois 1992)].

Via their *fourteen stage process of healing*, Bass and Davis (1988) offer an excellent, as well as a highly popular, self-help approach which outlines the specifics of achieving the goals of recovery, resolution, and thriving.[10] Included in this process are: (1) the decision to heal; (2) the emergency stage, or that period of time during which you begin "to deal with memories and suppressed feelings [which] can throw your life into utter turmoil"; (3) remembering the abuse (or the "process of getting back both memory and feeling"); (4) believing that the abuse occurred, an issue that is a serious problem for many survivors of child sexual abuse; (5) breaking the silence, or finally telling someone about what happened to you; (6) understanding that the abuse was *not* your fault; (7) making contact with your "child within" (i.e., getting to know her and healing her childhood wounds); (8) trusting yourself to know what the specifics of healing are for you; (9) grieving and mourning your losses; (10) being able to feel and express anger at the abuser and the other people who did *not* protect you from him/them; (11) disclosure of your childhood victimization to family members and confronting the abuser (if this latter one is an issue for you); (12) forgiving the abuser (again, if this is a priority for you); (13) developing spirituality (or "having a sense of a power greater than yourself") which may include "traditional religion, meditation, nature, or your support group"; and (14) resolution and moving on (Bass and Davis 1988:58–59).[11] Regarding this latter stage or the expected outcomes of the model, Bass and Davis (1988:59) suggest that: "Your feelings and perspectives will stabilize. You will come to terms with your abuser and other family members. While you won't erase your history, you will make deep and lasting changes in your life. Having gained awareness, compassion, and power through healing, you will have the opportunity to work toward a better world."

Swink and Leveille (1986) offer a *seven-stage model* to facilitate recovering from incest, and they suggest that recovery is most likely to be achieved in group therapy. Issues involved in the first stage are disclosing the secret and ending the denial. Second is relinquishing the guilt which comes via the realization that she was *not* at fault, but rather that the abuser was. The third step, or catharsis, entails expressing the range of feelings (e.g., pain, sorrow, betrayal, anger, and rage) that accompany the admission that she was sexually abused as a child. The fourth step is orphanization, or coming to the awareness that her family of origin has *not* been there for her. As was indicated earlier in this chapter, she comes to realize that she cannot transform them and that she must decide to stop trying to change them. Ultimately, this can mean breaking all ties with her family members. Fifth is reintegration, which refers to filling this "gap" by finding healthy people to fulfill her familial needs for nurturance, support, and guidance. If the original trauma and her later dissociative survival skills have caused her to split into more than one personality, integration also may refer to putting the various parts of herself back together. Sixth is confronting family members and/or the abuser(s). Swink and Leveille suggest that this can be done allegorically via psychodrama, role-playing, an unsent letter, or by directly confronting the abuser. The final stage in their model is rebuilding a new self. Swink and Leveille (1986:140) suggest that this is a gradual process which results in "a positive, stronger self who has learned self-acceptance, self-confidence, assertiveness, self-expression of feelings and self-love." The rebuilding of self also includes seeing self and the surrounding world with newly-found strength and self-respect, taking charge of your life, and participating in healthy relationships.

Although *Dinsmore* (1991) offers an *eight stage model of recovery from incest*, she adds that there is *not* one road to recovery and that we do a tremendous disservice when we offer rigid prescriptions that must be followed: "It is important to understand that incest recovery is a spiral process rather than a linear one. There are times when one makes it through a stage only to return to it later, but the second time around the stage is experienced in a different way, generally with more insight and clarity" (Dinsmore 1991:33). Notwithstanding this caveat, she offers an eight-stage process which is loosely based on the Kübler-Ross model of death and dying.

The first stage is acknowledgment, or ending the denial. Since many women have extensive histories of denying that the abuse occurred or have the memories of the abuse but decide that they must have "made them up," this step is a critical one. As Dinsmore (1991:34) expresses it: "Denial initially is a necessary defense mechanism, but it must be given up in order to allow healing to begin." The second stage, or crisis phase, is similar to Bass and Davis' emergency stage whereby the survivor becomes "obsessed" with the incest and its current effects on her. Likely responses include nightmares, flashbacks, panic attacks, depression, withdrawing from others, and suicidal ideation. Dinsmore (1991: 36) also notes that this can be a very dangerous stage: "[O]n many levels this present crisis feels as bad, if not worse, than the actual childhood experience, because as a child the survivor's coping methods protected her from feeling the pain." In order to make it to the next stage, then, the survivor must develop "life-enhancing coping skills" (e.g., enter into therapy and/or support groups, paint and draw, write, exercise, and generally take care of herself).

The third stage is disclosure; it refers not only to self-disclosure but also to telling someone else about the sexual abuse. Dinsmore (1991:37) suggests that telling is important and that numerous benefits can accrue from doing so: "Breaking the silence, telling the secret that she has been carrying with her for years and years, is crucial. Most survivors have kept the secret out of fear . . . The fear is as profound for her now as it was back then, for the child victim she was. The release can be empowering; the anticipation can be dreadful." The fourth step in this model is depression. Rather than depicting it as a negative component, Dinsmore regards depression as an important and unavoidable part of the recovery process. Again, although a critical element, this stage can be a dangerous one. In the more serious cases, the survivor may need medication and/or hospitalization; at minimum, she needs the loving kindness and support of others to help her get through this stage.

The next stage of this recovery process is anger. This, too, is a difficult step. First of all, as women raised in this culture, we have been socialized into denying our anger, as well as suppressing it if and when we feel it; second, we have learned that anger within the incestuous family has the potential to be "violent, explosive, and damaging" (Dinsmore 1991:39). Thus, learning to feel anger and to express it in safe ways become essential parts of recovery: "The job for incest survivors . . . is to learn to identify their anger and to express it in empowering ways . . . They need to understand that . . . it is not anger that must be controlled but rather how we express it that must be managed" (Dinsmore 1991: 39). This stage also may include confronting the abuser, but Dinsmore cautions that we should decide the merits of doing so individually.

The sixth stage in Dinsmore's (1991:43) recovery process is mourning. As she describes it:

> [O]nce the anger and rage are worked through, the survivor is able to get in touch with her deeper feelings. The sadness was covered by the anger, just as the anger was covered by the earlier depression. With the anger diminished, the survivor can now grieve for her lost childhood . . . She has become free to feel deep pain and to mourn for the little girl who was betrayed (Dinsmore 1991:43).

Acceptance is the penultimate stage in recovering from incest and child sexual abuse, and Dinsmore (1991:44) defines it as "letting go, or making peace with the past." She is quick to add, though, that this does *not* mean that we come to view incest as an "acceptable" phenomenon; instead, we come to accept that it happened, acknowledge its consequences, and truly understand that we did *not* cause it. The outcome of this process is moving on or integration. As Dinsmore (1991:46) defines it: ". . . [T]he final stage of healing . . . [is when] the survivor recognizes that being an incest survivor is only one piece of her and her life. She comes to realizes that, yes, she is a survivor but that she is also a woman, a lover, a friend, a mother, a professional, an advocate, a whole person."

The final model is *Engel's* (1989) *seven-step, self-help "journey to recovery."* The first step in this model is the essential one of facing the truth, a step that also enables you to feel the pain: "Aware or not, the abuse will continue to run your life until you come to terms with it. Only then can the pain be overcome and the victim emerge a freer human being" (Engel 1989:68). The second stage is releasing your anger. With the acknowledgment of what happened to you comes anger at the perpetrator, as well as at the people who did little or nothing to protect you. Although this anger is legitimate, Engel suggests that the goals should be to learn to release it in constructive ways so that you do no more damage to yourself, let go of your deeply-imbedded fears of retaliation and losing control, and promote healing and growth rather than staying focused on the anger. Third is confronting those who have hurt you. According to Engel (1989:69), doing so should "pave the way for a possible reconciliation with those who have hurt, neglected, and abused you[; and a]t the very least, confronting will bring closure to those relationships that plague you the most." These goals can be achieved via face-to-face contacts, telephone confrontations, writing letters, or by fantasy confrontation. Next, Engel suggests that you must resolve your relationships, which entails taking an inventory of all current ones (particularly with family members who were abusive or, at minimum, did *not* protect you from the abuser). During this stage, you make decisions about these people and can elect one of three approaches: a trial or temporary separation, permanent separation from them, or reconciliation. Fifth is self-discovery. If you elect to discontinue interacting with family members, the next task is to develop an identity that is separate from them. This entails becoming clear about who you are, who you want to be, letting yourself feel, and opening up your senses. This is a period of exploration wherein you can discover the critical parts of yourself that have been missing for so long. The sixth stage is self-care, and Engel describes it as learning what you already should have been taught. In other words, in dysfunctional families, children rarely learn how to care for and/or love themselves; instead, they learn to take care of everyone around them and that everyone else's needs are more important than their own. Accordingly, the major goal of this stage is learning how to parent yourself, with the hoped-for outcomes of coming to know and like yourself. The specifics involved in this are: (1) learning to ask for what you want, (2) ending the expectation that others will take care of you, (3) learning to say no, (4) knowing that you have choices and rights, and (5) coming to value yourself (Engel 1989:193–204). The final stage in this process is self-forgiveness. Engel does *not* assume that you have done "something wrong" or that the abuse was your "fault." Rather, she suggests that adults who were sexually abused as children feel so much guilt "for the abuse itself, for things they did as a child as a result of the abuse, and for things they have done as an adult to hurt themselves and others"; recovery, then, "depends on freeing yourself from that guilt, acknowledging what you are responsible for and what you are not" (Engel 1989:205).

According to Engel (1989:73–81), the benefits of achieving recovery are awesome. They include: higher self-esteem; better relationships; improved sexuality; increased abilities to understand, express, and release your emotions; relief from somatic complaints; a greater sense of control in your life; increased self-awareness; living in the present rather than in the past; learning healthy defenses and coping strategies; self-discovery; and peace of mind. In sum, she equates recovery with freedom: "It means knowing who you are and what you like. It means once again being able to enjoy your body, your sensations, your relationships, and the feeling of being alive . . . [Y]ou [will] have developed an inner strength and courage—a knowledge that comes from having endured and conquered one of the most devastating experiences imaginable" (Engel 1989:226).

As was the case with the rape recovery process, the models which outline how we respond to childhood sexual victimization and/or how to heal these wounds have positive as well as negative features. For example, Finkelhor and Browne's traumagenic dynamics model is an excellent one because it clearly outlines post-sexual-victimization issues which need to be resolved (traumatic sexualization, betrayal, stigmatization, and powerlessness), as well as the psychological impact and behavioral manifestation of these dynamics. Thus, their work not only helps us to understand the long-term impact of incest and child sexual abuse, but it also demystifies the roots of post-victimization responses, particularly ones which at first glance may seem to be "odd" (e.g., involvement in marginal groups and suicide attempts). The downside of this model, though, is that it does little to clarify how to resolve the long-term traumata of childhood sexual victimization.

Summit's child sexual abuse accommodation syndrome also is a good conceptualization because it clarifies the preconditions needed for child sexual victimization (particularly incest) to occur, i.e., secrecy and helplessness of the child. It also includes the sequence of events which often ensue once a child has been sexually victimized (i.e., entrapment and accommodation; delayed, conflicted, and unconvincing disclosure; and retraction). There also, though, are problems with this model. First of all, Summit infers that most children directly acknowledge that they have been sexually abused, yet we have a multitude of studies which dispute this. That is to say, many children "forget" or repress their memories of having been sexually victimized; others keep the secret because they are afraid to do anything else, while still others acknowledge the abuse but do so in very indirect ways, e.g., inappropriate knowledge of sexual behaviors (Bass and Davis 1988; Blume 1990; Briere 1989; Courtois 1988; Dinsmore 1991; Dolan 1991; Finkelhor 1987, 1988). Second, as was the case with Finkelhor's model, Summit does little to clarify how to actually recover from these experiences.

Regarding the merits of the PTSD model in explaining post-sexual-abuse consequences, it not only clarifies the connection between childhood trauma and difficulties experienced later in adulthood (e.g., intrusive thoughts, nightmares, and flashbacks), but it also emphasizes that these responses to extraordinary life events (i.e., ones for which we have no knowledge and are totally unprepared) are logical and normal. Again, though, there are problems when we apply this model to the victims and survivors of incest and child sexual abuse. For example (and as was noted earlier in this chapter), Finkelhor (1987, 1988) indicates that the PTSD model focuses mostly on the affective realm, while minimizing the cognitive dimension (e.g., issues such as self-esteem, self-blame and guilt, confusion, difficulty concentrating), and that many victims and survivors of incest and child sexual abuse do *not* evidence the "symptoms" of PTSD. To validate this latter point, he cites one study which investigated the responses of 126 women who had been sexually abused as children; only 10 percent of the women presently had PTSD-like symptoms, while such responses were ever-present for only 36 percent of them. In addition, we have Herman's (1992) work which indicates that the PTSD conceptualization may be too simplistic, particularly for childhood sexual victimizations which take place over an extended period of time and/or involve elements of brutality, terror, and captivity.

Of the remaining models, Bass and Davis' is the most popular, as well as the best known. Their model covers many of the critical issues involved when adult women begin to recover from their experiences of incest and child sexual abuse; it offers concrete solutions for how to work through the many facets of post-sexual-victimization trauma, and it is written in clear and accessible language. Their model, though, is somewhat problematic because of their suggestion that some women may need to confront and/or forgive their abusers. To reiterate an earlier point, I believe that these issues have been overstated and that a confrontation between abuser and survivor, as well as the slightest hint that she *should or must* forgive him, can end up doing more harm than good.

The remaining models of Courtois (1992), Swink and Leveille (1986), Dinsmore (1991), and Engel (1989) overlap in a number of ways with and evidence similarities to Bass and Davis' perspective. For example, all of these models include the emphases on disclosure, or ending the denial and beginning to feel and express anger, while three of of them (Courtois, Swink and Leveille, and Engel) stress the importance of relinquishing the guilt, self-forgiveness, forgiving the abuser, and/or confronting the abuser and other family members who did not protect us. In addition, each of these perspectives makes very specific contributions: Courtois outlines how and why pre-trauma work must be done, as well as why stabilization must occur, before the incest trauma can be dealt with directly; Swink and Leveille offer the much-needed option of "orphanization"; Dinsmore suggests that we must mourn and accept what happened to us; and Courtois and Engel introduce the important notions of "self-soothing" and "self-care," or learning to do what we should have been taught in childhood.

Again, though, there are problems with most of these perspectives. For example, Courtois infers that, in order to resolve childhood experiences, everyone who needs it will be able to access good therapy; but (and as is discussed in the next chapter) the reality of the situation is that this is *not* always true. In addition, Swink and Leveille stress the importance of catharsis or talking about our sexually abusive experiences with the goal of releasing the emotions that we have about them; yet Dolan (1991) contends that we have placed too much emphasis on this issue. Her preference is that we only remember and talk about *enough* of our memories to heal and that every effort is made for us to feel safe when we do so. In addition, chronologically, Engel places the issue of resolving relationships before such issues as self-discovery, self-care, and forgiving self. Although this may seem to be a picayune point, this ordering implies that relationships should be given a higher priority than the self in the process of recovering from incest and child sexual abuse. My perspective is that exactly the opposite is true; until we make the changes that will allow us to have accurate images of ourselves, we will have difficulties connecting with others in meaningful and healthy ways. Finally, regarding Dinsmore's model, I have no problems with it; in fact, I believe that it is one of the better ones currently available. What I particularly like about her model is that she normalizes crisis responses and suggests that feeling strong emotions when dealing with these issues is an essential part of this process. In addition, she illustrates the importance of feeling angry and directing that anger appropriately (at "them" rather than at ourselves), as well as the optimistic issue of thriving; and she offers very clear images of what the outcome of this process should be (i.e., integration and moving on).

Are Recovery and Healing the Same for the Victims and Survivors of Rape, Incest, and Child Sexual Abuse?

Regardless of whether you are recovering from rape, incest, or child sexual abuse, there are several *similarities* in achieving this goal. For example, many of the aforementioned works emphasize the need for: forgiving self; "breaking the silence" or talking about having been victimized; putting the blame where it belongs (i.e., on the perpetrator and this society rather than self); getting angry about what happened to you; empowering yourself; and involving suitable people in your process of recovery, growth, healing, thriving, and/or victory. In addition, many of the issues that must be resolved are similar in these models. Specifically, many if not most of the victims and survivors of rape, incest, and child sexual abuse evidence the short-term responses of fear, anxiety, and confusion, as well as the long-term consequences of depression, low self-esteem, and shattered assumptions about the world. And, in order for recovery to be possible, the causes of these reactions must be examined, understood, and addressed directly.

There also, though, are some critical *differences* in the process of recovery and healing. For example, I have suggested a number of times in this book that responses to childhood sexual victimization can be more devastating than are the reactions of adolescent females and adult women who have been raped. Again, the major explanations for this phenomenon are: (1) ofttimes, memories of our childhood experiences of sexual abuse are buried, but when they return, they often do so with a vengeance; (2) since most cases of incest and child sexual abuse occur prior to adolescence, the children who are so victimized are ill-equipped both cognitively and emotionally to comprehend these experiences; and (3) we are even less willing to believe "allegations" of incest and child sexual abuse than we are "claims" of rape, and this can result in further traumatization for the victims and survivors of these experiences.

Another difference is the issue of forgiveness that keeps "cropping up" in discussions about recovering from incest and child sexual abuse. Some authors (e.g., Finney) suggest that complete healing is impossible without forgiving our abuser(s), while the other side of the debate is that we need *not* concern ourselves with them or the others who may have failed to protect us from harm (e.g., Dinsmore, Swink and Leveille, Forward with Buck). It is interesting to note, though, that this issue does *not* even arise in the rape literature; in fact, the notion is almost laughable. In a similar vein, many works in the rape literature suggest that prosecution of rapists should be a critical concern for women who have been raped, while many reports in the child sexual abuse literature infer that the goal should be "treatment" for the offender, as well as our need to forgive him and/or to keep families together. As previously noted, we do a tremendous disservice to the victims and survivors of incest and child sexual abuse when we make the "demand" that they should forgive or understand their abuser(s). In fact, I often have found myself wondering why the focus hasn't been on what perpetrators can do to convince us that they feel true remorse for their acts; or why the goal isn't to seek admissions from them that they have treated us very cruelly?

A similar issue which again exists in the incest and child sexual abuse literatures is confronting one's attacker. Although several of the models mentioned in this chapter have this as a component, doing so can be risky, particularly if the perpetrator flatly denies the accusation or tries to convince his accuser that she is "imagining" it (Forward with Buck 1989; Herman 1992). In other words, how do we know when a girl, an adolescent female, or a woman is strong enough to endure these sorts of negative outcomes; do the risks outweigh the merits? Again, these are questions to be answered by each of us individually; there is *not* one "correct" way to resolve them. If we do opt to confront, though, we should be prepared to be called liars and to have our accusations denied; on the other hand, if we elect the options of orphanization and creating families of choice, we also should be supported for doing so.

Third, most of the works which examine the impact of sexual victimization on the spiritual dimension of our lives appear in the incest and child sexual abuse literatures. I am *not* sure why this is the case, but it is time to acknowledge that being raped also can cause spiritual consequences. When Herman (1992) and Reis (1991b) highlight the similarities in post-sexual-victimization responses in the spiritual dimension of our lives (regardless of whether we have been raped or have been sexually victimized as children), they are pointing us in this direction. Accordingly, in the future we need to pay more attention to this issue for adolescents and adult women who have been raped, as well as begin to examine the value of cleansing and/or rebirthing rituals and ceremonies in alleviating some of their distress.

Finally, most of the works which explore the long-term ramifications of sexual victimization, as well as the issues of recovery, growth, healing, and/or victory, are found in the incest and child sexual abuse literatures, while much less attention has been paid to these subjects in the rape victimization literature. Part of the problem has been our overreliance upon crisis theory to explain post-rape consequences. In other words, historically, we have tended to assume that recovery from rape is time-limited and that it is achieved fairly quickly. Although some experts have begun to rethink these assumptions (Burgess and Holmstrom 1979b; Forman 1983; Herman 1992; Kilpatrick and Veronen 1983; Koss and Harvey 1991; Resick and Schnicke 1990; Williams and Holmes 1981), it is important to note that many, if not most, rape crisis centers continue to use the crisis intervention model (Gornick et al. 1985; King and Webb 1981). We must begin to admit, though, that some of us who have been raped may have more difficulty recovering from these experiences and that existing services may have to be altered to meet our needs (Herman 1992).

Summary and Conclusions

Regardless of whether we focus on recovering from rape, incest, or child sexual abuse, it is a much more complicated process than simply dissipating "symptoms." In an earlier time, the bias seemed to be that we returned to "normal;" now, though, many, if not most, of the experts suggest that we end up as changed beings. That is to say, we change psychologically, physically, behaviorally, interpersonally, cognitively, self-perceptually, sexually, politically, and spiritually. In addition, at times, working toward recovery, healing, or victory can seem to be an overwhelming venture, and perhaps it is. But why *not* simply acknowledge that this is the case and focus on the fact that the alternatives (e.g., continuing to live half-lives dictated by fear and misgivings about ourselves and the world around us) are even worse?

Earlier in this book, I introduced the term "victory." For a long time, we seemed satisfied with such terms as victim and survivor; we defended their meanings and, until fairly recently, did *not* question their value-laden assumptions. Now, though, there is a movement to reconceptualize the outcome of sexual victimization and to view it in much more optimistic terms. That is to say, we now (particularly in the child sexual abuse and incest literatures) have such notions as *triumphing* (Blume 1990); *moving beyond survival* (Briere 1989; Farmer 1989); *thriving* (Bass and Davis 1988; Dinsmore 1991); *reclaiming our lives* (Poston and Lison 1989); and *recovery* (Herman 1992; Janoff-Bulman 1992). The bottom line is that, if we continue to use the language of victim and survivor, we infer that we should be satisfied with "hanging on for dear life"; when we begin to employ the more optimistic concepts of thriving, triumphing, recovery, and/or victory, though, we move to the next level of "really having a life." The fact that we were sexually victimized and the impact that it has had on our lives does *not* go away, but we can get to the point where it no longer dictates the shape and content of each and every moment of our present-day lives. We can feel joy again; we can love ourselves, as well as others who are worthy of that love; we can begin again to have full lives. When she introduces the concept of commonality, Herman (1992:235–236) clearly summarizes this perspective:

> Commonality with other people carries with it all of the meanings of the word *common*. It means belonging to a society, having a public role, being part of that which is universal. It means having a feeling of familiarity, of being known, of communion. It means taking part in the customary, the commonplace, the ordinary, and the everyday . . . The survivor who has achieved commonality with others can rest from her labors. Her recovery is accomplished; all that remains before her is her life.

In addition, we must *not* be lulled into thinking that recovery is an absolute construct or a time-limited process; rather, it is something that may continue throughout the remainder of your life. In fact, some experts now concede that you do *not* ever recover completely—you do the best that you can, or you become the best person that you can be (Dinsmore

1991; Herman 1992). Other reports, though, contend that some people do recover fully and/or are affected less by their traumatizing life events. As examples, Antonovsky (1987) writes about Nazi deathcamp survivors who learned to thrive and to develop a strong sense of coherence, while Werner and Smith (1982), as well as Herman (1992), speak about women and children who seem to be resilient, even in the face of extreme trauma. Although these are critical issues which demand our attention, we as yet know little about them. In other words, we know a great deal about the women and children who fail to get "better" and/or who repeat the pattern of victimization, while we know much less about the ones who choose a different way to live and/or the ones who go on to become well-functioning adults. It is time that we focus more on this latter group and come to decipher the reasons for their resiliency and/or their abilites to thrive.

Recovery, then, is neither a simple nor a linear process; it is a convoluted, meandering journey which has psychological, somatic, cognitive, interpersonal, behavioral, self-perceptual, sexual, political, and spiritual components. It is an intense period of self-exploration, self-discovery, and experimentation; and, if done well, it can teach us about the meaning of life, appreciating and loving ourselves, and the value of some of the people around us.

Treatment Issues: Trying to Resolve the Experiences of Rape, Incest, and/or Child Sexual Abuse

> For many survivors, the healing process is a battle of
> reclamation, of redirecting growth from the deeply
> gnarled roots of childhood . . . While there is often deep
> scarring, the survivor is more than a collection of wounds.
> She is also resilient and resourceful. The scar tissue is
> what remains of the ways in which she protected herself,
> distanced or withdrew, if needed, denied, forgot,
> minimized, sealed off. The scars are what allowed
> the survivor to reach our office or agency so that we
> might join her as she continues to heal (Butler 1989:xii).

> The first principle of recovery is the empowerment
> of the survivor. She must be the author and arbiter of
> her own recovery. Others may offer advice, support,
> assistance, affection, and care, but not cure . . . No
> intervention that takes power away from the survivor
> can possibly foster her recovery, no matter how much it
> appears to be in her immediate best interest (Herman
> 1992:133).

When I first began to consider which topics to include in this book, I decided that a chapter on the treatment of the aftermath of sexual victimization was a critical one because many of us who have been sexually victimized (particularly if it occurred in childhood) are unable to make the changes that lead to recovery by ourselves. We join support or therapy groups and/or initiate one-on-one relationships with therapists to facilitate this process. Perhaps because the issues of rape, incest, and child sexual abuse are so confusing, perhaps because these experiences tend to blur our boundaries and a sense of what is real, perhaps because our ideas about who we are become distorted afterwards, or perhaps it is a combination of these issues, many of us are forced to seek help to resolve these experiences. We must, though, remain cognizant that there are dangers and risks involved in entering therapy: danger in "breaking silence" because many of us have been threatened with all sorts of dire consequences if we "tell," the risk that our "allegations" will be minimized or disbelieved, and danger if we select therapists who have little understanding of the significance of sexual victimization (i.e., the potential that it has to harm us, and how to treat its aftermath).

Butler's and Herman's words highlight the importance of many of these issues. They not only pinpoint the need for therapists to confirm and to respect the survivors of sexual victimization and to acknowledge that their healing process is a battle for reclamation (i.e., even in the midst of upheaval, there is hope for healing), but they also congratulate the resiliency and resourcefulness of girls, adolescent females, and adult women who have survived. Finally, they suggest that therapists do *not* "heal" their clients; rather, they facilitate this process by teaching them how to heal themselves.

Before outlining many of the extant treatment modalities which have been developed to resolve the aftermath of sexual victimization, I want to clarify some other important therapeutic considerations. They include: (1) the specific philosophy of treatment that should be implemented when working with survivors of sexual victimization; (2) the importance of feminist principles and practices when treating the aftermath of rape, incest, and child sexual abuse; (3) how to select a therapist (if you elect and can afford to do so); (4) the specific issues to be resolved or the goals of the therapeutic process; and (5) problems that can arise during treatment for clients and practitioners alike.

The Philosophy of Treatment

Regardless of whether the format is individual or group therapy, when working with adult survivors of incest and child sexual abuse, several experts suggest critical guidelines or an appropriate philosophy of treatment that should be employed. As an example, Briere's (1989) philosophy is based upon the following principles: (1) utilizing an abuse perspective; (2) the question of truth; (3) the issue of responsibility; (4) using a phenomenologic perspective; (5) the importance of egalitarianism in the therapeutic process; (6) having the operating assumptions of growth and strength; and (7) having an awareness of the role and the context of our victimizing culture.

Regarding an abuse perspective, although Briere (1989) indicates that the therapeutic starting point must be the original trauma, he also contends that there is a need to examine later, as well as current, issues in survivors' lives. In addition, although many of us initiate therapy with a variety of presenting complaints and/or disguised presentations (e.g., substance abuse, depression, eating disorders); ofttimes, these "conditions" really are "symptoms" of other problems (e.g., self-hatred), or reflections of our histories of sexual victimization (i.e., compounded reactions). In part, this is due to the fact that many of us did *not* have access to memories of having been sexually victimized (i.e., those of us who have known for years that our lives were *not* "quite right" but had *no* clue as to why), or we may *not* have interpreted what transpired as sexual abuse (Bass and Davis 1988; Blume 1990; Briere 1989; Courtois 1989; Dolan 1991; Koss 1988; Warshaw 1988). The point is that therapists need *not* wait for their clients to disclose the fact that they were sexually victimized; rather, armed with the current knowledge about the frequency of sexual victimization, as well as the potential for and the nature of long-term consequences, they should be aware of it as a possibility.

The question of truth refers to the fact that often therapists are quite willing to accept the role of abuse experiences in causing certain psychological problems, yet there are other instances (particularly if the client evidences "histrionic" or "borderline" behaviors) when they tend to disbelieve her "allegation." According to Briere (1989:54), the impact of this latter experience can be insidious for the client: "Although little harm may come from accepting a distorted or technically false disclosure, much damage can be done by a trusted therapist who disagrees with a client about injurious experiences that have actually transpired."

The issue of responsibility highlights the penchant that we as a society have for blaming victims of "misfortune." In other words, ofttimes, observers want to emphasize what people have "done" to bring about their problems and/or blame them for them. In the case of sexual victimization, though, if practitioners present this type of attitude, the consequences for their clients can be devastating and perhaps life-threatening. According to Briere (1989: 55), the *correct, nonnegotiable* stance should be that: "Children have less power than adults, are dependent upon them, and are intellectually incapable of free and informed consent to have sex with them."

Briere's discussion of the phenomenologic perspective is particularly important. Specifically, he indicates that "many of the symptoms of post-abuse trauma . . . [are] logical, adaptive responses to victimization that become inappropriate in the post-abuse environment or as conditioned reactions to abuse-related stimuli that persist into later life"; thus, he demystifies and normalizes adult "psychopathology" and reconceptualizes it as an "extension of early reactions and solutions to aversive childhood events" (Briere 1989:56). This principle also mandates that we stay with the client's experience in adulthood, eschew abstractions or intellectualizations about their concerns and problems, and focus on the content, as well as the process, of therapy. In sum, Briere (1989:57) suggests that: "The therapeutic process must fit the client's current psychological and emotional state, so that the content and process of therapy are congruent with the client's immediate experience and her ability to process new information or feelings." This dictates that therapy be client-centered and that therapists not only be good leaders but also adept followers.

Fifth, since child sexual abuse usually occurs within the context of powerlessness and authoritarianism, at all costs, therapy for adult women who are trying to recover must be exactly the opposite. That is to say, what he calls "abuse-focused therapy" should take place "in an egalitarian atmosphere," wherein "the client is seen as an equal partner in treatment"

(Briere 1989:59). This is *not* merely a semantic difference but rather a different way to conceptualize the therapeutic process:

> From this perspective, 'cure by the therapist' is replaced with 'recovery by the survivor' with assistance from the therapist ... Ideally, the client is made aware early in treatment that good therapy is more an environment than an inherently curative procedure, and assuming that the clinician can provide a healing context and helpful guidance, the client is 'in charge of her own recovery' (Briere 1989:60).

Sixth, Briere (1989:60) argues that a therapist should hold and make explicit the assumptions of growth and strength; this means that the practitioner avoids viewing the woman as "sick" but rather sees her as "someone who ... made entirely appropriate accommodations to a toxic environment." An added emphasis, though, should be that their "accommodations" have become counterproductive in the adult world and that new ones must be learned. Regarding the equally important issue of strength, Briere (1989:61) indicates that the survivor's "resilience and willingness to struggle should be reinforced and relied upon by the therapist, whose task is lessened by the existence of the 'strong, healthy part' in most survivors."

Finally, as part of the therapeutic process to recover from childhood sexual victimization, Briere (1989) believes that the role our culture plays in causing and perpetuating this problem must be acknowledged directly. In other words, practitioners should *not* view the causes and the consequences of such problems as rape, child sexual abuse, and domestic violence as individual abberations or as phenomena which are based exclusively in intrapsychic factors; rather, they should regard them, as well as explain them to their clients, as logical extensions of a culture which permits and encourages violence.

Courtois (1988, 1992), too, highlights the need for a specific philosophy of treatment when doing retrospective incest therapy with adult women. Although many of her ideas are similar to Briere's, her viewpoint is unique because she aligns herself with several, extant treatment modalities (e.g., feminist treatment principles and family systems theory). Her philosophy can be summarized via four major principles:

(1) to treat the incest directly along with its original and compounded effects; (2) to use traumatic stress, feminist, and family systems models to understand the incest, its effects, and its symptoms, and to plan and implement treatment; (3) to individualize the treatment within the more general process and structure; and (4) to foster the development of a therapeutic alliance and a safe environment within which to conduct the treatment (Courtois 1988:165).

Courtois's first principle is identical to Briere's initial one: Therapists must be aware that girls' and women's responses to sexual victimization really are manifestations of current, as well as past, concerns. Her second point is that, in order to be effective in helping women to achieve recovery, we need eclectic models of causation and intervention. Third (and similar to Briere's fourth principle), she emphasizes the need for individualized treatment approaches which include an awareness of the social structure in causing and perpetuating the sexual victimization of children. Courtois's fourth point is probably her most important one: In order to encourage women to recover and grow, practitioners must be willing to work with them in nonthreatening and nonhierarchical ways. Thus, as does Briere, she believes that models of therapeutic practice which place the therapist at the center as the expert must be avoided at all costs.

Bass and Davis (1988:345–349), as well, offer several guidelines for clinicians who work with adult survivors of childhood sexual abuse. Some of their suggestions include that you must: (1) believe that healing from sexual victimization is possible; (2) be able to witness great pain; (3) be willing to believe that which may seem unbelievable; (4) be clear about your own attitudes and notions regarding such issues as child sexual abuse, good and evil, and feelings about men, heterosexuality, and homosexuality; (5) view the client as the expert; (6) believe and validate her experiences; (7) validate her needs, as well as the variety of ways that she has coped or survived, however negative they may seem to be; (8) *never* blame her for what happened; (9) offer information about what a child's life *should* be like; and (10) support her need to "speak out" on the subject.

Since he emphasizes the role of the therapist, particularly the need for "therapeutic acceptance" in working with women who were sexually abused as children, Summit's emphasis is a bit different. Specifically, he focuses on:

> *forgiveness*: conferring on the patient ... expiation for a deeply entrenched ... commitment to a felt reality of being bad and unforgivable. Acceptance also involves taking a share of the confusion and the pain in empathic interaction through repeated crises, demonstrating adult alternatives to both avoidance and defeat. Acceptance means learning from the child in the patient ... while maintaining the reassuring substance of the parent and the teacher [emphasis in original (Summit 1989:426)].

In sum, all of these authors offer important caveats about what girls and women who have been sexually abused need in their therapeutic relationships. Please note that many of these notions apply equally well for adolescent females and women who have been raped. Finally, although they offer specific treatment strategies (which are outlined later in this chapter), their ideas about the philosophy of treatment are particularly important because they illustrate the baseline assumptions that must exist in therapeutic relationships with survivors of sexual victimization, regardless of the specific strategies, theoretical perspectives, or treatment formats being employed. In sum: "Good therapy goes beyond any 'technique' and is a personalized, compassionate, and very human response to the client ... [; t]here is no substitute for each therapist's unique expression of human compassion and respect" (Dolan 1991:xvi).

Although these notions and principles are excellent ones that should be included in any treatment program for victims and survivors of sexual victimization, something is missing. That something is that we must make more explicit how these issues apply uniquely to women's and children's lives, and we need to remain cognizant of how our culture exacerbates the situation for all of us. Accordingly, in the section which follows, I outline the contributions that feminists, via their reformulations of many of the traditional psychotherapeutic principles and practices, have made generally, as well as specifically, in treating the survivors of sexual victimization.

Feminist Therapy as a Solution

Due to the influence of the "second wave" of feminism, i.e., the 1970s women's movement, we have become increasingly aware of the fact that many (if not most) traditional models of therapy do *not* work well for many women in resolving their life problems (Burt and Katz 1987; Chesler 1989; Conn 1991; Greenspan 1983, 1986; Jack 1991; Kaschak 1992; Laidlaw and Malmo 1990b; Laidlaw et al. 1990; Lerner 1989; Reis 1991b; Walker 1985). This is true because many of these approaches tend to: (1) place the responsibility (read blame) on the woman for having the "problem," as well as focus on her individual failings rather than situational variables, extenuating circumstances, and/or cultural forces that caused it; (2) encourage women to adjust to stereotypical gender roles which in many cases causes them *more* distress; (3) be highly sexist in their interpretation of women's emotions, behaviors, and roles, as well as in their definitions of psychopathology; and (4) assume that emotional distance between therapist and client is the healthiest approach (Adcock and Newbigging 1990; Bograd 1986; Broverman et al. 1970; Franks 1986; Green 1990; Greenspan 1986; Kitzinger 1990; Lerner 1989; Reis 1991b; Steinem 1992; Tallen 1990; Taylor 1990).

During the ensuing years, several feminist psychotherapeutic models have been developed and have clarified: why women are more likely to have certain problems; the role of the patriarchal culture in causing and perpetuating these problems; psychiatry's social control function (i.e., it keeps women in their place); the psychological, social, and economic costs of living in a patriarchal culture; and how and why women's lives are different from men's (Chesler 1989; Dinsmore 1991; Greenspan 1986; Jack 1991; Kaschak 1992; Lerner 1989; Reis 1991b; Tavris 1992; Taylor 1990). Based on these issues, feminist models of treatment have tried to include: (1) an awareness that women are an oppressed group and that this oppression has direct and significant emotional, social, and economic ramifications; (2) a therapeutic relationship based on openness, trust, reciprocity, and equality; (3) a rejection of *nonfeminist* models which encourage women to accept their "plight" and/or to conform to gender-typed expectations and norms; and (4) the client as the primary force in her own process of change (Butler 1985; Hertzberg 1990; Kaschak 1992; Laidlaw and Malmo 1990a; Lerner 1989; Reis 1991b; Rosewater 1990; Taylor 1990).

Regarding the specific subject of sexual victimization, feminists are credited with reconceptualizing it as a product of the culture rather than being "caused" by the individual [i.e., they have politicized it, as well as many other "women's" problems (Courtois 1988; Dinsmore 1991; Herman 1992; Kelly 1988; Koss and Harvey 1991; Russell 1984, 1986; Walker 1985). This new emphasis has had direct effects on how to go about working with or "treating" the victims and survivors of sexual victimization. As examples, feminist-based treatment approaches: minimize what the girl, adolescent female, or adult woman did to "cause" the sexual assault; focus on her and her needs; empower and permit her to have an active role in her own recovery; normalize her responses to sexual victimization rather than pathologize them (i.e., view them as "survival skills" rather than "symptoms"); place her experiences at the center of the treatment process; and focus on her reality and her subjective knowledge (Briere 1989; Courtois 1988; Dinsmore 1991; Herman 1992; Kelly 1988; Koss and Harvey 1991; Reis 1991b; Swink and Leville 1986; Taylor 1990; Walker 1985). These reconceptualizations are important because they should lead to a reduction in the client's senses of guilt and self-blame, problems that are common during the traditional, nonfeminist "brands" of treatment.

Reis (1991b:19–20) is one of the clearest voices about what the theoretical underpinnings of feminist therapy should be, as well as the value of, and the specifics of feminist interventions:

> First, because my work is grounded in feminist theory and thinking, I consider the work I do political. This does not mean that I propagandize the women who come to me. It does mean that I *never* disconnect—in my own mind—from the social and political pressures that are involved in every single piece of women's pain and struggle. Second, the work I do takes place in a private office ... The dangers in this set-up are many. The most important is the potential for what I call the 'privatization of pain.' Every issue a woman brings into the therapeutic container is tied

to her experience of being a woman in a culture that does
not love women, a culture that has imposed its power
relationships on her ... Third, I deeply believe in the
power of a therapeutic alliance to facilitate healing ... I
approach the work as a partner and companion ...

Although I agree with a feminist reformulation of therapy,
there is at least one potential problem. The literature which
summarizes the essentials needed when treating the survivors of
sexual victimization (particularly if this victimization occurred in
their early years) is replete with examples of clients who have
difficulty with their boundaries (i.e., they have trouble determining where they end and others begin); yet, feminist therapy
suggests that the counseling relationship be an equal one, that
there be a certain degree of closeness and reciprocity between
therapist and client. The potential problem is that, if girls,
adolescent females, and adult women are struggling with
boundary issues, too much equality may be confusing and
perhaps even counterproductive for them. I do *not* think that this
means that feminist therapists must return to the "distance
model" of intervention; rather, clinicians must remain cognizant
of the fact that egalitarianism (at least initially) may be confusing
and difficult to interpret for many of their clients.

As a final note, please be advised that many of the extant
treatment models that are summarized in this chapter explicitly
align themselves with feminist principles and practices, while
others do *not*. Authors who fall into the former category include:
Bass and Davis, Briere, Courtois, Dinsmore, Herman, Koss and
Harvey, Poston and Lison, Reis, and Swink and Leveille, while
the works authored by Burgess and Holmstrom, Dolan, Gil,
Kilpatrick and his associates, Ledray, and Miller fail to make this
connection. From my perspective, current treatment modalities
must include feminist emphases because doing so creates a more
humane atmosphere for the victims and survivors of sexual
victimization.

Selecting a Therapist

One of the most important elements that determines whether therapy will "work" is selecting a practitioner with whom you feel comfortable. This may be a more critical issue when trying to recover from sexual victimization because many of us, for years, have had problems trusting and getting close to anyone. In order to be effective, then, the clinician must have a clear understanding and vast knowledge not only about rape, incest, and child sexual abuse, but also about how to treat the aftermath of these experiences. I also would add to this list that a therapist should understand and support (at minimum, he/she should *not* oppose) a feminist view of the world, self, and counseling.

Several current works offer checklists and guidelines which can be useful when seeking a therapist. This selection process, though, is *not* an easy one for several reasons. First of all, while in the throes of distress, ofttimes, we have a sense of immediacy (i.e., I am in pain, and I have to find a therapist fast); and this can create the potential for error in determining whether a particular therapist will be "good" for us. In fact, in some cases, we end up making our selections based on who can see us quickly, which may or may not work out well in the long run.

Second, many works have the unstated bias that all of us have *equal* access to good therapy. As an example, although Finney (1990:211) offers the excellent suggestion of interviewing several therapists before making the determination about which one is best, she shows her class bias by noting that: "Yes, it will cost you perhaps $200 to $300, but if it prevents you from making a mistake and helps you find a therapist you really like, it will be well worth the effort and the price." The reality of the situation is that those of us with resources will be able to access the private mental health system, a system which tends to employ better practitioners and offer better services (Cockerham 1992), while those of us without adequate economic resources only can qualify for the public mental health system. This statement is *not* intended to downgrade the abilities and/or the motives of practitioners who are employed in public mental health or social service agencies; many of them are excellent, dedicated professionals. Rather, the point is to underscore the fact that we have a *two-tier* mental health system just as we have a two-tier system for physical illness (Cockerham 1981, 1992). In other words, in the U.S., if you can afford them (i.e., via adequate medical care coverage or out-of-pocket), there are wonderful physical and mental health services to be had; if, though, you *cannot* afford them (and more of us are increasingly unable to do so), you must rely on the humanity and kindness of individual private practitioners who may devote a percentage of their practice to "gratis" cases, or you must seek help in the crowded, understaffed public system and take your chances.[1]

Third, many of these reports assume that clients have homogenous attitudes about therapy and our need for it. In other words, these works infer that the stigma associated with "seeing" a therapist or being "in" counseling has disappeared. Again, the reality of the situation for many of us (particularly certain class groupings) is that we believe that we should be able to resolve our problems by ourselves (i.e., the pull yourself up by your bootstraps school of thought); "loved ones" do *not* believe that we need therapy and/or do *not* support or cooperate with our decision to initiate it; and/or many observers cling to the stereotype that anyone who is "seeing" a mental health practitioner must be "crazy" (Cockerham 1981; Herman 1992). With these sorts of notions in our heads, regardless of how severe our pain, many of us may *not* feel that therapy will be of any value.

Finally, many of the suggestions outlined below for selecting a therapist infer a certain level of functioning and/or intelligence on the part of the client. That is to say, several of them assume (again implicity rather than directly) that we will be able to ask intelligent questions (rather than assuming that we may be in the throes of "learned silence"), and that we will be able to understand and accurately interrupt the answers of these prospective therapists. Again, this observation is *not* meant to be derogatory. Rather, ofttimes, the realities of the situation are that: (1) we wait until we are "in crisis" before we decide to enter therapy; (2) many of us know very little about the qualifications of and differences among the various types of mental health practitioners; and (3) we may be *unable* to make such an important determination in one session. Regarding this latter issue, since such a large part of the success of what Briere calls abuse-focused therapy depends on building a relationship of trust with a therapist, particularly in cases of childhood sexual victimization, it may take weeks or perhaps months to achieve this goal. In addition, for many of us (particularly if we have buried these memories or never have told anyone about our experiences), this may be the first time that we "tell." So, how can we be expected to make such an "intelligent" choice about who is the best therapist so rapidly?

Notwithstanding these problems, a number of experts have suggested guidelines to follow when selecting a therapist. Please note, though, that most of the works that address this issue appear in the child sexual abuse literature. Again, the implication is that rape is a less serious experience and that one recovers from it fairly rapidly. As will be explained in detail later in this chapter, though, this probably has more to do with the existing bias that crisis intervention is the "best" model to treat the aftermath of rape victimization, a bias that is based predominantly upon conjecture rather than empirical research.

Specific suggestions include asking people that we know and trust (e.g., family members, friends, ministers, doctors) for recommendations (Bass and Davis 1988; Blume 1990; Finney 1990). This is similar to what Friedson (1961) has called the "lay referral system" for physical health problems (i.e., we ask people that we trust about whether we should seek medical attention, as well as which practitioner to see). Another way to create a list of potential therapists is to visit the local agency that handles child sexual abuse cases in your area and your local mental health association and ask about specific practitioners who specialize in this type of work (Finney 1990). Once you have made a short list of prospective therapists, the goal is to narrow it down. In order to do so, Bass and Davis (1988), Blume (1990), and Finney (1990) suggest that you prioritize your interview list by paying special attention to the names of practitioners that kept "popping up," as well as therapists about which significant others have said particularly positive things.

After doing so, you can interview three or four of them, either in person or by telephone (again, *if* you can afford this option). During this interview, Blume (1990:275–278) suggests that we ask the practitioner about his/her qualifications (i.e., whether the therapist has knowledge about and training in treating the aftermath of sexual victimization). She also focuses on the fact that, since girls and adults who are recovering from sexual victimization may have a blurred sense of where they "end" and others "begin," they must select clinicians who are very clear about their own "boundaries" (i.e., never select a therapist who believes that sexual contact with clients is acceptable and/or one that wants to be your "friend").

Bass and Davis (1988:459–460) offer specific questions that can be asked to help determine whether a counselor is suitable for you. They include: (1) have you worked with other survivors; (2) what kind of training have you had; (3) what specific techniques do you use in therapy; (4) do you think that children ever cause the abuse to happen; (5) is family reconciliation or forgiveness of the abuser necessary; (6) what do you think about touching clients (therapeutic touch only); (7) have you ever worked with lesbians; and (8) can I call you at home? The better practitioners will respond *yes* to questions one, seven, and eight; their answers to the fourth and fifth issues should be emphatic *nos*, while their attitudes about the second, third, and sixth issues will vary based on their professional training, biases, and experiences.

Bass and Davis (1988) and Finney (1990) also mention that it may be difficult for us as clients to determine whether a counselor is "good" or whether the process of therapy is really "helping" us. Part of the problem is that, since many of us feel so much pain when we try to talk about and sort through our sexually abusive experiences, and how they have affected us throughout our lives, we assume we are *not* doing well in therapy. Regardless of the difficulty we have in talking about these issues, though, we should feel understood and supported during this process, as well as feel as if we are making progress. As Bass and Davis (1988:461) express this point: "Counseling is not always comfortable, but you know you're with a good counselor when you develop more and more skills to heal yourself as time goes on. You become able to recognize your own patterns and to feel and interpret your emotions. Even if there's an initial period of strong dependency, you should eventually become more independent." If these are *not* your experiences (e.g., you are being told that your victimization or its aftermath is *not* that "bad," or if you are seeing a counselor who seems unable to deal with or is uncomfortable with your particular problems), find another therapist immediately.

Again, though, these authors implicitly assume that we will be able to make the rational decision to leave a therapist that is *not* helping us or one that may be actively harming us. Again, for many of us, the reality of the situation may be that we have become dependent on him/her and cannot make the "switch," we blame ourselves for being "bad" clients or being too "sick" to be helped, and/or we begin to accept the practitioner's biases about us and sexual victimization as "facts." To reiterate an earlier point, the inherent assumption is that we will have full use of all of our faculties, that we will always be able to make the right decision, and that we will *not* assume that we "deserve" bad therapy.

In sum, although the process of selecting a therapist is a critical one, we also must be realistic about it. Some girls and women (i.e., those who are better educated and/or have more economic resources) probably will do a better job of selecting a therapist. And the obverse is equally true: Those who may *not* trust mental health practitioners and/or lack the economic resources to initiate therapy with the better ones, probably will be shortchanged (Cockerham 1981). If we are sincere about trying to prevent further traumatization and subsequent victimization(s), though, this is an obvious issue that needs to be addressed and resolved for everyone in the population, not just the girls, adolescent females, and adult women who are "better off" educationally and economically.

Specific Issues Involved in and the Goals of Treatment

In the previous chapter, I examined the multitude of areas across which we need to recover and heal from sexual victimization. I refer again to the psychological, somatic, behavioral, interpersonal, cognitive, self-perceptual, sexual, political, and spiritual realms of our lives, as well as reducing the likelihood of subsequent victimization(s). In order to achieve recovery in these areas, though, many of us may require professional intervention. Notwithstanding the differences in content when doing therapy with girls, adolescent females, and adult women who have been sexually victimized, there are a number of general issues to examine and/or goals which ought to be emphasized. In many cases, these issues and goals dovetail well with the aforementioned dimensions of our lives.

Regarding the aftermath of *rape victimization*, it is important to state from the outset that many of the important issues and goals have *not* been clarified very well. Due to the facts that the primary treatment techniques have been derived from crisis intervention theory and that the literature which investigates the efficacy of these strategies is based mostly on conjecture and anecdotal data, we have assumed (rather than proven) the accuracy of many of its assumptions. As examples, this perspective assumes: (1) that our post-rape responses are "normal" given what has happened; (2) a "hurry-up" recovery process (i.e., it is to be completed in four to six weeks); and (3) that we stay in the "here and now" by focusing solely on the rape and its resultant effects (Aguilera and Messick 1978; Resick and Schnicke 1990). Of late, though, we have become more cognizant of the fact that some of these emphases are problematic and can even be detrimental, particularly for women who are experiencing subsequent victimizations, have other life issues with which they are grappling, and/or simply are having difficulty recovering "quickly" enough.

Even though the crisis approach does include the positive issues of helping the survivor of rape to accurately view her experiences (i.e., place the blame where it belongs—on the perpetrators and the society) and offering support and advocacy as she moves through the criminal justice system, problems exist because this perspective tends to minimize the woman's subjective experience. In other words, this perspective and its concomitant intervention strategies infer that she was "normal" and functioning well prior to being assaulted and that the rape experience has left her basically intact [i.e., she has *not* been severely damaged by it (Koss and Harvey 1991; Resick and

Schnicke 1990; Scurfield 1985)].² Accordingly, we have spent an *inadequate* amount of time considering whether these assumptions are true and what the salient goals should be. These flaws are even more pronounced when we consider that many of the concerns of adolescent females and women who have been raped are quite similar to those of females who are recovering from incest and childhood sexual abuse. Although we do know that the responses of this latter group can be more pronounced, the content of the reactions for both groups, as well as the areas across which they need to recover, are strikingly alike (Courtois 1988; Herman 1992; Janoff-Bulman 1992; Kelly 1988).

Regarding *incest and child sexual abuse*, much more attention has been paid to the specific issues that should be addressed in the treatment process. For example, when working with adult survivors of incest, Courtois (1988:177–182) indicates that there are several topics that should be uppermost for practitioners: (1) a commitment to treatment and the establishment of a therapeutic alliance; (2) acknowledging and accepting the occurrence of the incest; (3) helping the woman to recount her experiences; (4) breaking down the client's feelings of isolation and stigma; (5) aiding her to recognize, label, and express her feelings; (6) focusing on responsibility and survival issues; (7) allowing her to grieve; (8) cognitive restructuring of any residual, distorted beliefs and stress responses; (9) focusing on her self-determination and helping her to make behavioral changes; and (10) education and skill-building. In effect, Courtois highlights the emphases of helping women to become self-sufficient and well-functioning, as well as the feminist principles of valuing her and believing what she has to say.

Swink and Leveille (1986) indicate that there are some twenty-four emotional concerns that should be addressed, as well as several basic skills that should be taught, when adult women are recovering from their childhood experiences of incest. Some of the more critical emotional issues include: (1) clarifying the myths and facts of incest; (2) learning to trust and connect with others; (3) reexperiencing the abuse via dreams, nightmares, and flashbacks; (4) understanding the dynamics of incestuous families, and unlearning the role reversals which were taught in these households; (5) unlearning the patterns of helplessness and suppressing emotions; (6) unlearning the tendency to deal with the abuse in somatic ways; (7) unlearning self-destructive behaviors (everything from smoking to suicidal ideation and behaviors); (8) learning to experience anger and rage, as well as learning to direct them appropriately; (9) regaining our power; (10) developing a better self-concept; and (11) confronting the abuser. In effect, they emphasize the need for both personal and interpersonal changes. In addition, they suggest six basic skills that should be stressed during the therapeutic process: decision making, parenting skills, communication skills, assertiveness, relaxation training, and self-defense.

Dolan (1991) offers a particularly interesting perspective regarding the goals of treatment for adult survivors of childhood sexual abuse. First of all, she contends that therapy should be solution-focused and that therapists should provide a warm, supportive environment in which the woman can relay the details of her victimization. More importantly, she emphasizes the "active utilization of the client's present life resources and images of future goals and possibilities" (Dolan 1991:25). Since many of the works that investigate the consequences of and recovery from rape, incest, and child sexual abuse are oriented toward the past (i.e., going back and "trying" to fix, sort out, or, at minimum, come to grips with it), Dolan's emphasis on a *future* orientation (i.e., developing future images and models of who and what she wants to become) is both intriguing, refreshing, and a much needed reconceptualization.

Dinsmore (1991) also has words of wisdom regarding what is helpful in facilitating the healing process. Rather than focusing on a specific formula or particular treatment techniques, she regards therapy as a developmental process which may differ in content for each survivor:

> Some survivors confront their perpetrators, others do not. Some survivors have bonded with their mothers, others have not. Some survivors remain in the same towns as their families, others move clear across the continent to get away from their families. No matter what action is taken by the survivor, healing is related directly to her individual work, not to the actions of the perpetrator.

> Regardless of the specific steps, the recovery pattern is a developmental process that includes introspection, such as acknowledging the abuse and working through intense emotions, followed by an action, such as renegotiating family patterns or involvement in a survivor's mission (Dinsmore 1991:168).

Dinsmore also emphasizes a point that I regard as a very critical one and one that we often forget. Specifically, she notes the *heterogeneity* of the women with whom therapists work: Some are heterosexuals while others are lesbians; some are mothers, others are childless; some are able-bodied, others are *not*; some are involved in intimate love relationships, others cannot seem to bond with another; some are wealthy while others live in poverty; some are members of racial, ethnic, or religious minority groups while others are white. We do a tremendous disservice to everyone when we regard all women as being alike; the reality of the situation is that we and our lives can be quite different. We must not only take these ideas into consideration and be flexible enough to learn about women's "differences," but we also must be able to alter the therapy process to match their respective and ofttimes differing needs.

In summary, we seem to have inadequate information regarding the issues to be resolved in and the goals of the treatment of rape victimization, and this remains an obvious area for future theorizing and research. The incest and child sexual abuse literatures, though, are much clearer on this subject. Some of the important issues and goals highlighted therein include: (1) breaking silence and recounting the details of the experience(s), (2) cognitive restructuring, (3) assisting the girl, adolescent female, or adult woman in developing a better image of self and regaining her power, (4) learning to have better relationships, (5) education and skill-building, (6) unlearning old patterns that no longer work, (7) coming to grips with one's anger and finding constructive ways to express and deal with it, (8) having a future orientation or a model of self for which to strive, and (9) remaining cognizant of the differences among women.

Problem Areas That Can Arise during Therapy

Although the aforementioned issues to be resolved are excellent and laudatory goals for which to strive, we also need to be aware of the various pitfalls that can be encountered when trying to work through experiences of sexual victimization. In addition, if we speak of the possible difficulties that can arise, we need to focus on both of the involved parties. That is, some of the problems that can crop up are issues for clients; others really are problems for client and practitioner alike, while still others refer to the difficulties that therapists may encounter. Also, please note, that some of the concerns mentioned below are generic ones that can arise in any one-on-one therapeutic relationship, while others are specific to abuse-focused therapy. Finally, be advised that the following is *not* meant to be a comprehensive list of all the possible problems that can arise; rather, they are ones that are most frequently mentioned in the rape, incest, and child sexual abuse literatures.

Regarding the *client*, it is important that we acknowledge from the outset how truly "odd" the therapy relationship is. As is noted by Herman (1992:147): "Though the therapeutic alliance partakes of the customs of everyday contractual negotiations, it is not a simple business arrangement. And though it evokes all of the passions of human attachment, it is not a love affair or a parent-child relationship. It is a relationship of existential engagement, in which both partners commit themselves to the task of recovery." Although many lay people hold the bias that they should share details about themselves and their lives with loved ones, therapy mimics these sorts of relationships while simultaneously demanding that there be a certain amount of distance between the practitioner and the client. Part of this paradox can be resolved by implementing feminist principles and practices, but regardless of how feminist the therapist's orientation may be, one member of the dyad remains the trained professional while the other one is the client who has sought his/her expertise. In sum, given the characteristics and the nature of the relationship, it is no small wonder that therapy can produce all sorts of difficulties for both participants and that residual effects remain even within the context of feminist therapy.

An added problem for the client is the issue of being able to trust the therapist. As was mentioned earlier, trust between client and therapist is something that grows and matures over time; it is *not* a given that occurs automatically. I also would add that it is something that a therapist must earn. He/she does so by listening well, being helpful, being "there" when the client needs help, and by aiding the client in making the needed changes in her life. As noted in Chapter Five, though, one problem in achieving this goal is that the child, adolescent, or adult survivor of rape, incest, or child sexual abuse tends to be "deficient" at developing relationships and being able to trust. In addition, this sort of client often "tries" her therapist's patience by testing and retesting to make sure that he/she is trustworthy (Briere 1989; Courtois 1988, 1992). In reality, though, many of these tests really are unconscious attempts to get the therapist to reject her, a realistic expectation given many of her past experiences and relationships.

A third problem that the client may experience is being unable to make the needed changes that will facilitate recovery, growth, healing, and victory. Many girls and women who have been raped and/or have histories of child sexual victimization have had disrupted lives and have had their symptoms of "pathology" for a very long time. In addition, it is difficult to make the needed changes because many of them have never had a model of a "healthy" person in their lives, a "normal" relationship, and/or an image of what a "functional" family looks and acts like. Finally, some of them are more seriously impaired than others. I think that most practitioners would agree that a client whose primary complaints are fears or phobias which are related to the victimization, difficulty being sexually active, and/or difficulty trusting others are "easier" problems to deal with than are such "conditions" as MPD, BPD, or the shattered soul. I am *not* suggesting that therapy is doomed with clients who have reacted more "strongly"; rather, the point is that these sorts of problems will require a longer and a much more intensive form of treatment (Courtois 1988, 1992; Herman 1992).

Fourth, we need to recognize the fact that entering therapy to deal with the wounds of sexual victimization is inherently painful for all who do so. Thus, clinicians, particularly ones who are doing therapy with the victims and survivors of incest and child sexual abuse, need to applaud their clients' efforts for having continued to live, as well as congratulate them for having been able to survive these experiences (Bass and Davis 1988; Blume 1990; Briere 1989; Courtois 1988, 1992; Dinsmore 1991; Dolan 1991; Engel 1989; Finney 1990; Herman 1981, 1990; Miller 1990, 1991; Putnam 1989). In other words, before treatment can "work," and even before the actual work of therapy can begin, clinicians must acknowledge and validate the experiences of their clients and acknowledge that they have survived regardless of how "unpleasant" some of their tactics may have been. Therapists also must remain aware of how difficult it is for many of these girls and women to enter therapy because doing so infers that: they have been unable (for whatever reasons) to effect these changes by themselves, with significant others, and/or in support groups; they currently are in pain or are functioning poorly; and/or they just may have begun to have memories of the abuse and/or realized the impact that these experiences have been having on their lives.

Another problem is that, ofttimes, clients enter therapeutic relationships with distorted beliefs about what to expect. Sometimes they regard therapy as something that is "done" to them, i.e., as a "magical" process whereby someone "fixes" them. And, in some cases, particularly if the therapist views him/herself as the sole authority on the subject, that is precisely their experience. Increasingly, though, therapy is regarded as something that clients do for themselves; therapists simply act as the facilitators of the process.

The final, yet complicated problem that can arise for the client during treatment is transference. This is *not*, however, an issue that the client (at least initially) is aware of and/or regards as a problem; rather, it is one that the experts have defined for her as a problem. Briere (1989:65–66), for example, defines transference as "contextually inappropriate perceptions and expectations of significant others in one's adult life—including one's therapist—based on important interpersonal learning that occurred in childhood." He also divides transference into three types that have distinctively different consequences: (1) chronic distortions in adulthood that "reflect a general world view skewed by childhood experience, resulting in archaic responses to relevent interpersonal stimuli"; (2) intense emotionality which occurs when something in the present reactivates the earlier trauma; and (3) misperceptions about a significant other in the woman's life who has "similarities to a psychologically important person in the survivor's childhood" (Briere 1989:66). The first type of transference can result in highly distorted cognitions and a "warped" view of the world; the second set can produce "PTSD-like responses ... [or] reactions [that] are quite often brief and are perceived [by the client] as emotionally intense and psychologically intrusive," while the third type is what classic psychoanalysis refers to as transference in that a person in one's current life (often but *not* always the therapist) is responded to as if he/she were someone from the "past" (Briere 1989:66–67).

Briere (1989:67–68) goes so far as to suggest that this problem may be an unavoidable one:

> Psychotherapy, almost by definition, involves client interactions with a powerful, psychologically important person in an intimate context . . .
>
> Herein lies the 'catch' for the survivor: In order to find relief from injuries sustained in one or more abusive childhood relationships, he or she must voluntarily enter into what is, in some ways, an equally threatening one as an adult.

Courtois (1988:215) regards transference mostly as that which transpires between client and therapist: "Many aspects of the incest, the family experience, and individual personality style and functioning are brought to therapy and projected onto the therapist." In order to resolve this dilemma, Courtois cites the multitude of post-incest issues that can arise and offers information about how these issues affect the therapy process. First of all, she suggests that, through decades of experiences, the adult survivor of incest has learned that people are *not* to be trusted. This can cause therapy to be a slow, tedious process that neccesitates that the client learn to trust and rely upon the therapist. Second is traumatic transference (i.e., unconsciously, the client expects the therapist to exploit her) which creates the need "to create a safe environment and . . . a reliable, trustworthy [therapeutic] relationship" (Courtois 1988:217). Third, as a result of childhood victimization, girls learn to feel shame and self-hatred and to have low self-esteem which causes them as adults to "project their shame onto their therapists, expecting them to hold them in the same contempt they have for themselves and to behave disrespectfully as their family did" (Courtois 1988:217). To counter this, the therapist must work to show the client that he/she is worthy of that trust. Fourth, although some adult women evidence many post-incest interpersonal difficulties, some of them do have what Courtois refers to as "reparative relationships" (i.e., relationships that contradict their earlier experiences). She also adds that the "therapy relationship holds the potential to be such a reparative experience, possibly the survivor's first" (Courtois 1988:218). Fifth, post-sexual-victimization feelings of guilt, complicity, and responsibility cause problems in identity formation for most incest survivors. To counteract these issues, therapy should include cognitive restructuring which allows the woman to know the reality of the abuse (i.e., it was *not* her fault; it was the perpetrator's). Sixth, Courtois (1988: 223) speaks of the value of the post-incest defenses and accommodation mechanisms that survivors have implemented: "[They] were necessary at the time of the incest but have outlived their usefulness and become problematic in the post-abuse period." As a way to alter the present situation, the therapist must depathologize these mechanisms; educate her about their necessity, value, and normalcy, given what happened to her; and help her to learn new healthier patterns. Seventh, as a result of childhood sexual victimization, the girl may have learned to caretake and to feel responsible for others.[3] Accordingly, part of the treatment process must be devoted to helping her to *unlearn* these patterns, as well as to learn to take care of herself. Eighth, Courtois (1988:226) focuses on the very real sense of loss and grief that women who were sexually victimized as children come to experience during therapy; the most common issues include:

"lost childhood, lost innocence and trust, lost identity (i.e., I am *not* the person I might have been), lost potential (with family members, interpersonally, sexually, and occupationally), and lost good family and parenting" (Courtois 1988:226). Last are the issues of rage and anger. Typically, these arise as the woman comes to comprehend: her losses, how she was betrayed, and how she was neglected. The therapist's responsibilities, then, are being able to "sit quietly" with the woman's anger and rage (no easy task), teach the woman how to discharge these potent emotions safely, and help her learn how to gain some control over them (Courtois 1988).

In sum, although entering into a therapeutic relationship and cooperating during it can be arduous and painful work, the alternatives are much worse: continuing to "hang on for dear life" and having lives dictated by the scars of our past, if we have lives at all. Although the therapeutic process to heal these wounds is at minimum a difficult one, it is one that is necessary for many of us if we are ever to lead happy and productive lives.

Therapists, too, can experience all sorts of problems while doing abuse-focused therapy. For example, Briere (1989) notes the problems of isolation, as well as the impact that the details of the clients' experiences can have on them. Regarding the former issue, he notes that working "with victims [of sexual abuse] is a relatively autistic process, a closed system where the therapist absorbs the client's pain and often is unable to fully unburden it to others" (Briere 1989:168). He also suggests that, although part of this isolation comes from the discomfort of one's coworkers and supervisors regarding the details of the more severe cases of child sexual abuse, an equally important part arises out of this society which "discounts abuse and its effects . . . [and which] also discount[s] those who work with abuse victims" (Briere 1989:168). In sum, Briere (1989:167) notes that, although "[w]orking with sexual abuse survivors can be a gratifying experience . . . [t]here is a 'dark side' to such endeavors . . ."

Regarding the "material" itself, the bottom line is that doing this kind of work can be very draining for practitioners, particularly those who do it right (i.e., clinicians who really try to empathize with and understand their clients' pain), and that they must take steps to safeguard themselves. Briere (1989:171–177) offers several suggestions, including: (1) therapy for therapists which affords them the opportunity to vent feelings and to examine their own issues; (2) sharing the load or having "consultations with other abuse-focused clinicians" and/or their supervisors which permits them "to regularly discharge painful affect regarding his various 'cases,' to examine the impact of such work on his own psyche, and to hear useful suggestions and perspectives . . . [about] what to do next"; (3) making sure that they have mixed case loads which include "some relatively high functioning, nonabused clients" who can help them keep a healthy perspective about the "dangers of the world" and the "evilness of people;" (4) social partitioning which refers to (a) having other people in your life who do *not* do this kind of work, (b) getting involved in "noncognitive and physically demanding activities," and (c) taking needed "mental health breaks"; and (5) macrointerventions, or involving yourself in activities and projects that are larger than individual or group treatment and that focus on prevention of sexual abuse (e.g., research about the problem), are good ways to feel as if you are "directly addressing the problem—rather than solely treating effects—can be a powerful antidote to feelings of helplessness."

Steele (1989:20–21), as well, acknowledges that child sexual abuse can be traumatizing, not only for children and its adult survivors, but also for the professionals who come into contact with them afterward: "There is a vicious jolt that comes as we hear the unspeakable, . . . as we sit with someone who has experienced the intolerable . . . But what of that stunned moment when we suddenly realize there is more: when we come to a terrible knowing that we are not just repairing psychological damage, but that we are sitting face to face with a shattered soul." Steele (1989:24) not only identifies the problem but also offers eloquent and graphic advice about how one actually goes about doing the work of "sitting with a shattered soul:"

> Gently, with gracious and deep respect. Patiently, for time stands still for the shattered, and the momentum of healing will be slow at first. With the tender strength that comes from an openness to your own deepest wounding, and to your own deepest healing. Firmly, never wavering in the utmost conviction that evil is powerful, but there is

a good that is more powerful still. Stay connected to that Goodness with all your being, however it manifests itself to you. Acquaint yourself with the shadows that lie deep within you. And then, open yourself, all that is you, to the Light. Give freely. Take in abundantly. Find your safety, your refuge, and go there as you need. Hear what you can, and be honest about the rest: be honest at all costs. Words won't always come; sometimes there are no words in the face of such tragic evil. But in your willingness to be with them, they will hear you; from soul to soul they will hear that for which there are no words.

When you can, in your own time, turn and face that deep chasm within. Let go. Grieve, rage, shed tears, share tears. Find those you trust and let them be with you. Know laughter, the healing power of humor. Trust yourself. Trust the process. Embrace your world, this world that holds you safely now. Grasp the small tender mercies of the moment. Let you be loved. Let you love. The shattered soul will heal.

I came away from reading this passage with three very different thoughts. First, I found myself wondering whether Steele was talking about the therapist or the survivor. When I reread it, I found that her ideas really apply to both of them; in fact, she infers that the two really must become one before either of them can know the true meaning of healing. Second, Steele is suggesting that we need to rethink not only what it takes to deal with the more severe cases of child sexual abuse, but also who is truly capable of doing so. In other words, she reiterates the previously mentioned notion that traditional therapies and traditional "types" of therapists will *not* be very effective in dealing with the problem of childhood sexual abuse. Rather, what is needed is a certain kind of person who is truly able to hear, as well as feel, horrible pain; somebody who possesses the difficult to measure yet essential skills of "realness," empathy, kindness, spontaneity, humor, and flexibility. Finally, whether by design or by accident, Steele "mixes her metaphors" or "speaks in opposites" the way many survivors of child sexual abuse do. As examples, she discusses good and evil nearly in the same breath; she regards the shadows and the light as parts of the same whole; she speaks of hearing even when there are no words; and she writes about the importance of both laughter and tears in the healing of a shattered soul.

Although implicitly, Briere and Steele are addressing the issue of countertransference. There is, though, variation in how the experts define this concept. For instance, Briere (1989:73) speaks of it as "biased therapist behaviors that are based on [their own] earlier life experiences or learning," while Courtois (1988:229) depicts it as therapists implementing avoidance, attraction, and attack strategies:

> Avoidance refers to the desire to deny, escape from, or not see the situation as it really is . . . and is based on such emotions as anxiety, discomfort, repugnance, dread, and horror. Attraction connotes a moving towards or an arousal, a desire to become involved in or stimulated by the situation. Attack is motivated by anger and condemnation of the activity and connotes aggressive responses to those involved in it.

As examples of the variety of problems that therapists can encounter, Courtois (1988:229–243) notes their tendency to: (1) experience dread and horror; (2) try to deny and avoid that incest exists (a tradition that gained popularity via Freud and his writings); (3) project feelings of shame, pity, and disgust onto the incest survivor (which could be life threatening for her); (4) feel guilty, particularly if he/she had a normal, happy childhood; (5) feel rage about what happened to the client as a child; (6) feel grief when the client is relaying details of her abuse; (7) begin to think that all women are victims; (8) try to avoid the heinous nature of incest via muted language or euphemizing what happened; and (9) contact victimization or being "prone to lose faith in the world as safe and meaningful and in women and children as being personally invulnerable." Courtois adds that the problems experienced by clinicians who do abuse-focused therapy are similar to those encountered by therapists who have worked with Holocaust survivors.

In sum, doing this work is a double-edged sword; it can be rewarding and challenging, but practitioners who do this work also must be prepared for the worst. Regarding the former issue, Dinsmore (1991:167) notes that she has been inspired by many of her clients: "I have witnessed the enormous growth of women who were . . . brutalized as children as they emerge as strong, capable, loving women. It seems no less miraculous than watching a butterfly emerge from its cocoon . . . [W]orking with incest survivors has demonstrated to me the tremendous capabilities of the human spirit, particularly the spirit of women." When she speaks of the rewards of really engaging in this work, Herman (1992:153) concurs:

> The reward of engagement is the sense of an enriched life. Therapists who work with survivors report appreciating life more fully, taking life more seriously, having a greater scope of understanding of others and themselves, forming new friendships and deeper intimate relationships, and feeling inspired by the daily examples of their patients' courage, determination, and hope . . .

> [E]ngaged therapists [also] deepen their own integrity . . . Integrity is the capacity to affirm the value of life in the face of death, to be reconciled with the finite limits of one's own life and the tragic limitations of the human condition, and to accept these realities without despair . . . The interlocking of integrity and trust in caretaking relationships completes the cycle of generations and regenerates the sense of human community which trauma destroys.

Herman (1990:292) also outlines the downside of working with clients who are grappling with the problems of rape, incest, and child sexual abuse: "In bearing witness to the atrocities that our patients have suffered, we discover more than anyone wants to know about human evil . . . We seek continually to find a mode of communication that . . . allows all of us to come a little closer to facing the unspeakable."

Thus far in this chapter, I have focused on the issues of the appropriate philosophy of treatment, the merits of feminist psychotherapeutic principles and practices, selecting a therapist, the specific issues to be resolved during the therapy process, and potential problems that can arise in this relationship for clients and therapists alike. Although each of these is an important consideration, we also need to examine and evaluate the extant ways that treatment is done. Accordingly, the focus of the following section is on some of the specific treatment modalities

which have been found to be effective when treating the
aftermath of sexual victimization.

Specific Treatment Approaches and Models

It is important to acknowledge from the outset that there is
doubt and confusion regarding the quality of some of the
interventions to be discussed in this section. As noted by Resick
and Schnicke (1990:501): "This state of affairs may be due more
to the lack of comparative research on the topic than to the fact
that all theories are equal." Second, although feminist therapeutic principles and practices have been highly touted in recent
years, empirical investigations which prove their efficacy do *not*
as yet exist. Third, several current sources suggest that the
specific treatment approaches that are used with the victims and
the survivors of rape, incest, and child sexual abuse may *not* be
as important as are the philosophy of treatment, the
characteristics of individual therapists (particularly their abilities
to be empathic and understanding), and the therapist's
commitment and adherence to feminist emphases and principles
(Briere 1989; Courtois 1988; Courtois and Sprei 1988; Dinsmore
1991; Koss and Harvey 1991). Fourth, please note that many of
these works focus exclusively on *one* type of sexual victimization
(rape, incest, or child sexual abuse). In the following section, I,
too, focus on them as "separate" issues; I say "separate" because
at the end of this chapter, I highlight how similar these treatment
modalities really are or should be. Fifth, the treatment literature
can be confusing because there is disagreement as to what
constitutes treatment, as well as uncertainty about which
strategies may be more effective. Some works regard self-help as
a "treatment" option, while others focus exclusively on
professional intervention. As examples: (1) Bass and Davis,
Engel, Finney, and Poston and Lison offer self-help approaches
for women who were sexually victimized as children, while
Braswell and Ledray offer self-help models for adolescent girls
and women who have been raped; (2) Bagley and King, Briere,
Courtois, Dolan, and Jehu have authored excellent overviews of
professional treatment strategies which have been employed

with women who are trying to recover from childhood sexual victimization, while Calhoun and Atkeson and Koss and Harvey summarize these issues as they relate to the victims and survivors of rape; and (3) Koss and Harvey, Scurfield, and Stekette and Foa illustrate the specifics of group treatment for survivors of rape while Briere, Courtois, Gil, and Homstead and Werthamer outline these issues as they apply to the survivors of incest and child sexual abuse. Finally, there are differences in the literatures which summarize these processes for the victims and the survivors of the various forms of sexual victimization. For instance, while treatment aimed at resolving the crisis of rape has relied mostly on crisis intervention theory and/or feminist principles, many of the works in the incest and child sexual abuse literatures have drawn from traditional tactics in clinical psychology and have selected specific tactics which seem to work, while in many cases still adhering to feminist principles.

Notwithstanding these criticisms and the ethereal nature of what we know about the effective treatment of post-sexual-victimization trauma, the following discussion centers on several approaches which have been reported to be effective. This is *not* intended to be an exhaustive summary of all of the current treatment modalities. Rather, I have made judgments about the quality and the effectiveness of existing approaches, and have selected ones which represent different types of intervention (e.g., self-help, group therapy or support groups, and individual therapy) and have tried to summarize the very best ones.[4]

Treatment of Post-Rape-Victimization Trauma

As has already been noted, inadequate attention has been paid to recovery issues and the treatment of post-rape-victimization trauma. Again, due to what I and others now view as an *overreliance* on the crisis perspective to explain post-rape responses (Kilpartick and Veronen 1983; King and Webb 1981; Koss and Harvey 1991; Williams and Holmes 1981), historically, many practitioners have been locked into using crisis intervention tactics as their primary treatment tools. Several other treatment models, though, exist now and are receiving increasing atttention. They include: (1) the social learning model,

(2) treatment of PTSD, (3) Ledray's self-help approach, and (4) Koss and Harvey's treatment for nonrecent rapes, as well as their group intervention model. Each of these perspectives is discussed below.

Although it has its problems, the *crisis intervention model* remains the predominant approach used today to treat the aftermath of rape victimization, particularly in rape crisis centers. As is noted by Burgess and Holmstrom (1985:54): "The crisis model is issue-oriented treatment designed to ameliorate the symptoms of anxiety, fear, depression, loss of control, and decreased assertiveness." These goals are achieved via short-term intervention (three to four contacts, some of which can be conducted over the telephone), treatment in the "here and now" (i.e., the focus is on the rape rather than on earlier unresolved issues); and letting the woman know that she is *not* "crazy" but rather reacting to a disruptive, real-life experience (Burgess and Holmstrom 1979a, 1985; Calhoun and Atkeson 1991; Kilpatrick and Veronen 1983; Resick and Schnicke 1990; Turner and Avison 1992). This perspective also focuses on: medical problems which can result from rape; advocacy for the woman, particularly regarding legal matters; working with the woman's social support system; and, in some cases, providing added support for the woman via survivors' groups (Burgess and Holmstrom 1985; Koss and Harvey 1991).

The *social learning or behaviorism model* of Kilpatrick and his associates focuses predominantly on "unlearning" rape-related fears and phobias (Calhoun and Atkeson 1991; Kilpatrick and Veronen 1983; Kilpatrick et al. 1985). As was noted in the last chapter, this perspective suggests that stimuli that were present during the rape, if reexperienced, can produce the same responses of anxiety and fear that were felt during the rape. Over time, these reactions become crystallized, and rape survivors can become immobilized by their fears and phobias. In order to alter this situation, then, these logical, yet counterproductive, connections must be broken.

Kilpatrick and Veronen (1983) offer a behavioral treatment model which shortcircuits the fear and phobias of rape survivors. Their four to six-hour treatment package for recent rape victims, the Brief Behavioral Intervention Procedure (hereafter, BBIP), begins with the following assumptions: (1) practitioners must validate rather than question the woman's experience; (2) the woman who has been raped believes many of the myths which makes her think that she has "caused" her attack to occur; (3) most rape survivors lack information about normal reactions to rape; and (4) many survivors lack coping skills for their rape-related problems. Thus, "The overriding assumption is that providing victims with information and with coping skills will assist them in dealing with rape-induced problems" (Kilpatrick and Veronen 1983:179).

This treatment model also offers four specific treatment strategies. First is the "induced-affect interview" which entails having the woman relax via deep breathing and muscle relaxation. Then, the clinician asks her about the rape incident, and he/she constructs a picture about: (a) the situation which preceded the rape; (b) the first moment that the woman became aware of the danger; (c) the attack itself; and (d) what occurred immediately after the rape. The second part of this treatment module is the educational component wherein the practitioner explains to the woman that her reactions to the rape (particularly her fears and anxiety) are normal given the situation and that she need *not* be afraid of them. The third emphasis is cognitive. Specifically, the therapist helps the woman to examine the cultural influences which have made her feel responsible for the attack (e.g., how she has been socialized to regard rape as her fault, as well as cultural images such as Scarlet O'Hara and fables which reinforce this culture's distorted view of rape). The final step in this program is teaching her coping skills, including assertiveness training, controlling whom she tells about the rape, relaxation techniques such as deep breathing and muscle relaxation, and thought stoppage (Kilpatrick and Veronen 1983).[5]

Another popular approach is to *treat the post-rape symptoms of PTSD*. According to Scurfield (1985), there are two levels of treatment that may be required. First, practitioners need to address the immediate or acute symptoms. This involves restoring the "traumatized survivor to a pre-trauma level of functioning as quickly as possible . . . by taking advantage of the rapid therapeutic gains than can be accomplished during the time-limited period when the person's normal defenses are relatively permeable . . ." (Scurfield 1985:241).

The other level of treatment is dealing with the long-term aftermath of sexual victimization. In order to deal with these chronic reactions, as well as those that follow the delayed-onset pattern, there are five major principles that practitioners can employ. They include: (1) developing a therapeutic trust relationship with the client; (2) educating her regarding the stress recovery process (i.e., emphasizing the normalcy of her reactions); (3) stress management or stress reduction via imaginal flooding, systematic desensitization, thought stopping, and cognitive restructuring; (4) regression back to or reexperiencing the trauma, and (5) integrating the experience (Coons et al. 1989; Scurfield 1985; Stekette and Foa 1987). Regarding this latter principle, Scurfield (1985:246) suggests that this "'final step' in the stress recovery process is the integration of all aspects of the trauma experience, both positive and negative, with the survivor's notions of who he or she was before, during, and after the trauma experience. This involves accepting full responsibility for one's own actions and understanding what was beyond one's control."

Scurfield (1985) also notes that the symptomatology associated with PTSD can be effectively treated in a group format and that family members can be brought into the process. By this he means that working in groups can reduce the survivors' senses of isolation and stigma, as well as provide a built-in support system. As for involving family members, they can be added as part of the treatment process "concurrently, conjointly, or sequentially to PTSD treatment with the survivor," as well as via significant others groups.

Ledray's (1986) self-help approach for treating the aftermath of rape victimization involves giving advice to the survivor, as well as her significant other(s). For the woman who has been raped, Ledray suggests that her early considerations should be: (1) coming to believe that the rape was *not* her fault; (2) reporting the attack to the police for her own safety and for the safety of other women; (3) seeking medical care; and (4) making specific changes to insure her safety (e.g., environmental changes for her home such as deadbolt locks and a security system, staying somewhere else for awhile). For the significant other, Ledray's advice is similar and focuses on many of the same concerns: (1) do *not* blame the woman for having been raped and do *not* blame yourself for having been unable to protect her from it; (2) do *not* take the law into your own hands; (3) realize that you, too, will have feelings and responses to your loved one's victimization; and (4) try to provide the emotional support that she needs. Down the road, though, recovery issues for the rape survivor switch to the more complex issues of: sorting out feelings and responses (i.e., being aware that they are normal ways to feel and act); taking back control of her life via evaluating her resources, making changes, combatting both her fears and negative thoughts about self, expressing her anger in positive ways, rebuilding self-esteem, and seeking help from others (friends or professionals); and telling others (if she feels that doing so will help).

Koss and Harvey (1991) suggest a model for the clinical treatment of nonrecent rapes, as well as group treatment for the victims and survivors of rape. Regarding nonrecent rapes, they offer an integrative treatment plan which includes several stages. First of all, the practitioner must assess whether the nonrecent rape has been resolved. This determination is based on the woman's ability to talk about the rape, what her past and current post-rape responses were and are, the meaning that she has ascribed to the experience, how her social support system has responded to her needs, whether she currently is overreacting to minor events in her life, and the amount of time that has passed since the rape occurred. If the therapist determines that the woman continues to experience "residual" effects, Koss and Harvey suggest that treatment should move on to the second stage of building a relationship with the client. Third is getting the woman to process painful memories. Although this often entails arduous work and the painful catharsis of buried material, doing so is an essential part of recovering from rape. Fourth, they note the importance of the cognitive dimension or the woman's shattered beliefs that must be addressed. Particular issues to be examined and resolved include her attitudes about safety, trust, power, self-esteem, and intimacy. Fifth is helping to restore a sense of mastery by "guiding the survivor toward involvements that satisfy important needs and support changes in thinking" (Koss and Harvey 1991:191). The last step in their model is treating target symptoms of anxiety, depression, sexual dysfunction, and relationship difficulties.[6]

Although Koss and Harvey (1991) are careful to point out that there is a paucity of research which investigates the efficacy of group treatment approaches, they believe that there are convincing reasons for implementing them. Similar to some of the issues that Scurfield (1985) considers, group intervention can reduce the women's senses of isolation and self-blame, offer a clear source of support and an opportunity for safe attachments, validate women's feelings about having been sexually victimized, promote self-esteem, establish egalitarianism in the treatment process, provide an opportunity to share their grief, and allow assignment of meaning. They also emphasize that these benefits can accrue in self-help or support groups, as well as in psychotherapy groups.[7]

Treatment of Post-Sexual–Abuse-Victimization Trauma

Several recent works offer effective treatment strategies for post-sexual-abuse trauma. Please note, though, that most of these works offer suggestions about treatment for adult women who retrospectively are trying to heal these wounds, while far fewer of them focus on recent victims of incest or child sexual abuse.[8] As examples of some of the best approaches, we have the models of Bass and Davis (1988), Briere (1989), Courtois (1988), Dolan (1991), and Wheeler and Berliner (1988). Please note that Bass and Davis's model is predominantly a self-help approach, while the other four focus on professional intervention, whether it takes place in groups or on an individual basis. In addition, the models of Bass and Davis, Briere, Courtois, and Dolan focus on treating the aftermath for adult survivors, while Wheeler and Berliner's work examines treating the aftermath among children who recently have been victimized.

As was noted in detail in the last chapter, _Bass and Davis (1988)_ have written a popular, _self-help approach_ to deal with aftermath of incest and sexual abuse among adult women. The predominant technique that they recommend is writing exercises. Issues to be considered and written about include: (1) the effects of the abuse, (2) how you have coped, (3) the exact nature of the abuse, (4) your "child within," (5) grieving, (6) disclosures and confrontations, (7) reconstructing your family history, (8) changing patterns, and (9) your family now. The primary gains of doing these exercises are: finally acknowledging how the abuse has hurt you, as well as your strengths or the ways that you have coped; breaking the silence and perhaps even confronting the perpetrator; changing your counterproductive coping patterns; and becoming cognizant of what your family is now. Please note, as well, that although theirs is a self-help model, Bass and Davis also acknowledge the possible need for individual and/or group treatment for adult survivors of childhood sexual abuse.

In *The Courage to Heal Workbook*, Davis (1990) offers even more information about writing exercises and activities that can be implemented when recovering from childhood sexual victimization. Specifically, the workbook is broken into three sections: (1) survival skills for healing which focus on such issues as safety, building a support system, dealing with crisis, nurturing yourself, and acknowledging how far you already have come; (2) taking stock or analyzing your life when you were growing up, the effects that the abuse has had on you, the coping strategies that you have employed, and developing healthier coping strategies; and (3) aspects of healing or the specific tasks to be accomplished across Bass and Davis' (1988) stages of recovery (i.e., deciding to heal, remembering, believing that the abuse happened, breaking the silence, understanding that it was *not* your fault, learning to trust yourself, grieving and mourning your losses, anger, confrontations, dealing with your family now, and resolution and moving on).

The basic premise in Bass and Davis's works are that releasing the pain, developing insights, and coming to a deeper understanding of the consequences of childhood sexual victimization should create the potential and the groundwork for a better life. Via writing exercises and other recommended activities, women can learn to regard their abuse experiences as a part of their history (rather than having it immobilize them in the present), understand the effects that it has had on their present-day lives, deal with their current problems, have a more positive view of self, and learn to have good relationships. In other words, they learn to "thrive."

Briere's *(1989:82–110) model of treatment* focuses on several specific principles and techniques to treat adult women who were sexually victimized as children. They include: (1) normalization or destigmatization; (2) facilitating emotional discharge; (3) disrupting the abuse dichotomy; (4) role-playing; (5) desensitization; (6) tape recognition; (7) therapeutic restimulation; (8) reframing intrusive symptomatology as healthy and healing; (9) self-control techniques (e.g., grounding, distraction, relaxation, self-talk, "leaving the scene" or "time-out," writing, and "portable therapist"); and (10) working with the "inner child."

Regarding normalization or destigmatization, Briere (1989:83) describes it as "therapist interventions that help the survivor to understand that his current behavior is not 'weird' or 'abnormal' but, rather, an entirely understandable reaction to his childhood experience." This procedure includes the tasks of: (1) providing information about the high incidence of sexual abuse in our society, the culpability of the perpetrator(s), and the common effects of such abuse; (2) having interactions with other survivors which should help the woman realize that she is *not* alone; and (3) clarification, the goal of which is to restructure the illogical patterns of thinking that many adult survivors of childhood sexual victimization are left with.

According to Briere (1989) facilitating emotional discharge refers to releasing emotions about the abuse. He cautions, though, that this must be done carefully and in ways that maintain the safety of the client. Typical emotions which need to be recognized and released include the "surface" ones of anger and sadness, as well as the deeper feelings of terror and fears of abandonment and of being totally overwhelmed. The need to release these emotions, according to Briere, is predicated on the assumption that the woman is ready to do so and that a relationship of trust already has been established between her and the therapist.

The third therapeutic tactic in this model, disrupting the abuse dichotomy, or restructuring borderline ideation, may be required in severe cases of abuse. Specifically, it refers to correcting the following pattern of thinking: "'(1) I am being hurt by a parent or someone I care about, (2) therefore either (a) I am bad or (b) he/she is. However, (3) I have been taught that adults are always right and hurt you only as punishment when you are bad. Therefore (4) it must be my fault that I am being hurt, and thus it follows that (5) I am as bad as whatever was/is done to me'" (Briere 1989:88). The primary goal of changing these cognitions is to get the woman to see that the abuse was done to her rather than caused by her, and, as she gets closer to this insight, her self-perception about her "badness" should decline while her anger at the perpetrator(s), more than likely, will intensify.

Briere's fourth therapeutic strategy is role-playing. Although this approach may *not* be for everyone (particularly women whose connection to reality is tenuous or in cases where extreme dissociation exists), when warranted, it has two major goals: "(1) to support the integration of the various warring (or at least isolated) components of her psyche and (2) to increase her level of self-acceptance" (Briere 1989:90). Suggested tactics include: (a) "the observer" which means having the client watch herself in a therapy session and describe what she sees and thinks in the third person; (b) good person, bad person, which refers to the client verbalizing "her self-hating and self-accepting components in dialogue form," and (c) externalizing the anger or "addressing her abuser *in absentia* during the psychotherapy session"[9] (Briere 1989:91–94).

Fifth is desensitization. Similar to the model developed by Kilpatrick and his associates, the point is to reduce the woman's responses to certain stimuli associated with her childhood victimization(s). Specifically: "[Th]e client is taught relaxation techniques and then, while in a relaxed state, is gradually exposed to whatever it is that he is frightened of. Over time the repetitive pairing of the frightening stimulus with both relaxation and a safe therapeutic environment decreases the power of the stimulus to elicit anxiety" (Briere 1989:95). Thus, the goals of this technique are to reduce the overall level of anxiety that the woman feels and to lessen the impact of her dissociative experiences and flashbacks.

According to Briere (1989:96–97), tape recognition "is a form of cognitive treatment . . . which . . . teaches the client to identify and deal with abuse-related perpetrator statements and inferences that have become introjected and that the survivor now believes to be her own perceptions." The restructuring of these cognitions involves three stages: (1) recognition (i.e., distinguishing between one's real thoughts and learned ones that are left over from the experience with childhood sexual abuse); (2) identification which is "proactive . . . [and] teaches the client to anticipate and expect abuse related introjections and to specifically identify them as such as they occur"; and (3) disattention, or altering the client's "relationship to her introjected cognitions" [i.e., the woman is taught to ignore these thoughts] (Briere 1989:97–99).

The seventh strategy is therapeutic restimulation which can be used to introduce new issues into the therapy process or when the process itself has become "stuck." Briere illustrates the significance of the most popular form of therapeutic restimulation, the photograph method. Specifically, the therapist asks the client to bring pictures of herself and her family which were taken around the time of the abuse:

> [O]ver the years, [she has] 'forgotten' many aspects of her victimization and has developed a variety of strategies to bury the fear and rage she felt as a child. The experience of directly re-viewing the abuse scenario brings such memories and affects 'back,' where they can be worked with. Unlike their original presentation, however, these images and feelings are now recapitulated in an adult, and in a healing context (Briere 1989:100).

Eighth is reframing intrusive symptomatology as healthy and healing. This is a creative and productive tactic which reframes "symptoms" by regarding them as "healing strategies." Briere (1989:102) cites the examples of flashbacks and nightmares and asks us to reconceptualize them as the "mind's attempt to heal itself." This is similar to what was discussed in the last chapter as the need to challenge and reconceptualize the extant "symptoms approach" and to view symptoms as metaphors for underlying issues. Once identified, these symptoms, as well as the underlying meanings that they represent, can begin to be used in productive ways.

Self-control techniques refer to the fact that clients should be able to take their therapy with them. In Briere's (1989:103) words, "[T]he client should be able to take certain skills and coping strategies away from the therapy session that will be of use to him or her in daily living." Specific strategies that can be applied in everyday living are: (1) grounding or trying to stay in the "here and now" when dissociative episodes begin; (2) distraction, which "is most useful when the survivor is caught in an internal psychological process that feeds on itself, such as panic, compulsive behavior, or self-destructive rumination"; (3) relaxation; (4) self-talk or "talking back" in positive and self-affirming ways to one's negative cognitions; (5) leaving the scene or time-outs (i.e., "the client learns to physically leave the situation where the temptation to act out resides"); (6) writing or having the client explore by herself different issues and ideas which also has the simultaneous effect of reducing the likelihood of client dependency; and (7) "portable therapist" which "involves the client asking herself 'what would my therapist say?' at points of crisis or indecision outside of therapy" (Briere 1989:104–106).

The final strategy in Briere's model is dealing with the inner or hidden child.[10] Based on the inconsistency, confusion, and violence of their childhoods, some adult survivors of incest and sexual abuse at times appear to be small children, or they act in childlike or immature ways.[11] Please note that Briere (1989:107) is *not* talking about women who suffer from MPD and are switching to a different personality; rather he refers to "multiple, coexisting developmental states that variously influence . . . adult behavior." According to Briere (1989:108), the primary causes of this problem are: (1) "traumatic freezing" of development (i.e., due to the childhood sexual abuse, the woman is "stuck" at an earlier stage of development) and (2) "splitting-off" of the abuse experiences wherein parts of one's childhood experiences are separated from daily living. Via helping the woman to acknowledge the existence of her childlike parts and role-playing, Briere (1989:110) suggests that the inner child can be accessed and healed:

[W]orking with the 'child' is a way to break through archaic dissociative defenses and thereby integrate repressed childhood memories, affects, and cognitions with adult understanding. Through the process of 'acting as the child,' the survivor speaks the previously unspeakable and thus updates old perceptions and desensitizes primitive emotionality. As these split-off parts of the client are worked through, their ability to motivate primitive/archaic behaviors lessens, and the 'child' loses its status as a discrete entity.

In summary, Briere offers a number of excellent, specific strategies to help women to heal their childhood wounds of sexual victimization. In fact, of the approaches with which I am familiar, Briere's is one of the best, most sensitive guides for treating the aftermath of childhood sexual victimization. Not only does he offer a logical and concrete therapeutic approach, but he also emphasizes the need for therapists to be humanistic in their approach with clients who have survived these types of childhood trauma.

Courtois (1988) offers an *eclectic, traumatic stress approach* to heal the retrospective wounds of childhood incest for adult women. Specifically, she suggests five major principles to treat delayed or chronic "symptoms" of PTSD. First is the intake and diagnosis stage during which the therapist tries to learn as much as possible about the nature of the woman's prior sexual abuse, its impact on her life, and her current levels of functioning. During this initial contact, the therapist also should share information about the normalcy of the client's responses, as well as offer information about the course of treatment and how she may feel as they proceed through it.

The second stage in this model includes establishing and deepening the therapeutic relationship, involving the woman in a therapy or support group, and continuing to educate her about incest, its past and present consequences, and the specifics of the recovery process. According to Courtois (1988:173), the goals are "breaking silence and isolation by learning that she is not alone; working with presenting problems and symptoms; learning about family interactions and taking an 'adult look' at family dynamics and rules; and acknowledging the 'child within.'"

Similar to what Briere suggests, Courtois's third step is to work with the "child within." Within the safety of the therapeutic alliance, the woman "reconnects with her abused child and reexperiences the trauma and the feelings of childhood, in particular responsibility, guilt, confusion, ambivalence, shame, anger, sadness, and loss" (Courtois 1988:174). She adds that, although this is very difficult work and the client may regress while doing it (e.g., intrusive thoughts and symptoms may return and/or decompensation may occur), it is an important part of the recovery process, and it is the therapist's responsibility to take the woman through this stage in "doses" that she can bear.

The fourth component is integrating the helpless child with the nurturing adult. This "involves integrating the various aspects of the trauma experience, whether positive, negative or ambivalent, into the self and separating from family rules and patterns" (Courtois 1991:174). The goal is to get the woman to the point where she can see how the patterns and dynamics of her family of origin contributed to the abuse, as well as being able to "empathize with her difficult childhood position and view herself with compassion rather than self-loathing" (Courtois 1988:174). In effect, the goals are for the woman to feel less "bad" and to begin to "forgive" herself. Again, please note that forgiving self does *not* mean that the woman did anything wrong; rather, the emphasis is on altering her cognitions about the abuse, as well as her resultant self-perceptions.

The final step in Courtois's treatment model is disclosure about the abuse, as well as confronting family members and other involved parties. She suggests that these tasks can be accomplished symbolically in therapy or via direct confrontations. For Courtois (1988:175) the goal is that "the survivor breaks the silence to become the 'reactivated child' who reclaims her selfhood, her experience, and her voice." Yet, again, the importance of having a voice and developing a strong sense of self emerge as critical components of the recovery process.

In addition to outlining specific steps involved in the therapy process to resolve post-incest trauma, Courtois (1988:184) underscores the usefulness of "a very flexible, eclectic, multimodal therapy utilizing a broad range of techniques."

Specifically, she cites the merits of: (1) stress/coping strategies, (2) experiential/expressive-cathartic tactics, (3) exploratory/ psychodynamic modalities, and (4) cognitive/behavioral techniques.[12] *Stress/coping strategies* are valuable because, typically, the incest survivor has been plagued with multiple stressors for a very long time. In order to improve her abilities to deal with those stressors, Courtois (1988) draws elements from crisis intervention theory, trauma or victimization theory (particularly Horowitz's conceptualization of the stress process), stress management theory, and the interdisciplinary literature which examines coping with difficult life events. Her *experiential/ expressive-cathartic methods* draw "from gestalt and other experiential/humanistic therapies, from psychodrama, and from art, movement, music, and writing therapies [and] are those most useful in breaking through denial and promoting ventilation, catharisis, and abreaction of the trauma" (Courtois 1988:192). The goal, then, is to release the emotions associated with the original trauma in safe, productive ways. Third are the *exploratory/psychodynamic tactics* which focus on unconscious, as well as conscious, material. Specific strategies involve free association, dream analysis, and hyponosis. The *cognitive/ behavioral techniques* include a wide range of strategies (e.g., developmental skill-building, social learning, and behavior modification) and are effective ways of "reversing the developmental deficits and conditioned responses caused by the abuse and/or the dysfunctional family atmosphere and in challenging and correcting the faulty cognitions many survivors hold" (Courtois 1988:200). Specific tactics include going back and learning developmental material that was missed due to poor parenting, self-nurturing exercises, cognitive restructuring, normalizing and legitimizing the incest experience, guided imagery and metaphor, stress inoculation training, relaxation training, and improving her problem-solving and decision-making skills (Courtois 1988:201–209).

In sum, Courtois offers an important and eclectic model which draws from all sorts of existing treatment paradigms. In addition, she emphasizes feminist principles and practices to deal with the long-term aftermath of childhood sexual victimization. Hers not only is an excellent model but a thorough one which focuses on nearly every aspect of the survivor's present-day life.

Dolan's (1991) primary treatment approaches entail solution-focused therapy and Ericksonian hypnosis. While the former technique focuses on the conscious level and controlling the woman's "symptoms," the latter one incorporates the unconscious sources of these responses. Specific issues or elements involved in this model are: (1) the importance of the first interview, (2) utilizing supportive relationships, (3) dealing with non-supportive family members and the perpetrator, (4) making sure that the woman is safe in the present, (5) "healing the split," and (6) "therapeutic dissociation."

Assuming that the woman is aware of her victimization, Dolan suggests that the priority issues that should be addressed during the initial interview include letting the client talk about the details of her victimization, sorting out her feelings about the trauma, using her present resources, creating future images of herself and thinking about future goals, and letting the woman know that her responses are normal. In order to avoid further traumatizing the woman during this first session, though, Dolan offers (1991:26–28) the notions of "comfort in one part" which permits "the client's conscious exploration of memories while experiencing some conscious comfort" and a "symbol for the present" which is something in the room that the woman selects to keep her grounded in the present while she explores the past. Finally, this initial contact should be used to assess the woman's current level of functioning. This is an important consideration because "[b]efore undertaking therapy focused ... on the resolution of the past trauma, the client needs to acquire some physical and emotional stability [in the present], to feel somewhat 'in control'" (Dolan 1991:30). One way to do this is to administer the Solution-Focused Recovery Scale, a paper and pencil tool that helps the woman to realize that she already has begun the healing process, as well as highlights the areas across which she needs to heal in the future (Dolan 1991:32).

Second, Dolan believes that involving the woman's supportive, significant others in the therapy process can be useful. She is quick to add, though, that they are involved solely to benefit the client: "[T]he purpose of ... [their] participation is to emphasize and utilize the resources and strengths inherent in their relationship with the survivor, to provide support and validation, and whenever possible, to prevent 'fallout' from the original trauma from contaminating current relationships" (Dolan 1991:42). In addition, rather than focusing exclusively on the past, Dolan (1991:44–45) emphasizes that, once these significant others understand and validate their loved one's history of sexual abuse, they and the survivor should "refocus their shared energy away from the trauma of the past and toward the healing, comfort, and hope inherent in the present and future."

The third issue is to deal with nonsupportive family members, as well as the perpetrator. Specifically, Dolan contends that disclosing the "secret," as well as confronting these people is a critical step in the woman's recovery process. Although I am *not* as convinced as Dolan that these activities will produce positive outcomes, she offers suggestions about how to go about doing them safely. As examples, she notes that therapists should help their clients predict the possible reactions of these people and should educate the woman about how to maintain a self-supportive perspective during disclosure. In addition, if the woman feels a need to confront the perpetrator (with the explicit goal of putting the issue to "rest"), Dolan suggests safeguards that can be implemented *prior* to the actual confrontation. These include preparing her for the worst-case scenario, as well as arranging for psychological and physical ways to protect her if it comes to pass. Finally, similar to what Swink and Leveille (1986) refer to as "orphanization," Dolan (1991:82) suggests that, if family members are *unwilling* to be supportive, the woman may have to permanently separate from them, as well as establish "a new family" or "a nurturing and healthy circle of significant others with whom to celebrate traditional holidays and enjoy ongoing contact . . ."

The fourth major element in Dolan's treatment model is making sure that the woman is safe in the present. This includes helping her to *unlearn* dissociative coping strategies and the patterns of learned helplessness that have made her vulnerable to subsequent victimization(s), as well as aiding her to prevent similar traumas in the lives of her children. Specific approaches include: (1) "scaling" or having the woman rate the degree of problems that she is having and assisting her in finding solutions that will increase her sense of felt safety; (2) "externalization of safety" (i.e., "the process of making safety an abstract entity that the client can identify as being present or not present in her home and family in specific ways" and identifying ways that she can make sure that they are); and (3) developing safe ways which permit the survivor, as well as her children, to signal the therapist for help [e.g., a prearranged signal such as a postcard (Dolan 1991:86–94)]. Dolan notes that these tactics are reserved for instances when the therapist suspects that the client and/or her children currently are being victimized or if they are at risk for victimization but are helpless to acknowedge their victimization and/or to seek protection and help.

The fifth element in Dolan's (1991:96) model is healing the split or the "gap . . . between the client's awareness of psychological resources and healthy coping mechanisms while in the therapeutic session and her regressed state when under stress that unconsciously symbolizes or otherwise reminds the client of the original trauma." The goals are to keep grounded in the present and to access the coping resources that she has worked so hard to learn. As specific, practical strategies, Dolan (1991:97–101) suggests: (1) imagining and answering solution-focused questions (i.e., imagining what her therapist might ask which should get her thinking and focused on her own resources); (2) self-induced pattern interruption or literally stopping a negative behavior pattern and trying something different; (3) notes to the self (i.e., writing down specific ways to cope in difficult situations and reading these instructions when she is "in trouble"); (4) nondominant handwriting or "writing messages to herself with her less dominant hand . . . [which] in subsequent times of stress is very powerful and has a stronger effect than writing it with her dominant hand"; and (5) associational cues or imagining "an experience in which she felt 'relatively calm and secure'" which should heighten her senses of comfort and security in times of distress.

The final element in this model is therapeutic dissociation or using the client's ability to dissociate in positive ways. According to Dolan (1991:128), although these tactics originally were "healthy and adaptive response to survive childhood abuse, dissociation becomes a constricting and often frightening symptom after outlasting its usefulness"; accordingly, the therapist helps "the client to redirect the learned dissociative tendencies in useful and integrative ways, so that they become resources rather than bewildering afflictions."[13] Although at first glance this seems an unorthodox approach which could further entrench the client's ability to dissociate, it is important to point out that the survivor already knows how to do it quite well; Dolan's goal is to use that "skill" as a way to keep her safe and heading toward recovery.

In addition to the aforementioned issues and elements, Dolan (1991:129) also outlines several *therapeutic tasks* which she has found to be particularly helpful in working with survivors of sexual abuse (individually, as well as in groups): "A major advantage of therapeutic tasks is that they can function both during therapy sessions and apart from the therapy hour, enabling the client to integrate therapeutic learnings and changes in uniquely meaningful ways." Some of the possible tasks for clients (if and when they are willing to try doing some or all of them) are: (1) writing a rainy day letter (or "a letter the client writes to herself when she is feeling strong and hopeful . . . [which then] can be read as needed during subsequent periods of pain and doubt"); (2) making and using a "medicine bundle" (i.e., based upon native-American beliefs and traditions, the client makes a bundle which includes "symbolic articles and perhaps written words evocative of the client's healing resources"); (3) writing a letter *from* the future or writing a letter, perhaps to a friend, as if several years have passed, so that "the woman [can] create hopeful associations about her future self"); (4) holding an imaginary funeral for one's lost family of origin or creating a divorce ceremony which effectively removes them from her life; (5) artistic self-expression, again to release the pain, as well as to express her "eventual feelings associated with resolution;" (6) self-nurturing rituals (e.g., developing and routinizing ways in which she can be good to herself); (7) a present-focused activity such as taking a class or learning a new sport (i.e., "the client is asked to choose to learn something new that will require her full attention in the present in a rewarding way"); (8) write and burn which refers to writing about her feelings (particularly those of anger and rage), reading what she has written, and then destroying them; and (9) nurturing the inner child or comforting her by doing some "little kid activities" which the woman may have missed out on in her youth (Dolan 1991:130–138).

The final model is *Wheeler and Berliner's (1988)*, and it focuses on the *aftermath of sexual victimization among children*. They suggest that the "effects of child sexual abuse can be understood as a combination of classically conditioned responses to traumatic stress and socially learned behavioral and cognitive responses to the abuse experience" (Wheeler and Berliner 1988:227). They also hypothesize that "treatments that are directed at altering the conditioned and socially acquired responses to the victimization will alleviate initial symptoms and will reduce the likelihood of long-term or more serious disruptions in development" (Wheeler and Berliner 1988:228). In addition, they indicate that specific treatment strategies must be selected based on the age and developmental level of the child. Finally, although their treatment program is geared for children, they also emphasize the need for parents to be educated about their offsprings' potential responses, as well as ways that they can help to allay future consequences for them.

Wheeler and Berliner (1988) offer a three-pronged treatment approach. First is the initial intervention and assessment. This entails a complete psychological evaluation of the child to determine the extent of the current trauma, finding out about the caretaker's perspective regarding the child's present symptoms (as well as the ability of that person to act as a source of support), and exploring how the child is defining and perceiving the abuse. Next is anxiety-reduction strategies which involve "reducing the arousal to fear-producing cues and teaching management strategies for neutralizing the subjective feelings of anxiousness" (Wheeler and Berliner 1988:236). Specific strategies that they have found to be effective are desensitization, graduated exposure, modeling, thought stopping, and assertiveness training. The explicit goals of these tactics are to help the child make conscious connections between her current fears and her past experiences of sexual abuse, as well as help her feel safer in the present. Finally, they offer strategies to treat the child's socially learned responses about her "responsibility" for the abuse. As Wheeler and Berliner (1988:239) note, "It is important to provide sexually abused children with a straightforward explanation of what has happened and assurances that they are not culpable for their abuse." This entails explaining why adults always are responsible for such actions, as well as indicating why some adults are child molesters; exploring the ways in which the child regards her victimization, and helping her to see that she was violated without her consent rather than an active participant. Other emphases include restoring the child's sense of efficacy, helping her to develop a positive self-image, and helping her to deal with having been traumatically sexualized. These goals can be achieved through discussion, role-playing, and/or videotaping.

Summary and Conclusions

The primary goal of this chapter has been to present an overview of a number of diverse issues related to treating the aftermath of sexual victimization. Accordingly, several subjects were explored, including the appropriate philosophy of treatment for the victims and survivors of sexual victimization, the importance of feminist principles and practices in this process, selecting a therapist, the specific goals of therapy or the various issues which should be explored, and the problems that can arise during the treatment process.

In addition, several of the extant treatment modalities which currently are being employed with girls, adolescent females, and adult women who have been sexually victimized were summarized. As I noted earlier in this chapter, due to a paucity of research which investigates this issue, though, we are unable at the present time to determine with any degree of certainty which of the aforementioned treatment approaches are superior (Resick and Schnicke 1990; Wheeler and Berliner 1988). Part of the problem lies in the fact that many, if not most, of the people who "do" the therapy are *not* researchers interested in determining the efficacy of specific therapeutic approaches.

Thus, one future goal should be to link the practice of therapy with a research focus (i.e., get clinicians and researchers working together to try to determine the value of the various therapeutic strategies).

Notwithstanding this problem, we can see that, although the content of many of these models does differ, there also are many similarities among them. As examples, *all* of the aforementioned models (regardless of whether they describe treating the aftermath of rape, incest, or child sexual abuse) focus on the critical issues of: (1) educating the client regarding the normalcy of her reactions (i.e., depathologizing her "symptoms"); (2) validating her experiences and encouraging her to express how she feels about her responses; (3) cognitive restructuring or reinterpreting the event, particularly the emphasis that she was *not* at fault; (4) helping the child, adolescent female, or woman to come to terms with how her past experiences are affecting her now; (5) helping her to reduce current levels of "symptoms"; (6) assisting her in learning novel, more productive ways to deal with having been assaulted; and (7) aiding her in coming to grips with her history of sexual victimization.

There also, though, are several differences among these models. For instance, the crisis intervention model is the only one which emphasizes the "here-and-now." Again, since this perspective focuses on short-term intervention, this should *not* be surprising. Second, several of these treatment modalities (e.g., Bass and Davis and Courtois) highlight the importance of disclosing the "secret," as well as the possibility of confronting one's abusers (e.g., Bass and Davis, Courtois, and Dolan), while there is virtually *no* mention of these issues in the literature which focuses on treating post-rape-victimization trauma. As I indicated earlier, I believe that we must be very careful regarding these issues because disclosing this information and/or confronting one's attacker(s) can have detrimental effects on the survivor. Third, in the rape victimization literature there is much more of an emphasis on reporting the attack, as well as prosecuting the assailant. Again (and as was mentioned in the previous chapter), we do *not* focus nearly as much on these issues in the incest and child sexual abuse literatures. I believe, though, that it is time that we begin to do so. If we are indeed serious about preventing these problems, a much harder line must be taken with the perpetrators who sexually victimize infants, girls, and adolescent females. A fourth difference in these literatures is the suggestion that significant others should be brought into the therapy process. As examples, those who regard responses to sexual victimization via a PTSD model suggest this option, as do Ledray, Koss and Harvey, and Dolan. This seems such an obvious approach because these are the people with whom we spend most of our time, as well as the group that we go to for help and advice. A fifth difference is whether the models indicate the need to build a therapeutic relationship between therapist and client. In reality, though, this difference really reflects whether the treatment plan opts for long-term intervention or short-term assistance. Accordingly, crisis intervention avoids mention of the need to build this relationship, while the model to treat PTSD-like consequences, as well as the works of Koss and Harvey and Courtois, regard it as a critical element. Sixth, some of the aforementioned treatment modalities stress the need to unlearn fears and phobias, or desensitization. Specifically, the social learning perspective, as well as the models authored by Briere, Courtois, and Wheeler and Berliner, suggest that this as a critical component of the treatment process. Please note, though, that, while decreasing the client's levels of fears and anxiety is the predominant concern of the social learning model, these are simply two emphases among many contained in Briere's, Courtois's, and Wheeler's and Berliner's models. Finally, and as noted in the last chapter, some of the models which examine the aftermath of child sexual abuse focus on spiritual considerations (e.g., Bass and Davis and Dolan), while this issue rarely arises in discussions of how to treat post-rape consequences.

In addition (and based upon the age of the survivor of sexual victimization), other areas of difference should be expected. For instance, all of the aforementioned models which focus on the aftermath of child sexual abuse emphasize the need to access and/or work with the "child within" or the "inner child." As may seem obvious, and based upon the age requirement to regard an offense as rape, *no* such mention of this issue is made in the rape literature. Another treatment issue which exists in the literature on childhood victimization that does *not* appear in the rape literature is reconstructing one's family. Since many instances of childhood sexual victimization occur within the family, in order to heal their wounds, many survivors of incest decide to relinquish ties with their families and create new "families of choice." Even though we have a growing marital rape literature, the issues of relinquishing ties with family members and creating new families, for whatever reasons, do *not* arise there.

In addition, in the prior two chapters I mentioned that there are ten areas across which we can experience the consequences of sexual victimization. They are the psychological, somatic, behavioral, interpersonal, cognitive, self-perceptual, sexual, political, and spiritual dimensions of our lives, as well as subsequent victimization. I also indicated that the three most important areas across which the victims and survivors of rape, incest, and childhood sexual abuse experience disruption are the cognitive, self-perceptual, and spiritual ones. As can be seen in the summary of the various extant treatment strategies, a great deal of attention has been paid to the psychological, somatic, behavioral, interpersonal, cognitive, self-perceptual, and sexual aspects of our lives, while there has been much less interest (particularly in the rape literature) in the political and spiritual dimensions. Although a few works have begun to emphasize political (Bass and Davis 1988; Dinsmore 1991; Herman 1992; Kelly 1988), as well as spiritual concerns and solutions (Bass and Davis 1988; Dinsmore 1991; Dolan 1991; Finney 1990; Reis 1991b; Sanford 1990; Wisechild 1988), we need to improve our understanding of how these sorts of experiences affect us in these dimensions of our lives.

Finally, it is important to underscore the fact that a variety of therapeutic modalities have been mentioned (e.g., social learning, stress reduction, cognitive, behavioral, etc.), and that each of these perspectives not only has divergent theoretical assumptions but also different applications. To be specific, if my major area of disruption is cognitive, a cognitively-based treatment plan would be most effective for me; if, on the other hand, my primary problems are residual fears and phobias (e.g., the psychological and behavioral dimensions), the best bet probably is a social learning approach. More than likely, though, and as is noted by Courtois (1988, 1992), most survivors enter therapy with a *variety* of presenting complaints and underlying issues, and perhaps even a disguised presentation. Therefore, treatment must be geared to meet their specific needs and to address the primary problems that each individual is having. Courtois's solution is a valuable one: In order to address the multitude of needs that the client may have, we should draw from as many therapies as possible and implement an eclectic approach.

Although we have come a long way in understanding the need to treat the aftermath of sexual victimization and we have developed a number of treatment models in a relatively short period of time, we are no closer to proving the merits of certain approaches over others. This, then, must become a priority issue. If we are indeed serious about reducing the effects of such traumatizing experiences, we must be better able to determine which tactics are most effective for certain sorts of experiences and/or for certain girls, adolescent females, and adult women.

In addition, far too few resources acknowledge the link between personal and collective recovery. As is noted in the last chapter, several experts, particularly feminist ones, posit that a major component in recovering from sexual victimization is linking one's personal pain to larger structural issues. This necessitates that we come to regard sexual violence and victimization as social problems, rather than the individual problems of some women and children, and that we work toward healing this society, not just the individuals who have been violated.

Prevention of Rape, Incest, and Child Sexual Abuse: Personal, Interpersonal, Community, and Structural Considerations

> There is no indication that increased consciousness about the crime of rape has reduced the number of rapes that occur. Conventionally, prevention of rape has focused on altering the behavior of the victim. Through proscriptions of behavior resulting in vulnerability to attack (e.g., don't go out alone at night, . . . don't leave car doors unlocked), women are cautioned to restrict their activities to make themselves less accessible to rapists. Few efforts [though] have been directed to preventing the development of the behavior of rape in males. Conventional efforts have identified the rapist after the fact and focused on treatment at that point (Swift 1985:413).

> Child sexual abuse will continue as long as we simply focus on individual children, one at a time, applying crisis measures when abuse is revealed. It is also important, but not enough that children and families and offenders are healed after sexual abuse happens. A more general healing of society is required to change attitudes which promote and condone sexually abusive behaviors (Bagley and King 1990:203).

Swift's words indicate that the vast majority of the advice about rape prevention, historically, has been directed at girls and women, while little attention has been focused on the boys and men who commit these acts, as well as this society which encourages and permits the behavior. Accordingly, the mythology that for centuries has surrounded this subject (e.g., she must have done something to "cause" it, women "tease" men and then "cry" rape, men can't be held "accountable" for their sexual urges and actions) continues to be regarded as "truth." Similarly, by noting that we cannot view child sexual abuse solely as a personal problem, Bagley and King pinpoint the role of our social structure in causing the problem, as well as our need to focus on structural changes to reduce it. In effect, both of these quotations emphasize that we need to widen the net in terms of how we define and go about preventing sexual victimization. Both of them also point to where many of the current works in the field have been headed: the acknowledgment that our culture causes and perpetuates the problem. This is a critical redefinition; if we stay at the personal and interpersonal levels of analysis and only outline what girls and women can do to prevent their own sexual victimizations from happening, we end up placing the onus of responsibility on them and inferring that they are *the* primary problems. Such approaches and attitudes, though, can do little to resolve the underlying cultural traditions, practices, and standards which underscore the sexual victimization problem.

So, What Is Prevention of Sexual Victimization?

The glib answer to this question is anything that stops one from being sexually victimized. In reality, the prevention of sexual victimization is a highly complicated, multifaceted issue that includes everything from incarcerating the perpetrator to altering the very fabric of our society. If you investigate the *rape prevention* literature, though, what you see is a confusing body of knowledge, and it's difficult to extrapolate its primary message. Some of the works explore what Morgan (1986) calls the "traditional and empowered individual" approaches (what I refer to as the personal level of analysis), or what I can do to protect myself from being victimized or stop an assault once it has begun (Bart and O'Brien 1985; Warshaw 1988). Others examine what I refer to as interpersonal factors such as our current socialization patterns which "color code" our girls and boys and create "natural" victims and aggressors, as well as our current dating practices which have been linked to the rape problem (Alder 1985; Allgeier 1988; Shotland 1989; White and Humphrey 1991; Warshaw 1988). Finally, as was noted above, more works now acknowledge the insidious effects of our patriarchal culture, misogyny, and the devaluation of women and children, as well as pinpoint how these issues are causally related to many of our social problems, including rape (Kelly 1988; Parrot and Bechhofer 1991; Russell 1984, 1986). Morgan (1986) calls this the "collective problem," while I label them structurally-based prevention solutions.

The bottom line is that rape prevention can mean vastly different things. As an example, Koss and Harvey (1991) make the distinction between what individuals can do to protect themselves (rape avoidance) and changes that we as a society must make in order to eradicate the problem (rape elimination). Notwithstanding the different levels of analysis on which these two types of prevention focus, the authors suggest that there are certain aims that all rape prevention programs should contain. They are:

> to eliminate rape by challenging societal beliefs and cultural values that promote and condone sexual violence; to foil attempted rapes by educating potential victims about risk, risk avoidance, and self-defense; to reduce the emotional and physical trauma of rape by early and appropriate attention to the needs of individual rape victims; and/or to prevent recurrent instances of rape by offender incarceration and treatment (Koss and Harvey 1991:246).

The first aim is educational with the goal of changing attitudes and societal values, as well as a political one in that it will require activism to effect these sorts of changes; the second aim is to educate adolescent females and adult women about how they are at risk, as well as how they can reduce that risk; the third aim is to reduce the impact of a rape experience via education and intervention for those that have been raped, while the fourth aim is to put the assailant away which should reduce the problem naturally. It is important to add that aims two and three, although feasible, will *not* eradicate the problem; while the fourth one, although laudatory, is problematic because so many of the perpetrators are what Kanin calls "undetected rapists";

therefore, only the first aim or large-scale structural changes can truly eliminate the problem.

Regarding the *prevention of incest and child sexual abuse,* the information is even more confusing. For example, some of the current works explore such highly specific issues as whether educational programs aimed at preschool populations are worthwhile because these children may *not* be developed enough cognitively to grasp the abstract concepts of sexual victimization and its prevention (cf. Peraino 1990). Other approaches focus on children and adolescents (and sometimes their parents) and offer advice about how they can protect themselves from being sexually victimized by strangers, the inference being that children need *not* fear people in their own households and that they are the ones who must be responsible for stemming the problem (Berliner 1989; Finkelhor 1986). Still other works focus on how we need to change this society to reduce the prevalence of these problems (Bagley and King 1990; Butler 1985; Farmer 1989; Gelles and Straus 1988; Herman 1981; Russell 1984, 1986).

In their summaries of educationally-based child sexual abuse prevention programs, Conte (1988) and Finkelhor (1986) note that programs differ based upon such issues as the occupation of the prevention trainer, the age of the children for whom the program is planned, the length of the training, the intended audience (children and/or their parents), the language used to describe sexual victimization and its prevention, and the materials used to underscore the various concepts. Notwithstanding these differences, Daro (1989:260) suggests that there are at least six areas that should be included in child sexual abuse prevention programs:

> comprehensive safety instruction to children geared to a child's developmental level and cognitive abilities; education for parents regarding their responsibilities for protecting their children; education for all adolescents regarding healthy sexuality and appropriate displays of affection; comprehensive training programs for all professionals who work with children; institutional changes within child service and child welfare systems to prevent initial and subsequent victimization; and public awareness efforts emphasizing the message that

> preventing child sexual abuse, and all other forms of
> maltreatment, is everyone's responsibility.

To this list I would add prevention strategies that deal with
perpetrators via incarceration or treatment (if the latter approach
can be proven effective), and structural changes which make it
unlikely that the sexual victimization of children will occur.

What these various works really are doing is focusing on
different types of prevention (i.e., primary, secondary, and
tertiary). *Primary prevention* refers to attempts to reduce the
incidence of rape, incest, and child sexual abuse by promoting
healthier values in the general population, as well as increasing
the awareness of those who are at risk; *secondary prevention*
means developing effective treatment programs for the girls,
adolescent females, and adult women who have been victimized,
as well as early detection and treatment of men and boys who
have *not* yet raped or sexually abused but who have begun to
commit other sorts of sex offenses (e.g., exhibitionism, obscene
phone calls), while *tertiary prevention* includes rehabilitative
efforts to heal the earlier wounds of sexual victimization, as well
as treating the offending population (Bagley and King 1991; Koss
and Harvey 1991; Rozee et al. 1991). Koss and Harvey (1991: 253)
add that primary prevention is what many researchers regard as
"real" prevention, while the secondary variety is "regarded as
early or timely treatment and tertiary prevention is rehabilitative
treatment."

Each of these different types of prevention emphasizes
different issues and offers divergent information about how to
reduce, prevent, or eradicate the problem of sexual victimization.
What we need to do is acknowledge that each of these forms of
prevention is critical yet different, that each has value, and that,
in order to work toward the goal of prevention, all three types
must be considered and included. Although I regard structural
changes and solutions as the most critical ones, I also know that
if we focus exclusively on that level of analysis it will take a very
long time for these sorts of changes to occur (if they ever do). In
the meantime, we must continue to focus on personal,
interpersonal, and community solutions, as well as offer advice
regarding the likelihood of "certain" girls, adolescent females,
and adult women to be sexually victimized. This is *not* to infer

that these strategies will rid our society of the problem; rather, the point is that we need to offer a balanced presentation by including all three types of prevention. A case in point is the work of Gelles and Straus (1988). Although they examine the pros and cons of such issues as keeping the family together and protecting the victim, they also underscore the importance of making it so people can't commit family violence via such strategies as eliminating cultural norms that promote and accept violence and developing programs and policies which support families and reduce inequalities among them.

Accordingly, in the section which follows, prevention of the problems of rape, incest, and child sexual abuse is explored across several spheres, including the personal arena, inter-personal issues, community approaches, and structural changes that need to be made. In addition, each of these kinds of prevention is evaluated as it differentially solves the problems of rape, incest, and child sexual abuse. Please note, as well, that in most cases I have elected to focus on girls, adolescent females, and adult women while ignoring the prevention or treatment strategies which hope to reduce the problem among known and unknown offenders or potential offenders. The only exception to this is my discussion of rape prevention and education programs which are geared for high school and college audiences because most of those programs include both sexes.

Personal and Interpersonal Prevention Strategies

In this section, I focus on some of the ways that we can protect ourselves from being sexually victimized, as well as the ways that we can alter our interactions to reduce (or more optimistically eliminate) the likelihood that sexual victimizations will occur. I have elected to speak of personal approaches to prevention of sexual victimization along with the more interpersonally-based ones because I believe that it is difficult if not impossible to separate the two. Based on the fact that sexual victimization takes place in groups (usually but *not* always in dyads), and because of the interactionally-based nature of how we learn our culture's messages about and standards of sex and sexuality, many if not most of these prevention programs are administered in groups and/or focus on what we can do (particularly "at risk" populations) to safeguard ourselves.

For children, examples of educational approaches are just say no, run away, and tell someone; the Illusion Theater programs; and the good touch, bad touch continuum.[1] The goals of these programs are to educate children about the potential dangers, how they can try to protect themselves, and the need for them to tell someone if they are victimized. Several other programs are aimed at parents to make them more aware of the potential hazards for their children. Regardless of the audience, these programs attempt to educate children, particularly pre-teen groups (and in some cases their parents) about what incest and child sexual abuse are, the potential for children to be so victimized, and ways that they can be safeguarded. Be advised, though, that these educational efforts imply that the onus of responsibility for stopping such attacks rests with children and their parents.

We must be careful with these sorts of approaches for several reasons. One is that some studies have shown that preschoolers may be less able than older children to grasp the more abstract concepts that they need to understand in order to protect themselves from being sexually victimized, while other studies of this age group have found that some learning occurs and that they do retain at least some of the information anywhere from one week to a few months later (cf. Conte 1988; Daro 1989; Nyman 1989; Peraino 1990). This debate really may be an artifact of the types of educational programs that are administered, methodological differences among these approaches, the lack of reinforcing messages about prevention issues, and equating "success" with retention of the knowledge rather than the effectivnesss of specific prevention programs. Given that many adults would be unable to recall specific details from lectures that they attended weeks or months ago, it seems almost too obvious to suggest that these programs should *not* be "one-shot" efforts; rather, they should be an ongoing part of the curriculum for all parts of the educational system (preschool through post-college and professional programs).

Another issue is that some of the experts regard sexual abuse prevention programs as inherently flawed in that they create fears among the children who participate in them (cf. Blumberg et al. 1991; Conte 1988); yet there is little concrete data to support this allegation. The real issue becomes whether we should halt these sorts of prevention programs because they *may* cause distress for children, or whether we should err in the direction of protecting children, even if there may be psychological costs involved? For obvious reasons, I would elect the latter option; at the same time, though, we must validate empirically which approaches work better and cause fewer fears among the children who are served.

Another problem is that we may give children who already have been sexually abused the erroneous impression that they somehow were at "fault" for failing to say no, *not* getting away and/or *not* telling someone (Finkelhor 1986). Accordingly, when child sexual abuse prevention programs are administered, facilitators must remain cognizant of the fact that some children in the audience already have been abused. Thus, they must make these programs safe places where children can come forward and be helped without being made to feel that they did something wrong.

Even though the data are very clear that many, if not most, cases of child sexual abuse occur at the hands of a relative or other trusted adult and/or caretaker (Berliner 1989; Crewdson 1988; Russell 1984), another area of concern is that some of these programs infer that the potentially dangerous people are strangers. As an example, Peraino's (1990) prevention program within a preschool population employs the "We Help Ourselves" or WHO program which uses stuffed animal puppets and simple stories to educate children about preventing child sexual abuse. Although a wide range of topics are included in this program (e.g., differentiating between good and bad touch, identifying private parts of the body, the appropriateness of a doctor who is playing with a child to touch private parts of his/her body, a familiar adult touching private body parts while playing with a child, and what to do if someone for "no good reason" touches these private parts of your body), two out of three of the examples involve *strangers* trying to entice the child into a car, while the third scenario depicts a grandfather trying to get the child to come home with him for dinner. This is a thorny issue because little would be gained by teaching children that they should be suspicious and fearful of everyone in their lives; yet it is often a "loved one" who is much more likely to be the dangerous party.

In addition, since we already know that some children are more "vulnerable" to sexual abuse (e.g., girls, children who reside with a stepfather, and those who are between the ages of eight and twelve), programs must be developed which address their special needs. We must be particularly careful with this notion, though; if we assume that incest and child sexual abuse only are problems for particular "kinds" of children, we fail to see the larger picture or the fact that all children are potential victims.

An added problem is that relying on the dependent variable of how much knowledge and information the children retain may be an *ineffective* measure of prevention (Conte 1988). In reality, we do *not* know how children will react in similar, real-life situations, and ethically, we cannot put them in realistic scenarios which would answer this question; we only can hope that they will recall some of the information and the caveats and respond accordingly. In addition, it is *unlikely* that we will ever be able to determine with certainty how many children are *not* sexually abused because they went through these sorts of educational programs. These are the murky areas (at this point in time anyway) which defy quantification. Perhaps longitudinal analyses of the problem will provide better answers to some of these questions.

Finally, if we are serious about reducing or eradicating the problems of incest and child sexual abuse, we must remain cognizant of the fact that programs geared exclusively for children and their parents are insufficient. As Berliner (1989:252) suggests: "Prevention education aimed primarily at children is probably not the best way to tackle a complex social phenomenon. It might be best addressed through more research to understand factors that make such abusing possible." In other words, to effect these goals the perpetrators should be punished, and in order to truly protect our children, we must make structural changes that make the sexual victimization of children an impossibility.

Notwithstanding these problems, most of the experts concur that "something" (they're *not* clear yet as to what precisely this something is) can be gained from educational programs whose goals are to prevent sexual abuse (Berliner 1989; Conte 1988). According to Finkelhor (1986), though, in order for these programs to be effective, we must take into consideration the various audiences that we are trying to serve, as well as work toward developing programs which are age-specific and consider developmental and cognitive differences. Thus, it will take much more evaluation research to determine the effectivness of the various, currently popular approaches. In other words, we should *not* assume that all of these programs have the intended effect of educating children about and helping them to identify the dangers and what to do if sexually victimized; rather, we must prove their worth empirically.

For *adolescent females and adult women*, the information about preventing sexual victimization is even more questionable. Part of the problem lies in the fact that *less* empirical data exist to determine the effectiveness of such efforts. That in and of itself is an interesting observation; we simply have been less willing to examine the question of whether prevention programs are effective for adolescent and adult audiences. The research that does exist focuses mostly on high school and college students, even more specifically on young, white, middle-class students, while other racial and ethnic groups, classes, and age groups remain underrepresented. Notwithstanding these flaws, several studies have examined college students' attitudes about rape and have tried to determine whether their views can be altered (Jones 1991; NiCarthy 1991; Roden 1991; Sousa 1991).

The primary finding is that there is an attitudinal problem among young people in this country. In fact, a plethora of studies has found that many high school and college students believe the myths which surround the subjects of stranger and acquaintance rape, agree that sex-specific gender roles are acceptable, and/or uphold values which support interpersonal violence (Bridges and McGrail 1989; Briere et al. 1985; Burt 1991; Costin and Schwarz 1987; Craig 1990; Fonow et al. 1992;

Gilmartin-Zena 1987a, 1989c, 1990; Lottes 1988; Margolin et al. 1989; Mayerson and Taylor 1987; Muehlenhard et al. 1985; Muehlenhard and Linton 1987; Tetreault and Barnett 1987; White and Humphrey 1991). One of the most disturbing investigations of this problem to date, though, is the study of 1,700 junior and high school students that was conducted by the Rhode Island Rape Crisis Center. They found that:

> 51% of the boys and 41% of the girls believed that a man has a right to force a woman to kiss him if he had 'spent a lot of money' on her; 31% of the boys and 32% of the girls said it is not improper for a man to rape a woman who had past sexual experiences; 87% of the boys and 79% of the girls said rape is OK if a man and woman are married; and 65% of the boys and 47% of all of these seventh-to-ninth graders said it is okay for a man to rape a woman he has been dating for more than six months (White and Humphrey 1991:47).

Although these data are alarming, we must be aware of the fact that these attitudes do *not* develop and exist in a social vacuum; rather, they come from very clear messages that this culture gives young people via the various media, the socialization process, and expectations about gender-typed behaviors, issues that are discussed in detail later in this chapter.

In addition, be advised that these are not simply attitudinal "problems," because research shows that men who believe the various rape myths, support stereotypical gender roles, and agree with using interpersonal violence also are more likely to be sexually assaultive in their relationships with women (Check and Malamuth 1985; Malamuth and Check 1981). The results for women are equally troubling; if they share these beliefs, they may be more susceptible to being victimized, blame themselves (and other women) for being assaulted, and make all sorts of "defensive" changes in their lives (to try to reduce their likelihood of being attacked) which can end up reducing the quality of their lives (Brownmiller 1975; Gordon and Reiger 1989; Warshaw 1988).

Currently, we have more than enough studies that show that young people have problematic attitudes about rape; what we need to do now is to determine what can be done to alter these attitudes and proclivities. Several authors have begun to take this obvious next step. For example, utilizing an experimental, pretest, posttest research design, Fonow et al. (1992) have examined whether college students' attitudes about the various rape myths could be altered. One group of students viewed a twenty-five-minute *video* of a rape education workshop; a second experimental group received a *live*, twenty-five-minute workshop, while the third group acted as the control group. They determined that: (1) at the pretest, significant gender differences existed in the students' attitudes about the various rape myths, their views about who is to be blamed for an attack, their notions about the acceptability of adversarial sex, and their ideas about sex-role conservatism (i.e., women were *less likely* to believe the rape myths, blame the woman for the attack, regard adversarial sexual practices as acceptable, and opt for conservative sex roles); (2) both the video and live workshop groups had improved attitudes about the various rape myths at the three-week posttest assessment, but the latter approach was found to produce even more rejection of the various rape myths; and (3) women's attitudes changed more than men's which lead the authors to believe that these sorts of workshops need to address men's myths about rape even more directly.

I, too, have conducted a quasi-experimental, pretest, posttest analysis of this problem, and my findings are quite similar to Fonow et al.'s. Specifically, I studied a group of fifty-four introduction to sociology students to determine whether offering accurate information about the various rape myths (via two lectures and class discussions) would have the hoped-for effect of improving their views on this subject (Gilmartin-Zena 1989c, 1990). In addition, I examined their beliefs about stereotypical sex roles and their views about women. I found that: (1) at both the pretest and posttest assessments, women were more likely than men to have higher knowledge about the various rape myths; (2) attitudinal change was found at the posttest for both sexes (as was reported by Fonow et al.), but more so for the women; and (3) the students' views about women and gender roles did *not* change between the two assessments (which was *good* news because no effort was made to alter these perceptions).

Similarly, Harrison et al. (1991) have conducted a study to determine if college students' attitudes about the mythology which surrounds the subject of rape can be changed. Utilizing five different formats and groups, they determined that: (1) again, women had higher levels of knowledge about rape at the pretest and posttest assessments; (2) at the posttest assessment, men were significantly *less willing* to blame women for being sexually assaulted than they were at the onset of the study; and (3) for men, both formats (video only versus video and a discussion on the subject) seemed to work quite well.

There also, though, are problems with each of these analyses. For example, Fonow et al. (1992) and Harrison et al. (1991) posttested their students but did so shortly after the information was dispensed. Thus, as yet, we have no way of knowing whether these "new-found" attitudes stick and remain a permanent part of students' attributional schemas or whether periodic, reinforcing messages may be required. In addition, in my study, I did *not* include a later follow-up of the students, nor did I utilize a control group, both of which detract from the quality of the research design. Finally, all of these studies focus, yet again, on college students; the obvious question is whether similar findings would be gained in nonstudent populations. In sum, although there is little doubt that problematic attitudes about rape abound, the aforementioned studies offer hope that these views can be changed, if and when people are offered the opportunity to gain new knowledge on the subject.

Changing attitudes about rape, though, is *not* enough to stem the problem (particularly the acquaintance rape problem on America's college campuses). Accordingly, several experts have begun to alert us to the specific ways that we can alter our rape-supportive interactions with others. For instance, based on Koss et al.'s (1988) study of nearly 6,000 college students across the country, Warshaw (1988:161–164) concludes that we can take steps to make college campuses freer from sexual coercion.[2] In order to meet this goal, she offers a number of caveats for students of both sexes.[3] *For males*, she suggests that they should: (1) *never* force or pressure women to have sex; (2) stay sober; (3)

not buy the myth that a drunk woman deserves to be raped; (4) *not* join in if "invited" to participate in sexual behavior; (5) *not* confuse scoring with having a relationship; (6) *not* assume that you know what women want; (7) be aware of the fact that no means no; (8) inform women if they feel that they are getting mixed messages from them; (9) learn to communicate better with women; and (10) communicate with other men about the wrongness of coercive sex. Although this is a laudable list, it does nothing to acknowledge the overriding cultural images and assumptions that men have been encouraged to have about women (i.e., that they always are available sexually, that they are sex objects), which are the very bases or reasons why we have to offer such obvious suggestions. Thus, in order to really stem the problem, we must highlight how this culture adds to the problem.

Warshaw (1988:153–157) also offers caveats for the *women*: (1) be aware that you have the right to set sexual limits and to communicate these limits; (2) be assertive; (3) remain sober; (4) find out about new dates; (5) remain in control; (6) take care of yourself (i.e., learn to defend yourself *before* you actually need to do so); (7) trust your own feelings and judgments about men; and (8) since they have such high rates of victimization, for first-year college women, take special precautions. Again, though, the onus of responsibility is on the individual to see an attack coming and to stop its occurrence, while the role of the culture in causing and perpetuating the problem continues to be ignored.

Finally, Warshaw suggests that parents and educators can play key roles in preventing the acquaintance rape problem. She indicates that *parents*: (1) early on should talk to their children about their sexual rights and responsibilities; (2) as their children approach adolescence, should push for programming in their schools which address the issues of sex education, problems in dating, healthier sex roles, and date and acquaintance rape; (3) as their adult children enter college, should talk with them about the many new social situations, choices, and pressures they will encounter; and (4) should promote notions of healthy relationships. For *educators and institutions of secondary and higher education*, Warshaw (1988:173–175) has several ideas. As examples, she indicates the need: (1) for programs in junior and senior high schools which outline the problem of acquaintance and date rape; (2) to incorporate programs about acquaintance and date rape into first-year students' orientation workshops; (3) to establish adequately funded, on-campus rape counseling and education services; (4) to distribute information regarding rape, rape treatment, and university procedures for dealing with offenders; (5) for mandatory educational programs for social clubs and athletic teams; (6) to establish university control of fraternities and sororities; (7) an examination of the issue of dorm safety, as well as policies which could improve it; (8) a strong institutional stand against rape and sexual harassment; (9) for an investigation of how adequate current board policies and procedures are for handling cases of acquaintance rape; and (10) for self-defense and assertive training to be offered for women students on a regular basis.

Parrot (1991a, 1991b), as well, offers suggestions for stemming the acquaintance rape problem on America's college campuses. First of all, she indicates the need for college administrators to acknowledge that the problem exists, something that many of them have been unwilling and/or fearful to do. In addition, information about acquaintance rape and the institution's response to it must be made available to the students. She also addresses the link between alcohol consumption and acquaintance rape and recommends that administrative policies (if they do *not* already exist) should be created to limit the availability of alcohol to students. Further, she suggests the need for educational programs for both sexes because only "telling women how to avoid rape will not end the problem" (Parrot 1991a:360). In addition, she notes the importance of student input in developing rape prevention programs, as well as the value of peer educators in implementing them (Parrot 1990). Finally, according to Parrot (1991a), the more open and nonjudgmental the presentation of the material, the higher the likelihood that students will "hear" the message.

Other experts give advice to all girls and women, not just high school and college students. For example, since several reports have concluded that women who fight back or resist during an assault can ward off their assailant (Bart and O'Brien 1985; Ullman and Knight 1992), several experts acknowledge the value of adolescent girls and women learning to defend themselves (Ledray 1986). I believe, though, that we must be very careful with this suggestion. Although "quickie" self-defense courses or workshops do little to prepare girls and women to ably defend themselves, they could create the illusion of safety. The solution, then, is to offer long-term programs which would teach girls and women how to defend themselves. In addition, I believe that self-defense must be linked to other issues such as improving self-esteem and assertiveness training for girls and women. In other words, before we can teach them to defend themselves, we may have to back up and *convince* them that they are *valuable* enough to defend and that they have the *right* to do so. An added problem with this approach is that it gives the erroneous impression that women always will be able or have the opportunity to defend themselves. The reality of the situation is that, if a weapon is present or if she is the victim of a gang rape, the merits of fighting back would be negligible and even could place her in added physical danger. Finally, these approaches (yet again) place the onus of responsibility on women to stop rape rather than on men who commit these acts and/or on this society which encourages it.

Ledray (1986), as well, offers advice to adult women about how to reduce their individual likelihoods of being sexually victimized. For example, she notes that some women safeguard themselves by *not* going out alone at night, going out with men who can "protect" them, *not* living alone, and only going out with men that they "know" fairly well. She is quick to add, though, that these are confusing caveats. Although some of them may be realistic ways to reduce the risk of sexual victimization, she also notes that these approaches are passive rather than active ones, that they place the burden of responsibility on the potential victims, and that they could have negative effects such as isolating and limiting women's lives. Accordingly, she also offers more active tactics such as carrying something that could be used as a weapon, looking confident when you are out alone, keeping your car doors locked, and *not* identifying yourself as a single woman via the phonebook or your mailbox. It is important to add that some of Ledray's notions are questionable. For example, going out with men who will "protect" us and that we "know" fairly well is a major part of the acquaintance rape problem because, historically, women have *not* regarded them as potential assailants. Yet, the data are quite clear; in many cases, these are the very men who assault their "loved ones."

As was noted earlier in this book, there are a number of social-psychological constructs (e.g., self-esteem, sense of coherence, and mastery, to name a few) which are believed to be critical, particularly for girls and women, and the development of these traits may improve their ability to ward off sexual victimizations. Specifically, these characteristics may reduce the likelihood that we will be victimized, as well as enable us to recover more fully from these experiences if and when we should have the misfortune of being victimized. Accordingly, we must pay special attention to these sorts of concepts and try to instill them in our children, as well as encourage them among adolescent females and adult women via educational programs and policies. This ends up being a "stress innoculation" approach: We understand the need and the importance of immunizing our bodies against all sorts of physical maladies, but we do little to immunize girls, adolescent females, and adult women against psychological distress and/or educate them about efficient ways to cope with it.

Finally, and as was noted earlier in this book, there is increasing interest, particularly among feminists, in the subject of how important it is for girls and women to have a "voice." When Gilligan (1982) determined that Kohlberg's theory of moral development generically devalued the unique perspective of girls and women, she alerted us to the problem. Specifically, she found that his theory was biased against females because he, as had many of his predecessors (e.g., Freud and Erickson), regarded the male model of moral development as the norm, as well as the one that females should emulate. In addition, these earlier works and theorists regarded relationality (i.e., connecting with others and focusing on relationships as an essential part of one's life) as a *lesser* form of development; instead, they extolled the merits of individuation and separation. The problem is that relationality is one of the few arenas where girls and women have been encouraged and permitted to "shine" and to have a "voice." In effect, we have created a perfect Catch-22: If girls and women follow the cultural mandates and focus on relationships, they are emphasizing a "devalued" aspect of life; but, if they fail to do so and attempt to emulate a masculine or an androgynous style, they are regarded as being deviant, abrasive, and/or aggressive.

In more recent analyses of this issue, Gilligan and her associates have found that, early on, girls do have a voice, but, as they approach adolescence, they "lose" it, if and when they start to conform to what this society expects of them [i.e., stereotypical gender roles (Gilligan et al. 1988, 1990)]. In a similar vein, Hancock speaks of the need to go back and reclaim "the girl within." She describes this girl as being somewhere between the ages of eight and ten, and as:

> one who pulls on her blue jeans, packs her own lunch, and gets on her bike to ride to her best friend's house to build a fort or a tree house . . . A superb organizer, she is likely to have her own collection of stamps, stones, shells or snakeskins—or perhaps bugs or birds' nests. Often a tomboy, she may be a gymnast or a sleuth—or a junior scientist whose prize possession is her own microscope . . . Heady with the power that comes from genuine competence, she brims with initiative. The faster she can run, the higher she can jump, the more she is admired (Hancock 1989:7-8).

Suddenly, though, this girl is expected to discard her "childish" ways and to adopt the feminine role which suggests that she put the wants and needs of others before her own. In effect, she is asked to give up her "voice." Hancock (1989:4) adds that the "task of a woman's lifetime boils down to reclaiming the authentic identity she'd embodied as a girl" or that identity that existed before she incorporated the negative, cultural messages about femininity which end up reducing her aspirations, her chances for success in life, and the likelihood that she will develop an identity that is separate from others.

Regarding the issue of voice among adult women, Belenky et al. (1986) have shown the critical linkage between *not* having a voice (i.e., learned silence) and our culture which permits and even encourages violence against them and their children. In a recent analysis of the intersection among cultural imperatives to be feminine, gender, learned silence, and depression, Jack (1991), too, shows that accepting and following the social prescriptions for femininity is dangerous for women because doing so places them at risk for depression, as well as for living lesser lives. Finally, Steinem (1992) and Sidel (1990, 1992) acknowledge the role of our society in lowering girls' and women's aspirations, as well as the overall quality of their lives. What these authors have in common is that they acknowledge the role our society plays in perpetuating messages about "appropriate" feminine attitudes and behaviors, as well as the hazards for us if we follow this "advice." Although such concepts as having a voice and self-esteem are as old as time immemorial (Steinem 1992), we only have begun to investigate how these sorts of deficits have added to the second-class status of women and children in this culture. Although a disturbing subject, it also is heartening to see that many works are examining these issues, alerting us to the dangers, and, most importantly, offering solutions and suggestions for how to gain a voice and to develop a real identity (Belenky et al. 1986; Gilligan 1982; Gilligan et al. 1988, 1990; Jack 1991; Kaplan 1991; Miller, J. 1991; Reis 1991b; Surrey 1991).

Another interpersonal issue is how we raise our children. To summarize the problem, if we teach our daughters and sons to follow stereotypical gender roles, "Some of the travelers on the 'niceness' track and some of those on the 'aggression' track are on a collision course with each other" (Warshaw and Parrot (1991:74). The collision is stereotyped dating and interaction patterns which can make girls and women "natural" victims and boys and men "natural" assailants. As previously was mentioned, if they adhere to traditional dating patterns (i.e., the boy/man initiates the date, does all of the deciding about it, pays, drives, etc.), sometimes there is the *implicit* assumption that girls/women "agree" that the sexual component of their date also is his decision to make. As an even more basic explanation of the problem, Abbey (1991) has shown that there are dramatic differences in women's and men's perceptions of "friendliness," sexual availability, and sexual intent, with boys and men being much more likely to sexualize their interactions with girls and women. As ways to resolve this dilemma, there is a need for girls and women to be very clear in the messages about sexual availability and sexual intent, and we need to do a better job of offering alternative models for our children (Abbey 1991; Allgeier 1987, 1988; Parrot 1990). Again, though, the implication is that girls and women are the "gatekeepers" of sex and that they must be the ones to set the limits, reduce the confusion, and make sure that unwanted sexual activity does *not* take place. As Parrot (1990) indicates, if these sorts of approaches are to be effective, the boys and the men also must be brought into the picture and made to play responsible roles in their interactions with the opposite sex.

Farmer (1989) and Miller (1981, 1983, 1984, 1990, 1991) are two of the clearest voices about how we can go about the job of raising our children differently, raising them in nonviolent, noncoercive ways, and breaking the cycle of violence. For instance, Farmer (1989:191) notes that:

> We are fortunate to live at a time and in a society where there is an increasing awareness of the mistreatment that has been perpetrated on those most vulnerable and helpless of people—children . . .
>
> Your legacy and mine, our generation's commission, is to steadily increase and expand our love and respect for ourselves, for our children, and for all other human beings. Then we can end this destructive cycle of abuse and return to a more natural state of trust and innocence.

As specific strategies, Farmer (1989:177-190) suggests expressing the love we feel for our children and maintaining order as two of the secrets of good parenting. We can express that love by: noticing what they do that is right and praising them for it; really talking with them, which involves asking them questions, as well as listening to them; and touching them in loving, positive, and nonthreatening ways. As for maintaining order and respect, Farmer suggests that helpful tactics include: having reasonable expectations of our children; "catching" our children being good (i.e., we respond when they do "bad" things by yelling at them or correcting them, yet we often fail to acknowledge when they are behaving appropriately or when we are proud of them); setting up consistent consequences for our children when they do *not* follow the rules; taking time-outs when tensions run high (which reduces the risk of doing things that we may later regret); and looking for "win-win" solutions (i.e., working with our children to find solutions which benefit all of the involved parties). These sorts of parenting tactics not only reduce the risk that we will repeat the patterns of abuse that we may have learned as children, but they also increase the chances that our children will be able to grow into happy and healthy adolescents and adults.

For a long time now, Miller (1981, 1983, 1984, 1990, 1991) has been warning us about the need to raise our children in healthy ways and the costs involved when we fail to do so. She has done this by alerting us to the problem of "poisonous pedagody," or the negative lessons that many parents teach their children. Specifically, she indicts parenting which is based on controlling children, breaking their spirits, shaming them, and molding them into "obedient" beings, regardless of the costs. The results of these sorts of practices are that children learn to split off from themselves and to project all of their own failings and misfortunes onto others which, in turn, has the effect of perpetuating the intergenerational cycle of violence (Miller 1983). In a recent work, Miller (1990: 143) suggests that: "This liberation from old fears [i.e., her awareness of her own abusive childhood] has opened my eyes to many things: to the mute signals of the child, to the hidden mechanisms of society that destroy the soul of the child, and to the chance of saving children and thus our future . . ." The goal is to break the silence, to acknowledge the existence of poisonous pedagogy, and to act as "enlightened witnesses" for these children who are unable to help themselves.

I believe that we do a disservice to everyone, though, if we assume that parents socializing their children differently will resolve all of our problems. In other words, the family is *not* the only social institution which plays a role in causing and perpetuating the problem of sexual victimization. As one example, recent findings from a study sponsored by the American Association of University Women (1992) have shown that girls and boys are entering school systems with *similar* levels of self-esteem and equal aspirations. Somewhere between the ages of nine and fifteen, though, girls' average self-esteem scores drop by some 40 percent, while the comparable decline among boys is 20 percent. They also note equally dramatic shifts in the children's aspirations, particularly among the girls, whose future goals are suddenly lower. At least two interpretations of these data are possible. First of all, since children are *beginning* their educational careers with fairly equal aspirations and similar levels of self-esteem, parents must be doing things differently and correctly. And that something is that they are *less* likely to be training their sons and daughters into gender-specific roles. The second, more obvious conclusion (or the bad news) is that our school systems are doing a number of things wrong: If these children enter with good views of themselves and hopeful expectations about their futures, we must investigate what happens to stifle these positive perspectives, particularly among the girls.

Whether we emphasize personal or interpersonal prevention strategies and whether these tactics are offered to child, adolescent, or adult audiences, the goals are quite similar. That is, most of the suggested approaches are geared toward educating females of all ages about how they can protect themselves from and/or reduce their likelihood of being sexually assaulted. Other efforts, particularly programs which are developed for high school and college audiences, offer ways for them to alter their interactions with each other in ways that may reduce the likelihood of being raped or of raping. Finally, the issue of how we rear our children is examined, as is the potential we as parents have for breaking the cycle of violence by raising our children in loving and supportive ways. Although wonderful suggestions, these sorts of approaches fail to address what many now regard as the real underpinnings of the problem—the social, cultural, and structural factors which allow and even encourage the sexual victimization of women and children. Accordingly, in the next section, I will investigate what many experts, particularly feminist ones (Dinsmore 1991; Herman 1981; Kelly 1988; Koss and Harvey 1991; Madigan and Gamble 1991; Russell 1984, 1986; Women's Resource Centre 1989), have to say about the roots of the sexual victimization problem, as well as the possible solutions.

Community and Structural Prevention Strategies

Rozee et al. (1991:337) suggest that the very world that we live in perpetuates the rape problem for adolescent girls and adult women:

> We live in a patriarchal culture that has as its roots a nonconscious ideology of male supremacy. Our culture values males and . . . devalues females . . . Such ideology is reflected in media portrayals of the objectification of women, the presentation of women as victims, and the sexualizing of violence against women. The ideology of male supremacy [also] is supported by systematic discrimination against women in the legal and judicial handling of complaints of male violence. It is perpetuated in child-rearing and socialization practices that provide succeeding new generations of boys and men with the message that aggressive, sexually coercive behavior is acceptable and even desirable.

They also suggest that the related issues of sexual entitlement, power and control, hostility and anger, and acceptance of interpersonal violence wreak all sorts of havoc. As to the role of sexual entitlement, Rozee et al. (1991) argue that men have been taught to believe that rape is justifiable and that it is *not* their "fault." Power and control issues refer to our traditional dating patterns which "legitimize the use of force, power, and control by males in sexual advances toward females" (Rozee et al. 1991:339), while hostility and anger toward women in this culture are grounded in standard social customs and beliefs. Finally, the acceptance of interpersonal violence is a marker that men may be potential rapists, particularly the ones who believe that "the intermingling of sex and violence is normal" (Rozee et al. 1991:340). Accordingly, Rozee et al. (1991:340): "These factors in male gender-role socialization may be translated directly into the behavioral signals of acquaintance rape. Women who become aware of the signals may be in a better position to avoid further contact with such acquaintances."

Ledray (1986:206) concurs regarding the insidious effects of living in a culture which devalues and encourages violence against women: "Before we begin to prevent rape, we must first understand how we got to a point in our society where so many women are raped each year. We must understand what the threat of rape means, what its effects are, and what it reflects in our own and other cultures. We must understand how we differ from rape-free societies." As contributing sociocultural factors, Ledray points to attitudes about women, motives of the assailants, the status of women in the culture, and prevalent cultural views which support violence.

In addition to the need for structural changes, Ledray offers ways to effect change at the community level. As examples, she discusses the importance of the politicization of women and neighborhood activism. Regarding the politicization of women, Ledray (1986:216) indicates that:

> Individual women in positions of power and influence and groups of women must become more politically astute and active, demanding change. These concerned individuals need to develop public pressure groups with task forces, and initiate legislative lobbying efforts. They must demand accountability from public and private boards, businesses and organizations, and become familiar with the voting record of elected officials on women's rights issues.

As for neighborhood activism, Ledray suggests the need for and the effectiveness of neighborhood watches and taking responsibility for educating members of the community as to the dangers of rape, as well as ways to protect themselves.

Bagley and King (1989) offer many of the same causal explanations but do so for the problems of incest and child sexual abuse. As examples, they suggest that the root causes of child sexual abuse are cultural values which encourage sexual exploitation and the continued one-sided distribution of power and dominance among males. They also point to the respective roles of "power imbalance and objectification of human beings in modern society," as well as the widespread acceptance of interpersonal violence in our culture (Bagley and King 1989:207). The more critical part of their analysis, though, is what they say to do about these problems: "[H]ealing is possible only when society with some degree of consensus is able to look back as a collective entity at its own development in a self-critical manner, acknowledge rather than deny its own liabilities, and overcome its limitations by determining new directions to incorporate chosen values."

If the social structure is the problem, then, solutions must be aimed at restructuring its very fabric. I am reminded of George Bush's 1988 campaign promise of a "kinder and gentler America." His words accurately depicted what we needed then, and they continue to denote what we need today because we are no closer to achieving those goals. If we really are serious about building a kinder, gentler society, several very basic issues must be addressed and changed. First of all, and as noted by Bagley and King (1989: 208), we must acknowledge the very real intersection between the personal and the political arenas, as well as support the diversity of our population:

> Ultimately, the major change required is a personal one, at the level of social identity and the process of defining ourselves through our differences rather than our commonality. The community has, however, to be grounded in the principles of pluralism in which certain fundamental values are shared, but in which the uniqueness and autonomy of individuals and cultural groups is recognized and supported ... The political approach which this implies is necessarily one of pluralism, both social and interpersonal.

In addition, women and children must be valued for themselves and encouraged to become fuller human beings; negative and sexualized images of women and children must be eliminated and the "assumptions" that men and boys are better or more valuable than girls and women must be discarded. We also need to develop political and economic systems that are geared toward meeting the needs of all of their members rather than the needs of just a select few. As examples, health care services (whether they be for physical or mental health problems) must be provided for all who need them, and specific programs to reduce the poverty levels of women and their dependent children must be instituted to reduce their swelling ranks. In effect, I am speaking of dismantling the patriarchal, elitist culture that we currently have and replacing it with one

whose major priorities are the health, education, and the welfare
of its members.

Bagley and King (1989:219) eloquently summarize not only
the problems but also the solutions:

> It is clear . . . that society needs to move in a direction that
> is non-patriarchal, non-sexist, non-violent, and non-
> exploitive of the innocence and creativity of childhood . . .
> It is not enough that individuals begin to internalize new
> values and express them in their individual lives and
> relationships. Political changes are also required so that
> the whole process of socialization of men, women, and
> children will shift.
>
> Social change begins with awareness, but it must also be
> embodied in practice and reflected in legal and economic
> realities as well as in interpersonal values. The first change
> needed is that of remedying power imbalance. To be
> effective, programmes on sexual abuse must consciously
> embrace the issues of male power and sexual privilege and
> be directed towards the empowerment of women and
> children.

Summary and Conclusions

When I looked back at what I have written in this chapter,
I saw that I had devoted much more space and attention to the
personal and interpersonal strategies which can prevent the
sexual victimization of girls, adolescent females, and adult
women. This in part is due to the bias of many (if not most) of
the works in the prevention literature that the prevention of
rape, incest, and child sexual abuse requires personal awareness,
the ability to defend yourself, and changes in our interpersonal
relations with others.

Another explanation is that there is a great deal more
consensus in works that examine the structural causes and
solutions to the problem of sexual victimization. In other words,
the vast majority of these works pinpoint the causal connections
among patriarchy, misogyny, cultural images which objectify

and/or devalue women and children, power imbalances, the acceptance of interpersonal violence, and the prevalence of the crimes of rape, incest, and child sexual abuse. These same works also agree in large part about the solutions, i.e., that we need to restructure this society in ways that will produce lasting results.

In reality, and as I noted earlier in this chapter, though, we need all four levels of analysis, as well as prevention measures which focus on solutions across all of them. If we focus exclusively on rape, incest, and child sexual abuse as personal and interpersonal problems, we do a major disservice because we only will be changing people and their interactional patterns while ignoring the powerful influences of the community and the social structure. In addition, although the personal and interpersonal prevention strategies can be effective and empowering for all sorts of audiences, ultimately, to eliminate these problems, we must implement change at the community and structural levels.

Finally, at the present time, we have a multitude of works which investigate the personal and interpersonal methods of prevention. There is, though, a paucity of research which examines how these educational approaches affect us behaviorally, as well as the quality and the permanence of the messages that are given in them. In order to work toward the changes that we need to improve the lives of all members of our society, though, we need to devote more time and research to exploring the community and structural levels of analysis. By doing so, we should better understand and be able to implement specific tactics needed to produce long-lasting changes.

CHAPTER EIGHT

The Problem of Sexual Victimization: Where We've Been and Where We Need to Be

> Society provides us with warm, reasonably comfortable caves, in which we can huddle with our fellows, beating on the drums that drown out the howling hyenas of the surrounding darkness. 'Ecstasy' is the act of stepping outside the caves, alone, to face the night (Berger 1963:250).

Although I came across Berger's words many years ago, they still have the power to affect me deeply today. His message is that we can run and we can hide, but whatever it is that we are trying to face down or attempting to resolve will *not* just go away; rather, we must be actively involved in the process of doing something about it. Relating these words to rape, incest, and child sexual abuse, "ecstasy" involves doing things differently, changing our ways of thinking about those experiences, ourselves, and the world around us, and having the courage to try new solutions to old problems.

In order to heal the wounds of sexual victimization more fully, though, we must face our demons head-on, both individually and collectively. *Individually*, if girls, adolescent females, and adult women are still alive, they have survived these experiences, but it is time to move beyond "mere" survival or "just" being alive and to strive for something better. In other words, girls, adolescent females, and women need more than congratulations for still being "on their feet"; rather, many of them want to learn how to have real lives, lives that are fuller and more productive and permit positive connections with others. When theorists speak of the concepts of recovery, reclaiming your life, growth, healing, victory, and thriving, these are the sorts of issues to which they refer. In Berger's language, all of these concepts entail "stepping outside of the cave alone to face the night," to resolve that which has stopped us in our tracks.

Although critical, these sorts of changes only will resolve problems and alter lives on an individual basis. The other side of this issue is that we should step outside of the cave *with others* to collectively face the night. By that I mean that we must learn to think about and to resolve these issues together. As noted earlier in this work, several experts now extol the virtues of "breaking silence," "moving from individual survival to collective resistance," the "survivor's mission," and being "enlightened witnesses" (Barringer 1992; Bass and Davis 1988; Dinsmore 1991; Herman 1992; Kelly 1988; Miller, A. 1991). By focusing on others and caring about them, all of these authors are emphasizing the need to do something good about something bad. One of the clearest voices on the subject of connecting with others is Susan Griffin (1989:17), a woman whose work and spirit I admire:

> We were meant to hear one another, to feel. Our sexual feelings, our capacity for joy and pleasure, our love of beauty, move us toward a love that binds us to an existence. If there is a sound wave anywhere on this earth, if there is the sound of weeping or of laughter, this reaches my ears, reaches your ears. We are connected not only by the fact of our dependency on this biosphere and our participation in one field of matter and energy, in which no boundary exists between my skin and the air and you, but also by what we know and what we feel. Our knowledge, if we can once again possess it, is as vast as existence.

Thus, Griffin (as do most feminists) suggests that all of us are interconnected and that we need to not only be aware of this linkage but should also work diligently to encourage and strengthen it.

Throughout this book, I have focused on what I believe are the major issues of sexual victimization. I have summarized what we know about: (1) recent trends in this literature; (2) the extensiveness of the problems of rape, incest, and child sexual abuse in this country; (3) historical, as well as contemporary, perspectives which outline why we have these problems; (4) the possible consequences or the aftermath of rape, incest, and/or childhood sexual abuse; (5) the more optimistic issue of recovering from sexual victimization; (6) treatment strategies which facilitate recovery; and (7) the ways that we can go about preventing the problem of sexual victimization.

In the process of summarizing what we now know about these issues, I have shown that we have made a great deal of headway in understanding them, and in many cases rethinking and reconceptualizing them. First of all, we have come to realize that the language that we use to talk about sexual victimization is critical. If, for example, we speak about women and children as victims, along with this come imputations of helplessness and passivity. If we speak of survival, though, as well as the more optimistic concepts of reclaiming your life—recovery, healing, growth, and victory—we empower women and children and encourage them, in Finney's words, "to reach for the rainbow." Second, based on surveys of college students and residents of several communities across the country, we now know that rates of rape, incest, and child sexual abuse are much higher than the official estimates of these problems indicate. Third, regarding our notions of causality, we have moved away from perspectives which blame women and children for their own victimizations and have moved toward ones which highlight the social, social-psychological, and political components of these problems. Fourth, regarding the aftermath of sexual victimization, we now possess a much clearer understanding of the consequences (both immediate and long-term), as well as how "symptoms" can act as metaphors and represent underlying issues. Fifth, we also know that recovery is possible and that certain treatment approaches seem to work better than others. Finally, although uncertain about the specifics, we also now know that to be effective, prevention must cut across several levels of analysis (i.e., personal, interpersonal, community, and structural).

Although this list is laudatory, there is still much room for improvement, and there are many issues which currently remain nebulous or unresolved. For example, and as has been detailed elsewhere in this book, there are several serious methodological problems in the rape, incest, and child sexual abuse literatures. Although specifying "profitable avenues for future research" in the child sexual abuse literature, Gomes-Schwartz et al.'s (1990:168-169) ideas apply equally well to the topic of rape victimization. They suggest the need for: (1) studies which compare various treatment approaches; (2) prospective, longitudinal analyses; (3) large collaborative efforts which examine consequences and recovery in several treatment settings; (4) standardized measures; and (5) more focused studies which examine smaller segments of the problem. To this list, I also would add that we need to develop better measures to determine the extensiveness of these problems and better operational definitions of the variables involved, particularly the outcome variable of recovery, victory, healing, or growth.

In addition, more treatment modalities need to include collective aspects of healing and recovery. Rather than focusing exclusively on the plight of individual victims and survivors, we also should be emphasizing and examining the benefits of healing as a collective endeavor. At minimum, this requires that we involve interested, supportive family members and other significant others in the process. At maximum, this mandates that we become more cognizant of how sexual victimization affects all of us (not "just" the women and children who are so victimized), as well as the role of the social structure in causing and perpetuating this problem.

Third, we have a plethora of studies which show a causal link between our attitudes about women and children (as well as our views about other issues such as the acceptability of interpersonal violence, adversarial sexual beliefs, and expectations about gender roles), and our behaviors toward them. In other words, several reports have concluded that our negative attitudes and stereotypes about women and children are part of what causes the sexual victimization problem. This should be a concern for all of us because our attitudes are critical and play an important role in how victims and survivors of rape, incest, and child sexual abuse come to define and perceive these experiences. We, though, have far fewer reports which investigate the feasibility of changing these attitudes and behavioral proclivities. This is an area which is ripe for research, research which then needs to be applied via education and prevention programs.

Fourth, many of the current works in the sexual victimization literature have a negative focus. That is to say, many of them examine the destruction and mayhem that can ensue after sexual victimization, while far fewer works employ a coping or a recovery perspective (i.e., what women and children actively do to facilitate change and recovery and to reclaim their lives). In addition, several recent works suggest that we need to reconceptualize "symptoms" as coping resources and to acknowledge and validate whatever women and children have done to survive. As previously noted, if we are serious about healing, growth, recovery, and victory as the hoped-for goals after girls, adolescent females, and adult women have been sexually victimized, the specifics of how to achieve these goals should be a critical component of this literature. Again, the point is to apply a positive perspective rather than a negative one, i.e., emphasize the strengths of the victims and survivors of rape, incest, and child sexual abuse rather than their weaknesses.

Fifth, a related concern is that we need to do empirical analyses of the various extant treatment strategies and determine whether the ones which seem to be positive really are effective in facilitating recovery, growth, and healing. We must be careful with this issue, though, because if we strictly adhere to the principle of experimental research, this may mean that some women and children will *not* receive treatment. In other words, the classic, experimental research design mandates that at least one group (i.e., the experimental group) receives the specific treatment, while at least one other group (i.e, the control group) does *not* and acts as the comparison group. Although this approach does *not* seem to present problems for many medical researchers, some experts who treat the aftermath of sexual victimization have noted the ethical dilemma of withholding treatment from some women and children who have been sexually victimized (Courtois 1988; Jehu 1989).

Sixth, since we have begun to rethink the potential for long-term consequences of rape, and the possible problems with the crisis intervention perspective in treating its aftermath, we have become more realistic about the impact of being raped. We also, though, need more research which determines the specific nature, content, and duration of post-rape-victimization trauma.

By acknowledging the likelihood of long-term reactions, a delayed-response pattern, and the potential for varied response patterns, current works which have begun to reconceptualize rape responses via the PTSD model or as responses to trauma which form a continuum are moving in the right direction.

Seventh, we need to spend more time clarifying and examining how "symptoms" may act as metaphors. As has been noted throughout this work, the "symptoms approach" forces us to examine and treat the visible responses of women and children who have been sexually victimized, while it fails to delve into the deeper, underlying issues that these "symptoms" may represent. As examples, before we treat the "symptoms" and "disorders" of depression, fears, phobias, drug and alcohol abuse or addiction, low self-esteem, bulimia, and various sexual "dysfunctions," we must come to understand what these responses really mean. That is to say, most of them also can be interpreted as "signs" that our views of ourselves and the world around us have been altered, if *not* shattered, we no longer have cognitive maps or spiritual guidelines to follow, and our psyches and our bodies are continuing to react because we have *not* come to terms with the fact that we have been victimized. This is particularly true in cases of sexual victimization which are "extreme" in both their content and duration.

All of this entails that we really listen to the victims and survivors of rape, incest, and sexual abuse, as well as realize that their "words" and their "descriptions" of their experiences actually may represent their feelings of terror, shame, and guilt. As such, we must avoid intellectual abstractions about them and their lives, continue to care about them even after they have related the "gory" details of their experiences, and come to a deeper understanding of the emotions and beliefs that they associate with those experiences. Herman (1992:69) has some particularly powerful advice about these issues:

> The survivor's shame and guilt may be exacerbated by the harsh judgment of others, but it is not fully assuaged by simple pronouncements absolving her from responsibility, because simple pronouncements, even favorable ones, represent a refusal to engage with the survivor in the lacerating moral complexities of the situation. From those

who bear witness, the survivor seeks not absolution but fairness, compassion, and the willingness to share the guilty knowledge of what happens to people in extremity.

Eighth is the area of prevention. We need to improve our understanding of what really works, and what more we can do to keep women and children safe. We also need to spend much more of our time and effort extrapolating why the perpetrators of sexual violence come to regard these violations as acceptable practices. As was noted in the previous chapter, there are a number of approaches that have been suggested (e.g., personal, interpersonal, community, and structural tactics) to prevent these acts of violence against women and children. In addition, we must pressure our local, state, and federal governments to view violence against women and children as critical, important problems; we also must pressure them to make a financial commitment to change the situation and to work toward recovery for individuals who have had the misfortune of being sexually victimized.

Finally, in order to make the changes necessary to alter the current epidemic proportions of the sexual victimization problem in this country, we have to understand, focus on, and work at the social, cultural, and political levels. Although psychological issues (e.g., understanding possible responses to sexual victimization and how such an experience is viewed by the individual), the interpersonal level of analysis, and the involved learning factors are highly critical in clarifying the problems of rape, incest, and child sexual abuse, until we are willing to acknowledge the added and equally powerful social, cultural, and political influences of these problems, we will get nowhere.

I am reminded of Miller's (1990:9) advice which places the onus of responsibility on the shoulders of parents: "[W]e suddenly realize that it is up to us adults, depending on how we treat our newborn infants, either to turn them into future monsters or to allow them to grow up into feeling, and hence responsible human beings." Although I agree with her thesis, I believe that it also is essential for us to go a step further; we *cannot* just assume that individual parents and families are the sole causes of the abuse problem in this country. We also have to include the existing and ofttimes negative cultural images of women and children in this society, our historical unwillingness to do something about the sexual victimization of women and children, the lack of economic and social options available to women and children in this society, and the dearth of policies which aid women, children, and families in the U.S. In other words, when we expand our focus, we can readily see that many of the roots of the problems of rape, incest, and child sexual abuse lie in the basic values and emphases which permeate this society.

We have the power to make permanent changes in this world. Since we now are armed with information about how prevalent a problem sexual victimization is, since we now know a great deal about the consequences of rape, incest, and child sexual abuse, and since we now have much clearer images about what recovering from sexual victimization entails, we can make a difference for the present generation, as well as the generations to come. As expressed by Engel (1989:67):

> Through greater awareness you will be among the first generation of people to have the opportunity to recover from the devastation of childhood sexual abuse. The chances are high that your parents, grandparents, and great-grandparents were also sexually abused, but at a time when society was not ready to examine the problem. For them, there was little hope. Unrecovered, they took their anger, pain, and frustration out on you and other children. And this is why the cycle of abuse has continued up to the present day. Today, however, people all over the country are recovering from the damage caused by such abuse.

I also am reminded of Miller's plea that we take control of our lives and *not* repeat the patterns of anger, violence, and pain, and that we take the responsibility in our individual lives. To this list I also would add the need for collective action—that we do things together to create change.

Concluding Remarks

I noted in the Preface of this book that I wanted to write a book that made a difference. I have tried to achieve this goal by clarifying the scope of the sexual victimization problem; what can happen to us afterwards; the steps that must be taken if we are to achieve the higher goals of growth, thriving, victory, recovery, and healing; the sorts of therapeutic principles and practices that seem to work well with the victims and survivors of rape, incest, and child sexual abuse; and prevention issues. All of these are critical issues that we must care about and do something about. Although we have come a long way in understanding, acknowledging, and offering solutions to the problems of rape, incest, and child sexual abuse, our work is *not* done; there is still much left to do.

I, for one, have a vested interest in these issues because I would like the world to be a safer place for my daughter and me; I would like our lives and the lives of other women and children in this country to be freer from these sorts of pains. I want to live in a world where the victims, survivors, and victors of rape, incest, and child sexual abuse no longer are made to feel guilty and ashamed for having been victimized; I want the shame to be placed where it rightfully belongs—on the perpetrators of these crimes, on the people who have elected to ignore that we have been victimized, and on this society that has been so unwilling to acknowledge these nefarious acts. Along with all of this, though, we must remain aware of the fact that we are the future, that we are the ones who will have to make the difference.

Notes

Preface

1. If interested in the prevalence of sexual victimization among males, its impact upon them, and their recovery issues, see the works of Bolton, Morris, and Maceachron (1989); Bera, Gonsiorek, and Letorneau (1991); Finkelhor (1979, 1984); Grubman-Black (1990); Hunter (1990); Lew (1988); and Risin and Koss (1988).

2. For information about women as the perpetrators of child sexual abuse, see the works of Bass and Davis (1988), Finkelhor (1984), Finkelhor and Williams, with Burns (1988), and Russell (1986).

3. One example is that, since girls and adolescent females have yet to fully develop coherent and integrated views of themselves, incest and child sexual abuse are regarded as being more devastating and disruptive experiences for them than rape is for adult women (Briere 1989; Courtois 1988; Finkelhor 1984; Herman 1992; van der Kolk 1989; Ledray 1986; Putnam 1990; Shengold 1989; Wilson et al. 1985).

4. For overviews about the men who commit these crimes, see the works of Beneke (1982); Groth (1979); Horton, Johnson, Roundy, and Williams (1990); and West, Roy, and Nichols (1978).

5. If interested in self-help works, there are several good books which give general information, as well as discuss specific tactics to facilitate recovery. For *adult women who were sexually abused as children*, the works of Bass and Davis (1988), Engel (1989), Finney (1990), Poston and Lison (1989), and Tower (1988) are particularly valuable resources. Regarding *recovering from rape*, the works of Kelly (1988), Koss and Harvey (1991), and Ledray (1986) are excellent self-help overviews.

6. There are a number of excellent resources as to what significant others can do for their loved ones who are recovering from rape, incest, and child sexual abuse. They include works by Davis (1991), Gil (1992), and Ledray (1986).

Chapter 1

1. Several works have examined the rape crisis center, its history and goals and the variety of services that it renders, as well as the differing ideologies which can dictate its course. For overviews of these subjects, see the works of Burt et al. (1987), Gornick et al. (1985), Harvey (1985), and King and Webb (1981).

2. For excellent discussions about multiple personality disorder see the works of Cohen et al. (1991) and Putnam (1989). Cohen et al.'s book is a compilation of responses from 150 people across the country (many of whom are multiples), and it focuses on their experiences and what they think their therapists and significant others should know about their multiplicity. Although Putnam's book is quite different, it is equally useful because he does an excellent job of summarizing and synthesizing the available information about the causes and consequences of multiple personality disorder, the types of personalities that may exist, treatment strategies that he has found to be effective, and what integration is like.

3. Katz and Mazur offer the frequently cited works of Sutherland and Scherl (1970) and Ennis (1967). Although both of these studies included only 13 cases of rape, the authors draw all sorts of far-reaching conclusions.

4. An enormous literature investigates the problematic attitudes that the general public, men (including convicted rapists), and the involved professionals have regarding sexual victimization. For discussions of these issues, please see the works of Baron and Straus (1989); Bechhofer and Parrot (1991); Best et al. (1992); Bridges and McGrail (1989); Burt (1980, 1983, 1991); Calhoun and Townsley (1991); Check and Malamuth (1985); Feild (1978); Feldman-Summers and Palmer (1980); Fonow et al. (1992); Gilmartin-Zena (1983a, 1988, 1989a, 1989b); Holmstrom and Burgess (1978); Jenkins and Dambrot (1987); Lottes (1988); Madigan and Gamble (1991), Marolla and Scully (1986); Masson (1984); Muehlenhard (1989); Russell (1986); Scully and Marolla (1984, 1985) and Williams and Holmes (1981).

Chapter 2

1. I do *not* believe that determining the "real" rate of rape ever will be feasible. No matter which data source you examine, each has its

flaws and is unlikely to count all cases of sexual victimization. For example, we now know that many children "bury" their experiences of childhood sexual abuse; some of them recover these memories as adults while others may never do so. Thus, if you ask a group of adult women about their sexually coercive experiences, you would *not* get a completely accurate figure. In other cases, women and children would be hesitant to discuss issues of sexual victimization and/or would *not* define what happened to them as rape, incest, or child sexual abuse. Therefore, the best that we can do is to come up with *estimates* about the incidence and prevalence of these problems.

2. For detailed discussions of the extent of the offenses of rape, incest, and child sexual abuse, see the works of Bagley and King (1990), Courtois (1988), Crewdson (1988), Haugaard and Reppucci (1988), Koss and Harvey (1991), Russell (1984, 1986), and Warshaw (1988).

3. Preliminary victimization data from 1991, though, show that rapes and attempted rapes soared by an unprecedented 59 percent (Law Enforcement News 1992).

4. Interestingly enough, in the index of Ageton's book, the words incest and child sexual abuse do *not* even appear.

5. Please note that Russell's estimates of the problems of incest and child sexual abuse are based on the same sample of 930 women described in the earlier discussion of community estimates of the rape problem.

Chapter 3

1. For excellent overviews of the marital rape problem, see Russell (1982b, 1991), and Finkelhor and Yllo (1985).

2. Russell (1984:164–165) notes that the historical roots of the victim-precipitated view of crime and rape can be traced back to Freud.

3. I often have wondered why more men do *not* resent this particular element in Amir's work. From my vantage point, this explanation of rape is quite insulting to men and their abilities to live as rational, cognitive, and feeling human beings.

4. Of the 156 societies studied, Sanday found that 18 percent were rape-prone, 35 percent evidenced mixed patterns (i.e., rape existed but was infrequent), and 47 percent were rape-free.

5. For example, Check and Malamuth (1983) found, on the average, that 30 percent of the college-age men that they studied self-

reported a likelihood to commit rape. When they considered the impact of the men's attitudes about sex roles, though, 44 percent of the men who evidenced high sex-role stereotyping admitted a tendency to be sexually assaultive, while only 12 percent of the men who support low sex-role stereotyping reported such a tendency.

6. Since there are varying "degrees" or "brands" of feminism (e.g., equal rights or liberal, socialist, and radical), we can assume that their respective perspectives about rape also will vary (cf. Andersen 1988; Kamen 1991; Sapiro 1990).

7. For an overview of the mythology which surrounds the subject of child sexual abuse, see Bagley and King (1990:48–49).

Chapter 4

1. Since so many studies (particularly investigations of the long-term consequences of child sexual abuse) point to suicidal ideation and attempted suicides as aftereffects, we should acknowledge that some of the suicides which have shocked and confused us (i.e., ones to which people have exclaimed "she seemed so normal," "her life seemed so full") may very well be the result of their earlier experiences of sexual victimization. Practitioners, then, should be aware of this possible link.

2. As examples, Burt and Katz (1987) have developed three valuable scales ("How Do I See Myself Now," "How I Deal with Things," and "Changes that Have Come from Your Efforts to Recover") that explore how women recover from rape and how they perceive themselves afterward. In addition, Calhoun and Atkeson (1991:54–58) and Koss and Harvey (1991:85–88) summarize a number of different objective measures of post-rape-victimization "symptoms." Further, Blume (1990:xvii-xxi) offers the "Incest Survivors' Aftereffects Checklist"; Dolan (1991:32) has given us the "Solution-Focused Recovery Scale for Survivors of Sexual Abuse"; Ratner (1990:12–14) has developed a symptoms checklist; Briere (1989: 186–187) has formulated the "Trauma Symptom Checklist"; and Jehu (1988:48) offers the "Distorted Beliefs Scale."

3. Although it is artificial to separate the various dimensions of our lives and speak of them as if they are independent, I have elected to do so for purposes of clarity and management of a large volume of information.

4. Although many, if not most, of the better studies which have investigated women's post-rape reactions are included in this table, I do *not* suggest that this list is all-inclusive.

5. Examples of this type of research are the works of Burgess and Holmstrom (1979b); Kilpatrick et al. (1979, 1981, 1985); Koss and her associates (1987, 1988); and Russell (1984).

6. I believe that, in part, this discrepancy can be explained via the divergent time frames these studies utilize. For example, if I measure a woman's responses shortly after her assault, she might be in shock or the impact of the experience may *not* have registered as yet. If, on the other hand, I investigate this same woman's reactions one week later, she may be in the throes of disruption or be completely numb.

7. It is important to note, though, that some experts, particularly feminists (e.g., Kelly 1988; Russell 1974), view some of these consequences (e.g., fear and anger) as positive and realistic outcomes rather than negative ones. More will be said about this issue later.

8. Again, some of these consequences are *not* all bad. In addition, it is important to reiterate the feminist caveat about the value-laden nature and masculine bias of such terms as "frigidity" and "promiscuity" (Kelly 1988; Russell 1974). In sum, these terms tend to be labels applied by others rather than survivors' depictions of their own lives.

9. Again, some of the experts point out that we should *not* feel too safe, because the reality of the world as we currently know it is that girls and women are vulnerable to sexual victimization. In addition, some reports have shown that women who evidence some level of self-blame (particularly behavioral self-blame or thinking that their behavior may have been problematic, rather than viewing self as the problem) may recover more fully from being raped (Janoff-Bulman 1992).

10. The authors interpret these findings to mean that: (1) after many negative life events, being raped is similar to the "straw that breaks the camel's back" (i.e., we are overloaded and break down); (2) having experienced few pre-rape stressors means that we have had little opportunity to develop coping skills; and (3) those of us who report moderate levels of pre-rape stress in our lives have been able to hone our coping skills, thereby reducing the current impact of being sexually assaulted.

11. Kendall-Tackett (1991) has developed a profile of when adults molested as children seek treatment for this problem. She suggests that "early presenters" are young adults who were older when they were sexually abused, experienced a lengthy period of abuse, had reported their abuse to law enforcement authorities, and had experienced a

greater number of acts. The "late presenters" are women whose abuse began when they were quite young, did *not* last very long, was *not* reported to official authorities, and included fewer sexual acts.

12. Although there is a burgeoning literature which examines the causes, the development, and the treatment of MPD, it is interesting to note that many lay people and professionals alike continue to question whether this disorder is "real" (cf. Bliss 1986; Kluft 1985a, 1990; Mayer 1991; Putnam 1989). In fact, Goodwin (1985:4) illustrates the similarity between the incredulity of professionals about whether MPD exists and their earlier unwillingness to acknowledge that childhood sexual abuse was possible. What is particularly noteworthy about her analysis is that the language used to discredit the existence of both childhood sexual abuse and MPD is nearly identical, i.e., it is rare; it doesn't exist; that's impossible; she's lying and/or faking.

Chapter 5

1. As has been noted already, there are exceptions to this criticism. In the past few years, for example, a number of books have been published which summarize not only the consequences of sexual victimization but also the equally important issues of how and why many of us do recover from these experiences. Most notably, works which offer messages of hope and/or information about recovery are those of Bagley and King (1990), Bass and Davis (1988), Briere (1989), Burgess and Holmstrom (1979b), Courtois (1988), Davis (1990), Dolan (1991), Finney (1990), Gil (1992), Herman (1992), Janoff-Bulman (1992), Kelly (1988), Koss and Harvey (1991), Ledray (1986), Ratner (1991), and Sanford (1990).

2. It is important to add that some authors now are suggesting that some of these physiological changes may be *permanent* ones. As an example, Janoff-Bulman (1992:65–69) summarizes recent works which suggest that trauma (particularly events involving extreme threat) gets encoded chemically and neurologically in our bodies and can result in catecholamine depletion. This, in turn, can cause hypersensitivity to subsequent situations of stress. In sum, "a single case of overwhelming terror may be capable of changing brain chemistry such that some survivors are more sensitive to adrenaline surges even decades later. Increasingly, there is a suggestion that traumatic stress may result in permanent structural changes in the brain" (Janoff-Bulman 1992:68).

3. For detailed discussions of the ways that we can reclaim our bodies, see Bass and Davis (1988:207–222), Wisechild (1988), and Dolan (1991).

4. Some recent works go so far as to suggest that we cannot resolve our problems with prior sexual victimization (particularly experiences of incest and childhood sexual abuse) until we begin to control our substance abuse problems (Courtois 1992; Farmer 1989; Ratner 1990). The rationale is that we will continue to deny the significance of our experiences, as well as backslide, until we eliminate the crutches of drug addiction and alcoholism. When, though, Root (1989:544) notes that "an individual with an unresolved history of sexual victimization is likely to feel affectively much worse when immediate abstention from alcohol, drugs, or food removes the means for mitigation of symptoms associated with earlier traumas," she offers a dissenting opinion. She also suggests that these same women will be highly susceptible to subsequent relapses.

5. For detailed analyses of how to go about reclaiming the sexual part of ourselves, see Bass and Davis (1988:239–269), Maltz (1991), and Maltz and Holman (1987:81–106).

6. Herman (1992), Janoff-Bulman (1992), and Reis (1991b) are notable exceptions because they realize the importance of healing from *all* sorts of sexual victimizations (i.e., all the way from living in a society that values pornography through acts of sexual victimization).

7. Please note that Sutherland and Scherl based their model upon interviews with thirteen women who had been raped. In addition, they suggested that two major themes occur during this latter stage of recovery: (1) the woman must integrate a new view of herself (which includes accepting the event, as well as acknowledging her "complicity" in it), and (2) she must resolve her "feelings" about the assailant and her "relationship" with him. This latter issue is particularly troubling; again, the inference is that women who have been raped must come to "understand" and/or "forgive" him.

8. In an early work, Burgess and Holmstrom (1974) suggested that the rape trauma syndrome has the two phases of impact and reorganization. In a later work, though, they suggest that some women may experience a "compounded reaction to rape," particularly ones with "a past or current difficulty with a psychiatric condition, a physical condition, or behavioral patterns which created difficulty for them living in this society" (Burgess and Holmstrom 1979b:45). Burgess and Holmstrom also add that this woman may need more than crisis counseling to aid her in recovering from her sexual assault.

9. Other models exist which outline the recovery process for survivors of childhood sexual victimization (e.g., Farmer 1989; Poston and Lison 1989; Ratner 1990; Sgroi 1988, 1989). Since many of their emphases are similar to ones outlined later in this section, their inclusion would be redundant.

10. Please note that Bass and Davis (1988:58) suggest that we do *not* have to go through all of these stages: "Although most of these stages are necessary for every survivor, a few of them (i.e., the emergency stage, remembering the abuse, confronting your family, and forgiveness) are *not* applicable for every woman."

11. Although Bass and Davis (1988) apply this model of recovery exclusively to adult survivors of incest and child sexual abuse, these same stages (with some modification) apply equally well to the victims and survivors of rape. For example, remembering is *not* usually a problem for survivors of rape because they typically do *not* "bury" the experience. In addition, the issues of disclosure and confrontations, as well as forgiveness of the perpetrator, do *not* readily apply, but many of the other issues do (e.g., deciding to heal, the emergency stage, and breaking the silence).

Chapter 6

1. The obvious solution to this problem is to develop some sort of national health insurance program which would provide access to physical and mental health services for all citizens. Rather than an innovation, we in the U.S. would simply be catching up with every other Western, industrialized nation on the planet (Cockerham 1992).

2. We now, though, have evidence that the impact of such an experience can be severe, can last a long time, and/or may follow a delayed-onset pattern for a sizable number of us; yet, we have continued to implement crisis intervention strategies as if they are the most efficient ones. I tend to side with Williams and Holmes (1981) who argue that these techniques have been selected *not* for their efficiency, but rather because of their relative inexpensiveness.

3. It is important to note that caretaking and being responsible for others often are considered "correct" behaviors for women in a patriarchal culture because these are the only options available to them. As Jack (1991) suggests, though, these also are important, underlying issues in the sex differential to develop depression.

4. There are several other works which offer extensive summaries of this subject. Regarding rape victimization, the works of Burkhart (1991), Katz (1984), Braswell (1989), Calhoun and Atkeson (1991), Forman (1980, 1983), Janoff-Bulman (1985), and Resick and Schnicke (1990) offer treatment information, while works which summarize how to treat post-sexual-abuse trauma include Alexander et al. (1991), Dinsmore (1991), Donaldson and Gardner (1985), Engel (1989), Friedrich (1990), Gil (1988), Jehu (1988), Steele (1987, 1988), Poston and Lison (1989), and Tower (1988).

5. Calhoun and Atkeson (1991) offer other treatment strategies which are based on social learning theory. They include: (1) systematic desensitization, (2) exposure treatment (also referred to as flooding or implosion), and (3) stress inoculation training (which is similar to Kilpatrick and Veronen's BBIP).

6. Although beyond the scope of this book, Koss and Harvey (1991:194–204) offer several tactics that can be used to reduce the "symptoms" of anxiety, depression, sexual dysfunction, and relationship difficulties.

7. For specifics of designing groups for survivors of rape, please see Koss and Harvey (1991:231–234).

8. The work of Gomes-Schwartz et al. (1990) is an exception to this criticism because it examines the longitudinal consequences of sexual victimization among 156 recently abused children. They, though, do *not* discuss the treatment strategy employed in this combined research/treatment program.

9. Briere (1989:94) suggests that role-playing the anger that the survivor has for the perpetrator can be superior to an actual confrontation because the latter strategy can result in "further enmeshment and damage" of the woman. Briere is one of the few in the child sexual victimization literature who expresses this sentiment.

10. Briere (1989:109–110) offers a number of specific strategies to work with the inner child.

11. This childlike behavior may be similar to what Finney (1990:142–145) has called ego states, i.e., the child does *not* split apart literally into multiple personalities but rather splits off particular memories, emotions, or pains.

12. Courtois (1988:212–213) also notes the merits of adjunctive therapies, including group therapy, support groups, and other specialized programs which address only one problem (e.g., eating disorders, substance abuse or addiction), marital or family therapy, and educational groups and courses.

13. Although beyond the scope of this work, Dolan (1991:162–165) offers examples of how to utilize the client's dissociative abilities positively.

Chapter 7

1. For overviews of how these particular prevention programs for children work, as well as their content, see Koss and Harvey (1991) and Blumberg et al. (1991).

2. Please note that Warshaw (1988:175–178) also discusses specific, successful rape education and prevention that have been implemented at several colleges and universities across the country.

3. Other authors have offered suggestions regarding how students can alter their dating patterns. Specifically, they suggest that, if we move away from nonegalitarian styles (i.e., the man initiates the date, makes all decisions about the date, pays for everything, and drives), we may be able to reduce the likelihood of acquaintance rapes occurring on dates (Allgeier 1987; Muehlenhard 1989; Muehlenhard et al. 1985; and Muehlenhard and Linton 1987).

References

Abbey, Antonia. 1991. "Misperceptions as an Antecedent of Acquaintance Rape: A Consequence of Ambiguity in Communication between Women and Men." Pp. 96–111 in *Acquaintance Rape: The Hidden Crime*, edited by A. Parrot and L. Bechhofer. New York: John Wiley and Sons.

Abramsom, Lyn Y., Martin E.P. Seligman, and John D. Teasdale. 1978. "Learned Helplessness in Humans: Critique and Reformulation." *Journal of Abnormal Psychology* 87:49–74.

Adcock, Christine and Karen Newbigging. 1990. "Women in the Shadows: Women, Feminism and Clinical Psychology." Pp.172–188 in *Feminists and Psychological Practice*, edited by E. Burman. London: Sage.

Adler, Frieda, Gerhard O.W. Muehler, and William S. Laufer. 1991. *Criminology*. New York: McGraw-Hill.

Ageton, Suzanne S. 1983. *Sexual Assault Among Adolescents*. Lexington, MA: Lexington.

Aguilera, Donna C. and Janice M. Messick. 1978. *Crisis Intervention: Theory and Methodology*. St. Louis: C.V. Mosby.

Alder, Christine. 1985. "An Exploration of Self-Reported Sexually Aggressive Behavior." *Crime and Delinquency* 31:306–331.

Alexander, Pamela C., Robert A. Neimeyer, and Victoria M. Follette. 1991. "Group Therapy for Women Sexually Abused as Children: A Controlled Study and Investigation of Individual Differences." *Journal of Interpersonal Violence* 6:218–231.

Allen, Charlotte Vale. 1980. *Daddy's Girl*. New York: Berkeley.

Allen, Deborah and Judy Bessai Okawa. 1987. "A Counseling Center Looks at Sexual Harassment." *Journal of NAWDAC* Fall:9–16.

Allender, Dan B. 1990. *The Wounded Heart: Hope for Adult Victims of Childhood Sexual Abuse*. Colorado Springs, CO: Navpress.

320 *Rape, Incest, and Child Sexual Abuse*

Allgeier, Elizabeth Rice. 1987. "Coercive versus Consensual Sexual Interactions." Pp. 9–63 in *The G. Stanley Hall Lecture Series,* edited by V.P. Makosky. Washington, D.C.: American Psychological Association.

_____. 1988. "Acquaintance Assault Reduction Strategies." Paper presented at the annual meetings of the Ohio Coalition on Sexual Assault, September 20, Columbus, OH.

American Association of University Women. 1992. "The AAUW Report, How Schools Shortchange Girls, Executive Summary." American Association of University Women Educational Foundation.

Amir, Menachem. 1967. "Victim Precipitated Forcible Rape." *Journal of Criminal Law, Criminology, and Police Science* 58:493–502.

_____. 1971. *Patterns in Forcible Rape.* Chicago: University of Chicago.

Andersen, Margaret L. 1988. *Thinking About Women: Sociological Perspectives on Sex and Gender.* New York: Macmillan.

Antonovsky, Aaron. 1979. *Health, Stress and Coping.* San Francisco: Jossey-Bass.

_____. 1984. "A Call for a New Question—Salutogenesis—and a Proposed Answer—the Sense of Coherence." *Journal of Preventive Pyschiatry* 2:1–13.

_____. 1987. *Unraveling the Mystery of Health: How People Manage Stress and Stay Well.* San Francisco: Jossey-Bass.

Arliss, Laurie P. 1991. *Gender Communication.* Englewood Cliffs, NJ: Prentice-Hall.

Armstrong, Louise. 1978. *Kiss Daddy Goodnight.* New York: Hawthorne.

Asher, Shirley Joseph. 1988. "The Effects of Childhood Sexual Abuse: A Review of the Issues and Evidence." Pp. 3–18 in *Handbook on Sexual Abuse of Children: Assessment and Treatment Issues,* edited by L.E.A. Walker. New York: Springer.

Atkeson, Beverly M., Karen S. Calhoun, Patricia Resick, and Elizabeth M. Ellis. 1982. "Victims of Rape: Repeated Assessment of Depressive Symptoms." *Journal of Consulting and Clinical Psychology* 50:96–102.

Bagley, Christopher and Kathleen King. 1990. *Child Sexual Abuse: The Search for Healing.* London: Routledge.

Baier, John L., Marianne G. Rosenzweig, and Edward G. Whipple. 1991. "Patterns of Sexual Behavior, Coercion, and Victimization of University Students." *Journal of College Student Development* 32:310–322.

Baron, Larry and Murray A. Straus. 1987. "Four Theories of Rape: A Macrosociological Analysis." *Social Problems* 34:467–489.

_____. 1989. *Four Theories of Rape in American Society: A State-Level Analysis.* New Haven: Yale University.

Barringer, Carol E. 1992. "The Survivor's Voice: Breaking the Incest Taboo." *NWSA Journal* 4:4–22.

Bart, Pauline and Patricia O'Brien. 1985. *Stopping Rape: Successful Survival Strategies.* Elmsford, NY: Pergamon.

Bass, Ellen and Laura Davis. 1988. *The Courage to Heal: A Guide for Women Survivors of Child Sexual Abuse.* New York: Harper and Row.

Bechhofer, Laurie and Andrea Parrot. 1991. "What is Acquaintance Rape?" Pp. 9–25 in *Acquaintance Rape: The Hidden Crime,* edited by A. Parrot and L. Bechhofer. New York: John Wiley and Sons.

Becker, Judith V., Gene G. Abel, and Linda S. Skinner. 1979. "The Impact of a Sexual Assault on the Victim's Sexual Life." *Victimology: An International Journal* 4:229–235.

Becker, Judith V., Linda J. Skinner, Gene G. Abel, Julia Howell, and Kathy Bruce. 1982. "The Effects of Sexual Assault on Rape and Attempted Rape Victims." *Victimology: An International Journal* 7:106–113.

Becker, Robert E. and Richard G. Heimberg. 1985. "Cognitive-Behavioral Treatments for Depression: A Review of Controlled Clinical Research." Pp. 209–234 in *Depression in Multidisciplinary Perspective,* edited by A. Dean. New York: Brunner/Mazel.

Belenky, Mary Field , Blythe McVicker Clinchy, Nancy Rule Goldberger, and Jill Mattuck Tarule. 1986. *Women's Ways of Knowing: The Development of Self, Voice, and Mind.* New York: Basic.

Beneke, Timothy. 1982. *Men on Rape: What They Have to Say about Sexual Violence.* New York: St. Martin's.

Bera, Walter H., John G. Gonsiorek, and Don Letourneau. 1991. *Male Adolescent Sexual Abuse: Clinical Perspectives.* Beverly Hills, CA: Sage.

Berger, Peter. 1963. *Invitation to Sociology: A Humanistic Perspective.* Garden City, NY: Anchor.

Berger, Ronald J., Patricia Searles, Richard G. Salem, and Beth Ann Pierce. 1986. "Sexual Assault in a College Community." *Sociological Focus* 19:1–26.

Berliner, Lucy. 1989. "Child Abuse Prevention Education: How Can We Make It Work?" *Journal of Interpersonal Violence* 4:251–253.

Best, Connie L., Bonnie S. Dansky, and Dean G. Kilpatrick. 1992. "Medical Students' Attitudes about Female Rape Victims." *Journal of Interpersonal Violence* 7:175–188.

Bliss, Eugene L. 1986. *Multiple Personality, Allied Disorders and Hypnosis.* New York: Oxford.

Blumberg, Elaine J., Michele W. Chadwick, Linda A. Fogarty, Timothy W. Speth, and David L. Chadwick. 1991. "The Touch Discrimination Component of Sexual Prevention Training: Unanticipated Positive Consequences." *Journal of Interpersonal Violence* 6:12–28.

Blume, E. Sue. 1990. *Secret Survivors: Uncovering Incest and Its Aftereffects in Women.* New York: John Wiley and Sons.

Bograd, Michele. 1986. "A Feminist Examination of Family Therapy: What Is Women's Place?" Pp. 95–106 in *A Guide to Dynamics of Feminist Therapy,* edited by D. Howard. New York: Harrington Park.

Bolton, Frank G., Larry A. Morris, and Ann E. MacEachron. 1989. *Males at Risk: The Other Side of Child Sexual Abuse.* Beverly Hills, CA: Sage.

Bolz, Barbara. 1991. "Healing Ourselves; Healing the World: An Interview with Laura Davis." *On the Issues* (Fall) XX:17–40.

Braswell, Linda. 1989. *Quest for Respect: A Healing Guide for Survivors of Rape.* Ventura, CA: Pathfinders.

Braun, Bennett G. 1985. "The Transgenerational Incidence of Dissociation and Multiple Personality Disorder: A Preliminary Report." Pp. 127–150 in *Childhood Antecedents of Multiple Personality,* edited by R.P. Kluft. Washington, D.C.: American Psychiatric Association.

————. 1989. "Psychotherapy of the Survivor of Incest with a Dissociative Disorder." *Psychiatric Clinics of North America* 12:307–324.

————. 1990. "Dissociative Disorders as Sequelae to Incest." Pp. 227–245 in *Incest-Related Syndrome in Adult Psychopathology,* edited by R.P. Kluft. Washington, D.C.: American Psychiatric Association.

Braun, Bennett G. and Roberta G. Sachs. 1985. "The Development of Multiple Personality Disorder: Predisposing, Precipitating, and Perpetuating Factors." Pp. 37–64 in *Childhood Antecedents of Multiple Personality,* edited by R.P. Kluft. Washington, D.C.: American Psychiatric Association.

Bridges, Judith S. and Christine A. McGrail. 1989. "Attributions of Responsibility for Date and Stranger Rape." *Sex Roles* 21:273–286.

Briere, John. 1989. *Therapy for Adults Molested as Children: Beyond Survival.* New York: Springer.

Briere, John and Neil M. Malamuth. 1983. "Self-Reported Likelihood of Sexually Aggressive Behavior: Attitudinal versus Sexual Explanations." *Journal of Research in Personality* 17:315–323.

Briere, John, Neil Malamuth, and James V.P. Check. 1985. "Sexuality and Rape Supportive Beliefs." *International Journal of Women's Studies* 8:398–403.

Briere, John and Marsha Runtz. 1988a. "Post Sexual Abuse Trauma." Pp. 85–100 in *Lasting Effects of Child Sexual Abuse*, edited by G.E. Wyatt and G.J. Powell. Beverly Hills, CA: Sage.

_____. 1988b. "Symptomatology Associated with Childhood Sexual Victimization in a Nonclinical Adult Sample." *Child Abuse and Neglect* 12:51–59.

_____. 1989. "The Trauma Symptom Checklist (TSC-33): Early Data on a New Scale." *Journal of Interpersonal Violence* 4:151–163.

Broverman, Inge K., Donald M. Broverman, Frau L. Clarkson, Paul Rosenkrantz, and Susan R. Vogel. 1970. "Sex Role Stereotypes and Clinical Judgments of Mental Health Professionals." *Journal of Consulting and Clinical Psychology* 34:1–7.

Brown, George W. and Tirril Harris. 1978. *Social Origins of Depression: A Study of Psychiatric Disorder in Women.* New York: Free Press.

Browne, Angela and David Finkelhor. 1986. "Initial and Long-Term Effects: A Review of the Research." Pp. 143–179 in *A Sourcebook on Child Sexual Abuse*, edited by D. Finkelhor and associates. Beverly Hills, CA: Sage.

Brownmiller, Susan. 1975. *Against Our Will: Men, Women and Rape.* New York: Simon and Schuster.

Bureau of the Census. 1981. *Statistical Abstract of the United States* (102nd ed.) Washington, D.C.: U.S. Department of Commerce.

Bureau of the Census. 1991. *Statistical Abstract of the United States* (111th ed.) Washington, D.C: U.S. Department of Commerce, Economic and Statistics Administration.

Burgess, Ann Wolbert and Lynda Lytle Holmstrom. 1974. "Rape Trauma Syndrome." *American Journal of Psychiatry* 131:981–986.

_____. 1979a. "Adaptive Strategies and Recovery from Rape." *American Journal of Psychiatry* 136:1278–1282.

_____. 1979b. *Rape: Crisis and Recovery*. Bowie, MD: Robert J. Brady.

_____. 1985. "Rape Trauma Syndrome and Post Traumatic Stress Response." Pp. 46–60 in *Rape and Sexual Assault: A Research Handbook*, A.W. Burgess. New York: Garland.

Burkhart, Barry R. 1991. "Conceptual and Practical Analysis of Therapy for Acquaintance Rape Victims." Pp. 287–303 in *Acquaintance Rape: The Hidden Crime*, edited by A. Parrot and L. Bechhofer. New York: John Wiley and Sons.

Burnam, M. Audrey, Judith A. Stein, Jacqueline M. Golding, Judith M. Siegel, Susan Sorenson, Alan B. Forsythe, and Cynthia A. Telles. 1988. "Sexual Assault and Mental Disorders in a Community Population." *Journal of Consulting and Clinical Psychology* 56:843–850.

Burt, Martha. 1980. "Cultural Myths and Supports for Rape." *Journal of Personality and Social Psychology* 38:217–230.

_____. 1983. "Justifying Personal Violence: A Comparison of Rapists and the General Public." *Victimology: An International Journal* 8:131–150.

_____. 1991. "Rape Myths and Acquaintance Rape." Pp. 26–40 in *Acquaintance Rape: The Hidden Crime*, edited by A. Parrot and L. Bechhofer. New York: John Wiley and Sons.

Burt, Martha R., Janet Gornick, and Karen J. Pittman. 1987. "Feminism and Rape Crisis Centers." *Sexual Coercion and Assault* 2:8–13.

Burt, Martha R. and Bonnie L. Katz. 1987. "Dimensions of Recovery from Rape: Focus on Growth Outcomes." *Journal of Interpersonal Violence* 2:57–81.

Butler, Marylou. 1985. "Guidelines for Feminist Therapy." Pp. 32–38 in *Handbook of Feminist Therapy*, edited by L.B. Rosewater and L.E.A. Walker. New York: Springer.

Butler, Sandra. 1985. *Conspiracy of Silence: The Trauma of Incest*. Volcano, CA: Volcano.

_____. 1989. "Preface." Pp. xi-xiii in *Therapy for Adults Molested as Children: Beyond Survival*, authored by J. Briere. New York: Springer.

Calhoun, Karen S. and Beverly M. Atkeson. 1991. *Treatment of Rape Victims: Facilitating Psychosocial Adjustment*. New York: Pergamon.

Calhoun, Karen S., Beverly M. Atkeson, and Patricia A. Resick. 1982. "A Longitudinal Examination of Fear Reactions in Victims of Rape." *Journal of Counseling Psychology* 29:655–661.

Calhoun, Karen S. and Ruth M. Townsley. 1991. "Attributions of Responsibility for Acquaintance Rape." Pp. 57–69 in *Acquaintance Rape: The Hidden Crime*, edited by A. Parrot and L. Bechhofer. New York: John Wiley and Sons.

Cammaert, Lorna P. 1985. "How Widespread is Sexual Harassment on Campus?" *International Journal of Women's Studies* 8:388–397.

Caplan, Gerald. 1964. *Principles of Preventive Psychiatry*. New York: Basic Books.

Carmen, Elaine (Hilberman) and Patricia Perri Rieker. 1989. "A Psychosocial Model of the Victim-to-Patient Process: Implications for Treatment." *Psychiatric Clinics of North America* 12:431–443.

Carrow, Deborah M. 1980. *Rape: Guidelines for a Community Response*. U.S. Department of Justice: Law Enforcement Assistance Administration.

Celano, Marianne P. 1992. "A Developmental Model of Victims' Internal Attributions of Responsibility for Sexual Abuse." *Journal of Interpersonal Violence* 7:57–70.

Charon, Joel. 1977. *Symbolic Interactionism: An Introduction, an Interpretation, an Integration*. Englewood Cliffs, NJ: Prentice-Hall.

Check, James V.P. and Neil M. Malamuth. 1983. "Sex-Role Stereotyping and Reactions to Depictions of Stranger versus Acquaintance Rape." *Journal of Personality and Social Psychology* 45:344–356.

_____. 1985. "An Empirical Assessment of Some Feminist Hypotheses about Rape." *International Journal of Women's Studies* 8:414–423.

Chesler, Phyllis. 1989. *Women and Madness*. San Diego: Harcourt Brace Jovanovich.

Clark, Lorenne and Debra Lewis. 1977. *Rape: The Price of Coercive Sexuality*. Toronto: Women's Press.

Cobb, Kenneth A. and Nancy R. Schauer. 1977. "Michigan's Criminal Sexual Assault Law." Pp. 170–186 in *Forcible Rape: The Crime, the Victim, and the Offender*, edited by D. Chappell, R. Geis, and G. Geis. New York: Columbia University.

Cockerham, William C. 1981. *Sociology of Mental Disorders*. Englewood Cliffs, NJ: Prentice-Hall.

_____. 1992. *Medical Sociology* (5th ed.) Englewood Cliffs, NJ: Prentice Hall.

Cohen, Barry M., Esther Giller, and Lynn W., editors. 1991. *Multiple Personality Disorder from the Inside Out*. Baltimore, MD: Sidran.

Cohen, Lawrence H., editor. 1988. *Life Events and Psychological Functioning: Theoretical and Methodological Issues.* Beverly Hills, CA: Sage.

Cohen, Lawrence H. and Dean W. Nelson. 1983. "Crisis Intervention: An Overview of Theory and Technique." Pp. 13–25 in *Crisis Intervention* (2nd ed.), edited by L.H. Cohen, W.L. Claiborn, and G.A. Specter. New York: Human Sciences.

Cohen, Lawrence J. and Susan Roth. 1987. "The Psychological Aftermath of Rape: Long-Term Effects and Individual Differences in Recovery." *Journal of Social and Clinical Psychology* 5:525–534.

Coles, Robert. 1990. *The Spiritual Life of Children.* Boston: Houghton Mifflin.

Conn, Sarah A. 1991. "The Self-World in Connection: Implications for Mental Health and Psychotherapy." *Woman of Power* 20:71–76.

Connell, Noreen and Cassandra Wilson, editors. 1974. *Rape: The First Sourcebook for Women.* New York: Plume.

Conrad, Peter and Joseph W. Schneider. 1980. *Deviance and Medicalization: From Badness to Sickness.* St. Louis: C.V. Mosby.

Conte, Jon R. 1988. "Research on the Prevention of Sexual Abuse of Children." Pp. 300–309 in *Coping with Family Violence: Research and Policy Perspectives*, G.T. Hotaling, D. Finkelhor, J.T. Kirkpatrick, and M.A. Straus (eds.). Newbury Park, CA: Sage.

Conte, Jon R. and Lucy Berliner. 1988. "The Impact of Sexual Abuse on Children: Empirical Findings." Pp. 72–93 in *Handbook on Sexual Abuse of Children: Assessment and Treatment Issues*, edited by L.E.A. Walker. New York: Springer.

Conte, Jon R. and John R. Schuerman. 1987. "The Effects of Sexual Abuse on Children." *Journal of Interpersonal Violence* 2:380–390.

_____. 1988. "The Effects of Sexual Abuse on Children: A Multidimensional View." Pp. 157–170 in *Lasting Effects of Child Sexual Abuse*, edited by G.E. Wyatt and G.J. Powell. Newbury Park, CA: Sage.

Cooley, Charles Horton. 1902. *Human Nature and the Social Order.* New York: Charles Scribner's Sons.

Coons, Philip M., Elizabeth S. Bowman, Terri A. Pellows, and Paul Schneider. 1989. "Post-Traumatic Aspects of the Treatment of Victims of Sexual Abuse and Incest." *Psychiatric Clinics of North America* 12:325–335.

Coons, Philip M., Carol Cole, Terri Pellow, and Victor Milstein. 1990. "Symptoms of Posttraumatic Stress and Dissociation in Women Victims of Abuse." Pp. 205–225 in *Incest-Related Syndrome in Adult Psychopathology*, edited by Richard P. Kluft. Washington, D.C.: American Psychiatric Association.

Costin, Frank and Norbert Schwarz. 1987. "Beliefs about Rape and Women's Social Roles: A Four-Nation Study." *Journal of Interpersonal Violence* 2:45–56.

Courtois, Christine A. 1988. *Healing the Incest Wound: Adult Survivors in Therapy*. New York: W.W. Norton.

_____. 1992. "Surviving: The Impact of Abuse on Adult Development and Parenting." Workshop presented at the National Symposium on Child Victimization, May, Washington, D.C.

Courtois, Christine A. and Judith E. Sprei. 1988. "Retrospective Incest Therapy for Women." Pp. 270–307 in *Handbook on Sexual Abuse of Children: Assessment and Treatment Issues*, edited by L.E.A. Walker. New York: Springer.

Craig, Mary. 1990. "Coercive Sexuality in Dating Relationships: A Situational Model." *Clinical Psychology Review* 10:395–423.

Crewdson, John. 1988. *By Silence Betrayed: Sexual Abuse of Children in America*. New York: Harper and Row.

Daro, Deborah. 1989. "When Should Prevention Education Begin?" *Journal of Interpersonal Violence* 4:257–260.

Davis, Laura. 1990. *The Courage to Heal Workbook: For Women and Men Survivors of Child Sexual Abuse*. New York: Harper and Row.

_____. 1991. *Allies in Healing: When the Person You Love Was Sexually Abused as a Child*. New York: Harper Perennial.

de Young, Mary. 1982. *The Sexual Victimization of Children*. Jefferson, NC: McFarland and Company.

Dean, Alfred. 1985. "On the Epidemiology of Depression." Pp. 5–31 in *Depression in Multidisciplinary Perspective*, edited by A. Dean. New York: Brunner/Mazel.

_____. 1986. "Measuring Psychological Resources." Pp. 97–111 in *Social Support, Life Events, and Depression*, edited by N. Lin, A. Dean, and W. Ensel. Orlando: Academic.

DeSalvo, Louise. 1989. *Virginia Woolf: The Impact of Childhood Sexual Abuse on her Life and Work*. Boston: Beacon.

Dinsmore, Christine. 1991. *From Surviving to Thriving: Incest, Feminism, and Recovery*. Albany, NY: State University of New York.

Dohrenwend, Barbara Snell and Bruce P. Dohrenwend. 1984. *Stressful Life Events and Their Contexts.* New Brunswick, NJ: Rutgers University.

Dolan, Yvonne M. 1991. *Resolving Sexual Abuse: Solution-Focused Therapy and Ericksonian Hypnosis for Adult Survivors.* New York: W.W. Norton.

Donaldson, Mary Ann and Russell Gardner, Jr. 1985. "Diagnosis and Treatment of Traumatic Stress among Women after Childhood Incest." Pp. 356–377 in *Trauma and Its Wake: The Study and Treatment of Post-Traumatic Stress Disorder,* edited by C.R. Figley. New York: Brunner/Mazel.

Donnerstein, Edward and Daniel Linz. 1989. "Mass Media, Sexual Violence and Male Viewers: Current Theory and Research." Pp. 488–500 in *Men's Lives,* edited by M.S. Kimmel and M.A. Messner. New York: Macmillan.

Donnerstein, Edward, Daniel Linz, and Steven Penrod. 1987. *The Question of Pornography: Research Findings and Policy Implications.* New York: Free Press.

Downey, Geraldine and Phyllis Moen. 1987. "Personal Efficacy, Income and Family Transitions: A Longitudinal Study of Women Heading Households." *Journal of Health and Social Behavior* 28:320–333.

Dukes, Richard L. and Christine L. Mattley. 1977. "Predicting Rape Victim Reportage." *Sociology and Social Research* 62:63–84.

Ellis, Elizabeth M. 1983. "A Review of Empirical Rape Research: Victims' Reactions and Response to Treatment." *Clinical Psychology Review* 3:473–490.

Ellis, Elizabeth M., Beverly M. Atkeson, and Karen S. Calhoun. 1981. "An Assessment of Long-Term Reactions to Rape." *Journal of Abnormal Psychology* 90:263–266.

Ellis, Lee. 1989. *Theories of Rape: Inquiries into the Causes of Sexual Aggression.* New York: Hemisphere.

Empey, Lamar. 1978. *American Delinquency: Its Meaning and Construction.* Homewood, IL: Dorsey.

Engel, Beverly. 1989. *The Right to Innocence: Healing the Trauma of Childhood Sexual Abuse.* New York: Ivy.

Ennis, Philip. 1967. *Criminal Victimization in the United States: A Report of a National Survey.* Washington, D.C.: U.S. Government Printing Office.

Estrich, Susan. 1987. *Real Rape: How the Legal System Victimizes Women Who Say No.* Cambridge, MA: Harvard University.

Faller, Kathleen Coulborn. 1990. *Understanding Child Sexual Maltreatment.* Newbury Park, CA: Sage.

Faludi, Susan. 1991. *Backlash: The Undeclared War against American Women.* New York: Crown.

Farmer, Steven. 1989. *Adult Children of Abusive Parents: A Healing Program for Those Who Have Been Physically, Sexually, or Emotionally Abused.* New York: Ballantine Books.

Federal Bureau of Investigation. 1992. *Crime in the United States 1991.* Washington, D.C.: U.S. Department of Justice.

Feild, Hubert S. 1978. "Attitudes Toward Rape: A Comparative Analysis of Police, Rapists, Crisis Counselors, and Citizens." *Journal of Personality and Social Psychology* 36:156–179.

Feldman-Summers, Shirley and Gayle C. Palmer. 1980. "Rape as Viewed by Judges, Prosecutors, and Police Officers." *Criminal Justice and Behavior* 7:19–40.

Fenstermaker, Sarah. 1989. "Acquaintance Rape on Campus: Responsibility and Attributions of Crime." Pp. 257–271 in *Violence in Dating Relationships: Emerging Issues,* edited by M.A. Pirog-Good and J.E. Stets. New York: Praeger.

Fine, Catherine G. 1990. "The Cognitive Sequelae of Incest." Pp. 161–182 in *Incest-Related Syndrome in Adult Psychopathology,* edited by R.P. Kluft. Washington, D.C.: American Psychiatric Association.

Finkelhor, David. 1979. *Sexually Victimized Children.* New York: Free Press.

———. 1984. *Child Sexual Abuse: New Theory and Research.* New York: Free Press.

———. 1986. "Prevention: A Review of Programs and Research." Pp. 224–254 in *A Sourcebook on Child Sexual Abuse,* edited by D. Finkelhor and associates. Beverly Hills, CA: Sage.

———. 1987. "The Trauma of Child Sexual Abuse." *Journal of Interpersonal Violence* 2:348–366.

———. 1988. "The Trauma of Child Sexual Abuse: Two Models." Pp. 61–82 in *Lasting Effects of Child Sexual Abuse,* G.E. Wyatt and G.J. Powell. Beverly Hills, CA: Sage.

Finkelhor, David and Larry Baron. 1986. "High-Risk Children." Pp. 60–88 in *A Sourcebook on Child Sexual Abuse,* edited by D. Finkelhor and associates. Beverly Hills, CA: Sage.

Finkelhor, David and Angela Browne. 1986. "Initial and Long-Term Effects: A Conceptual Framework." Pp. 143–180 in *A Sourcebook on Child Sexual Abuse*, edited by D. Finkelhor and associates. Beverly Hills, CA: Sage.

_____. 1988. "Assessing the Long-Term Impact of Child Sexual Abuse: A Review and Conceptualization." Pp. 55–71 in *Handbook on Sexual Abuse of Children: Assessment and Treatment Issues*, edited by L.E.A. Walker. New York: Springer.

Finkelhor, David, Gerald T. Hotaling, I.A. Lewis, and Christine Smith. 1989. "Sexual Abuse and Its Relationship to Later Sexual Satisfaction, Marital Status, Religion, and Attitudes." *Journal of Interpersonal Violence* 4:379–399.

Finkelhor, David and Linda Meyer Williams with Nanci Burns. 1988. *Nursery Crimes: Sexual Abuse in Day Care*. Newbury Park, CA: Sage.

Finkelhor, David and Kersti Yllo. 1985. *License to Rape: Sexual Abuse of Wives*. New York: Holt, Reinhart and Winston.

Finney, Lynne D. 1990. *Reach for the Rainbow: Advanced Healing for Survivors of Sexual Abuse*. Park City, UT: Changes.

Fiorentino, L.M. 1986. "Stress: The High Cost to Industry." *Occupational Nursing* 34:217–220.

Folkman, Susan, Richard S. Lazarus, Rand J. Gruen, and Anita DeLongis. 1986. "Appraisal, Coping, Health Status, and Psychological Symptoms." *Journal of Personality and Social Psychology* 50:571–579.

Fonow, Mary Margaret, Laurel Richardson, and Virginia Wemmerus. 1992. "Feminist Rape Education: Does It Work?" *Gender and Society* 6:108–121.

Forman, Bruce D. 1980. "Psychotherapy with Rape Victims." *Psychotherapy: Theory, Research, and Practice* 17:304–311.

_____. 1983. "Assessing the Impact of Rape and Its Significance in Psychotherapy." *Psychotherapy: Theory, Research, and Practice* 20:515–519.

Forward, Susan and Craig Buck. 1978. *Betrayal of Innocence: Incest and Its Devastation*. New York: Penguin.

Forward, Susan with Craig Buck. 1989. *Toxic Parents: Overcoming Their Hurtful Legacy and Reclaiming Your Life*. New York: Bantam.

Frank, Ellen and Barbara Payak Anderson. 1987. "Psychiatric Disorders in Rape Victims: Past History and Current Symptomatology." *Comprehensive Psychiatry* 28:77–82.

Franks, Violet. 1986. "Sex Stereotyping and Diagnosis of Psychopathology." Pp. 219–232 in *A Guide to Dynamics of Feminist Therapy*, edited by D. Howard. New York: Harrington Park.

Friedrich, William N. 1990. *Psychotherapy of Sexually Abused Children and Their Families*. New York: W.W. Norton.

Friedson, Elliot. 1961. *Patients' View of Medical Practice*. New York: Russell Sage Foundation.

Fromuth, Mary Ellen. 1986. "The Relationship of Childhood Sexual Abuse with Later Psychological and Sexual Adjustment in a Sample of College Women." *Child Abuse and Neglect* 10:5–15.

Fuller, Beth. 1990. "Reflections with Psalms 27: What Is There to Heal From? Why Are You So Angry at God?" Unpublished manuscript.

Gagnon, J. Patrick. 1989. *Soul Survivors: A New Beginning for Adults Abused as Children*. New York: Prentice-Hall.

Gagnon, John H. 1965. "Female Child Victims of Sex Offenses." *Social Problems* 13:176–192.

Gebhard, Paul H., John H. Gagnon, Wardell B. Pomeroy, and Cornelia V. Christenson. 1965. *Sex Offenders: An Analysis of Types*. New York: Harper and Row.

Gelles, Richard J. and Murray A. Straus. 1988. *Intimate Violence: The Causes and Consequences of Abuse in the American Family*. New York: Touchstone.

Gidycz, Christine A. and Mary P. Koss. 1990. "A Comparison of Group and Individual Sexual Assault Victims." *Psychology of Women Quarterly* 14:325–342.

————. 1991. "The Effects of Acquaintance Rape on the Female Victim." Pp. 270–284 in *Acquaintance Rape: The Hidden Crime*, edited by A. Parrot and L. Bechhofer. New York: John Wiley and Sons.

Gil, Eliana. 1988. *Treatment of Adult Survivors of Childhood Abuse*. Walnut Creek, CA: Launch.

————. 1992. *Outgrowing the Pain Together: A Book for Spouses and Partners of Adults Abused as Children*. New York: Dell.

Gilligan, Carol. 1982. *In a Different Voice: Psychological Theory and Women's Development*. Cambridge, MA: Harvard University.

Gilligan, Carol, Janie Victoria Ward, and Jill McLean Taylor, with Betty Bardige, editors. 1988. *Mapping the Moral Domain*. Cambridge,

MA: Center for the Study of Gender, Education and Human Development.

Gilligan, Carol, Nona P. Lyons, and Trudy J. Hanmer, editors. 1990. *Making Connections: The Relational Worlds of Adolescent Girls at Emma Willard School.* Cambridge, MA: Harvard University.

Gilmartin, Pat. 1991. "Women and Social Change: What Rape and Child Sexual Abuse Can Teach Us." Paper presented at the conference, Women and Images: Vision and Social Change, May, Youngstown State University, Youngstown, OH.

Gilmartin-Zena, Pat. 1983a. "Attribution Theory and Rape Victim Responsibility." *Deviant Behavior* 4:357–374.

_____. 1983b. *Immediate Reactions to Rape: A Symbolic Interactionist Perspective.* Unpublished dissertation, Kent State University, Kent, OH.

_____. 1985. "Rape Impact: Immediately and Two Months Later." *Deviant Behavior* 6:347–361.

_____. 1987a. "Attitudes Toward Rape: Student Characteristics as Predictors." *Free Inquiry in Creative Sociology* 15:175–182.

_____. 1987b. "Changing Definitions of Rape: Their Content and Impact." *Sexual Coercion and Assault* 2:1–7.

_____. 1988. "Gender Differences in Students' Attitudes Toward Rape." *Sociological Focus* 21:279–292.

_____. 1989a. "Attitudes about Rape Myths: Are Women's Studies Students Different?" *Free Inquiry in Creative Sociology* 17:65–72.

_____. 1989b. "Changing College Students' Attitudes about Rape: The Results of an Experimental Research Design." Paper presented at the annual meetings of the Society for the Study of Social Problems, San Francisco.

_____. 1989c. "Gender Differences in College Students' Perceptions about Rape: The Results of an Experimental Research Design." Paper presented at the annual meetings of the North Central Sociological Association, Akron, OH, March.

_____. 1990. "College Students' Views about Rape: Can their Attitudes Be Changed?" Workshop presented at the Fourth National Conference on Campus Violence, Towson, MD, January.

Girelli, Steven A., Patricia A. Resick, Susan Marhoefer-Dvorak, and Cathleen Kotsis Hutter. 1986. "Subjective Distress and Violence During Rape: Their Effects on Long-Term Fear." *Violence and Victims* 1:35–46.

Golan, Naomi. 1978. *Treatment in Crisis Situations*. New York: Free Press.

Gold, Erica R. 1986. "Long-Term Effects of Sexual Victimization in Childhood: An Attributional Approach." *Journal of Consulting and Clinical Psychology* 54:471–475.

Gomes-Schwartz, Beverly, Jonathan M. Horowitz, and Albert P. Cardarelli. 1990. *Child Sexual Abuse: The Initial Effects*. Newbury Park, CA: Sage.

Goodwin, Jean. 1985. "Credibility Problems in Multiple Personality Disorder Patients and Abused Children." Pp. 1–20 in *Childhood Antecedents of Multiple Personality*, edited by Richard P. Kluft. Washington, D.C.: American Psychiatric Association.

Gordon, Margaret T. and Stephanie Riger. 1989. *The Female Fear*. New York: Free Press.

Gornick, Janet, Martha R. Burt, and Karen J. Pittman. 1985. "Structure and Activities of Rape Crisis Centers in the Early 1980s." *Crime and Delinquency* 31:247–268.

Green, G. Dorsey. 1990. "Is Separation Really So Great?" Pp. 87–104 in *Diversity and Complexity in Feminist Therapy*, edited by L.S. Brown and M.P.P. Root. New York: Harrington Park.

Greenspan, Miriam. 1983. *A New Approach to Women and Therapy*. New York: McGraw-Hill.

_____. 1986. "Should Therapists Be Personal? Self Disclosure and Therapeutic Distance in Feminist Therapy." Pp. 5–18 in *A Guide to Dynamics of Feminist Therapy*, edited by D. Howard. New York: Harrington Park.

Greenwald, Evan and Harold Leitenberg. 1990. "Posttraumatic Stress Disorder in a Nonclinical and Nonstudent Sample of Adult Women Sexually Abused as Children." *Journal of Interpersonal Violence* 5:217–228.

Griffin, Susan. 1971. "Rape: The All-American Crime." *Ramparts* 10 (September):26–36.

_____. 1979. *Rape: The Power of Consciousness*. New York: Harper and Row.

_____. 1989. "Split Culture." Pp. 7–17 in *Healing the Wounds: The Promise of Ecofeminism*, edited by J. Plant. Philadelphia: New Society.

Groth, Nicholas A. 1979. *Men Who Rape: The Psychology of the Offender*. New York: Harper and Row.

Grubman-Black, Stephen. 1990. *Recovery from Childhood Sexual Abuse: Broken Boys/Mending Men*. New York: Ivy.

Hall, Eleanor R., Judith A. Howard, and Sherrie L. Boezio. 1986. "Tolerance of Rape: A Sexist or Antisocial Attitude?" *Psychology of Women Quarterly* 10:101–118.

Hancock, Emily. 1989. *The Girl Within*. New York: Fawcett Columbine.

Harney, Patricia A. and Charlene L. Muehlenhard. 1991. "Factors that Increase the Likelihood of Victimization." Pp. 159–175 in *Acquaintance Rape: The Hidden Crime*, edited by A. Parrot and L. Bechhofer. New York: John Wiley and Sons.

Harrison, Patrick J., Jeannette Downes, and Michael D. Williams. 1991. "Date and Acquaintance Rape: Perceptions and Attitude Change Strategies." *Journal of College Student Development* 32:131–139.

Harvey, Mary. 1985. *Exemplary Rape Crisis Programs: Cross-Cite Analysis and Case Studies*. Washington, D.C.

Haugaard, Jeffrey J. and N. Dickon Reppucci. 1988. *The Sexual Abuse of Children: A Comprehensive Guide to Current Knowledge and Intervention Strategies*. San Francisco: Jossey-Bass.

Herman, Judith Lewis. 1981. *Father-Daughter Incest*. Cambridge, MA: Harvard University.

_____. 1990. "Discussion." Pp. 289–293 in *Incest-Related Syndrome in Adult Psychopathology*, edited by R.P. Kluft. Washington, D.C.: American Psychiatric Association.

_____. 1992. *Trauma and Recovery*. New York: Basic.

Hertzberg, Joan F. 1990. "Feminist Psychotherapy and Diversity: Treatment Considerations from a Self Psychology Perspective." Pp. 275– 298 in *Diversity and Complexity in Feminist Therapy*, edited by L.S. Brown and M.P.P. Root. New York: Harrington Park.

Hindelang, Michael J. and Bruce L. Davis. 1977. "Forcible Rape in the United States: A Statistical Profile." Pp. 87–114 in *Forcible Rape: The Crime, the Victim, and the Offender*, edited by D. Chappell, R. Geis, and G. Geis. New York: Columbia University.

Hoff, Lee Ann. 1978. *People in Crisis: Understanding and Helping*. Menlo Park, CA: Addison-Wesley.

Holmstrom, Lynda L. and Ann W. Burgess. 1978. *The Victim of Rape: Institutional Reactions*. New York: John Wiley and Sons.

Homstead, Kerry Christensen and Lynn Werthamer. 1989. "Time-Limited Group Therapy for Adolescent Victims of Child Sexual

Abuse." Pp. 65–84 in *Vulnerable Populations: Sexual Abuse Treatment for Children, Adult Survivors, Offenders, and Persons with Mental Retardation, Volume 2*, edited by S.M. Sgroi. Lexington, MA: Lexington.

Horowitz, Mardi Jon. 1986. *Stress Response Syndromes* (2nd ed.) New York: Jason Aronson.

Horton, Anne L., Barry L. Johnson, Lynne M. Roundy, and Doran Williams, editors. 1990. *The Incest Perpetrator: A Family Member No One Wants to Treat*. Newbury Park, CA: Sage.

Hunter, Mic. 1990. *Abused Boys: The Neglected Victims of Sexual Abuse*. New York: Fawcett.

Jack, Dana Crowley. 1991. *Silencing the Self: Women and Depression*. Cambridge, MA: Harvard University.

Janoff-Bulman, Ronnie. 1979. "Characterological versus Behavioral Self-Blame: Inquiries into Depression and Rape." *Journal of Personality and Social Psychology* 37:1798–1809.

————. 1985. "The Aftermath of Victimization: Rebuilding Shattered Assumptions." Pp. 16–35 in *Trauma and Its Wake: The Study and Treatment of Post-Traumatic Stress Disorder*, edited by C.R. Figley. New York: Brunner/Mazel.

————. 1992. *Shattered Assumptions: Towards a New Psychology of Trauma*. New York: Free Press.

Jehu, Derek. 1988. *Beyond Sexual Abuse: Therapy with Women Who Were Childhood Victims*. New York: John Wiley and Sons.

————. 1989. "Mood Disturbances Among Women Clients Sexually Abused in Childhood." *Journal of Interpersonal Violence* 4:164–184.

Jenkins, Megan J. and Faye H. Dambrot. 1987. "The Attribution of Date Rape: Observers' Attitudes and Sexual Experiences and the Dating Situation." *Journal of Applied Social Psychology* 17:875–895.

Johnson, Allan C. 1980. "On the Prevalence of Rape in the U.S." *Signs: Journal of Women in Culture and Society* 6:140–153.

Jones, Linda E. 1991. "The Minnesota School Curriculum Project: A Statewide Domestic Violence Prevention Project in Secondary Schools." Pp. 258–266 in *Dating Violence: Young Women in Danger*, edited by B. Levy. Seattle: Seal Press.

Josselson, Ruthellen. 1987. *Finding Herself: Pathways to Identity Development in Women*. San Francisco: Jossey-Bass.

Kamen, Paula. 1991. *Feminist Fatale: Voices from the "Twentysomething" Generation Explore the Future of the 'Women's Movement.'* New York: Donald I. Fine.

Kanin, Eugene. 1957. "Male Aggression in Dating-Courtship Relations." *American Journal of Sociology* 63:197–204

————. 1984. "Date Rape: Unofficial Criminals and Victims." *Victimology: An International Journal* 9:95–108.

————. 1985. "Date Rapists: Differential Sexual Socialization and Relative Deprivation." *Archives of Sexual Behavior* 14:219–231.

Kaplan, Alexandra G. 1991. "The 'Self-in-Relation': Implications for Depression in Women." Pp. 206–222 in *Women's Growth in Connection: Writings from the Stone Center*, edited by J.V. Jordan, A.G. Kaplan, J.B. Miller, I.P. Stiver, and J.L. Surrey. New York: Guilford.

Kaplan, Howard B., editor. 1983. *Psychosocial Stress: Trends in Theory and Research*. New York: Academic.

Kaschak, Ellyn. 1992. *Engendered Lives: A New Psychology of Women's Experience*. New York: Basic.

Katz, Bonnie P. 1991. "The Psychological Impact of Stranger versus Nonstranger Rape on Victims' Recovery." Pp. 251–269 in *Acquaintance Rape: The Hidden Crime*, edited by A. Parrot and L. Bechhofer. New York: John Wiley and Sons.

Katz, Judy. 1984. *No Fairy Godmothers, No Magic Wands: The Healing Process After Rape*. Saratoga, CA: R & E.

Katz, Sedelle and Mary Ann Mazur. 1979. *Understanding the Rape Victim: A Synthesis of Research Findings*. New York: John Wiley and Sons.

Kelley, Susan J. 1988. "Ritualistic Abuse of Children: Dynamics and Impact." *Cultic Studies Journal* 5:228–236.

————. 1989. "Stress Responses of Children to Sexual Abuse and Ritualistic Abuse in Day Care Centers." *Journal of Interpersonal Violence* 4:502–513.

————. 1992. "Ritualistic Abuse." Workshop presented at the National Symposium on Child Victimization, May, Washington, D.C.

Kelly, Liz. 1988. *Surviving Sexual Violence*. Minneapolis: University of Minnesota.

Kendall-Tackett, Kathleen A. 1991. "Characteristics of Abuse that Influence When Adults Molested as Children Seek Treatment." *Journal of Interpersonal Violence* 6:486–493.

Kercher, Glen A. and M. McShane. 1984. "The Prevalence of Child Sexual Abuse Victimization in an Adult Sample of Texas Residents." *Child Abuse and Neglect* 8:495–501.

Kessler, Ronald C. and Marilyn Essex. 1982. "Marital Status and Depression: The Importance of Coping Resources." *Social Forces* 61:484–507.

Kessler, Ronald C., Richard H. Price, and Camille B. Wortman. 1985. "Social Factors in Psychopathology: Stress, Social Support and Coping Process." *Annual Reviews of Psychology* 36:531–572.

Kilborne, Jean. 1979. *Killing Us Softly* (movie). Cambridge, MA: Cambridge Documentary

_____. 1987. *Still Killing Us Softly* (movie). Cambridge, MA: Cambridge Documentary

Kilpatrick, Dean G., Connie L. Best, and Lois J. Veronen. "Rape Victims: Have We Studied the Tip or the Iceberg?" Paper presented at the annual meeting of the American Psychological Association, Anaheim, CA, August 1983.

Kilpatrick, Dean G., Patricia A. Resick, and Lois J. Veronen. 1981. "Effects of a Rape Experience: A Longitudinal Study." *Journal of Social Issues* 37:105–122.

Kilpatrick, Dean G. and Lois L. Veronen. 1983. "Treatment for Rape-Related Problems: Crisis Intervention Is Not Enough." Pp. 165–185 in *Crisis Intervention* (2nd ed.), edited by L. Cohen, W. Claiborn, and G.A. Specter. New York: Human Sciences.

Kilpatrick, Dean G., Lois J. Veronen, and Connie L. Best. 1985. "Factors Predicting Psychological Distress among Rape Victims." Pp. 113–141 in *Trauma and Its Wake: The Study and Treatment of Post-Traumatic Stress Disorder*, edited by C.R. Figley. New York: Brunner/Mazel.

Kilpatrick, Dean G., Lois J. Veronen, and Patricia A. Resick. 1979. "The Aftermath of Rape: Recent Empirical Findings." *American Journal of Orthopsychiatry* 49:658–669.

King, H. Elizabeth and Carol Webb. 1981. "Rape Crisis Centers: Progress and Problems." *Journal of Social Issues* 37:93–104.

Kinsey, Alfred C., Wardel Pomeroy, Clyde Martin, and Paul Gebhard. 1953. *Sexual Behavior in the Human Female*. Philadelphia: W.B. Saunders.

Kirkpatrick, Clifford and Eugene Kanin. 1957. "Male Sexual Aggression on a University Campus." *American Sociological Review* 22:52–58.

Kitzinger, Celia. 1990. "Resisting the Discipline." Pp. 119–136 in *Feminists and Psychological Practice*, edited by E. Burman. London: Sage.

Klein, Dorie. 1981. "Violence Against Women: Some Considerations Regarding Its Causes and Elimination." *Crime and Delinquency* January:64–80.

Kluft, Richard P., editor. 1985a. *Childhood Antecedents of Multiple Personality*. Washington, D.C.: American Psychiatric Association.

————. 1985b. "Childhood Multiple Personality Disorder: Predictors, Clinical Findings, and Treatment Results." Pp. 167–196 in *Childhood Antecedents of Multiple Personality*, edited by R.P. Kluft. Washington, D.C.: American Psychiatric Association.

————. 1985c. "The Natural History of Multiple Personality Disorder." Pp. 197–238 in *Childhood Antecedents of Multiple Personality*, edited by R.P. Kluft. Washington, D.C.: American Psychiatric Association.

————. 1990. *Incest-Related Syndromes of Adult Psychopathology*. Washington, D.C.: American Psychiatric Association.

Koss, Mary P. 1985a. "Hidden Rape: The Rest of the Iceberg." Paper presented at the conference, An American Dilemma in the Mid 80s: Rape and Sexual Assault, April 11, Kent State University.

————. 1985b. "The Hidden Rape Victim: Personality, Attitudinal, and Situational Characteristics." *Psychology of Women Quarterly* 9:193–212.

————. 1988. "Hidden Rape: Sexual Aggression and Victimization in a National Sample of Students in Higher Education." Pp. 3–25 in *Rape and Sexual Assault II*, edited by A.W. Burgess. New York: Garland.

Koss, Mary P., Thomas E. Dinero, and Cynthia A. Seibel. 1988. "Stranger and Acquaintance Rape: Are There Differences in the Victim's Experience?" *Psychology of Women Quarterly* 12:1–24.

Koss, Mary P., Christine A. Gidyca, and Nadine Wisiewski. 1987. "The Scope of Rape: Incidence and Prevalence of Sexual Aggression and Victimization in a National Sample of Higher Education Students." *Journal of Consulting and Clinical Psychology* 55:162–170.

Koss, Mary P. and Mary R. Harvey. 1991. *The Rape Victim: Clinical and Community Interventions* (2nd ed.) Newbury Park, CA: Sage.

Kramer, Teresa L. and Bonnie L. Green. 1991. "Posttraumatic Stress Disorder as an Early Response to Sexual Assault." *Journal of Interpersonal Violence* 6:160–173.

Kreisman, Jerold J. and Hal Straus. 1989. *I Hate You—Don't Leave Me: Understanding the Borderline Personality.* New York: Avon.

Kroll, Jerome. 1988. *The Challenge of the Borderline Patient: Competency in Diagnosis and Treatment.* New York: W.W. Norton.

Kunzman, Kristin A. 1990. *The Healing Way: Adult Recovery from Childhood Sexual Abuse.* San Francisco: Harper and Row.

LaFree, Gary, Barbara F. Reskin, and Christy A. Visher. 1985. "Jurors' Responses to Victims' Behavior and Legal Issues in Sexual Assault Trials." *Social Problems* 32:389–407.

Laidlaw, Toni Ann and Cheryl Malmo. 1990a. "Introduction: Feminist Therapy and Psychological Healing." Pp. 1–12 in *Healing Voices: Feminist Approaches to Therapy with Women*, edited by T.A. Laidlaw, C. Malmo, and Associates. San Francisco: Jossey-Bass.

———. 1990b. "Afterword: Empowering Women through the Healing Process." Pp. 320–323 in *Healing Voices: Feminist Approaches to Therapy with Women*, edited by T.A. Laidlaw, C. Malmo, and Associates. San Francisco: Jossey-Bass.

Laidlaw, Toni Ann, Cheryl Malmo, and associates, editors. 1990. *Healing Voices: Feminist Approaches to Therapy with Women.* San Francisco: Jossey-Bass.

Landis, Carney, Agnes T. Landis, M. Marjorie Bolles, Harriet F. Metzger, Marjorie Wallace Pitts, D. Anthony D'Esopo, Howard C. Moloy, Sophia J. Kleegman, and Robert L. Dickinson. 1940. *Sex in Development: A Study of the Growth and Development of the Emotional and Sexual Aspects of Personality Together with Physiological, Anatomical, and Medical Information on a Group of 153 Normal Women and 142 Female Psychiatric Patients.* New York: Paul B. Hoeber.

Landis, Judson T. 1956. "Experiences of 500 Children with Adult Sexual Deviation." *Psychiatric Quarterly Supplement* 30:91–109.

Lane, K.E. and P.A. Gwartney-Gibbs. 1985. "Violence in the Context of Dating and Sex." *Journal of Family Issues* 6:45–59.

Largen, Mary Ann. 1988. "Rape-Law Reforms: An Analysis." Pp. 271–292 in *Rape and Sexual Assault II*, edited by A.W. Burgess. New York: Garland.

Law Enforcement News. 1992. "UCR Shows Sixth Straight Crime Jump; BJS Reports Rape Up by 59 Percent." May 15.

Ledray, Linda E. 1986. *Recovering from Rape: Practical Advice on Overcoming the Trauma and Coping with Police, Hospitals, and*

Court—for Survivors of Sexual Assault and for Their Families, Lovers, and Friends. New York: Henry Holt.

————. 1988. "Responding to the Needs of Rape Victims." Pp. 169–190 in *Rape and Sexual Assault II*, edited by A.W. Burgess. New York: Garland.

Ledray, Linda, Sander Lund, and Thomas Kiresuk. 1986. "Impact of Rape on Victims and Families: Treatment and Research Considerations." Pp. 134–149 In *Women in Health and Illness: Life Experiences and Crises*, edited by D.K. Kjervik and I.M. Martinson. Philadelphia: W.B. Saunders.

Lefcourt, Herbert M. 1985. "Intimacy, Social Support, and Locus of Control as Moderators of Stress." Pp. 155–171 in *Social Support: Theory, Research and Applications*, edited by I.G. Saronson and B.R. Saronson. Boston: Martinus Nijhoff.

Lerman, Hannah. 1988. "The Psychoanalytic Legacy: From Whence We Come." Pp. 38–52 in *Handbook on Sexual Abuse of Children: Assessment and Treatment Issues*, edited by L.E.A. Walker. New York: Springer.

Lerner, Harriet Goldner. 1989. *Women in Therapy*. New York: Perennial Library.

Lerner, Melvin. 1980. *The Belief in a Just World: A Fundamental Delusion*. New York: Plenum.

Levy, Barrie, editor. 1991. *Dating Violence: Young Women in Danger*. Seattle: Seal Press.

Lew, Mike. 1988. *Victims No Longer: Men Recovering from Incest and Other Sexual Childhood Abuse*. New York: Nevraumont.

Lifton, Robert Jay. 1967. *Survivors of Hiroshima: Death in Life*. New York: Touchstone.

————. 1986. *The Nazi Doctors: Medical Killing and the Psychology of Genocide*. New York: Basic.

Lindemann, E. 1944. "Symptomatology and Measurement of Acute Grief." *American Journal of Psychiatry* 28:417–425.

Lipovsky, Julie A., Benjamin E. Saunders, and Shane M. Murphy. 1989. "Depression, Anxiety, and Behavior Problems among Victims of Father-Child Sexual Assault and Nonabused Siblings." *Journal of Interpersonal Violence* 4:452–468.

Lizotte, Alan J. 1985. "The Uniquness of Rape: Reporting Assaultive Violence to the Police." *Crime and Delinquency* 31:169–190.

Lott, Bernice, Mary Ellen Reilly, and Dale R. Howard. 1982. "Sexual Assault and Harassment: A Campus Community Case Study." *Signs: Journal of Women in Culture and Society* 8:296–319.

Lottes, Ilsa L. 1988. "Sexual Socialization and Attitudes Toward Rape." Pp. 193–220 in *Rape and Sexual Assault II*, edited by A.W. Burgess. New York: Garland.

Lundberg-Love, Paula and Robert Geffner. 1989. "Date Rape: Prevalence, Risk Factors, and a Proposed Model." Pp. 169–184 in *Violence in Dating Relationships: Emerging Social Issues*, edited by M.A. Pirog-Good and J.E. Stets. New York: Praeger.

Madigan, Lee and Nancy Gamble. 1991. *The Second Rape: Society's Continued Betrayal of the Victim*. Lexington, MA: Lexington.

Mahoney, E.R., Michael D. Shively, and Marsha Traw. 1986. "Sexual Coercion and Assault: Male Socialization and Female Risk." *Sexual Coercion and Assault* 1:2–8.

Malamuth, Neil M. 1981. "Rape Proclivity among Males." *Journal of Social Issues* 37:138–157.

_____. 1989. "Predictors of Naturalistic Sexual Aggression." Pp. 217–240 in *Violence in Dating Relationships: Emerging Social Issues*, edited by M.A. Pirog-Good and J.E. Stets. New York: Praeger.

Malamuth, Neil M. and James V.P. Check. 1981. "The Effects of Mass Media Exposure on Acceptance of Violence against Women: A Field Experiment." *Journal of Research in Personality* 15:436–446.

Malamuth, Neil M. and Karol E. Dean. 1991. "Attraction to Sexual Aggression." Pp. 229–247 in *Acquaintance Rape: The Hidden Crime*, edited by A. Parrot and L. Bechhofer. New York: John Wiley and Sons.

Maltz, Wendy. 1991. *The Sexual Healing Journey: A Guide for Survivors of Sexual Abuse*. New York: Harper Collins.

Maltz, Wendy and Beverly Holman. 1987. *Incest and Sexuality: A Guide to Understanding and Healing*. Lexington, MA: D.C. Heath.

Mannarino, Anthony P., Judith A. Cohen, and Michele Gregor. 1989. "Emotional and Behavioral Difficulties in Sexually Abused Girls." *Journal of Interpersonal Violence* 4:437–451.

Mannarino, Anthony P., Judith A. Cohen, Judith A. Smith, and Susan Moore-Motily. 1991. "Six- and Twelve-Month Follow-Up of Sexually Abused Girls." *Journal of Interpersonal Violence* 6:494–511.

Margalit, Malka. 1985. "Perception of Parents' Behavior, Familial Satisfaction, and Sense of Coherence." *Journal of School Psychology* 23:355–364.

Margolin, Leslie, Melody Miller, and Patricia B. Moran. 1989. "When a Kiss Is Not Just a Kiss: Relating Violations of Consent in Kissing to Rape Myth Acceptance." *Sex Roles* 20:231–243.

Marolla, Joseph and Diana Scully. 1986. "Attitudes toward Women, Violence, and Rape: A Comparison of Convicted Rapists and Other Felons." *Deviant Behavior* 7:337–355.

Masson, Jeffrey Moussaieff. 1984. *The Assault on Truth: Freud's Suppression of the Seduction Theory*. New York: Farrar, Straus, and Giroux.

Mayer, Robert S. 1991. *Satan's Children: Case Studies in Multiple Personality*. New York: G.P. Putnam's Sons.

Mayerson, Suzin E. and Dalmas A. Taylor. 1987. "The Effects of Rape Myth Pornography on Women's Attitudes and the Mediating Role of Sex Role Stereotyping." *Sex Roles* 17:321–338.

McCahill, Thomas W., Linda C. Meyer, and Arthur M. Fischman. 1979. *The Aftermath of Rape*. Lexington, MA: D.C. Heath.

McDermott, M. Joan. 1979. *Rape Victimization in 26 American Cities: Applications of the National Crime Survey Victimization and Attitude Data*. U.S. Department of Justice: Law Enforcement Assistance Administration.

Mead, George Herbert. 1932. *The Philosophy of the Present*. Cambridge, MA: Harvard University.

————. 1934. *Mind, Self, and Society*. Chicago: University of Chicago.

Mechanic, David and Stephen Hansell. 1989. "Divorce, Family Conflict and Adolescents' Well-Being." *Journal of Health and Social Behavior* 30:105–116.

Medea, Andra and Kathleen Thompson. 1974. *Against Rape: A Survival Manual For Women: How to Avoid Entrapment and How to Cope with Rape Physically and Emotionally*. New York: Farrar, Straus and Giroux.

Meltzer, Bernard N., John W. Petras, and Larry T. Reynolds. 1977. *Symbolic Interactionism: Genesis, Varieties and Criticism*. London: Routledge and Kegan Paul.

Miller, Alice. 1981. *The Drama of the Gifted Child*. New York: Basic.

————. 1983. *For Your Own Good: Hidden Cruelty in Childrearing and the Roots of Violence*. New York: Farrar, Straus and Giroux.

————. 1984. *Thou Shalt Not Be Aware: Society's Betrayal of the Child*. New York: Meridian.

_____. 1990. *Banished Knowledge: Facing Childhood Injuries*. New York: Doubleday.

_____. 1991. *Breaking Down the Wall of Silence: The Liberating Experience of Facing Painful Truth*. New York: Dutton.

Miller, Jean Baker. 1991. "The Development of Women's Sense of Self." Pp. 11–26 in *Women's Growth in Connection: Writings from the Stone Center*, edited by J.V. Jordan, A.G. Kaplan, J.B. Miller, I.P. Stiver, and J.L. Surrey. New York: Guilford Press.

Millett, Kate. 1970. *Sexual Politics*. New York: Ballantine.

Moos, Rudolf and Andrew Billings. 1982. "Conceptualizing and Measuring Coping Resources and Process." Pp. 212–230 in *Handbook of Stress: Theoretical and Critical Aspects*, edited by L. Goldberger and S. Breznitz. New York: Free Press.

Morgan, Marcia K. 1986. "Conflict and Confusion: What Rape Prevention Experts Are Telling Women." *Sexual Coercion and Assault* 1:160–168.

Morrison, Toni. 1987. *Beloved*. New York: Alfred A. Knopf.

Mosher, Donald L. and R.D. Anderson. 1986. "Macho Personality, Sexual Aggression, and Reactions to Guided Imagery of Realistic Rape." *Journal of Research in Personality* 20:120–135.

Muehlenhard, Charlene L. 1989. "Misinterpreted Dating Behaviors and the Risk of Date Rape." Pp. 241–256 in *Violence in Dating Relationships: Emerging Social Issues*, edited by M.A. Pirog-Good and J.E. Stets. New York: Praeger.

Muehlenhard, Charlene L., Debra E. Friedman, and Celeste M. Thomas. 1985. "Is Date Rape Justifiable? The Effects of Dating Activity, Who Initiated, Who Paid and Men's Attitudes toward Women." *Psychology of Women Quarterly* 9:297–310.

Muehlenhard, Charlene L. and Melaney A. Linton. 1987. "Date Rape and Sexual Aggression in Dating Situations: Incidence and Risk Factors." *Journal of Counseling Psychology* 34:186–196.

Nadelson, Carol C., Malkah T. Notman, Hannah Zackson, and Janet Gornick. 1982. "A Follow-Up Study of Rape Victims." *American Journal of Psychiatry* 139:1266–1270.

NiCarthy, Ginny. 1991. "Addictive Love and Abuse: A Course for Teenage Women." Pp. 240–252 in *Dating Violence: Young Women in Danger*, edited by B. Levy. Seattle: Seal Press.

Norris, Jeanette and Shirley Feldman-Summers. 1981. "Factors Related to the Psychological Impacts of Rape on the Victim." *Journal of Abnormal Psychology* 90:562–567.

Notman, Malkah T. and Carol Nadelson. 1976. "The Rape Victim: Psychodynamic Considerations." *American Journal of Psychiatry* 133:408–413.

Nyman, Nina W. 1989. "Prevention Education: A Developmental View." *Journal of Interpersonal Violence* 4:254–256.

O'Brien, Robert M. 1985. *Crime and Victimization Data.* Beverly Hills, CA: Sage.

Parrot, Andrea. 1990. "Changing Attitudes about Rape." Workshop presented at the Fourth Annual Conference on Campus Violence, January, Towson, MD.

————. 1991a. "Institutional Response: How Can Acquaintance Rape Be Prevented?" Pp. 355–367 in *Acquaintance Rape: The Hidden Crime*, edited by A. Parrot and L. Bechhofer. New York: John Wiley and Sons.

————. 1991b. "Recommendations for College Policies and Procedures to Deal with Acquaintance Rape." Pp. 368–380 in *Acquaintance Rape: The Hidden Crime*, edited by A. Parrot and L. Bechhofer. New York: John Wiley and Sons.

Parrot, Andrea and Laurie Bechhofer, editors. 1991. *Acquaintance Rape: The Hidden Crime*. New York: John Wiley and Sons.

Peraino, Joseph M. 1990. "Evaluation of a Preschool Antivictimization Prevention Program." *Journal of Interpersonal Violence* 5:520–528.

Peters, Stefanie Doyle. 1988. "Child Sexual Abuse and Later Psychological Problems." Pp. 101–118 in *Lasting Effects of Child Sexual Abuse*, edited by G.E. Wyatt and G.J. Powell. Beverly Hills, CA: Sage.

Peters, Stefanie Doyle, Gail Elizabeth Wyatt, and David Finkelhor. 1986. "Prevalence." Pp. 15–59 in A *Sourcebook on Child Sexual Abuse*, edited by D. Finkelhor and associates. Beverly Hills, CA: Sage.

Pfohl, Stephen J. 1977. "The 'Discovery' of Child Abuse." *Social Problems* 24:310–323.

Popiel, Debra A. and E.C. Suskind. 1985. "The Impact of Rape: Social Support as a Moderator of Stress." *American Journal of Community Psychology* 13:645–676.

Poston, Carol and Karen Lison. 1989. *Reclaiming Our Lives: Hope for Adult Survivors of Incest.* New York: Bantam.

Powell, Gloria Johnson. 1988. "Child Sexual Abuse Research: The Implications for Clinical Practice." Pp. 271–282 in *Lasting Effects of Child Sexual Abuse*, edited by G.E. Wyatt and G.J. Powell. Beverly Hills, CA: Sage.

Putnam, Frank W. 1985. "Dissociation as a Response to Extreme Trauma." Pp. 65–98 in *Childhood Antecedents of Multiple Personality*, edited by R.P. Kluft. Washington, D.C.: American Psychiatric Association.

————. 1989. *Diagnosis and Treatment of Multiple Personality Disorder*. New York: Guilford.

————. 1990. "Disturbances of 'Self' in Victims of Childhood Sexual Abuse." Pp. 113–131 in *Incest-Related Syndrome in Adult Psychopathology*, edited by R.P. Kluft. Washington, D.C.: American Psychiatric Association.

Putnam, Frank W., Juliet J. Guroff, Edward K. Silberman, Lisa Barban, and Robert M. Post. 1986. "The Clinical Phenomenology of Multiple Personality Disorder: A Review of 100 Recent Cases." *Journal of Clinical Psychiatry* 47: 285–293.

Randall, Susan Carol and Vicki McNickle Rose. 1981. "Barriers to Becoming a 'Successful' Rape Victim." Pp. 336–354 in *Women and Crime in America*, edited by L.H. Bowker. New York: Macmillan.

Rapaport, Karen and Barry R. Burkhart. 1984. "Personality and Attitudinal Characteristics of Sexually Coercive College Males." *Journal of Abnormal Psychology* 93:216–221.

Rapaport, Karen R. and C. Dale Posey. 1991. "Sexually Coercive College Males." Pp. 217–228 in *Acquaintance Rape: The Hidden Crime*, edited by A. Parrot and L. Bechhofer. New York: John Wiley and Sons.

Ratner, Ellen. 1990. *The Other Side of the Family: A Book for Recovery from Abuse, Incest and Neglect*. Deerfield Beach, FL: Health Communications.

Reis, Patricia. 1991a. "In Dreams Begin Responsibilities: Healing Sexual Abuse." Paper presented at the conference, Women and Images: Vision and Social Change, May 4, Youngstown State University, Youngstown, OH.

————. 1991b. *Through the Goddess: A Woman's Way of Healing*. New York: Continuum.

Resick, Patricia A. 1983. "The Rape Reaction: Research Findings and Implications for Intervention." *The Behavior Therapist* 6:129–132.

Resick, Patricia A., Karen S. Calhoun, Beverly M. Atkeson, and Elizabeth M. Ellis. 1981. "Social Adjustment in Victims of Sexual Assault." *Journal of Consulting and Clinical Psychology* 49:705–712.

Resick, Patricia A. and Monica K. Schnicke. 1990. "Treating Symptoms in Adult Victims of Sexual Assault." *Journal of Interpersonal Violence* 5:488–506.

Risin, Leslie I. and Mary P. Koss. 1988. "The Sexual Abuse of Boys: Childhood Victimizations Reported by a National Sample." Pp. 91–104 in *Rape and Sexual Assault II*, edited by A.W. Burgess. New York: Garland.

Roberts, Cathy. 1989. *Women and Rape*. Washington Square, NY: New York University.

Roden, Marybeth. 1991. "A Model Secondary School Date Rape Prevention Program." Pp. 267–278 in *Dating Violence: Young Women in Danger*, edited by B. Levy. Seattle: Seal Press.

Root, Maria P.P. 1989. "Treatment Failures: The Role of Sexual Victimization in Women's Addictive Behavior." *American Journal of Orthopsychiatry* 59:542–549.

Rose, Vicki McNickle. 1977. "Rape as a Social Probelm: A By-Product of the Feminist Movement." *Social Problems* 25:75–89.

Rosewater, Lynne Bravo. 1990. "Diversifying Feminist Theory and Practice: Broadening the Concept of Victimization." Pp. 299–312 in *Diversity and Complexity in Feminist Therapy*, edited by L.S. Brown and M.P.P. Root. New York: Harrington Park.

Rozee, Patricia D., Py Bateman, and Theresa Gilmore. 1991. "The Personal Perspective of Acquaintance Rape Prevention: A Three-Tier Approach." Pp. 337–354 in *Acquaintance Rape: The Hidden Crime*, edited by A. Parrot and L. Bechhofer. New York: John Wiley and Sons.

Ruch, Libby O. and Susan Meyers Chandler. 1983. "Sexual Assault Trauma During the Acute Phase: An Exploratory Model and Multivariate Analysis." *Journal of Health and Social Behavior* 24:174–185.

Ruch, Libby O., Susan Meyers Chandler, and Richard A. Harter. 1980. "Life Change and Rape Impact." *Journal of Health and Social Behavior* 21:248–260.

Ruch, Libby O. and Michael Hennessy. 1983. "Sexual Assault: Victim and Attack Dimensions." *Victimology: An International Journal* 7:94–105.

Ruch, Libby O. and Joseph J. Leon. 1983. "Type of Sexual Assault Trauma: A Multidimensional Analysis of a Short-Term Panel." *Victimology: An International Journal* 8:237–250.

Rumbaut, Ruben G., John P. Anderson, Robert M. Kaplan, and Jacqueline K. Turek. 1981. "Stress, Adaptation, and the 'Sense of Coherence': Operationalizing a New Construct for Research on Health and Aging." Paper presented at the Society for the Study of Social Problems, August, Toronto.

Runtz, Marsha and John Briere. 1986. "Adolescent 'Acting-Out' and Childhood History of Sexual Abuse." *Journal of Interpersonal Violence* 1:326–334.

Rush, Florence. 1980. *The Best Kept Secret: Sexual Abuse of Children.* New York: McGraw-Hill.

Russell, Diana E.H. 1974. *The Politics of Rape: The Victim's Perspective.* New York: Stein & Day.

_____. 1982a. "The Prevalence and Incidence of Forcible Rape and Attempted Rape of Females." *Victimology: An International Journal* 7:81–93.

_____. 1982b. *Rape in Marriage.* New York: Macmillan.

_____. 1984. *Sexual Exploitation: Rape, Child Sexual Abuse, and Workplace Harassment.* Beverly Hills, CA: Sage.

_____. 1986. *The Secret Trauma: Incest in the Lives of Girls and Women.* New York: Basic.

_____. 1991. "Wife Rape." Pp.129–139 in *Acquaintance Rape: The Hidden Crime*, edited by A. Parrot and L. Bechhofer. New York: John Wiley and Sons.

Russell, Diana E.H. and Nancy Howell. 1983. "The Prevalence of Rape in the United States Revisited." *Signs: Journal of Women in Culture and Society* 8:688–695.

Sales, Esther, Martha Baum, and Barbara Shore. 1984. "Victim Readjustment Following Assault." *Journal of Social Forces* 40:117–136.

Sanday, Peggy Reeves. 1981. "The Socio-Cultural Context of Rape." *Journal of Social Issues* 37:5–27.

_____. 1986. "Rape and the Silencing of the Feminine." Pp. 84–101 in *Rape: An Historical and Social Enquiry*, edited by S. Tomaselli and R. Porter. Oxford: Basil Blackwell.

_____. 1990. *Fraternity Gang Rape: Sex, Brotherhood, and Privilege on Campus.* New York: New York University.

Sanford, Linda T. 1990. *Strong at the Broken Places: Overcoming the Trauma of Childhood Abuse.* New York: Random House.

Sanford, Linda Tschirhart and Mary Ellen Donovan. 1985. *Women and Self-Esteem: Understanding and Improving the Way We Think and Feel About Ourselves.* New York: Penguin.

Sapiro, Virginia. 1990. *Women in American Society* (2nd. ed.) Mountain View, CA: Mayfield.

Saunders, Benjamin E., Catalina Mandoki Arata, and Dean G. Kilpatrick. 1990. "Development of a Crime-Related Post-Traumatic Stress Disorder Scale for Women within the Symptom Checklist-90–Revised." *Journal of Traumatic Stress* 3:439–448.

Saunders, Benjamin E., Lorenz A. Villiponteauz, Julie A. Lipovsky, Dean G. Kilpatrick, and Lois J. Veronen. 1992. "Child Sexual Assault as a Risk Factor for Mental Disorders among Women: A Community Study." *Journal of Interpersonal Violence* 7:189–204.

Scheier, Michael F. and Charles Carver. 1985. "Optimism, Coping and Health: Assessment and Implications of Generalized Outcome Expectancies." *Health Psychology* 4:219–247.

———. 1986. "Dispositional Optimism and Physical Well-Being: The Influence of Generalized Outcome Expectancies on Health." *Journal of Personality* 55:169–209.

Scheier, Michael F., Jagdish Kumari Weintraub, and Charles S. Carver. 1986. "Coping with Stress: Divergent Strategies of Optimists and Pessimists." *Journal of Personality and Social Psychology* 51:1257–1264.

Schetky, Diane H. 1990. "A Review of the Literature on the Long-Term Effects of Childhood Sexual Abuse." Pp. 35–54 in *Incest-Related Syndromes of Adult Psychopathology,* edited by R.P. Kluft. Washington, D.C.: American Psychiatric Association.

Schwartz, Pepper. 1980. "The Scientific Study of Rape." Pp. 145–179 in *Methodology in Rape Research: Proceedings of the Conference Held in Chevy Chase, Maryland, November 18 and 19, 1977,* edited by R. Green and J. Wiener. Rockville, MD: National Institute of Mental Health.

Schwendinger, Julia R. and Herman Schwendinger. 1983. *Rape and Inequality.* Beverly Hills, CA: Sage.

Scully, Diana and Joseph Marolla. 1984. "Convicted Rapists' Vocabulary of Motive: Excuses and Justifications." *Social Problems* 31:530–544.

———. 1985. "Riding the Bull at Gilley's: Convicted Rapists Describe the Rewards of Rape." *Social Problems* 32:251–263.

Scurfield, Raymond M. 1985. "Post-Trauma Stress Assessment and Treatment: Overview and Formulations." Pp. 219–256 in *Trauma and Its Wake: The Study and Treatment of Post-Traumatic Stress Disorder*, edited by C.R. Figley. New York: Brunner/Mazel.

Seligman, Martin E.P. 1975. *Helplessness: On Depression, Development, and Death*. San Francisco: W.H. Freeman.

———. 1991. *Learned Optimism*. New York: Knopf.

Sexual Coercion and Assault Staff. 1986. "Rape Law Reform: Has It Made Any Difference? Highlights on Recent Research." *Sexual Coercion and Assault* 1:28.

Sgroi, Suzanne M., editor. 1988. *Vulnerable Populations: Evaluation and Treatment of Sexually Abused Children and Adult Survivors, Volume I*. Lexington, MA: Lexington.

———. 1989. *Vulnerable Populations: Evaluation and Treatment of Sexually Abused Children and Adult Survivors, Volume 2*. Lexington, MA: Lexington.

Shengold, Leonard. 1989. *Soul Murder: The Effects of Childhood Abuse and Deprivation*. New Haven: Yale University.

Shotland, R. Lance. 1989. "A Model of the Causes of Date Rape in Developing and Close Relationships." Pp. 247–270 in *Close Relationships*, edited by C. Hendrick. Newbury Park, CA: Sage.

Sidel, Ruth. 1990. *On Her Own: Growing Up in the Shadow of the American Dream*. New York: Viking.

———. 1992. *Women and Children Last: The Plight of Poor Women in Affluent America* (revised and updated edition). New York: Penguin.

Siegle, Judith M., Jacqueline M. Golding, Judith A. Stein, M. Audrey Burnam, and Susan Sorenson. 1990. "Reactions to Sexual Assault: A Community Study." *Journal of Interpersonal Violence* 5:229–246.

Simons, Ronald D. and Les B. Whitbeck. 1991. "Sexual Abuse as a Precursor to Prostitution and Victimization among Adolescent and Adult Homeless Women." *Journal of Family Issues* 12:361–379.

Skelton, Carol A. and Barry R. Burkhart. 1980. "Sexual Assault: Determinants of Victim Disclosure." *Criminal Justice and Behavior* 7:229–236.

Snow, Barbara and Teena Sorensen. 1990. "Ritualistic Child Abuse in a Neighborhood Setting." *Journal of Interpersonal Violence* 5:474–487.

Soeken, K.L. and S.P. Damrosh. 1986. "Randomized Response Technique: Applications to Research on Rape." *Psychology of Women Quarterly* 10:119–126.

Sousa, Carole. 1991. "The Dating Violence Intervention Project." Pp. 223–231 in *Dating Violence: Young Women in Danger*, edited by B. Levy. Seattle: Seal Press.

Steele, Kathy. 1987. "Sitting with the Shattered Soul." *Pilgrimage: Journal of Exploration and Psychotherapy* 15:19–25.

_____. 1988. "The Healing Pool." *Voices* 24:74–78.

Stein, Judith A., Jacqueline M. Golding, Judith M. Siegel, M. Audrey Burnam, and Susan B. Sorenson. 1988. "Long-Term Psychological Sequelae of Child Sexual Abuse: The Los Angeles Epidemiologic Catchment Area Study." Pp. 135–154 in *Lasting Effects of Child Sexual Abuse*, edited by G.E. Wyatt and G.J. Powell. Beverly Hills, CA: Sage.

Steinem, Gloria. 1992. *Revolution from Within: A Book of Self-Esteem.* Boston: Little, Brown and Company.

Stekette, Gail and Edna B. Foa. 1987. "Rape Victims: Post-Traumatic Stress Responses and Their Treatment: A Review of the Literature." *Journal of Anxiety Disorders* 1:69–86.

Stone, Michael H. 1990. "Incest in the Borderline Patient." Pp. 183–204 in *Incest-Related Syndrome in Adult Psychopathology*, edited by R.P. Kluft. Washington, D.C.: American Psychiatric Association.

Stryker, Sheldon. 1980. *Symbolic Interactionsim: A Social Structural Version.* Menlo Park, CA: Benjamin/Cummings.

Sugarman, David B. and Gerald T. Hotaling. 1991. "Dating Violence: A Review of Contextual and Risk Factors." Pp. 100–118 in *Dating Violence: Young Women in Danger*, edited by B. Levy. Seattle, WA: Seal Press.

Summit, Roland C. 1983. "The Child Sexual Abuse Accommodation Syndrome." *Child Abuse and Neglect* 7:177–193.

_____. 1988. "Hidden Victims, Hidden Pain: Societal Avoidance of Child Sexual Abuse." Pp. 39–60 in *Lasting Effects of Child Sexual Abuse*, edited by G.E. Wyatt and G.J. Powell. Beverly Hills, CA: Sage.

_____. 1989. "The Centrality of Victimization: Regaining the Focal Point of Recovery for Survivors of Child Sexual Abuse." *Psychiatric Clinics of North America* 12:413–430.

Surrey, Janet L. 1991. "The 'Self-in-Relation': A Theory of Women's Development." Pp. 51–66 in *Women's Growth in Connection: Writings from the Stone Center*, edited by J.V. Jordan, A.G. Kaplan, J.B. Miller, I.P. Stiver, and J.L. Surrey. New York: Guilford.

Sutherland, Sandra and Donald Scherl. 1970. "Patterns of Responses Among Victims of Rape." *American Journal of Orthopsychiatry* 40:503–511.

————. 1972. "Crisis Intervention with Victims of Rape." *Social Work* 17:37–42.

Swift, Carolyn. 1985. "The Prevention of Rape." Pp. 413–426 in *Rape and Sexual Assault: A Research Handbook*, edited by A.W. Burgess. New York: Garland.

Swink, Kathy K. and Antoinette E. Leveille. 1986. "From Victim to Survivor: A New Look at the Issues and Recovery Process for Adult Incest Survivors." Pp. 119–141 in *A Guide to Dynamics of Feminist Therapy*, edited by D. Howard. New York: Harrington Park Press.

Tallen, Bette S. 1990. "Twelve Step Programs: A Lesbian Feminist Critique." *NWSA Journal* 2:390–407.

Tannen, Deborah. 1990. *You Just Don't Understand: Women and Men in Conversation*. New York: William Morrow.

Tavris, Carol. 1992. *The Mismeasure of Women*. New York: Simon and Schuster.

Taylor, Maye. 1990. "Fantasy or Reality? The Problem with Psychoanalytic Interpretation in Psychotherapy with Women." Pp. 104–118 in *Feminists and Psychological Practice*, edited by E. Burman. London: Sage.

Temkin, Jennifer. 1986. "Women, Rape and Law Reform." Pp. 16–40 in *Rape: An Historical and Social Enquiry*, edited by S. Tomaselli and R. Porter. Oxford: Basil Blackwell.

Terr, Lenore. 1990. *Too Scared to Cry: Psychic Trauma in Childhood*. New York: Basic.

Tessier, L.J. "Tess." 1992. "Women Sexually Abused as Children: The Spiritual Consequences." *Second Opinion* 17:11–23.

Thoits, Peggy A. 1983. "Dimensions of Life Events that Influence Psychological Distress: An Evaluation and Synthesis of the Literature." Pp. 33–103 in *Psychosocial Stress: Trends in Theory and Research*, edited by H.B. Kaplan. New York: Academic.

————. 1987. "Gender and Marital Differences in Control and Distress: Common Stress versus Unique Stress Explanations." *Journal of Health and Social Behavior* 28:7–22.

Tower, Cynthia Crosson. 1988. *Secret Scars: A Guide for Survivors of Child Sexual Abuse*. New York: Penguin.

Trimble, Michael R. 1985. "Post-Traumatic Stress Disorder: History of a Concept." Pp. 5–14 in *Trauma and Its Wake: The Study and Treatment of Post-Traumatic Stress Disorder*, edited by Charles R. Figley. New York: Brunner/Mazel.

Tsai, Mavis, Shirley Feldman-Summers, and Margaret Edgar. 1979. "Childhood Molestation: Variables Related to Differential Impacts on Psychosexual Functioning in Adult Women." *Journal of Abnormal Psychology* 88:407–417.

Turner, R. Jay and William R. Avison. 1992. "Innovations in the Measurement of Life Stress: Crisis Theory and the Significance of Event Resolution." *Journal of Health and Social Behavior* 33:36–50.

Ullman, Sarah E. and Raymond A. Knight. 1992. "Fighting Back: Women's Resistance to Rape." *Journal of Interpersonal Violence* 7:31–43.

U.S. Department of Justice. 1992. *Criminal Victimization in the United States, 1990*. Office of Justice Programs: Bureau of Justice Statistics.

van der Kolk, Bessel. 1989. "The Compulsion to Repeat the Trauma: Re-enactment, Revictimization, and Masochism." *Psychiatric Clinics of North America* 12:389–411.

Walker, Lenore E. Auerbach. 1985. "Feminist Therapy with Victims/Survivors of Interpersonal Violence." Pp. 203–214 in *Handbook of Feminist Therapy: Women's Issues in Psychotherapy*, edited by L.B. Rosewater and L.E.A. Walker. New York: Springer.

Warshaw, Robin. 1988. *I Never Called It Rape: The MS Report on Recognizing, Fighting, and Surviving Date and Acquaintance Rape*. New York: Harper and Row.

Warshaw, Robin and Andrea Parrot. 1991. "The Contribution of Sex-Role Socialization to Acquaintance Rape." Pp. 73–82 in *Acquaintance Rape: The Hidden Crime*, edited by A. Parrot and L. Bechhofer. New York: John Wiley and Sons.

Weis, Kurt and Sandra S. Borges. 1973. "Victimology and Rape: The Case of the Legitimate Victim." *Issues in Criminology* 8:71–115.

Werner, Emmy E. and Ruth S. Smith. 1982. *Vulnerable But Invincible: A Longitudinal Study of Resilient Children and Youth*. New York: McGraw-Hill.

West, D.J., C. Roy, and F.L. Nichols, 1978. *Understanding Sexual Assaults*. London: Heinemann.

Wheaton, Blair. 1985. "Personal Resources and Mental Health: Can There Be Too Much of a Good Thing?" *Research in Community Mental Health* 5:139–184.

Wheeler, J. Robert and Lucy Berliner. 1988. "Treating the Effects of Sexual Abuse on Children." Pp. 227–248 in *Lasting Effects of Child Sexual Abuse*, edited by G.E. Wyatt and G.J. Powell. Beverly Hills, CA: Sage.

White, Jacqueline and John A. Humphrey. 1991. "Young People's Attitudes toward Acquaintance Rape." Pp. 43–56 in *Acquaintance Rape: The Hidden Crime*, edited by A. Parrot and L. Bechhofer. New York: John Wiley and Sons.

White, Barbara B. and Donald L. Mosher. 1986. "Experimental Validation of a Model for Predicting the Reporting of Rape." *Sexual Coercion and Assault* 1:43–55.

Williams, Linda S. 1984. "The Classic Rape: When Do Victims Report?" *Social Problems* 31:459–467.

Williams, Joyce E. and Karen A. Holmes. 1981. *The Second Assault: Rape and Public Attitudes*. Westport, CT: Greenwood.

Wilson, John P., W. Ken Smith, and Suzanne K. Johnson. 1985. "A Comparative Analysis of PTSD among Various Survivor Groups." Pp. 142–172 in *Trauma and Its Wake: The Study and Treatment of Post-Traumatic Stress Disorder*, edited by C.R. Figley. New York: Brunner/Mazel.

Wilson, Kenneth, Rebecca Faison, and G.M. Britton. 1983. "Cultural Aspects of Male Sexual Aggression." *Deviant Behavior* 4:241–255.

Wirtz, Philip W. and Adele V. Harrell. 1987a. "Assaultive versus Non-assaultive Victimization: A Profile of Psychological Response." *Journal of Interpersonal Violence* 2:264–277.

———. 1987b. "Effects of Postassault Exposure to Attack—Similar Stimuli on Long-Term Recovery of Victims." *Journal of Consulting and Clinical Psychology* 55: 10–16.

Wisechild, Louise M. 1988. *The Obsidian Mirror: An Adult Healing from Incest*. Seattle: Seal Press.

———. 1991. *Healing from Incest through Creativity*. Seattle: Seal Press.

Wolfgang, Marvin E. 1958. *Patterns in Criminal Homicide*. Philadelphia: University of Pennsylvania.

Women's Research Centre. 1989. *Recollecting Our Lives: Women's Experience of Childhood Sexual Abuse*. Vancouver: Press Gang.

Wyatt, Gail E. 1985. "The Sexual Abuse of Afro-American and White Women in Childhood." *Child Abuse and Neglect: The International Journal* 9:507–519.

Wyatt, Gail Elizabeth and M. Ray Mickey. 1988. "The Support by Parents and Others as It Mediates the Effects of Child Sexual Abuse: An Exploratory Study." Pp. 211–226 in *Lasting Effects of Child Sexual Abuse*, edited by G.E. Wyatt and G.J. Powell. Beverly Hills, CA: Sage.

Wyatt, Gail Elizabeth, Cindy M. Notgrass, and Michael Newcomb. 1990. "Internal and External Mediators of Women's Rape Experiences." *Psychology of Women Quarterly* 14:153–175.

Wyatt, Gail Elizabeth and Gloria Johnson Powell. 1988. "Identifying the Lasting Effects of Child Sexual Abuse." Pp. 11–17 in *Lasting Effects of Child Sexual Abuse*, edited by G.E. Wyatt and G.J. Powell. Beverly Hills, CA: Sage.

Zigler, Edward, Nancy Rubin, and Joan Kaufman. 1988. "Do Abused Children Become Abusive Parents?" *Parents* 100–104.

Zinn, Maxine Baca and E. Stanley Eitzen. 1990. *Diversity in Families* (2nd ed.) New York: Harper and Row.

Index